On Global Order

On Global Order

Power, Values, and the Constitution
of International Society

Andrew Hurrell

OXFORD
UNIVERSITY PRESS

OXFORD

UNIVERSITY PRESS

Great Clarendon Street, Oxford ox2 6DP

Oxford University Press is a department of the University of Oxford.
It furthers the University's objective of excellence in research, scholarship,
and education by publishing worldwide in

Oxford New York

Auckland Cape Town Dar es Salaam Hong Kong Karachi
Kuala Lumpur Madrid Melbourne Mexico City Nairobi
New Delhi Shanghai Taipei Toronto

With offices in

Argentina Austria Brazil Chile Czech Republic France Greece
Guatemala Hungary Italy Japan Poland Portugal Singapore
South Korea Switzerland Thailand Turkey Ukraine Vietnam

Published in the United States
by Oxford University Press Inc., New York

British Library Cataloguing in Publication Data

Data available

Library of Congress Cataloging in Publication Data

Data available

Typeset by SPI Publisher Services, Pondicherry, India
Printed in Great Britain
on acid-free paper by
Biddles Ltd., King's Lynn, Norfolk

ISBN 978–0–19–923310–6
ISBN 978–0–19–923311–3 (Pbk.)

10 9 8 7 6 5 4 3 2 1

Contents

Acknowledgements

This book is concerned with the ways in which the inherited society of sovereign states has adapted to the changes associated with globalization, with the evolving character of global political order, and with the principal political and moral dilemmas facing contemporary international society.

My most important intellectual debt is to my teacher in this field, Hedley Bull, whose brilliance was most apparent in his rigorous scepticism, his capacity to ask searching questions, and his insistence on a style of academic enquiry that looks beyond both transient policy debates and current academic fashions. As will be readily apparent from the following chapters, this book builds on the hugely enjoyable collaborative work that I have undertaken over past years: on comparative regionalism with Louise Fawcett; on globalization and inequality with Ngaire Woods; on the Global South with Amrita Narlikar; on European integration and on the European state with Anand Menon; and on the environment and on international law with Benedict Kingsbury. I am especially grateful to Benedict Kingsbury. He is amongst the most original of all contemporary thinkers on international law and society and many of the arguments and formulations in this book stem from collaboration, conversations, and joint teaching in Oxford and New York. I have also drawn heavily on the ideas and writings of my colleagues, in particular Laurence Whitehead, Kalypso Nicolaidis, Adam Roberts, Rosemary Foot, and Jennifer Welsh; and on shared teaching, countless workshops and conferences, and much fruitful discussion with many other friends and colleagues in many diverse places. These include: (in Oxford) Richard Caplan, Martin Ceadel, Audrey Cronin, John Darwin, Anne Deighton, Diego Gambetta, Alexandra Gheciu, Evelyn Goh, Guy Goodwin-Gill, Sudhir Hazareesingh, Yuen Foong Khong, Markus Kornprobst, Gil Loescher, Vaughan Lowe, Neil MacFarlane, Walter Mattli, David Miller, Rana Mitter, Karma Nabulsi, Patricia Owens, Sarah Percy, James Piscatori, Jochen Prantl, Avi Shlaim, Henry Shue, Hew Strachan, and Federico Varese; and (outside Oxford) Philip Allott, Amitav Acharya, Emanuel Adler, Mike Barnett, Charles Beitz, Erica Benner, Mats Berdal, Tom Biersteker, Jane Boulden, Allen Buchanan, Michael Byers, Barry Buzan, Lars-Erik Cederman, Molly Cochran, James Der Derian, Gelson Fonseca, Pierre Hassner, Robert Jackson, Eddie Keene, Robert Keohane, Harold Koh, Martti

Koskenniemi, Nico Krisch, Andrew Linklater, James Mayall, David Malone, Monica Serrano, Diana Tussie, Joseph Weiler, and Nicholas Wheeler.

I have been especially fortunate to have worked with many wonderful doctoral students, whose ideas have contributed directly to the core themes of this book. They include: Tim Dunne, Alison van Rooy, Sukumar Perival, Naoko Shimazu, Stephen Hopgood, James Lin, Kai Alderson, Chimène Keitner, Robert Falkner, Stephanie Kuttner, Vivien Collingwood, Carolyn Deere, Terry MacDonald, Alex Betts, Matias Spektor, Rahul Rao, and Par Engstrom. Institutionally, I owe a great debt to Nuffield College, both for its generous material support and for nudging me gently into the world of social science. The following institutions have also provided both a stimulating environment and perceptive audiences: NYU School of Law, the Watson Center at Brown University, the universities of Brasília and São Paulo, and El Colégio de Mexico.

An earlier version of Chapter 10 was given as the 2006 Martin Wight Lecture, published as 'One World? Many Worlds? The Place of Regions in the Study of International Society', *International Affairs*, 83/1 (January 2007), 151–66. An earlier version of Chapter 11 was published as 'Pax Americana or the Empire of Insecurity?', *International Relations of the Asia Pacific*, 5/2 (2005), 153–76. Other chapters build in different ways on a range of my earlier writings on international society. Miriam Prys, Matias Spektor, and Sandeep Sengupta provided excellent research assistance. Dominic Byatt has shown enormous patience and good humour in coaxing the manuscript from me and I would like to thank him and his colleagues at OUP for all their work in the production of this book.

My greatest debt is to my family, Yasmin, Alex, and Anita, for their boundless love, patience, and support. They make everything worthwhile.

AJH
February 2007

1

Governing the globe

There is endless discussion of the need to deal with the global challenges of the twenty-first century—climate change, nuclear proliferation, the spread of infectious diseases, and economic globalization. Much of this debate is necessarily technical and issue-specific. But it also begs a set of very large and very difficult *political* questions. How is the world organized politically? How should it be organized? What forms of political organization are required to meet the challenges faced by humankind in the twenty-first century? Drawing on work in International Relations, International Law, and Global Governance, this book aims to provide a clear and wide-ranging introduction to the analysis of global political order—how patterns of governance and institutionalization in world politics have already changed; what the most important challenges are; and what the way forward might look like.

The unprecedented nature of the political challenge needs to be under-scored. It is an obvious exaggeration to suggest that the problem of domestic political order has been 'solved'. But we can at least point to the existence of successful states that have both provided stable political order and institution-alized many other values such as political democracy or social welfare. Even if models are hard to replicate and transfer, we know that Canada and Sweden exist. At the global level, the intellectual, practical, and normative challenges are of an entirely different order. We cannot make any easy assumptions as to whether the sorts of global governance that many consider indispensable are in fact likely to be possible. Yes, we can point to the growth of international law and institutions; yet the weaknesses and failures are all too evident and the health of many of the limited institutions that currently exist is hardly encouraging. Yes, we can point to elaborate schemes of institutionalized gov-ernance within particular regions—Europe above all; yet the circumstances of their emergence were historically contingent and the degree to which Europe represents a viable model for other regions, let alone for the world as a whole, remains highly questionable.

At its heart, this book is concerned with the ability of the inherited anarchi-cal society of sovereign states to provide a practically viable and normatively acceptable framework for global political order in an era of globalization. In contrast to the technocratic and interest-driven literature on global governance and institutionalism, I will emphasize and illustrate the threefold nature of the challenge facing international society: the need to capture shared and common interests, to manage unequal power, and to mediate cultural diversity and value conflict. It is the difficulty of finding a legitimate form of global politics capable of meeting these three challenges together which makes the problem of order a quintessentially political problem.

Political order

So how might we start to think about international political order? Many analyses of social order, whether in International Relations (as with Hedley Bull) or in social theory (as with Jon Elster), begin with a beguilingly simple distinction between order as fact and order as value.[1] On the one hand, social order can be understood in the sense of stable and regular patterns of human behaviour. In this depiction, it is contrasted with chaos, instability, or lack of predictability. On the other hand, social order requires the existence of a particular kind of purposive pattern that human beings have infused with meaning, that involves a particular set of goals, objectives, and values, and that leads to a particular outcome. It is a beguilingly simple distinction because, as we shall see, order as fact and order as value are often rather hard to disentangle.

If order is to be understood in terms of some purposive pattern, what sorts of purposes, goals, and values might be relevant to international life? In 1965, Raymond Aron posed the question of international order in the following manner: 'under what conditions would men [sic] (divided in so many ways) be able not merely to avoid destruction, but to live together relatively well in one planet?'[2] For Aron, living 'relatively well' was to be viewed in distinctly minimalist terms. Order was understood as 'the minimum conditions of coexistence' that might be obtained in the anarchical system of states. He took states to be the principal agents of order, hence making international order and global order for all practical purposes synonymous. And he proposed a definition of order which deliberately sought

---

[1] Hedley Bull, *The Anarchical Society: A Study of Order in World Politics*, 3rd edn. (Basingstoke, UK: Macmillan, 2003), esp. 3–21; Jon Elster, *The Cement of Society: A Study of Social Order* (Cambridge: Cambridge University Press, 1989), 1–16. More generally, see Dennis Wrong, *The Problem of Order: What Unites and Divides Society* (New York: Free Press, 1994); N. J. Rengger, *International Relations, Political Theory and the Problem of Order* (London: Routledge, 2000); T. V. Paul and John Hall (eds.), *International Order and the Future of World Politics* (Cambridge: Cambridge University Press, 1999).

[2] Raymond Aron, as reported in Stanley Hoffmann, 'Conference Report on The Conditions of World Order', *Daedalus*, 95/2 (1966), 456.

to avoid any discussion of shared values or of the necessary conditions for the promotion of some shared vision of how global society might ideally be organized.

A few years later, Hedley Bull defined order as 'A pattern [in the relations of human individuals or groups] that leads to a particular result, an arrangement of social life such that it promotes certain goals or values'.[3] Bull was somewhat more optimistic than Aron, but his analysis of these 'certain goals and values' also pointed in a constrained and minimalist direction. Bull's classic study of order in world politics concentrated on the common framework of rules and institutions that had developed within the anarchical society of states. It was anarchical in that there was no common power to enforce law or to underwrite cooperation; but it was a society in so far as states were conscious of common rules and values, cooperated in the working of common institutions, and perceived common interests in observing these rules and working through these institutions. It was, however, a necessarily thin and fragile society in which the three fundamental goals of international social life were limited to the preservation of the society of states itself, the maintenance of the independence of individual states, and the regulation—but not elimination—of war and violence amongst states and societies.[4]

It is on the basis of these ideas that we can identify the first analytical framework for thinking about international order: the idea of a pluralist and limited society of sovereign states. We can understand the political constitution of world politics by thinking primarily in terms of a world made up of separate, sovereign states which are, in turn, linked through various kinds of political practices and institutionalized structures. We can understand the question of global political order by assessing the manner and degree to which these political practices and institutions have reduced conflict and facilitated some degree of cooperation and stability. What kinds of ordered and cooperative relations have states and their governments established amongst themselves? What kinds of shared purposes and values (if any) can be discerned in the norms, rules, and institutions by which states and other actors have sought to structure and regulate their interaction?

For those who think in this way, interstate cooperation and international law are never likely to provide a stable and universal peace. At best, they can mitigate the conflicts that are likely to arise from the existence of a multiplicity of sovereignties. The relevant question is not: how might human beings create forms of international society or schemes of international cooperation

---

[3] Bull (2003: 3–4). See also Stanley Hoffmann's definition of order: 'the norms, practices, and processes that ensure the satisfaction of the basic needs of the social group in question'. Stanley Hoffmann, 'Is there an International Order?', in *Janus and Minerva: Essays in the Theory and Practice of International Politics* (Boulder, CO: Westview, 1987), 85.

[4] For a detailed analysis of Bull's view, see Kai Alderson and Andrew Hurrell (eds.), *Hedley Bull on International Society* (Basingstoke, UK: Macmillan, 2000), chs. 1–3.

that embody all their aspirations for justice or which universalize some particular conception of the good society? It is rather: how might states and other groups do each other the least possible harm and, in an age of total war and nuclear weapons, survive as a species? So the core goals of international social order are survival and coexistence; and the political framework is made up of the core institutions of a pluralist international society of states—international law, Great Powers, the balance of power, diplomacy, and war.

Although limited and pessimistic, it is important to distinguish this position from those who have seen international life as a condition of immutable struggle and conflict in which there is no element of society, and, still more, from those who have viewed war as having a positive value in the lives of both individuals and societies. There continue to be many celebrants of violence and many others who are willing to use war and violence for the pursuit of their political, economic, or religious goals. But in contrast to the relatively recent past, there are few who would uphold war and conflict as a normatively desirable feature of how the world as a whole should be ordered.

The narrowness and limited ambition of this pluralist society of sovereign states undoubtedly reflected the intense ideological and geopolitical conflicts of the Cold War. But it also drew upon a deep-rooted tradition in Western thought which had long viewed international society in pluralist or minimalist terms. A central strand of the history of thought on international relations was concerned with the idea of what, by the start of the eighteenth century, was commonly referred to as a society of states or, more commonly in the nineteenth century as a Family of Nations. This society involved the creation of certain minimalist rules, understandings, and institutions designed to limit the inevitable conflict that was to be expected within such a pluralist and fragmented political system. The normative structure of this society was built around the mutual recognition of states as independent and legally equal members of international society, on their freedom to promote their own ends subject to minimal constraints, and on the unavoidable reliance on self-preservation and self-help.

Chapter 2 unpacks this pluralist conception of international society in greater depth. It tries to get beyond the caricatured image of the 'Westphalian system' and to give a flavour of the richness of classical pluralism as an ongoing tradition of thought and practice. It explains why pluralism has remained such a powerful and influential way of thinking about international order and continues to be viewed by some as normatively attractive. For the modern heirs of this tradition, we are condemned to accept a limited and minimalist form of international society because of a pessimistic view of the constraints of power-politics and a deep scepticism regarding the depth of the value consensus that is ever likely to exist across the states and societies of the world. The chapter explains what is involved in making these claims about power and values.

This limited conception of what international society could, or should, aspire to have long faced numerous powerful critics. But it was in the course of the twentieth century that the forces making for change grew stronger. At the level of practice, there was a dramatic and sustained move towards more and more far-reaching international institutions and an exponential increase in the scope, range, and intrusiveness of international rules, norms, and institutions. At the level of normative ambition, the changes were still more far-reaching and led inexorably to the belief that international order had to be reconceived and reconceptualized. A minimally acceptable order was seen increasingly as requiring both limits on the freedom of states to resort to war and the creation of international rules that affected the domestic structures and organization of states, that invested individuals and groups within states with rights and duties, and that sought to embody some notion of a general common good. The scope of legitimate expectations increased exponentially.[5] Indeed, it is easy to lose sight of just how profound and radical these changes have been.

In order to capture these changes, Chapter 3 examines a second way of thinking about international society—the idea of a liberal solidarist society of states. The core idea of solidarism can be seen in the constant appeals to the existence of an 'international community' capable of fulfilling a broader range of political and moral purposes. Crudely speaking, it is a state system that can be made to work better and that strives to narrow the gap between law and power on the one hand and law and morality on the other—even if that gap can never be fully eliminated. Solidarism has deep historical roots and has taken a variety of forms. But it was liberal solidarism that characterized many of the academic and policy debates in the 1990s, reflecting the sense of liberal optimism engendered by the end of the Cold War and by the degree to which liberal ideas had, apparently, conquered the world. Chapter 3 unpacks some of the most important features of liberal solidarism and looks at the principal theoretical logics that have been used to explain shifts in patterns of governance and institutionalization. It also develops the critical concept of legitimacy in more detail—analysing five dimensions of legitimacy and suggesting how solidarist practices and solidarist claims have influenced our understandings of what a legitimate form of global political order would involve.

This book is about the nature and possibilities of international order, not about world politics in general. Theorists of international society are not

---

[5] Contrast earlier minimalist emphasis on coexistence with this recent definition: ' "World order", for these purposes, describes a system of global governance that institutionalizes cooperation and sufficiently contains conflict such that all nations and their peoples may achieve greater peace and prosperity, improve their stewardship of the earth, and reach minimal standards of human dignity', Anne-Marie Slaughter, *A New World Order* (Princeton, NJ: Princeton University Press, 2004), 15.

trying to arrive at any overall theory of world politics (whatever that might look like and whatever it might plausibly seek to explain), but are asking a discrete set of questions about political order and about the rules and norms that support it. Equally, to start from the traditional focus on states does not mean that states are the only legitimate objects of study in world politics nor that they necessarily remain 'in control'. Here it is important to distinguish between the agents of order and the domains of what is to be ordered. Within the classical European state system, states were the primary agents of order and the institutions that were created were concerned with a relatively narrow range of interactions, clustered, as the titles of so many texts and treatises suggest, under the headings of war, peace, and diplomacy. The twentieth century witnessed an enormous expansion in the range of issues and problems that are subject to regulation and institutionalization. One of the central questions therefore becomes how a state-based political order struggled to adapt to these changes and how an originally sovereignty-based legal order sought to regulate transnational forces and transnational spaces.

Social order, however, cannot be seen solely within the framework of the state. Since at least the end of the eighteenth century, Western understandings of social order have been structured around the relationship between three domains: the state, the market, and civil society. From this perspective we need to consider the role of market exchange, mutuality, and solidarity, rather than simply imperative political control and negotiated political coordination. This way of thinking stresses the complex patterns of social relations that exist and structure social life, often quite separate from the power and laws of the state. As the scope of interstate regulation within the global system has expanded, so it has come more and more into contact with the ordering mechanisms of these other two domains: markets and civil society. As we shall see in relation to the global economy, there has been a constant shifting back and forth between public (state-based) and private (market actor-based) modes of regulation, and indeed the development of many hybrid varieties. And it is impossible to make sense of the ways in which many environmental problems are 'governed' without understanding the actions and activities of civil society groups and non-state organizations operating both nationally and transnationally.

Chapter 4 looks at the third way of thinking about global political order: the idea of complex governance around and beyond the state. The analysis develops but pushes further many of the features of liberal solidarism: the complexity of global rule-making; the role of private market actors and civil society groups in articulating values which are then assimilated in interstate institutions; and the increased range of informal, yet norm-governed, governance mechanisms often built around complex networks, both transnational and trans-governmental. Tied closely to processes of social and economic globalization, this view sees traditional interstate governance as increasingly subsumed within a broader process in which there is a steady erosion of old distinctions between the domestic and the international, between public and private international law, and between public and private spheres more generally. The state loses its place as the privileged sovereign institution and instead becomes one of many actors and one participant in a broader and more complex social and legal process. The chapter examines this difficult and contested terrain under three headings: the deepening of interstate governance, the roles played by civil society, and the importance of markets and economic governance.

Having elaborated these three frameworks, the five chapters in Part II go on to examine some of the central and difficult issues that arise in any discussion of global political order: nationalism and the politics of identity, human rights and democratization, war and insecurity, economic globalization, and the ecological challenge. In each case, I begin by giving a sense of the historical background to the problem; I then illustrate how the ideas and practices of international society in relation to that issue have evolved and developed; and I discuss the nature of the problems involved and the limits to change.

Part III shifts the focus and opens up two cross-cutting perspectives. Chapter 10 examines the relationship between the one world of the global system and the many worlds of different regions. On the one side, we have the one world of globalizing capitalism, of global security dynamics, of global institutions and global governance, and a political system that, for many, revolves around a single superpower. On the other side, the regional level of political order has become more firmly established within the architecture of world politics and there are important elements of an emerging multi-regional system of international relations. The chapter traces how one-world forces and factors play out across different regions and how the many regional worlds play into the evolving set of debates on global political order. Although this chapter is focused on the particular issue of regionalism, the one world/many worlds relationship and the need to see problems from both perspectives shape the treatment of many of the issues analysed in this book, for example, in relation to nationalism, globalization, the environment, or human rights.

Chapter 11 considers the relationship between empire and global political order. This inevitably involves looking at the role of the United States. But, as elsewhere, my aim is to set the role and position of the United States in a broader conceptual and historical context. Historically, I suggest that order within the pluralist view has always been concerned with hierarchy as well as with the balance of power. Moreover, if globalization increases the demand for governance and if that demand cannot be met through the creation of multilateral institutions, then hierarchy represents one alternative model. However, the core argument of the chapter is to express deep scepticism both about the reality of US power and about the viability of hegemonic ordering. Although the power of the United States is immense, it is the limits, instability, and uncertainties of that power that are most striking. These limits apply most directly to the exercise of coercive power but their implications are broader and call into question the simplistic image of the United States as an unrivalled and all-powerful hegemonic power capable of acting as the pivot of an effective and legitimate order.

Central arguments

This book is primarily an exercise in clarifying complexity. In so far as it seeks to develop an overall argument, this can be summarized under three headings: how international society has changed, what the principal difficulties and challenges are, and what the way forward might look like.

First, the nature and extent of change. Even focusing directly on questions of order and governance, it is clear that there have been very great changes in the character of international society that are hard to make sense of within the framework of state-based pluralism. This is particularly true of governance of the global economy, of the management of the global environment, and of complex structures of governance that have been developed within regions. But it has also affected security—the heartland of traditional International Relations. And it is also visible in the way in which understandings of what states are and the relationship between governments and their citizens have been transformed. The arguments for structural and systemic change have to be taken seriously. Those who deny that there has been significant change in the character of international political relations rely on such a narrow view of the agenda of international order, such a one-dimensional view of the logic of power-political competition amongst states, and such a constrained account of the role of international law and institutions that it becomes impossible to make sense of the far-reaching changes that have taken place in the character of international society, above all in the period since 1945.[6]

---

[6] On the inescapability and continuity of interstate conflict, see John J. Mearsheimer, *The Tragedy of Great Power Politics* (New York: W.W. Norton, 2001). 'The sad fact is that international politics has always been a ruthless and dangerous business, and it is likely to remain that way. Although the intensity of their competition waxes and wanes, great powers fear each other and always compete with each other for power', 2. However, even if neo-realists such as Mearsheimer are right to be gloomy, it does not follow that neo-realism provides an accurate understanding either of the reasons for that gloom or the best way to confront it. For the most important neo-realist view of institutional change, or rather non-change, see Stephen D. Krasner, *Sovereignty: Organized Hypocrisy* (Princeton, NJ: Princeton University Press, 1999). From a Krasnerian view, sovereignty was never more than a convention or reference point and was always rife with anomalies or exceptions that could be explained in terms of power; powerful states went against international law when it suited them and the sovereignty-based legal order was never a confining or a constraining system; authority structures have never been able to dominate power asymmetries; as this has been true throughout the history of the modern state system, it makes little sense to think in terms of real or deep change.

No satisfactory account of international society can fail to consider the far-reaching challenges that derive from globalization—in its economic, social, political, and ecological dimensions. The density of international and world society has undoubtedly increased along both solidarist and transnational dimensions, reflecting the increasing complexity of world society, the involvement of a wider range of actors and processes, and far-reaching changes in the scope and range of international law and institutions. It is impossible to think seriously about international relations without reference to the changes in norms relating to conquest and security management, to self-determination and human rights, and to the elaborate institutions and regimes created to deal with global economic and ecological problems. There is a political as well as a legal and moral reality to solidarist and transnational norms and, even on purely pragmatic grounds, states need to justify their actions in terms of those norms and to seek the legitimacy from those international bodies that are the repositories and developers of those norms.

But, on the other side, a state-based pluralism continues to play a fundamental role in the political, legal, and normative structure of contemporary international society. The transformationist rhetoric about 'post-Westphalia' substantially overstates the degree to which we have in fact moved beyond a state- and sovereignty-based order—in terms of politics, law, and morality. Moreover, the precarious and insecure political foundations of both liberal solidarism and other alternative modes of governance mean that the aspirations of this normatively ambitious international society remain deeply contaminated by the preferences and interests of powerful states; that where solidarist cooperation is weak or breaks down, the older imperatives of pluralist international society continue to flourish; that even when genuinely consensual, the promotion of solidarist values both depends on, and reinforces, the power and privileges of the dominant state or groups of states. We are therefore not dealing with a vanished or vanishing Westphalian world, as much transformationist writing suggests, but rather with a world in which solidarist and cosmopolitan conceptions of governance coexist, often rather unhappily, with many aspects of the old pluralist order.

Following from this, the second set of arguments developed in the book concerns the principal difficulties and problems facing international society. As many have noted, all is not well with even the limited institutions that the world currently has. There appears to be a malaise in terms of both global institutions such as the United Nations (UN), the Nuclear Non-Proliferation Treaty (NPT), the World Trade Organisation (WTO), the World Bank, and the International Monetary Fund (IMF) and in terms of even the most elaborate and effective regional groupings such as the European Union (EU), North Atlantic Treaty Organisation (NATO), or North American Free

Trade Agreement (NAFTA). More generally, there is an increasingly serious and increasingly well-recognized governance deficit and an under-provision of cooperation—relative to the goals embodied in the legal and normative system, relative to what many functional theories of governance would lead us to expect, and relative to many reasonable and common sense views of what order in the twenty-first century is likely to require.

Contemporary international society is characterized by a complex plurality of ideas, views, and values. It is also characterized by a plurality of political identities in search of recognition, some relatively secure within established states, many others standing in ambiguous or highly conflictual relation to existing institutional and political structures. Global inequality remains extreme, with much of the day-to-day process of governance and many fundamental social choices being made in the shadow of unequal and often coercively exercised power. Many moral ideas and norms are now embedded within the institutions and practices of international society, but the plurality of views, values, and identities cannot be reconciled on the basis of any straightforward appeal to shared moral principles. And, although interest-driven cooperative logics play a fundamental role, global governance cannot be reduced to the provision of international public goods or the resolution of well-understood collective action problems. Subsequent chapters trace how liberal interest-driven accounts of the problems of global governance all too often disguise or evade the deep conflict over values, underlying purposes, and ways of seeing the world, and how the creation of stable and legitimate forms of cooperation is hindered by the enormous inequalities of power and wealth that characterize the international political system, the globalized world economy, and what has come to be called global civil society.

My account of the challenges, then, lays particular emphasis on conflicting values and on unequal power. In stressing the role of values, it is important not just to focus on the most obvious examples of clashing values and deeply incompatible world views—as in popular debates about 'clashing civilizations', the 'struggle for civilization', or the 'West against the rest'. Albeit in less dramatic form, the emergence of both solidarist and more complex modes of governance inevitably raises questions of how conflicting societal values are to be ordered. As the 'waterline of sovereignty' is lowered and as global governance is involved more and more in how societies are organized domestically, so the political salience of societal difference and value conflict rises. Divergent values also become more salient as the legal order moves down from high-minded sloganizing towards detailed and extremely intrusive operational rules and towards stronger mechanisms for their implementation. In some areas, such as human rights, the problem is widely recognized. But the intractability of the problem extends well beyond human rights. Thus, the politics of security is not only driven by problems of trust and credible contracting but also by deep disputes as to the values that are to be incorporated into understandings of security: whose security is to be promoted—that of states? nations? regimes? individuals? co-religionists? Equally, liberal approaches to global environmental negotiations can easily overlook the absence of a shared cultural or cognitive script that allows the largely rhetorical consensus value of 'sustainability' to be translated into stable and effective operational rules.

Inequality is a central fact of international political life. Of course there are many debates over the extent of global economic inequality and how it may be changing. But inequality of power and of condition continues to be one of the distinguishing features of international life and the big picture is reasonably clear. Roughly 85 per cent of the world's income goes to the richest 20 per cent of the world's population, whilst 6 per cent goes to the poorest 60 per cent. High-income countries consume over half of the world's total energy output and produce just under half of all carbon dioxide. Moreover, it is the political dimensions of inequality that feed most directly into the problem of global political order—first, inequality in the capacity of states to adapt to the many changes and challenges of both the international system and globalized capitalism; and, second, the way in which the structures of governance that have developed within international society both reflect and reinforce the broader patterns of inequality that mark the global system. Institutions are not, as liberal theory often suggests, neutral arenas for the solution of common problems but rather sites of power and dominance. The vast majority of weaker actors are increasingly 'rule takers' over a whole range of issues that affect all aspects of social, economic, and political life.

Together with the seriousness of value conflict, global inequality represents the other great obstacle to the achievement of legitimate forms of global political order. On one hand, inequality is implicated in many of the most serious challenges, for example in relation to conflict and insecurity, environmental problems, and violations of human rights. On the other, the legitimacy of traditional modes of international order based on hierarchy and inequality has come under increasing challenge. In 1950, the population of today's high-income countries constituted around 32 per cent of the world's population; today it is around 20 per cent; by 2050, it is likely to be around 13 per cent. In 2050, Western Europe may constitute just 4 per cent of world population and Japan just over 1 per cent. This again suggests that those who are concerned with the stability of the 'one world' will need to pay increased attention to the voices and views of the 'many worlds', and to those peoples and groups that have historically been marginalized in both the practices of global political order and the debates surrounding that order.

The third strand of the argument concerns normative implications and issues, and involves asking what sort of global political order we should be aiming at. Although I seek to demonstrate the continued vitality of

11

pluralist understandings and practices, the nature of the challenges facing international society means that a retreat to a thin, state-based pluralism is extremely problematic. The structural conditions associated with globalization, the changed nature of security challenges, and the very diverse but expansive normative aspirations embodied in powerful political forces (both state and non-state) make it very difficult to accept the prescriptive bottom line with which Hedley Bull ended *The Anarchical Society* in 1977: that a thin pluralist international society of states provides the best available means of upholding world order.

Much more importantly, the core normative issue involves asking who is the 'we' that is to be at the centre of the attempt to create a practically more viable and morally more acceptable form of global political order. Here, I highlight the importance of developing the links between political and moral cosmopolitanism. What does this mean? It means that it is not enough simply to lay out a view or a vision of where we think the world ought to be heading, however sophisticated and well-argued it may be and however attractive it is to us and those like us. Rather, the task is to think very hard about the conditions under which moral principles and moral ideas can be meaningfully and persuasively defended, justified, and criticized within global society as a whole. In the concluding chapter I suggest that three conditions are of fundamental importance: moral accessibility, institutional stability, and effective political agency.

Taking international society forward

This study takes the core idea of international society and applies it to the conditions of global politics in the early years of the twenty-first century. In doing so it is heavily indebted to earlier work on international society and can be broadly situated within the so-called English School.[7] This debt is visible in a number of ways: first, in the broad manner in which the problematique of order is understood; second, in the insistence on the importance of identifying conceptions of international society that are obviously in one sense analytical constructs but that also have a long history and a complex and shifting relationship to practice and to the understandings of actors engaged in practice; and, third, in arguing that political theory is not an activity that can be neatly divided into the empirical analysis of international politics on

---

[7] On the English School generally, see Brunello Vigezzi, *The British Committee on the Theory of International Politics (1954–1985): The Rediscovery of History* (Milan: Edizioni Unicopli, 2005); Tim Dunne, *Inventing International Society: A History of the English School* (Basingstoke, UK: Macmillan, 1998); Barry Buzan, *From International to World Society? English School Theory and the Social Structure of Globalization* (Cambridge: Cambridge University Press, 2004); and Andrew Linklater and Hidemi Suganami, *The English School of International Relations: A Contemporary Reassessment* (Cambridge: Cambridge University Press, 2006).

the one side and a purely normative exercise on the other, but rather one that revolves around an inherited set of political debates and that will necessarily remain open-ended and inconclusive.

But there are also a number of differences. In the first place, I seek to take forward the elaboration of different conceptions of international society. For writers such as Wight and Bull, the central challenge was to recover and defend the Grotian idea of international society and to set it against, on the one hand, the Hobbesian emphasis on the element of war and conflict and, on the other, the Kantian or revolutionist emphasis on transnational solidarity and the transcendence of the society of states. The difficulty with this trilectic is not just that it involves the serious miscasting of some of its central characters,[8] but, more importantly, that the Grotian *via media* remained extremely broad and encompassed a very wide range of often inconsistent, even contradictory, elements.

A second difference concerns the treatment of power. One of the most serious weaknesses of the Hedley Bull/Martin Wight trilectic is the tendency to see power as belonging to a separate 'element' or 'stream' of international life. Thus, the Grotian strand of international law and society is contrasted with the Hobbesian element of power and power competition and the Kantian emphasis on the idea of a global community. Although it is certainly the case that there are times and situations where the starkness of power appears all-dominant, such a move fails to appreciate the social aspects of power and the crucial links between power on the one hand and norms, rules, and institutions on the other. For both realists and liberals, power is all too often understood in simple contradistinction to law. Political power cannot be understood only in terms of material forces and factors. It is an inherently social concept. And, whenever power is exercised, questions inevitably arise as to its justification and legitimization.

In addition to English School writing, there is also an obvious overlap between this study and the literature on institutionalism and global

---

[8] The past twenty years have seen a great deal of sophisticated work on Grotius. See, in particular, Richard Tuck, *The Rights of War and Peace: Political Thought and International Order from Grotius to Kant* (Oxford: Oxford University Press, 1999); Benedict Kingsbury, 'A Grotian Tradition of Theory and Practice: Grotius, Law and Moral Skepticism in the Thought of Hedley Bull', in Ian Clark and Iver B. Neumann (eds.), *Classical Theories of International Relations* (Basingstoke, UK: Macmillan, 1996), 42–70; and Edward Keene, *Beyond the Anarchical Society: Grotius, Colonialism and Order in World Politics* (Cambridge: Cambridge University Press, 2002). But it is the analysis of the other traditions that has given 'textbook International Relations' its most misleading picture of the history of thought on the subject. For more nuanced views of Hobbes, see, in particular, Noel Malcolm, 'Hobbes' Theory of International Relations', in *Aspects of Hobbes* (Oxford: Oxford University Press, 2002), 432–56; on Kant, see James Bohman and Matthias Lutz-Bachmann (eds.), *Perpetual Peace: Essays on Kant's Cosmopolitan Ideal* (Cambridge, MA: MIT Press, 1997); and Andrew Hurrell, 'Kant and the Kantian Paradigm in International Relations', *Review of International Studies*, 16 (1990), 183–205.

governance.[9] Much of this work seeks to make sense of the immense complexity of global society by identifying the underlying mechanisms and logics that permit cooperation to take place and allow social order to be created and sustained.[10] Norms and institutions are conceived as negotiated and contracted in the process of social interaction, rather than as 'given' by the society to which individual actors or groups belong. As James Coleman puts it: 'Social norms ... specify what actions are regarded by a set of persons as proper or correct, or improper or incorrect. They are purposively generated, in that those persons who initiate or help maintain a norm see themselves as benefiting from its being observed or harmed by its being violated'.[11] Applied to international life, this approach is concerned with the ways in which institutions make it rational for states to cooperate out of self-interest. States are understood as rational actors driven by a calculating logic of consequences. Rationalist institutionalism views norms and institutions as purposively generated solutions to different kinds of collective action problems. As the leading proponent of this approach puts it:

Institutionalists do not elevate international regimes to mythical positions of authority over states: on the contrary, such regimes are established by states to achieve their purposes. Facing dilemmas of coordination and collaboration under conditions of interdependence, governments demand international institutions to enable them to achieve their interests through limited collective action.[12]

It is precisely this kind of reasoning that explains why so much of the recent discussion has been framed around the concepts of governance (as opposed to government) and global governance.

At the most general level, governance involves the establishment and operation of social institutions (in the sense of rules of the game that serve to define social practices, assign roles, and guide interactions among the occupants of those roles) capable of

---

[9] See e.g. Oran Young, *Governance in World Affairs* (Ithaca, NY: Cornell University Press, 1999); Joseph S. Nye and John D. Donahue (eds.), *Governance in a Globalizing World* (Washington, DC: Brookings, 2000); and Paul F. Diehl (ed.), *The Politics of Global Governance: International Organizations in an Interdependent World* (Boulder, CO: Lynne Rienner, 1997).

[10] See e.g. Karol Soltan, Eric M. Uslaner, and Virginia Haufler (eds.), *Institutions and Social Order* (Ann Arbor, MI: University of Michigan Press, 1998).

[11] James S. Coleman, *Foundations of Social Theory* (Cambridge, MA: Harvard University Press, 1990), 242.

[12] Robert O. Keohane, 'Institutionalist Theory and the Realist Challenge after the Cold War', in David A. Baldwin (ed.), *Neorealism and Neoliberalism: The Contemporary Debate* (New York: Columbia University Press, 1993), 273–4; and Robert O. Keohane, *Power and Governance in a Partially Globalized World* (London: Routledge, 2002); cf. Robert Axelrod: 'what works well for a player is more likely to be used again, while what turns out poorly is more likely to be discarded', 'An Evolutionary Approach to Norms', *American Political Science Review*, 80 (December 1986), 1097.

resolving conflicts, facilitating cooperation, or, more generally, alleviating collective-action problems in a world of interdependent actors.[13]

Seen from this perspective, global governance is best understood as a response to the increasingly serious collective action problems generated by growing societal, ecological, and economic interdependence. Such interdependence creates huge scope for joint gains but cooperation under conditions of formal anarchy is difficult because of the problem of enforcing agreements and the temptations to cheat and free ride. Globalization does not lead to an automatic harmony of interests, but it does create increasing demand for cooperation and also decreases the degree of concern with relative gains—who gains how much and with what kinds of power-political implications—that, for realists, has long been the most potent obstacle to effective cooperation. The view of international society presented in this book challenges the analytical and political liberalism that dominated much of the writing on global governance in the 1990s. Although analytically extremely impressive, this literature tended to skirt rather easily over the problem of managing power, especially unequal power, and the difficulties of mediating between conflicting values.[14] Politically, it tended to assume far too easily that the end of the Cold War had led to an underlying consensus on certain core liberal values and that the power of the liberal West could be harnessed, relatively unproblematically, to shared and common purposes.[15]

A third approach to international order focuses not on purposes and persistent patterns nor on the incentives facing agents in situations of collective action, but rather on the broad political, economic, and social forces, the historical movements, and the structural trends that shape the choices of human agents.[16] From this perspective, we can understand the behaviour of the parts by uncovering the logic of the whole and the laws that shape that logic—the

[13] Oran Young, *International Governance: Protecting the Environment in a Stateless Society* (Ithaca, NY and London: Cornell University Press, 1994), 15. See also James N. Rosenau and Ernst-Otto Czempiel (eds.), *Governance without Government: Order and Change in World Politics* (Cambridge: Cambridge University Press, 1992); and the further discussion of governance in Chapter 4.

[14] Michael Barnett and Raymond Duvall (eds.), *Power and Global Governance* (Cambridge: Cambridge University Press, 2005), esp. ch. 1 on both the use of 'global governance' and the current academic debate about power.

[15] The close relationship between academic fashions and political trends is no coincidence. Academic International Relations (especially in the United States) has since its creation as an academic field been very closely connected to the priorities, preferences, and prejudices of US politics and foreign policy. For the classic discussion, see Stanley Hoffmann, 'An American Social Science: International Relations', in *Janus and Minerva: Essays in the Theory and Practice of International Politics* (Boulder, CO: Westview, 1987); and Miles Kahler, 'Inventing International Relations: International Relations Since 1945', in Michael W. Doyle and G. John Ikenberry (eds.), *New Thinking in International Relations* (Boulder, CO: Westview, 1997), 20–53.

[16] Buzan seeks to set out a structural interpretation of English School ideas (Buzan 2004).

15

structural political forces related to the rise and fall of hegemonic powers;[17] the structural economic logics of global capitalism;[18] the transnational social forces that help us make sense of the mobilization of previously subordinated peoples in the struggle against colonialism and the various 'waves' of democratization; and, last but not least, the complex dynamics of the biosphere within which all social activity must take place. It is impossible to provide an account of international political order without referring extensively to these structural forces and without taking a position as to their origins, their significance, and their durability. But they are not themselves the central focus of this study.

Theoretical underpinnings

My focus, then, is less on theoretical explanation of how particular institutions or governance regimes emerge and develop, and more on assessing the changing character of institutionalization in world politics, the normative commitments of different varieties of institutionalism and ideas about global governance, and the adequacy of existing institutions for meeting practical and normative challenges. This approach reflects a broader set of theoretical commitments that I cannot defend in any detail here.[19] But five general points should be noted.

In the first place, it involves a clear rejection of the view that the international system can be viewed solely in material terms as a decentralized, anarchic structure in which functionally undifferentiated states vary only according to the distribution of power. Central to the 'system' is a historically created, and evolving, structure of common understandings, rules, norms, and mutual expectations. The concepts of state sovereignty, international law, or war are not given by the game of power-politics. Rather, shared and historically grounded understandings of war or sovereignty shape what the nature of the game is, how it is to be played, and, very critically, how it has changed and evolved. International Relations cannot therefore be taught or analysed as part of an abstract game independent of its human or historical origins. It grows out of its past, although never fully outgrows it and the system is the result of complex historical processes of change and development. There are certainly

[17] See e.g. Robert Gilpin, *War and Change in World Politics* (New York: Cambridge University Press, 1981).

[18] See e.g. Robert Cox, *Production, Power, and World Order* (New York: Columbia University Press, 1987) and (with T. Sinclair), *Approaches to World Order* (Cambridge: Cambridge University Press, 1996).

[19] For a fuller analysis, including fuller references to the relevant academic literatures, see Andrew Hurrell, 'Norms and Ethics in International Relations', in Walter Carlsnaes, Thomas Risse, and Beth Simmons (eds.), *Handbook of International Relations* (London: Sage, 2002), 137–54.

very powerful and recurring political logics of conflict and cooperation, but these cannot be cashed out in the form of historical and immutable systemic laws. History matters because of the extent to which all human societies, including international society, rely on historical stories about themselves to legitimize notions of where they are and where they might be going. An important element in the study of International Relations is therefore the uncovering of actors' understandings of international politics and the ways in which these understandings have been gathered into intelligible patterns, traditions, or ideologies. The past also matters because of the changing, contested, plural, and completely un-straightforward nature of the concepts which we use to map the international political, legal, and moral landscape—and which are indelibly shaped by who 'we' are. To stress the importance of history is not to buy into an argument about eternal recurrence and endless reproduction. It does not mean that nothing ever changes. The point is rather that we can only understand change by looking carefully at the past, tracing the changing constitution of international society, and being as clear-headed as we can about the nature and seriousness of the political difficulties involved.

Second, although material structures matter, they cannot be understood outside the shared knowledge and shared understandings held by the actors themselves. In this, I follow a broadly constructivist approach that sees international social structures not as 'natural' features of world politics, but as produced and reproduced in the concrete social practices of social actors and in inter-subjective meanings. These meanings are not purely subjective ideas held by individuals but rather shared ideas that exist between actors and that are embedded in historical practice and in historically constructed normative structures—in international legal rules and practices, in international political norms, and in the dominant ideologies and practices that animate them. Trying to give a sense of the major changes that have taken place in the international legal order is a central task. But it is also important to avoid an excessively legalist approach. The normative structure includes political norms—a classic example of which would be the emergence amongst major powers of understandings about spheres of influence. It also includes practices such as the expansion of conditionality (discussed in Chapters 3 and 8), whose importance is widely recognized by international lawyers but which fit uneasily into the structure of law.

And it includes traditions of moral deliberation. Thus, war and conflict take place within an inherited tradition of ideas that may well have emerged from within the European and indeed Christian world but which have become deeply embedded in the institutions and practices of international society. The continual involvement of individuals and societies in war and conflict, the moral and political necessity of trying to make sense of what war involves, and the limited range of plausible arguments have led over time

17

to the creation of intelligible patterns, traditions, and ideologies. These form the core of legal debates over the use of force and also of moral debates, including understandings of what might constitute just war. As Michael Walzer puts it: 'Reiterated over time, our arguments and judgements shape what I want to call *the moral reality of war*—that is, all those experiences of which moral language is descriptive or within which it is necessarily employed'.[20]

Third, it is important to remember the multiple roles played by norms, rules, and institutions in international life. They may well serve as regulatory rules designed to constrain choices or as the parameters within which individual agents pursue their own preferences. This is the view of rules that lies behind the common claim that international law in relation to, say, the use of force is not able to 'control' what states do. Whilst this may very often be true, the critical point is that norms and rules have many other roles and do much more than this. Norms and rules help explain how actors are constituted: who can act and in what kinds of social and political activities. They help us make sense of the identity of actors and hence of the sources of their preferences. In addition, norms do not simply constrain action and constitute actors but they also enable and empower action. Norms are therefore central to understanding the power to mobilize, to justify, and to legitimize action.

Fourth, this theoretical approach reflects a view about the role of ideas in understanding and explaining political action. We can understand the actions of states or patterns of international order not only in terms of what state leaders have been forced to do or what calculations of power and interest have led them to do but also in terms of the ideas, values, and principles which they have believed in and that they have striven after. As Robert Musil put it: 'If there is to be a sense of reality, then there must also be a sense of possibility'.[21] For this reason we should be cautious about accepting too clear-cut a distinction between a rational logic of consequences and a norm-following logic of appropriateness.[22] Elster contrasts instrumentally rational action that is hypersensitive to consequences with norms understood as internalized Kantian imperatives ('blind, compulsive, mechanical, or even unconscious'); and Krasner distinguishes between consequential action on the one hand and 'taken for granted', 'deeply embedded', or 'internalized'

---

[20] Michael Walzer, *Just and Unjust Wars: A Moral Argument with Historical Illustrations* (New York: Basic Books, 1977), 15.

[21] Robert Musil, *The Man without Qualities*, translated by Sophie Wilkins and Burton Pike (London: Picador, 1995); cf. E. H. Carr on the limitations of realism: 'Most of all, consistent realism breaks down because it fails to provide any ground for purposive or meaningful action', *The Twenty Years' Crisis, 1919–1939* (Basingstoke, UK: Palgrave, 2001), 86.

[22] James G. March and Johan P. Olson, *Rediscovering Institutions: The Organizational Basis of Politics* (New York: Free Press, 1989).

norms on the other (which is how he interprets English School writing).[23] And yet how we calculate consequences is often far from obvious and not easily separable from our understanding of legal or moral norms. Time and process are especially important in understanding how logics of consequences and of appropriateness interrelate. At any point in time it may indeed be helpful to think of actors making choices between consequentialist calculations of interest and normative evaluations of appropriateness. But over time the obviousness of certain sorts of norms (in relation to, say, slavery, human rights, or military conquest) becomes such an accepted and natural feature of the international political and legal landscape that it becomes part of how actors routinely calculate consequences, and the costs and benefits of alternative policy choices.

Even if we suspect that appeals to political ideas, to legal principles, and to moral purposes are no more than rationalizations of self-interest, they may still affect political behaviour because of the powerful need to legitimate action. As Skinner puts it:

It does not...follow from the fact that an agent's professed principles may be *ex post facto* rationalizations that they have no role to play in explaining his behaviour. As I have sought to emphasize, this argument ignores the implications of the fact that any agent possesses a standard motive for attempting to legitimate his untoward social or political actions. This implies first of all that he will be committed to claiming that his apparently untoward actions were in fact motivated by some accepted set of social or political principles. And this in turn implies that, even if the agent is not in fact motivated by any of the principles he professes, he will nevertheless be obliged to behave in such a way that his actions remain compatible with the claim that these principles genuinely motivated him. To recognize these implications is to accept that the courses of action open to any rational agent in this type of situation must in part be determined by the range of principles that he can profess with plausibility.[24]

Fifth, and finally, this book reflects a particular view of the relationship between the role that normative ideas play in the practice of politics ('how have moral ideas about international order influenced political behaviour?') and rational debate as to the nature of ethical conduct ('what ought we to do?') This view of normative theory (which I will draw together in the concluding chapter) focuses on the need to understand, but not uncritically accept, the normative consensus that has come to develop within international society, and to build arguments and proposals for greater justice out of the values and

---

[23] Elster (1989: 100) and Krasner (1999: 44–8).

[24] Quentin Skinner, 'Some Problems in the Analysis of Political Thought and Action', in James Tully (ed.), *Meaning and Context: Quentin Skinner and His Critics* (Cambridge: Polity Press, 1988), 116–17. As Skinner notes, one consequence is that 'Every revolutionary is to this extent obliged to march backwards into battle', 112. The concept of legitimacy is developed more fully in Chapter 3.

modes of reasoning that have already begun to take root within the shared practices of international and global society.

This book is concerned with the changing constitution of international society in the three senses of the term identified by Joseph Weiler: first, constitution in the sense of the broad institutional practices, norms, and conventions of behaviour which, taken together, define how a polity has been constituted; second, constitution in the sense of the processes by which a polity is constituted and through which change take place; and, third, constitution in the sense of the vitality, strength, or healthiness of the polity.[25] This is an immodest undertaking. But there is a simple defence. One, although only one, of the purposes of International Relations as an academic subject is to provide a sense of what makes the world hang together, to use John Ruggie's wonderfully apt phrase.[26] The immense complexity of the global system means that any such synthesis is bound to be partial and incomplete. And yet, especially at a time when disciplinary fragmentation has proceeded so far and when research within disciplines has become ever more specialized, the need for synthesis has grown. It is important for students of International Relations to avoid seeing the subject as a series of disparate and disconnected, if evermore theoretically sophisticated, domains with no clear sense of how they might relate to each other. It is also important that the mental maps and broad images of the world that do so much to shape political practice are both taken seriously but also subjected to critical academic scrutiny.

This is particularly the case because the language of 'international order' or 'global governance' is never politically neutral. Indeed a capacity to produce and project proposals, conceptions, and theories of order is a central part of the practice of power. Unsurprisingly, in debates on world order, it is the voices of the most powerful that dominate the discussion, either talking about the world or taking their ideas to the world. In addition, the rhetoric of 'order' and 'governance' can easily lead to an exaggerated belief in the possibility of a neat, tidy arrangement of political life that is unlikely within domestic society and deeply implausible beyond it. It implies an image of politics that is very hard to reconcile with the immense complexity of the global system, with the multiplicity of logics—of power, of interest, and of identity—that operate within it, and with the dynamism and unpredictability of the forces that shape it. This long-standing challenge has been made harder by the speed of change and by our limited understanding of large-scale social systems characterized by complexity, non-linearity, and unpredictability. There is also a

---

[25] J. H. H. Weiler, *The Constitution of Europe: 'Do the New Clothes Have an Emperor?' and Other Essays on European Integration* (Cambridge: Cambridge University Press, 1999).

[26] John Ruggie, 'Embedded Liberalism and the Postwar Economic Regimes', reprinted in *Constructing the World Polity: Essays in International Institutionalization* (London: Routledge, 1998), 1.

need to be persistently alert to the variable and unstable meanings of the core political concepts around which debates on global order are organized—state, nation, power, hegemony, security, democracy. Our language and concepts struggle to cope with the difficulties involved and, to paraphrase Novalis, the best we can do is to try to grasp at the rough and ever-changing contours of political order that shimmer through the veil of chaos.

Part I
Frameworks

2

The anarchical society revisited

This chapter lays out the principal features of a state-based pluralist conception of international society and introduces some of the major issues, debates, and dilemmas to which it has given rise. My first purpose is to establish an initial framework against which subsequent developments and alternative conceptions can be evaluated. The second goal is to give a sense of just why pluralism has remained such a powerful and influential way of thinking about international order. Although this book argues that there can be no retreat to a pluralist world, it is crucial to understand the case for pluralism and to appreciate its continued vitality in political and legal practice, and in political theory. It continues to be viewed by many as both politically powerful and normatively attractive. The chapter is divided into four sections, looking in turn at pluralism and the state, pluralism and power, pluralism and values, and pluralism and law.

Pluralism and the state

'The view of world order to which we have fallen heir is dominated by the conception of statehood.'[1] The deeply entrenched statism of both political theory and international relations has many sources. For some it rests simply on the historical rise of the modern state as the dominant form of social and political order and on its continued power in the face of would-be challengers or competitors, be they transnational firms, international organizations, or transnational social movements and non-governmental organizations (NGOs). For others it rests on the role of the national state as the primary focus for human loyalty and communal allegiance. But, whatever its foundations, it is impossible to ignore the immense power of the idea and ideology of the state in the Western political imagination and the way in which this ideology became globalized in the course of European imperial

[1] Neil MacCormick, 'Liberalism, Nationalism and the Post-sovereign State', *Political Studies*, 44 (1996), 554.

expansion and in the process of decolonization. The emergence of the modern state was complex, the history of state formation contested, and the variety of actually existing states and the inequalities amongst them have always been hard to square with the ideal-typical character of the 'modern state'. But, once established, the state came to dominate the ontological landscape of politics, as well as many of the most powerful traditions of political theory, moral reflection, and international legal analysis.

Many of the arguments about the irrelevance or outdatedness of the pluralist conception of international order are based on empirical assessments about the changing and diminishing role of the state. As we see in chapters dealing with globalization, human rights, and security, many commentators take it as axiomatic that the state is in retreat, that it is powerless, that it is hollow (to paraphrase the titles of recent books). Suffice it to say here that the pluralist remains unimpressed. Yes, the character of the state and the conditions that it faces have changed, but the most striking point is the resilience of the state in the face of these changes and challenges. Witness the continued power of political nationalism both in movements seeking to form new states and in providing the powerful ideological cement for many old ones, the continued economic role of the state even in the face of liberal globalization, and the continued importance of military power both in defining what a state is (Weber's classic definition of the state as the possessor of the monopoly of legitimate violence) and as a core instrument of public policy.

In addition, it became, and has remained, extremely difficult to avoid seeing the world except through the eyes of the state. James Scott has highlighted how states needed to make societies visible and legible in order to control them 'The premodern state was, in crucial respects, partially blind; it knew precious little about its subjects, their wealth, their landholdings and yields, their location, their very identity. It lacked anything like a detailed "map" of its terrain and its people. It lacked, for the most part, a measure, a metric, that would allow it to "translate" what it knew into a common standard necessary for a synoptic view.'[2] The development of the state and the expansion of its goals and roles involved the creation and institutionalization of many of the simplified categories through which both the social and natural worlds could be understood and manipulated—including through maps, censuses, surveys, and systems of national statistics; through the categorization of individuals for the purposes of taxation, conscription, and citizenship; and through the imposition of national languages and the creation of national education systems. 'The categories used by state agents are not merely means to make their environment legible; they are an authoritative tune to which most of

[2] James C. Scott, *Seeing Like a State: How Certain Schemes to Improve the Human Condition Have Failed* (New Haven, CT: Yale University Press, 1998), 2.

the population must dance.'[3] As a consequence the world that we see and experience is still in countless ways the world created by those who have sought to build up, control, and administer states.

But the resilience of the state cannot be explained by empirical arguments about its continued political centrality or by claims concerning its cognitive embeddedness. For the pluralist, there are extremely powerful prudential and moral reasons why the state should continue to be placed at the heart of any enquiry into global political order.

The first argument is straightforwardly Hobbesian. It stresses the state as a bulwark against anarchy and as the best hope for the provision of security. On this view, it is unproductive to enquire into the origins of states and dangerous to flirt with hypothetical alternatives. Domestic order and external defence are the two defining purposes of the state and from the early theorists of the state such as Bodin and Hobbes, the legitimacy of the state is dependent above all on its capacity to uphold civil peace and to promote international security. As the Islamic saying has it: sixty years of tyranny is better than a single night of anarchy.[4] It is certainly the case that the state can all too easily become a threat to the security of its citizens and that concentrations of unaccountable state power have been responsible for large-scale political violence, both within domestic societies and in terms of interstate war. It may be true then, as John Keane suggests, that 'states are positively dangerous instruments of pacification'.[5] Nevertheless, for the pluralist, there is very little to suggest that politics without the state (certainly in the absence of secure and sustainable external suppliers of public order) represents a sustainable road to the containing or curtailing of social violence. Rather, the declining capacity of the state to enforce legitimate order has led in many parts of the world to the privatization of violence as diverse social groups are increasingly able to mobilize armed force, and to the privatization of security as social groups seek to protect themselves, whether through the growth of vigilantism, the formation of paramilitary groups, or the purchase of security within an expanding commercial marketplace. Where privatized security has been most visible, it is the weak and the poor who are the most vulnerable. In this case, as in others, the state can certainly be a major part of the problem but remains an unavoidable part of the solution. This Hobbesian view of the state also has important consequences for the understanding of the limits of purely legal conceptions of sovereignty. It is true that many constitutional

---

[3] Scott (1998: 82–3).

[4] Quoted by James Piscatori, 'Order, Justice and Global Islam', in Rosemary Foot, John Lewis Gaddis, and Andrew Hurrell (eds.), *Order and Justice in International Relations* (Oxford: Oxford University Press, 2003), 267.

[5] John Keane, *Reflections on Violence* (London: Verso, 1996), 26; cf Rudolph J. Rummel: 'In the twentieth century, governments murdered as a prudent estimate 174 million men, women and children. It could be over 340 million'. *Never Again: Ending War, Democide and Famine Through Democratic Freedom* (Coral Springs: Llumina Press, 2005): 145.

systems will seek to constrain and control the sovereign power. This is what liberal constitutional orders are all about. Nevertheless it is also true that, when faced by a decisive internal or external challenge, effective coercive power and the will and capacity to act have to exist somewhere if the survival of the state is to be guaranteed. This was, of course, how Weber defined the state—a territorially based form of political order maintained by the threat and application of physical force. For those working within this tradition, it is precisely this characteristic that differentiates political life within the state from international institutions and from different forms of governance beyond the state.

A second major argument concerns diversity and pluralism. The state as an institution (but not necessarily any particular state) and the apparatus of state sovereignty provide a container for pluralism and a framework for the protection of diversity. What animates this claim is the idea that peoples, nations, and communities have an identity and justifiably seek the protective and expressive power of the state to further that identity. If states and state sovereignty provide the basic institutional framework, it is some notion of political community and a belief in the moral value of self-determination— most commonly national but often shading into cultural and religious—that has come evermore to provide the political power and the moral meaning to the idea of living in a world made up of separate nation-states. As we see in Chapter 4, such arguments have come to exercise a profound impact on all discussion about the identity of the actors and about the character and moral purposes of those actors. It is a fundamental feature of the discourse by which claims to political authority and to the control of territory are articulated and justified. The importance of a thick national community (and the inevitable myth-making that goes with it) may be seen as having some intrinsic or essentialist value. This is clearly the case with many illiberal brands of nationalism. But it is also true of liberal communitarians and ethical particularists whose view of a good and worthwhile society stresses the importance of a common culture and shared ethical standards. Dense forms of political community can be favoured for instrumental reasons, as for those liberal nationalists who believe that it is only identification with a national community that can foster meaningful citizenship and provide a secure basis for both grounding and implementing conceptions of social justice.[6] Or, as for anti-colonial nationalists, their value may lie in the creation of the solidarity and effective agency needed to resist external oppression.

A third argument stresses the importance of collective self-governance: a pluralist international society furthers the right of a people or community to govern itself whilst minimizing the dangers of imposition and interference from other, and especially, more powerful states, or from the threat that

[6] See especially David Miller, *On Nationality* (Oxford: Clarendon Press, 1995).

would come from the creation of a world government or from a greater centralized global power. The greater the emphasis on popular sovereignty, the more important the political community represented by the state becomes. Laws that express and reflect the will of the people will always have a far higher legitimacy and value than those that emerge from horse-trading and agreements amongst the representatives of often dubious states. But there are other conceptions of politics that work to reinforce the attractions of a state-based pluralism. For example, those influenced by the republican tradition will be likely to place a high priority on forms of political responsibility and patriotism that are located within a specific country. Republicans from Rousseau onwards are always likely to place a high value on active and engaged citizens within a small and cohesive polity and to be suspicious of distant and distanced institutions. Finally, this view of political self-government is reinforced by those who share Mill's view that 'real' and effective democracy must be home-grown and who are therefore sceptical over attempts to export democracy or to incorporate democratic norms into international law and society.

Pluralism and power

Even if we accept a view of global political order built around the state, it is not clear why we should be content with only a very thin and minimalist view of international society. After all, pluralist writers on international society clearly recognize the reality of shared interests. As it developed historically (especially in the period from Hobbes to Vattel), the idea of international society begins with the argument that a brutalist depiction of international life is empirically wrong and underplays the possibilities of cooperation. States cooperate because, however different their values and however problematic their power relations, they see the possibility of gain. Rules, laws, and conventions can, and often do, emerge without an overarching authority. They are of mutual benefit because they help shape expectations, increase the predictability of international life, and thereby reduce uncertainty and insecurity. However, capturing common interest is rarely simple, first, because of the problem of managing conflicts of power and second, because of the problem of mediating amongst diverse and often contested values.

The first part of the pluralist answer, then, has to do with the problem of power and of managing unequal power. The core intuition is that diffidence, fear, and suspicion are extremely difficult to dislodge in social settings characterized by great inequalities of power, weak institutions, and deep societal differences. On this traditional account, anarchy—in the sense of the absence of centralized government—creates a self-help system in which each state has no alternative but to look to its own security. Unequal power and the material capabilities of opponents create potential threats to national security. If a state is much more powerful than its neighbours, that power is likely to be seen as dangerous and to inspire fear: 'By fear we mean not an unreasoning emotion, but a rational apprehension of future evil.'[7] This in turn leads to security competition and to emergence of the balance of power as a central political mechanism of the system. As von Gentz put it in 1806: 'The state which is not prevented by any external consideration from oppressing a weaker, is always, however weak it may be, too strong for the interests of the whole.'[8] In addition, the enormous inequalities of power in international relations have the potential to fuel interstate rivalry and stand in the way of attempts to move towards collective security and to domesticate international relations. The textbook portrayal of International Relations has tended to lay too much emphasis on anarchy and too little on inequality.

Internally, inequality is an important part of the political story, though far from being the whole of it. Internal politics is also the realm of authority and law, of established institutions, of socially settled and established ways of doing things. Internationally, inequality is more nearly the whole of the political story. Differences of national strength and power and of national capability and competence are what the study and practice of international politics are almost entirely about. This is so not only because international politics lacks the effective laws and institutions found within nations but also because inequalities across nations are greater than inequalities within them.[9]

Even if the hard-line realist position overstates the intensity and continuity of such insecurity, the tremendous differences in the scale of inequality between domestic and international settings do have a crucial negative impact on the possibility of any centralized system of law and order as well as other less structured forms of governance. Inequality means that some states have far less need for the cooperation and forbearance of others, that the strength of the violators of law can easily come to exceed that of the upholders of law, and that, even if this is not the case, attempts at coercive sanctions against violators will involve large-scale conflict. On this account, then, the structure of power and interests and the extent of inequality will often make the resolution of many conflicts difficult, if not impossible. All politics, but especially world politics, is the arena for struggles amongst differing social and political ideals, and the character of competition for power between these rival views and the manner in which power is deployed will remain *a*—but not necessarily *the*—central focus of enquiry.

Because the realist position is so often caricatured and because realists themselves (and especially neo-realists) are often guilty of self-caricature, it

---

[7] Martin Wight, *Power Politics* (London: Penguin Books, 1979), 139.

[8] Friedrich von Gentz, *Fragments upon the Balance of Power in Europe* (London: M. Peltier, 1806), 60–1.

[9] Kenneth Waltz, *Theory of International Politics* (Reading, MA: Addison-Wesley, 1979), 143.

is important to note what this view does *not* imply. It does not depend on the argument that there is an absolute and eternal divide between 'domestic order' on the one hand and 'international anarchy' on the other. After all, Morgenthau's political realism was just as much a response to the breakdown of constitutional government on the streets of Weimar Germany as it was to the failings of the League of Nations in Geneva. Rather, it reflects a powerful sense of the fragility of all social orders, including within the developed and prosperous West. Both during the 1990s, but especially after September 11, it became common to draw a sharp contrast between a modern, rational West and on outside world composed of premodern states and irrational, even barbaric, cultures. Such a move, however, underplays the extent to which the repudiation of Enlightenment rationalism has been a central part of the Western philosophical and political tradition and skirts too easily around the fact that the 'triumph' of liberal capitalist democracy was not predestined but rather the product of a great deal of chance and contingency.[10] War and non-democratic politics have belonged as much to the mainstream of the Western tradition as have democracy, peace, and human rights; and the idea of a world safely and securely divided between zones of peace and tranquillity and zones of conflict and turmoil is comforting but illusory—as the reappearance in the 1990s of concentration camps and racist violence in the heart of Europe should remind us. There is indeed a profound sense in which it is the possibility of war and conflict that continues to define the meaning of 'normal' politics and our understanding of political order. As Pasquale Pasquino puts it, war is 'the concept that makes it possible to understand the forms as well as the existence of peace and order.'[11]

Nor does a continued concern with power depend on the view that the only hard currency in international life is provided by military power and that it is fear of subjugation that fuels the suspicion of unequal power. Instead, concern might stem from fear that a more powerful state, even a powerful state with shared values, will be able to 'lay down the law' to weaker states, to slant the distribution of interaction and cooperation in its own favour, to impose its own values and ways of doing things, and to undermine the procedural rules on which long-term, stable, and legitimate cooperation depends. If unequal power is not harnessed to some collective authority or firmly embedded within stable structures of interstate or societal cooperation, then the potential political implications of that unequal power cannot be

[10] See John Burrow, *The Crisis of Reason: European Thought, 1848–1914* (New Haven, CT: Yale University Press, 2000); and Mark Mazower, *Dark Continent: Europe's Twentieth Century* (Harmondsworth, UK: Penguin Books, 1999).

[11] Pasquale Pasquino, 'Political Theory of Peace and War: Foucault and the History of Modern Political Theory', *Economy and Society*, 22/1 (February 1993), 80. See also Carl Schmitt, *The Concept of the Political*, translated by Georg Schwab (New Brunswick, NJ: Rutgers University Press, 1976), esp. 32–5; and Ian Shapiro and Russell Hardin (eds.), *Political Order, Nomos*, vol. 38 (New York: New York University Press, 1993), part I.

ignored—not because they lead inevitably to war and conflict, but because the pathologies of power will tend to affect the nature and functioning of the legal and normative order.

What, then, does this concern imply for international society? Most obviously it points to the importance of the balance of power.[12] The link between pluralist conceptions of international society and the balance of power was historically very close, with the balance of power being seen as a principal means of preserving the independence of states (but not of all states), as a means of constraining and restraining the most powerful and would-be hegemonic, as an inducement to moderation and restraint into foreign policy, and, finally, as an essential background condition for the operation of international law and institutions. The balance of power was not simply a deeply rooted pattern of state behaviour (order as regularity) but became a consciously maintained institution governed by its own political norms (order as purposive pattern). From this perspective, it matters a great deal that states come to have a shared sense of the balance of power, that this develops into a coherent and well-established doctrine, and that it may even form part of the institutional, or as Butterfield put it, constitutional structure of the state system.[13] Crucial, then, is the emphasis placed by international society writers on the balance of power not as the expression of some automatic or mechanistic logic of power competition, but rather as an institution with its own shared rules, mutual understandings, and unspoken assumptions that could assist power-political bargaining and legitimize agreed outcomes.[14] In a similar vein, the stability of nuclear deterrence depended not on the mechanics of nuclear delivery systems but on the emergence of a shared set of understandings as to what constitutes acceptable behaviour. The most serious Cold War crises and deterrence failures arose precisely from the lack or erosion of such understandings.

Closely connected with the history of the balance of power was a particular understanding of war. One of the core features of a pluralist order is the emergence of war as a distinct legal and social category, involving violence by organized groups for political purposes and distinguished from private war.

[12] For an excellent analysis of power-based understandings of order which is then contrasted with his own constitutionalist view, see G. J. Ikenberry, *After Victory: Institutions, Strategic Restraint and the Rebuilding of Order after Major Wars* (Princeton, NJ: Princeton University Press, 2001), 10–17 and 21–49.

[13] Herbert Butterfield, 'The Balance of Power', in Herbert Butterfield and Martin Wight (eds.), *Diplomatic Investigations: Essays in the Theory of International Politics* (London: Allen and Unwin, 1966), 132–48. See also Bull (2003: ch. 5); Robert Jervis, 'A Political Science Perspective on the Balance of Power', *American Journal of Political Science*, 97/3 (June 1992: 716–24); Waltz (1979: ch. 6).

[14] Paul Schroeder, *The Transformation of European Politics 1763–1848* (Oxford: Clarendon Press, 1994). See also Kissinger's view, 'An international structure held together only by a balance of forces will sooner or later collapse in catastrophe', in *American Foreign Policy*, 3rd edn. (New York: W.W. Norton, 1977), 395.

Within the pluralist world, military force represented a legitimate instrument that could be resorted to, controlled, and used with at least the expectation of effectiveness to promote state objectives and for the self-enforcement of basic rights, above all the right of self-defence and the maintenance of the balance of power. Politically, it was, in Clausewitz's famous phrase, 'a real political instrument'; legally, it was, as one leading nineteenth-century international lawyer put it, a 'permitted mode of giving effect to decisions'. Central to pluralist statecraft was the idea that there is an internal logic of political violence, with coercion and politics being very closely allied. It is for these reasons that war is understood by a pluralist such as Bull as one of the institutions of international society—central to politics of individual states, to the operation of the balance of power, to the ways in which change occurs in the structure of the system, and, at least potentially, to the implementation of collective security and the promotion of shared purposes.

For progressivist liberals talking in terms of acceptable, controlled violence is morally questionable and serves as little more than a thinly disguised celebration of crude *Realpolitik*. But to the pluralist, this is dangerous wishful thinking that misunderstands the nature of politics. The statesperson needs to understand the rationality of violence, partly to learn how to succeed politically, but partly because thinking in terms of interests and in terms of rationality (including the rationality of violence) will make politics more rather than less tolerable. For the classical tradition of *raison d'état*, rationality was not something that could simply be assumed; central to politics is the immensely difficult task of imposing some kind of rationality and order on the chaos and contingency of political life and of countering the perverse internal logics of power and the destructive role of rhetoric in political affairs.[15] Equally, it was around such arguments that a powerful tradition of prudential and situational ethics emerged, captured most clearly in Weber's ethic of responsibility as a substitute for the controlling force of determining formal rules or binding ethical principles. Moral politics should be closely tied to the practice of statecraft and to the responsibility of the statesperson to their own political community. The (unavoidable) use of political violence always carries with it the danger of perverse and unintended consequences and is, in Weber's words, 'morally suspect or at least morally dangerous'. On the strong account of this position, there are no overarching global principles of justice that apply to foreign policy. Political morality is the art of successfully navigating very stormy seas and prudence becomes the supreme political virtue. But, even if there are some shared principles of justice beyond the state, acting upon them in the face of the contingency and perverse consequences that characterize political action will still involve a great deal of prudential

[15] See, in particular, Jonathan Haslam, *No Virtue Like Necessity: Realist Thought in International Relations Since Machiavelli* (New Haven, CT: Yale University Press, 2002), chs. 1 and 2.

judgement, pragmatic adaptation, and painful trade-offs amongst competing goals.

Whilst academic International Relations has devoted enormous attention to the balance of power, it has tended to neglect the links between inequality and order. Equally, international law has been so focused around the idea of international law as a horizontal system of coordination and so keen to escape from mistaken municipal analogies that stress enforcement that it has also tended to divert its eyes from the issue of inequality. Inequality was very often seen within the classical European state system as a source of disorder. Small and weak states may invite attack that greater power would have deterred. They may also become the focus for geopolitical competition amongst the major powers. But inequality has long been central to the analysis of international order. In the first place, it was precisely the inequality of states that, for the classical theorists of international society, differentiated international life from the state of nature amongst individuals. For Hobbes, it was the equality of fear resulting from the equal ability to kill possessed by everyone that persuaded men in the state of nature to bind themselves into a commonwealth. As Hobbes famously put it: 'From Equality proceeds Diffidence. From Diffidence Warre'.[16] And yet the disparity of power between states compared to individuals in the state of nature was one of the crucial differences that opened up the possibility of international society as a distinct form of political association.

Second, institutionalized forms of hierarchy were central to pluralist understandings of how international order might be nurtured and sustained and to the political norms through which those understandings were institutionalized. Although the logic of the balance of power might indeed operate automatically, its dangers and inevitable frictions could be minimized by the recognized managerial role of the Great Powers. Great Powers could promote order both by managing relations between themselves (through diplomacy, conferences, missions, joint interventions) and by exploiting their own unequal power over subordinate states within their spheres of influence and alliance systems. More important still, the classical state system was an imperial order. International Relations theorists of many persuasions tell stories based around balanced or balancing power and around the hegemonic struggles of the core states. All too often they neglect the second face of the European state system: its imperial face and the extent to which colonialism was one of the principal institutions of international society. To the extent that order could be said to exist within the classical state system, it was a function of both balanced power *and* unequal or hierarchical power.

---

[16] Thomas Hobbes, *Leviathan* edited by Richard Tuck (Cambridge: Cambridge University Press, 1996), 87.

The classical state system was a system that was both marked by inequality and structured around inequality. The combination of rapid industrial development, the emergence of more efficient administrative and organizational state structures, the consolidation of national states, and changes in military technology and organization—all of these factors led to the emergence of a small number of major powers that dominated the international political landscape. Moreover, if inequality marked the core of the state system, the relations between the European core and the periphery were still more unequal. The industrial revolution and technological innovations in armaments provided the base for unparalleled dominance of the European powers over the rest of the world. The European colonial order was built around subordinate territories which played no formed role in international relations, an economic system marked by the enforced opening of peripheral economies and by demographic openness, and a series of cultural assumptions that stressed the superiority of Western and white culture and a natural belief that progress entailed the replication of European models—an assumption that was as true of Marx as it was of Mill.[17]

Now it is true that much changed during the challenge to the Western dominance of the international system that characterized the period from 1900 to 1990—especially in relation to decolonization but also in terms of the struggle for equal sovereignty and racial equality. It is also the case, as we see, that equality has entered into many aspects of the normative structure of international society. And yet, although disguised by the rhetoric of sovereign equality, this older hierarchical conception of order remained extraordinarily powerful and influential throughout the twentieth century. Thus, for example, the Cold War 'order' and the long peace of 1945–89 were constructed in very traditional fashion around attempts to regulate the balance of power between the superpowers (through arms control agreements, summits, and mechanisms of crisis management) and through the exploitation of hierarchy (through the mutual, if tacit, recognition of spheres of influence and through the creation of an oligarchical non-proliferation system designed to limit access to the nuclear club). Moreover, even as international institutions expanded so dramatically in both number and scope, hierarchy and inequality have remained central to both their conception and their functioning. This was clearly the case during the League of Nations.

The League of Nations did not represent a total departure from the previous international system. Symbolically, its Covenant was not a separate compact, but formed part of the Paris peace treaties, which in turn stemmed from a conference dominated by the five principal victors.... Even after the signature of the peace treaties, many

---

[17] Keene stresses the crucial need to set the history of the 'anarchical society' of European states side by side with the role played by hierarchy and empire in the relationship between Europe and the non-European world. Keene (2002).

consequential problems continued to be settled by the Supreme Council of the Allied and Associated Powers or its deputy, the Conference of Ambassadors in Paris, and its offshoot the Reparations Commission.[18]

This continued to be the case in the post-1945 period. Sometimes the ordering role of hierarchy was formalized, as in the special rights and duties of the permanent members of the UN Security Council (UNSC), or the weighted voting structures of the IMF or World Bank, or the expansion of the role of the G8.[19] Hierarchy is also reflected in the way in which international financial management is dominated by closed groups of the powerful (as in the Bank of International Settlements or Financial Stability Forum) or the de facto decision-making rules of the WTO. Finally, hierarchy and the central ordering role of major powers can be seen in the continuing importance of informal groupings of states—Contact Groups, Core Groups, and Groups of Friends—that act in and around formal institutions.

But if power is really so important, why bother with the idea of international society at all? Why not come clean and simply focus on material power either in relation to the international political system (as realists and neo-realists have done) or in relation to the structural dynamics of the capitalist world economy (as Marxists and neo-Marxists have done)?

In the first place, the problem of power cannot be understood solely in terms of material capabilities, as neo-realists suggest. Constructivism, with its emphasis on norms and rules, is often associated with a more optimistic view of international relations. But a constructivist view of power and of the problem of power is potentially more troubled, even tragic, than that the comfortingly rationalist vision of the neo-realists, especially so-called defensive neo-realists.[20] It is, after all, the very clash of meanings, ideologies, and claims to justice, interacting with patterns of unequal power, which makes stable cooperation so problematic. Recall Weber's scathing critique of those who would reduce all politics to 'power-politics', a move which reveals 'a most wretched and superficial lack of concern for the *meaning* of human action, a blasé attitude that knows nothing of the tragedy in which all action, but quite particularly political action, is in truth enmeshed'.[21] A concern for meaning leads naturally to the problem of language. Language cannot be understood as

---

[18] John Dunbabin, 'The League of Nations' Place in the International System', *History*, 78/254 (October 1993), 425.

[19] For a conceptual analysis of the role of hierarchy, see David A. Lake, 'Anarchy, Hierarchy, and the Variety of International Relations', *International Organization*, 50/1 (Winter 1996), 1–33.

[20] On the distinctions between varieties of neo-realism, see Mearsheimer (2001: ch. 2).

[21] Max Weber, 'The Profession and Vocation of Politics', in Peter Lassman and Ronald Spiers (eds.), *Weber: Political Writings* (Cambridge: Cambridge University Press, 1994), 354–5.

a straightforward or easy facilitator of communication and collective action, and the relationship of political language to the world it seeks to describe is imprecise and approximate, relying all too often on Nietzsche's 'mobile unstable army of metaphors'. Whilst the use of political language (including the culturally specific resources of particular languages) is central to the attainment and stabilization of power, it has a dynamic and, at times, un-masterable quality. As George Steiner reminds us:

Words carry us forward towards ideological confrontations from which there is no retreat. This is the root of the tragedy of politics. Slogans, clichés, rhetorical abstractions, false antitheses come to possess the mind.... Political conduct is no longer spontaneous or responsive to reality. It freezes around a core of dead rhetoric. Instead of making politics dubious and provisional in the manner of Montaigne (who knew that principles are endurable only when they are tentative), language encloses politicians in the blindness of certainty or the illusion of justice. The life of the mind is narrowed or arrested by the weight of its eloquence. Instead of becoming masters of language, we become its servants.[22]

It is precisely for these reasons that diplomacy and the elaborate artificiality of diplomatic language and practice played such an important role in traditional analyses of the institutions of international society. Diplomacy is essential to international society because it underpins the minimal conditions and prerequisites of any cooperative social order: the capacity to communicate, the necessity of shared conventions for communication (linguistic and procedural), and the provision of an institutional framework to allow political negotiation to take place in strained and often very difficult circumstances. It also plays an expressive and symbolic role, especially in terms of upholding the idea of a shared international community, again particularly at times (e.g. during the Cold War or the so-called 'long war against global terrorism') when its very existence is under threat and held in doubt.

Second, norms and institutions are central to understanding the form and character of power-politics at a particular time. The case of war provides perhaps the clearest example. War and violent conflict often appear to be bereft of all rules and norms. And yet war as a particular form of social conflict, its relationship to other forms of violence, and its connection to the practices of 'normal' politics is impossible to understand outside a complex set

---

[22] George Steiner, *The Death of Tragedy* (London: Faber and Faber, 1961), 56–7. Language is closely connected with the problem of cultural diversity and values conflict discussed in the next section. Here it is not necessary to accept determinist claims about the way in which different languages map the world differently or predetermine certain modes of observation and interpretation. The point is rather to stress the complex ways in which language affects the way people think and act, the role of particular languages in both symbolizing culture and producing culture, the difficulties of translating political ideas across linguistic boundaries, and the very different value connotations of apparently similar words and concepts.

of historically evolving legal and moral norms and rules. At least in the forms that we know it, war is an inherently normative phenomenon. A focus on international society does not therefore—as is so often mistakenly assumed—lead to a soft, liberal Grotianism concerned solely with the promotion of law and morality. To believe in the importance of a common framework of rules and social norms does not imply that power, coercion, and conflict do not play a major, often dominant, role in international relations. Social norms are just as central to understanding imperialism, the balance of power, or the role of Great Powers as they are to the study of, say, human rights.

Third, norms are central to understanding the power of political mobilization and of coordinated action. As Hardin notes, 'identification with a group matters because it can lead to coordination of great power'.[23] Strong identification with an ethnic group, with a nationalist movement, or with a nation-state makes it easier for political leaders to extract resources, to build armies, and to persuade many thousands to fight and to sacrifice their lives. Realists have notably little to say about this associational aspect of power. Norms are also constitutive. As Hollis puts it, 'They enable not only by making collective action easier but also by creating forms of activity'.[24] Norms and rules help explain how actors are constituted: who can act and in what kinds of social and political activities. They help us make sense of the identity of actors and hence of the sources of their preferences. Norms can be understood as expressions of what states and other groups are, where they belong, and of the kinds of roles they play. In the so-called war on terror, think of the immense political power of normative claims that establish identity: 'good vs evil', 'civilized vs barbarian', 'infidel vs believer', and 'them against us'. The point, then, is to recognize the multiple roles played by norms, rules, and institutions. Norms may well serve as regulatory rules designed to constrain choices and/or as parameters within which individual agents pursue their own preferences. This is the view of rules that lies behind the common claim that international law regarding the use of force is not able to 'control' what states do. Whilst this may often be true, the critical point is that norms have many other roles and do much more than this.

Finally, and most importantly, norms and institutions are central to the stabilization and legitimization of power. On the standard realist and

---

[23] Russell Hardin, *One for All: The Logic of Group Conflict* (Princeton, NJ: Princeton University Press, 1995), 9; cf. Jennifer Widner: 'Hobbes's war of all against all in the context of extreme individualism is a mild form of social conflict compared to what can ensue from clashes between several social groups, each of whose members display high levels of social trust internally, and no trust or active distrust towards outsiders. Conflict becomes more devastating where the possibility for coordinated action exists.' 'States and Statelessness in Africa', *Daedalus*, 124/3 (Summer 1995), 148.

[24] Martin Hollis, 'Why Elster Is Stuck and Needs to Recover His Faith', *London Review of Books*, 13/2 (24 January 1991), 13.

neo-realist account, institutions are always and inevitably simple reflections of state power and of the interests of powerful states. As power shifts and as the interests of the most powerful evolve, dominant patterns of institution-alization will automatically follow. Institutions, based on this view, do not 'matter': they have no autonomy or compliance pull of their own, either by affecting the incentives or calculations of actors or by influencing the way in which interests are understood or preferences constructed. Neo-realist writers are right to stress that power matters and that powerful states will always have more options: to determine which issues get negotiated via formal interstate bodies and which are, for example, managed via market mechanisms; to influence both the rules of the bargaining game and what is allowed onto the agenda; to deploy a wide range of sticks and carrots in the bargaining process, including the threat of direct coercion; and, finally, to walk away from any institution that becomes too constraining. Institutions are not just concerned with liberal purposes of solving common problems or promoting shared values. They are also sites of power and reflect and entrench power hierarchies and the interests of powerful states.

However, such a view seriously underestimates the importance of insti-tutions to the stabilization and the legitimization of power in general and of unequal or hegemonic power in particular. Power is, after all, a social attribute. To understand power in international relations, we must place it side by side with other quintessentially social concepts such as prestige, authority, and legitimacy. A great deal of the struggle for political power is the quest for legitimate and authoritative control that avoids costly and dangerous reliance on brute force and coercion. To a much greater extent than realists acknowledge, states need international law and institutions both to share the material and political costs of protecting their interests and to gain the authority and legitimacy that the possession of crude power can never secure on its own. All major powers face the imperative of trying to turn a capacity for crude coercion into legitimate authority. As Wight puts it: 'The fundamental problem of politics is the justification of power.... Power is not self-justifying; it must be justified by reference to some source outside or beyond itself, and thus be transformed into "authority" '.[25] For this reason, it is a mistake to view 'law' as something that is, or can be, wholly separated from some separate other thing called 'political interest'. It is one of the great paradoxes of academic International Relations that, because it so resolutely neglects the social dimensions of power, realism is unable to give a full or convincing account of its own proclaimed central category.

---

[25] Martin Wight, *International Theory: The Three Traditions*, edited by Gabriele Wight and Brian Porter (Leicester, UK: Leicester University Press, 1991), 99. A fuller analysis of both the relation of power and institutions and of legitimacy is given in Chapter 3.

Pluralism and values

If one of the driving forces behind the limited pluralist conception of order has been a pessimistic view of power-politics and of the political difficulties of sustained cooperation, a second follows from deep scepticism about claims regarding the existence of consensus and shared values across international and global society. All communities and polities have to find ways of dealing with diversity and with value conflict. Conflict is, after all, intrinsic to all morality, and even within a single cultural system conflicts arise: how different principles are to be related to one another; how shared principles are to be applied to the facts of a particular case. For international society, the problem has always run much deeper, and the creation of any kind of universal society of states or any other kind of world society has had to face up to the existence of fundamental differences in religion, social organization, culture, and moral outlook. These difficulties may be based on what Amartya Sen has called 'the empirical fact of pervasive human diversity'.[26] They may reflect, as for Isaiah Berlin, a belief in the plurality, contradictoriness, even incommensurability of human goods. Or they may be based on the view that it is precisely *differences* in social practices, values, beliefs, and institutions that represent the most important expression of our *common* humanity.[27] What makes us different is precisely what makes us human.

The concern with values has a historical, a theoretical, and a normative dimension.

Historically, it was axiomatic to the classical European writers on international society that the existence and solidity of the society of states was in some way related to shared values. A common culture might support international society by narrowing the range of conflict over substantive values, by assisting the mutual acceptance of the players as legitimate actors, or by providing a common language for both bargaining and contracting and for reasoning and persuasion. Some stressed the role of a shared international political or diplomatic culture orchestrated by specialized elites with at least some commitment to shared values and perhaps to a shared world view. Others emphasized shared societal values, whether those of Christianity, Europe, or civilization.[28] In the eighteenth century, writers on international society often spoke of Europe as a *grande république* united by what Gibbon called 'a general resemblance of religion, language and manner'. In the

---

[26] Amartya Sen, *Inequality Reexamined* (Oxford: Oxford University Press, 1992), xi.

[27] For an account of how Enlightenment 'universalism' can be read in this way, see Sankar Muthu, *Enlightenment against Empire* (Princeton, NJ: Princeton University Press, 2003).

[28] For Wight, 'a state-system will not come into being without a degree of cultural unity amongst its members', or, more strongly, 'a states-system presupposes a common culture', Martin Wight, *Systems of States* (Leiciester, UK: Leicester University Press, 1977), 3 and 46. See also Adam Watson, *The Evolution of International Society: A Comparative Historical Analysis* (London: Routledge, 1992).

nineteenth century, international society was routinely viewed as referring to a European family of civilized nations. Indeed, many influential nineteenth-century international lawyers rejected the idea that international law could be understood as the product of the will or consent of states and sovereigns. Instead, they saw international law as the product of a historical and cultural community. Law drew not only its strength from the gathering pace of contemporary processes of social and economic progress and integration but also reflected the dense set of shared historical, cultural, and legal traditions, most especially in relation to the shared inheritance of Roman law. 'If law was the effect of a common consciousness, and the existence of a common European consciousness seemed an undeniable fact, then international law's reality was firmly grounded in a social and cultural fact.'[29]

As we consider the historical evolution of international society and its contemporary dilemmas, three sets of questions arise. The first concerns membership. If a common culture and shared values play an important role in underpinning the core of an international society, they naturally give rise to questions about boundaries and membership. The creation of international society and, especially, the successful consolidation of an increasingly dense international society in particular parts of the world lead naturally to divisions between insiders and outsiders. If there is an international society, what are its limits? Does it incorporate the entire human race or is it limited to a particular area? If it is limited, what are the principles of inclusion and exclusion? To what extent does the existence of such a division itself become a source of instability and insecurity? On the one side, there is a long Western tradition of doctrines and ideas that rested on principles of exclusiveness, based on being Christian, being European, or being 'civilized'; on the other hand, there is the powerful countercurrent in Western thought that has maintained the existence of a universal community of humankind and that has drawn its primary inspiration from the long tradition of natural law. A related question concerns patterns of interaction 'across the divide'. At one extreme, realist doctrines have often denied all legal and moral rights to those without the power to force respect for their independence. At the other extreme, revolutionist doctrines have insisted on an absolute equality of rights, both as individuals and as communities, and on a duty to assist their liberation. In between liberals have been (and remain) deeply divided. Some have argued for a strong (if never quite absolute) respect for pluralism and equality between communities and cultures, and have laid great emphasis on the norms of sovereignty and the non-intervention. Others accord only conditional or secondary rights to those outside the inner core and have argued for intervention or imperialism to promote the intrinsically superior

---

[29] Martti Koskenniemi, *The Gentle Civilizer of Nations: The Rise and Fall of International Law, 1870–1960* (Cambridge: Cambridge University Press, 2002), 51.

values of the inner core.[30] As we shall see, the emergence of a more ambitious solidarist international society has led to a re-emergence of these old questions of membership and relations between insiders and outsiders. To what extent does liberal solidarism with its notions of conditional sovereignty involve a new standard of civilization? To what extent should threats to international society be interpreted in the language of rogue states, pariahs, and outlaws? To what extent do the principles of membership justify interventionism, or indeed a return to empire?

A second set of questions concerns the expansion of international society. In contrast to much mainstream analysis of international relations, writers on international society insisted that the transition from a European to a global international society represented one of the most important developments of the twentieth century. This transition involved five sets of struggles— for decolonization and the end of empire, for equal sovereignty, for racial equality, for economic justice, and for cultural liberation. Although success across these areas was highly variable, the process of decolonization and the emergence of important centres of power in the non-Western world consti- tuted a challenge to the Western dominance of the international system that had seemed such a striking and self-evident feature of the world at the turn of the twentieth century. But for those who believed that culture mattered, this transition also opened up a number of deeply problematic questions. To what extent had decolonization and the emergence of the Third World disrupted and challenged the common rules and institutions of international society? What were the long-term implications for international society of its expanded membership? Had international society outgrown the European or Western culture upon which it was once founded, and if so, what cultural foundations, if any, could it be said to have?[31]

In the post–Cold War world, much attention has been given to the notion of a cultural backlash against Westernization, whether manifested as part of the anti-globalization movement or as one element in a radicalized, anti-Western Islamism. Much attention has also been given to the intensification of strug- gles for cultural recognition and the sharpening of the politics of identity (the subject of Chapter 5). Less commented upon but equally central is the question of what has happened to the states and societies that were in the

---

[30] For an excellent analysis of the liberal shift to empire, see Jennifer Pitts, *A Turn to Empire: The Rise of Imperial Liberalism in Britain and France* (Princeton, NJ: Princeton University Press, 2005).

[31] Hedley Bull, 'The Third World and International Society', in George W. Keeton and Georg Schwarzenberger (eds.), *The Year Book of World Affairs* 1979 (London: Stevens and Sons, 1979), 15. Hedley Bull and Adam Watson (eds.), *The Expansion of International Society* (Oxford: Oxford University Press, 1984). For a more critical view of international law as part of the ideology of European civilization, see Yasuaki Onuma, 'Eurocentrism in the History of International Law', in *A Normative Approach to War: Peace, War and Justice in Hugo Grotius* (Oxford: Clarendon Press, 1993), 371–86.

vanguard of the revolt against Western dominance—the developing world in general and especially large developing states such as China, India, and Brazil. How far have the end of the Cold War and the evolution of globalization helped to underpin a new consensus on the desirability of a solidarist liberal international society? How far has what is now often termed the Global South accommodated itself to economic and political liberalism? If so, is this based on the unavoidable need to come to terms with the hegemonic position of the United States? Or does it reflect a genuine internalization of the values of liberal solidarism and the spread of a common culture of West-ernization or, more broadly, of modernity? I will return to these questions in Chapter 8.

Talk of an international society expanding beyond its historical Western core leads to a final set of questions, namely the extent to which civilizations or cultural entities should be viewed as the ultimate units of global order, rather than states or nation-states. Most influential in the recent period has been Samuel Huntington's view that the world is divided along cultural and civilizational lines and that it is conflict amongst cultures and civilizations that has come to dominate global politics.[32] But earlier examples can be seen in Spengler's identification of a universal history proceeding through a series of eight cultures or cultural organisms, each 'windowless', self-enclosed, and with little possibility of mutual understanding, or in Toynbee's belief that nation-states are to be seen as part of larger, civilizational entities and that history is structured around the rise and decline of these civilizations.[33] The problems with 'civilizational history' have been well rehearsed; and the criticisms of the image of clashing civilizations are well known. It is difficult to identify clear territorial boundaries to civilizations, and harder still to imbue them with the capacity to act as a coherent unit. Huntington places far too much in the undifferentiated category of civilization ('civilization and culture both refer to the overall way of life of a people')—thereby reifying and essentializing cultures and downplaying the multiplicity of trends, conflicts, and contradictions with any particular cultural tradition. It is difficult to view the world as consisting of a limited number of cultures, each with its own immutable core, particularly given the expansion of channels and forces by which norms and ideas are diffused across the world.

Nevertheless, the immense popularity of Spengler in the 1920s, of Toynbee in the 1940s, and of Huntington in the 1990s underscores the very powerful

---

[32] Samuel P. Huntington, *The Clash of Civilizations and the Remaking of World Order* (New York: Simon and Shuster, 1996).

[33] Oswald Spengler, *Der Untergang des Abendlandes* (Munich: C. H. Beck, [1922] 1963); Arnold Toynbee, *A Study of History* (Oxford: Oxford University Press, 1934); and W. H. McNeill, *The Rise of the West: A History of the Human Community* (Chicago, IL: Chicago University Press, 1963) and his biography of Toybnee, *Arnold J Toynbee: A Life* (Oxford: Oxford University Press, 1989). See also Ian Hall's analysis of Toynbee's influence on Martin Wight, *The International Thought of Martin Wight* (Basingstoke, UK: Palgrave, 2006), esp. chs. 3 and 6.

normative appeal of viewing global order in terms of civilizations and cultural entities. In all of these cases their language, ideas, and images reflected a deep affinity with historically constructed but powerfully felt cultural beliefs and collective imaginaries, and, of course, provided an extremely powerful set of ideological resources in the battle for political power. As is evident in the allegedly 'civilizational' struggle of the 'West' against 'Islamic terrorism', both sides feed off, and depend on, the other. Both sides are engaged in an intense struggle to manipulate culturally rooted ideologies and utopias.

This leads to the second dimension of the question of values, namely the *theoretical*. The role of values in political action is complex. As Michael Hechter argues, values are *ex ante* reasons for taking action, or relatively general and durable internal criteria for evaluating action.[34] Whereas rationality is conditional and future oriented, values are the product of history. They are what differentiates one society from another and one international system from another. They might indeed be incommensurable, or, more often, they may shape the meanings of rational action in ways that can either help or hinder cooperative endeavours.[35]

It is certainly the case that order cannot simply be equated with the existence of a common value system and with normative consensus. Value systems, after all, do not just happen. They are fostered by social agents for particular purposes and they are maintained because it will often pay people in some way to ensure that they are.[36] Think, for example, of the way in which understandings of 'Islam' are politically constructed with a wide variety of political actors using religious ideas for instrumental and strategic purposes. Accounts of order that focus solely on the role of shared values run the risk of circularity, of *post hoc* reasoning, or of reducing human agents to automata blindly following internalized values. Nevertheless, to reduce clashes over values to simple conflict over power is superficial and risks underestimating both the depth of conflict and its scope. As Aron emphasized, power is only a means to an end and the study of international society has to be concerned

[34] Michael Hechter, 'The Role of Values in Rational Choice Theory', *Rationality and Society*, 6/3 (July 1994), 318–33. Elster usefully highlights the role of the past in the operation of social norms. 'Rationality is essentially conditional and future oriented. Its imperatives are hypothetical, that is conditional on future outcomes one wants to realize. The imperatives expressed in social norms either are unconditional, or, if conditional, are not future-oriented. In the latter case, norms make the action dependent on past events or (more rarely) on hypothetical outcomes. Rational actors follow the principle of letting bygones be bygones, cutting one's losses and ignoring sunk costs. In the operation of social norms, by contrast, the past plays an essential role.' Elster (1989: 98–9).

[35] For an example of how values and rational action interact, see Avner Offer, 'Going to War in 1914: A Matter of Honour?', *Politics and Society*, 23/2 (June 1995), 213–41.

[36] Brian Barry, *Sociologists, Economists and Democracy* (London: Macmillan, 1970), 75–98; and James S. Coleman, *Foundations of Social Theory* (Cambridge, MA: Harvard University Press, 1990), chs. 10 and 11.

with what those ends actually are, with the inescapable plurality of such ends, and with the conflicts that arise amongst them.[37]

Values are fundamental to understanding both the nature of conflict and the possibilities for cooperation. As is so clearly illustrated by terrorism, the important point is to avoid assuming that the rationality of violence or the calculus of political consequences looks the same from all perspectives and in all cultural, historical, and economic contexts. Analytically what is needed is not a rigid dichotomy between a political rationality that makes sense to 'us' on the one hand and irrationality and fanaticism on the other, but rather a greater contextual understanding of the links between values and action. Values are crucial for understanding the intensity and durability of many kinds of conflict. It is true, for example, that there is a great deal of strategic rationality in many ethnic and nationalist conflicts. Such conflicts are not the expression of irrational or atavistic hatred and there is a great deal of explanatory power in rationalist accounts of ethnic conflict. However, much of this rationality is 'value rational' behaviour (to use Weber's term) in which values such as dignity and self-respect increase the willingness of individuals to endure high costs and to make tremendous sacrifices, often over long periods.[38] Many such conflicts are driven by demands for cultural recognition, for status, and for equal standing; and it is one of the consequences of such demands that the drive of one group for recognition so often involves the dehumanization of the other side, a descent into a vicious spiral of hatred and violence, and the progressive erosion of the power of logic and language. Recognition and respect have been equally central to the demands of revisionist states. Challenges to the legitimacy of international order have rarely resulted from the protests of the weak. They have come more often from those states or peoples with the capacity and political organization to demand a revision of the established order and of its dominant norms in ways that reflected their own interests, concerns, and values. Thus, a central theme of twentieth-century international history was the struggle of revisionist states for *Gleichberechtigung* involving the redistribution of territory, the recognition of regional spheres of influence, and the drive for equality of status within international institutions both formal and informal.

If values are important to understanding conflict, they are also central to many aspects of cooperation in a global system. This problem is often underplayed by the rationalist approaches to law and institutions that have been so influential in International Relations. Such approaches may indeed provide powerful accounts of how cooperation is possible *after* the parties have come

[37] Raymond Aron, *Peace and War: A Theory of International Relations* (London: Weidenfeld & Nicolson, 1966), esp. ch. 3.
[38] See Hardin (1995) and Ashutosh Varshney, 'Nationalism, Ethnic Conflict and Rationality', *Perspectives on Politics*, 1/1 (March 2003), 85–99.

to believe that they form part of a shared project or community in which there is a common interest that can be furthered by cooperative behaviour. They assume the accepted legitimacy of the players, a common language for bargaining, a shared perception of potential gains, and some mechanism for at least potentially securing contracting. Once there is a common identification of, and commitment to, some kind of moral community (however minimalist in character) within which perceptions of potential common interest can emerge, there may indeed be prudential reasons for the players to cooperate collectively. But rational prudence alone cannot explain the initiation of the game and why each player individually might choose to begin to cooperate. Rationalist approaches neglect the factors which explain how and why contracting is possible in the first place, the potential barriers that can block the emergence of any such a shared project, and the role of values in understanding those barriers.

Accounts of international relations that give prominence to culture and values face many potential snares. First, it is important to separate culture from context. Culture does not necessarily matter but difference and diversity do. Understandings of world order vary enormously from one part of the world to another, reflecting differences in national and regional histories, in social and economic circumstances and conditions, and in political contexts and trajectories. A careful emphasis on context can help navigate the treacherous waters between a reductionist universalism on the one hand and culturalist essentialism on the other.[39] Second, it is important not to so overload a definition of culture that it becomes impossibly broad, nor to conflate elements that should be kept separate (as with the need to separate religion from culture in current debates on Islam). Nor, as noted above, is the Huntingtonian view of civilizations particularly helpful. Finally, it is equally unhelpful to view the emergence of cultural particularism and of groups that appeal to nationalist or religious cultural values in terms of a dichotomy between modern and premodern societies. Fundamentalism arises out of intimate connection with modernity not just in terms of the factors that may drive its emergence but also in terms of the way in which globalization provides new channels for mobilization, new forms of political action, and also new possibilities of community.[40]

---

[39] See Laurence Whitehead, 'Afterword: On Cultures and Contexts', in Hans Antlöv and Tak-Wing Ngo (eds.), *The Cultural Construction of Politics in Asia* (Richmond, UK: Curzon Press, 2000), 223–40.

[40] See Olivier Roy, *Globalised Islam: The Search for a New Ummah* (London: Hurst, 2002), 13–29. If Islamism is best understood as a response to modernity, it makes still less sense to view radical jihadists in premodern terms: 'However old-fashioned their theology may seem to Westerners, and whatever they may think of themselves, radical Euro-Islamists are clearly more of a postmodern phenomenon than a premodern one', 303.

The third dimension of the pluralist concern with culture and values is *normative*. The pluralist sensibility tends strongly towards the view that diversity is a fundamental feature of humanity and that the clash of moral, national, and religious loyalties is not the result of ignorance or irrationality but rather reflects the plurality of values by which all political arrangements and notions of the good life are to be judged. They see it as a persistent illusion of liberals and Marxists that modernization and development will lead naturally and/or easily to a convergence of social, cultural, and ethical outlooks. One of the perennial attractions of a state-based pluralism is that it seems to provide one way—and perhaps the least bad way—of organizing global politics in a world where actual consensus on fundamental values is limited or where there is widespread scepticism as to how a cross-cultural morality might be grounded. It does this in three ways. The first is captured by the old adages of 'live and let live' and 'good fences makes good neighbours'. If diversity and value conflicts are such important features of international life, then we should seek to organize global politics in such a way as to give groups scope for collective self-government and cultural autonomy in their own affairs and to reduce the degree to which they will clash over how the world should be ordered. Hence we see arguments for a strong version of sovereignty and the reciprocal commitment to non-intervention or to limited intervention; and for the centrality of the balance of power as a means of constraining the predations of the powerful. If ways of life are irreducibly varied, if there can be no easy appeal to a shared 'ordinary morality', and if rational argument cannot produce agreement, then surely the best course of action is to lower our sights and seek peaceful coexistence? The principled importance of acknowledging and providing space for difference therefore merges with the prudential argument for peace, allowing different groups to form their own states and political communities is one way of reducing conflict.

A second pluralist strategy is to argue that moral values should, so far as possible, be kept out of particular international institutions. The realist emphasis on the idea of an objective national interest has always been easy to criticize on empirical grounds. But, like so much in the world of the so-called 'realists', it expresses a normative idea, namely that international life will be better, or again less bad, if states try to put aside arguments about fundamental values or deep ideological commitments and instead concentrate on bargaining over limited interests; and that it might be possible to link the character of these interests to a shared understanding of legitimacy and legitimate foreign policy behaviour. As we see in the next section, a similar normative argument has been made concerning the normative virtues of positivist international law.

Third, the sceptical pluralist is attracted to the idea that it might also be possible to develop a cross-cultural consensus over the minimal rules around which such a limited international society might be built. It is for this reason that Hart's notion of a minimum content of natural law built around Hobbesian assumptions plays such a crucial role in Bull's thinking.[41] We can see this idea being played out in Bull's emphasis on the 'elementary conditions of social life'; his attempt to isolate the elementary, primary, and universal goals of a society of states; and his analytical effort to link these goals to the historical institutions of international society. There is therefore an *analytical* move (what are the minimum conditions that would have to exist before any society could be meaningfully so described?), a *historical* move (how far can one isolate an acceptance of these conditions in the practices of states?), and a *normative* move (on what minimum conditions of coexistence might the holders of sharply conflicting values be able to agree?).

The normative case for pluralism is often based on scepticism and a sense of the limits of politics. The limited interstate order underpinned by the society of states provides a morally significant means of promoting coexistence and limiting conflict in a world in which consensus on more elaborate forms of cooperation does not exist and in which more elaborate international institutions are liable to be captured by the special interests and particular values of the most powerful. The law of the jungle may not be deflected by very much and morality may well remain firmly on the margins. But, in the absence of any firm reason for believing in the viability of a transformed international society, these small gains remain morally highly significant. The order upheld by a pluralist society does not, however, only have a consequentialist or instrumental value. For its defenders, it has the potential not just to help manage international conduct in a restrained way but also to create the conditions for a more legitimate and morally more ambitious political community to emerge: by providing a stable institutional framework within which substantive norms can be negotiated; by developing a common language in which claims and counterclaims can be made and debated with some degree of accessibility and authority; and by embedding a set of formal rules that embody at least elements of equality and some restraints on the power and ambitions of the strong.

The pluralist remains insistent, then, that the question of how to mediate amongst opposing moral, social, and political values remains one of the greatest and most difficult challenges facing world order. It is central to practical questions: How broad and how deep is international society? How strong is the consensus on the nature of a desirable world order and the means by which it might we achieved? And it is central to normative questions: What value should be accorded to the traditions and practices of particular human communities? How might we balance obligations owed to such communities with obligations owed to humankind in general? Even if Locke's 'great and

---

[41] H. L. A. Hart, *The Concept of Law* (Oxford: Oxford University Press, 1961), 188–95.

natural community' of humankind does exist, it is, to use John Dunn's words, 'an extravagantly variegated natural community'.[42]

Pluralism and law

The main features of a pluralist conception of the international legal order follow directly from what has already been discussed. It is a view of international law built around the state and the concept of state sovereignty. International law is the law of a society of states or a 'Family of Nations', with each state enjoying a measure of independence from other states and the powers of supreme government over its territory and its people. Sovereignty was defined by one of the most influential writers on international law as 'supreme authority, an authority which is independent of any other earthly authority... [it] includes therefore independence all round, within and without the borders of the country.'[43] Sovereignty thus comprises independence and authority over territory and supremacy over persons.

The basic problem is, of course, how such a claim to supreme authority can be reconciled with the idea of international law and society. The tension between sovereign will and legal obligation was 'solved' within the pluralist tradition by the notion of consent. The basis of the law of nations is 'is the common consent of the States that a body of legal rules shall regulate their intercourse with one another'. Law is understood in positivist terms—a human contrivance to serve particular social ends rather than as deriving from metaphysics, natural law, or abstract reason.[44] The authority of law is not related to its content but to an agreed system of social recognition. Central to a positivist, consent-based international law is therefore an emphasis on sources (treaties and agreements, customary rules, and international judicial decisions) and on the practices of legal argument that allow those sources to be identified and legally evaluated. International law is interpreted as a horizontal public order (often modelled on the idea of a set of bilateral contracts) within which no sovereign would submit except to those rules to which it had consented. On this basis, sovereignty cannot by definition be unconditional and can only be meaningful if it is recognized by others. It is a shared social quality and absolute independence and supreme authority must be limited for the same quality to inhere in other states and for international law to impose any kinds of restrictions on states. One major element of

---

[42] John Dunn, 'Nation State and Human Community', published in Italian in John Dunn, *Stato Nazionale e Communitá Umana* (Milan: Anabasi, 1994).

[43] Lassa Oppenheim, *International Law: A Treatise*, vol. 1 (London: Longman, Green & Co., 1905), 101.

[44] For an overview of positivism and where it fits into the broader history of international law, see Stephen C. Neff, 'A Short History of International Law', in Malcom Evans (ed.), *International Law* (Oxford: Oxford University Press, 2003), 41–5.

classical international law, then, involved the elaboration of rules concerning the constitution of state and sovereignty. Establishing the limits to territorial authority forms an essential part of the structure of rules and institutions that enable separate political communities to coexist. As Jennings put it: 'The mission and purpose of traditional international law has been the delimitation of the exercise of sovereign power on a territorial basis.'[45] Another major element concerns those rules necessary for states to communicate with each other (through the law of diplomacy) and to interact both in times of war and peace.

It has to be said, however, that many pluralist discussions of the state and of sovereignty have an empty and unilluminating quality. They go ritualistically through distinctions between internal and external sovereignty; they list the definitions of the state as, for example, given in the 1933 Montevideo Convention (a permanent population, a defined territory, a government, and a capacity to enter into relations with other states); and they stress the importance of the efficiency of governments and the effective control of territory in determining questions of recognition and membership of international society. But they seem divorced from any meaningful theory of the state, and they are difficult to relate to state practice—for example, the extent to which the recognition of new states and practices of intervention were from the early nineteenth century evermore concerned with notions of what the state actually was or should be and with the complexity of relations between state, nation, regime, and society. No doubt this reflected the continual and complex agonizing about the very possibility of law within a world of jealous and often warring sovereigns. Yet this doctrinal hesitation also reflected the difficulty of generating the consensus necessary to incorporate values relating to the domestic organization of state and society into the fabric of positive international law—in marked contrast, as we see, to the conceptions of law discussed in Chapter 3. Thus pluralist international society rests on a presumed fit between the people and its government and on a narrow view of legal agency according to which the government is taken as the legitimate expression of sovereign power.[46]

This is a view of law that stays close to power—so close indeed that, for its critics, it is little more than the reporting of practice and a mere apologia for the deeds and, more often, the misdeeds of politicians. This 'realism' is most evident in relation to the balance of power and to the treatment of war. Sometimes the balance of power is seen as directly related to the legal order and it is for this reason that pluralist writers on international society have been attracted to the writings of Vattel and Oppenheim. More often,

[45] R. Y. Jennings, *The Acquisition of Territory in International Law* (Manchester, UK: Manchester University Press, 1963), 2.

[46] Michael Walzer, 'The Moral Standing of States: A Response to Four Critics', *Philosophy and Public Affairs*, 9/3 (1980), 210–16.

the balance of power is seen as an enabling condition or a background state, without which international law and institutions could not function. The relative autonomy of international law will therefore be threatened either when balance of power-politics are highly conflictual (as during the Cold War) or when power is radically unbalanced (as in the post–Cold War period).[47] At the harder realist end of pluralism, there is clear priority for the balance of power, war, and Great Power management over law.

A further important aspect of the pluralist legal order, concerned the regulation of interaction between and amongst states, in peace (especially the regularization of diplomacy), and in war. A central aspect of the legal order was the constitution of 'war' as a particular form of social violence. A war involves violence by organized groups (whether states or of other kinds) for political purposes. It is a clash between agents of political groups. This is one of the ways in which public war was to be distinguished from private violence against which there was a common purpose—hence the characterization of pirates (and, of course, more recently terrorists) as the enemies of all humankind, *hostis humani generi*. In terms of law and war, the period from the end of the eighteenth century to the mid-twentieth century witnessed a marked move away from *jus ad bellum*—because of the perceived lack of consensus over the values that would allow judgement as to the justice of going to war and because of the belief that attempts to enforce such judgements would create still more conflict; and towards a heavy concentration on the *jus in bello*—because of the belief that international society could be threatened by the manner in which war is undertaken, because there are very powerful self-interested reasons for restraint (a great deal of the laws of war draw their force from reciprocal interest), and because the failure to abide by restraints given the inherent expansionist logic of conflict would risk an intensification of conflict. As Kant put it: 'For it must still remain possible, even in wartime, to have some sort of trust in the attitude of the enemy, otherwise peace could not be concluded and the hostilities would turn into a war of extermination (*bellum internicinum*).'[48]

In the pre-1914 world, the 'apologetic' and power-reflecting side of international law was very visible: the special role and status of Great Powers as the managers of international security, the dominant role of major states in establishing by their practice or agreement the rules of international law, and the extent to which that law reflected the interests of the powerful, imposing few restrictions on the use of force and the resorting to war, and upholding the validity of treaties signed under duress. Equally, most definitions of formal

---

[47] The scarcity of literature reflects the reluctance of lawyers to confront the question. But see Alfred Vagts and Detlev F. Vagts, 'The Balance of Power in International Law: A History of an Idea', *American Journal of International Law*, 73/4 (October 1979), 555–80.

[48] Immanuel Kant, 'Perpetual Peace: A Philosophical Sketch', in Hans Reiss (ed.), *Kant: Political Writings*, 2nd edn. (Cambridge: Cambridge University Press, 1991), 96.

empire depend on both a *de facto* ability to coerce and control and a set of *de jure* claims to lawful authority that are accepted by others and incorporated into the dominant norms of the system. But, just as crucially, informal empire was built around a wide range of legally structured and institutionalized controls over weaker states and semi-colonies involving unequal treaties, imposed export regimes, enforced concessions, and 'temporary occupations'. Finally, there was no place for notions of self-determination and the dominant powers determined the criteria by which non-European political communities could be admitted to membership of international society.

For its defenders, unless law reconciled itself with the realities of the power-political order, it would, to quote Julius Stone, 'have a moth-like existence, fluttering inevitably and precariously year by year into the destructive flame of power'.

To avoid so shiftless an existence, the international legal order takes the extraordinary course of providing by its own rules for its collision with overwhelming power. It allows the military victory through the imposed treaty of peace to incorporate his dictated terms into the body of international law, thus preserving at any rate the rest of the rules and its own continued existence. By this built-in device it incorporates into the legal order the net result of what otherwise would be an extra-legal, or even illegal, revolution.[49]

In consequence of this emphasis on the centrality of power, this is a view that sees law as having only a limited role in the sustaining of international order. International law is not sufficient for international order. Many important norms are political rather than legal (e.g. those relating to spheres of influence, crisis management or the balance of power; or the cases such as the human rights provisions of the Helsinki Process that played an important part in the unwinding of the Cold War in Europe but which did not embody formal legal rules). And law can sometimes be an obstacle to order—as when the demands of a collective security system stand in the way of, or otherwise impede, the operation of the balance of power (e.g. in the interwar period). Nor, on this view, should international law be concerned with the regulation of all aspects of international life. Rather, it provides a set of instruments and tools that states may find useful at particular times to help resolve disputes. Within this 'foreign office model of international law', theory and practice are closely interwoven; there is a heavy emphasis on the settlement of disputes (by bilateral negotiation, multilateral decision-making, political mediation,

---

[49] Julius Stone, 'Approaches to the Notion of International Justice', in C. E. Black and Richard Falk (eds.), *The Future of the International Legal Order* (Princeton, NJ: Princeton University Press, 1969), p. 386; cf. Brierly, 'The truth is that international law can no more refuse to recognize that a finally successful conquest does change the title to territory than municipal law can a change of regime brought about by successful revolution.' J. L. Brierly, *The Law of Nations: An Introduction to the International Law of Peace*, 6th edn. (Oxford: Clarendon Press, 1963), 172–3.

or legal adjudication or arbitration); and legal reasoning is focused on directly applicable rules and relevant sources. If we can talk at all of the constitution of international society, then it is much more like a common law constitution, that is to say a pattern of institutional practices, laws, conventions, and political norms that together define how a society is constituted. More generally, the practice-oriented lawyer will insist that law has been, and continues to be, judged by the wrong standards. Law is not best understood as an abstract normative system. It is only one way of doing things and is driven by practical reasoning. Even domestically, no one should expect all political disputes and controversies to be resolved by the judicial system. Indeed, if courts are asked to rule on particularly divisive political issues, this is a sign that something has gone wrong with the political, not the legal, system. This is still more the case internationally. The failure of collective security is not a failure of law, but of politics.

At times the pluralist account so reduces international law to a limited list of roles and functions, and so emphasizes the priority of power and interest that any notion of normativity is lost. After all, the idea of law has to involve some claim about legal obligation if it is to differ from cooperative contracting driven by self-interest. Moreover, even in its positivist heyday, the idea of law as a useful toolkit for solving disputes represented only one strand. International law has always expressed the constitutive rules of the society of states. It has provided a language for normative reflection on political practice. Not only did many lawyers view law as an instrument for the implementation of substantive goals but they saw themselves as committed to the values embodied in the idea of a legal order and the rule of law.

However, the crucial point is to underscore the extent to which the normative virtues of this limited account of law can be defended on similar lines to the more general account of international society discussed earlier. Writing as the pluralist conception of international law was emerging, Vattel, for example, continued to uphold the importance of natural law 'so that we may never confuse what is just and good in itself with what is merely tolerated through necessity'.[50] But he also argued that states would have to put up with many things '... in themselves unjust and worthy of condemnation, because they cannot oppose them by force without transgressing the liberty of individual Nations and thus destroying the foundations of their natural society.'[51] This view did not depend, therefore, on some all-encompassing moral scepticism, but rather on a pragmatic or prudential judgement as to the

---

[50] Emerich de Vattel, *The Law of Nations or The Principles of Natural Law*, vol. III, translated by Charles G. Fenwick (Washington, DC: Carnegie Institution, 1916), 11. See Andrew Hurrell, 'Vattel: Pluralism and Its Limits', in Ian Clark and Iver Neumann (eds.), *Classical Theories of International Relations* (Basingstoke, UK: Macmillan, 1996), 233–55.

[51] Ibid. 8.

limits of what could or should be formally incorporated within the international legal order. A more elaborate case of this kind can be built around the apparently narrow sources-based positivist international law of Oppenheim. If international law was ever to establish itself as a mode of regulating and moderating international affairs, then consensus would be most likely to be built around a system of law built around state consent and a clearly defined set of sources.[52]

Conclusions

This chapter has sought to lay out some of the most important features of a pluralist view of the anarchical society of states. It has not attempted to trace these features historically, nor does it suggest that pluralism can be used as a label to capture a particular phase in the historical development of international society. The relationship of these ideas to the historical development of the state system is an enormously complex subject. Many of the features of the pluralist conception reflect political, legal, and moral practices and traditions that developed during the history of the European state system, especially during the period from around 1750 to 1914. Many of the sharpest analyses of these debates and dilemmas are provided by the great tradition of classical theorists during this period. But the theory and practice of international relations in this period is far too rich and complex to be gathered up under a single heading or made to fit an entire historical period. The past twenty years has seen a great deal of work on the history of thought on international relations, including far more critical accounts of how the mythology of Westphalia and the conventional history of international society came to be constructed.[53]

In International Relations textbooks, it is very hard to escape from the mythology of Westphalia—that modern international relations began in 1648, that the Peace of Westphalia contained an early official statement of the core principles that came to dominate world affairs, and that we should therefore understand contemporary changes in terms of moving 'beyond Westphalia'. All fields have their founding myths, but the endless references to Westphalia betray an intellectual sloppiness that has had damaging consequences. It encourages a misleading view of origins. Westphalia did not mark the beginning of the state system. The Peace of Westphalia certainly did not mark the beginning of a system of nation-states. It may have contributed to the development of the positive law of nations, to the secularization of

---

[52] Benedict Kingsbury, 'Legal Positivism as Normative Politics: International Society, Balance of Power, and Lassa Oppenheim's Positive International Law', *European Journal of International Law*, 13/2 (April 2002), esp. 422–33.

[53] See, in particular, Keene (2002).

international society, to the erosion of the unity of Christendom, to the evolution of diplomacy as an institution, and, indirectly, to the emergence of the sovereign state as the basic member of international society. But, as Osiander notes, it does not refer to sovereignty at all, still less to any notion of equal sovereignty; it is built around intervention and the rights of religious minorities rather than non-intervention; and there is nothing concerning the balance of power.[54] It encourages a misleading view of the development of international society and of change: if you have never thought hard about sovereignty in the past, then it is easy to conclude that sovereignty today has suddenly become complex and contested. More importantly, although many of the practices and ideas that animate a pluralist conception of international society can be found within the history of the classical European state system, one of the core purposes of this chapter was to give some sense of the continuing vitality of that conception, whatever its limits, inconsistencies, and moral failings.

The pluralist account of international society does not deny the reality of shared interests, or the importance of seeking to build institutions around the idea of common interests and common values. But it is the difficulties of such efforts that are most central, together with the dangers of what Bull called 'premature global solidarism'. These difficulties stem from the problem of managing unequal power on the one hand and mediating between conflicting values on the other. Nor, as we have seen, does the pluralist deny either the important role that moral values play in international life or the necessity to develop morally more acceptable values. But pluralists remain sceptical of the argument that, having dismissed an extreme 'Hobbesian' depiction of international life, the political theorist is cleared for take-off and can fly unencumbered by any serious concern with the pathologies of power and the deep contestation of values that continue to characterize international life. Within International Relations, Hobbes has come to be associated with highly implausible and historically inaccurate images of all out and absolute conflict and the ever-present danger of war. But one of the most important features of Hobbes's writing was his appreciation of the limits of human knowledge and capacities. Politics is not about ultimate ends, but rather about the achievement of more limited goals: domestically the suppression of violence amongst proponents of competing and conflicting ends; internationally, the attempt to isolate limited, if always fragile, 'pathways to peace'.

As we proceed in the following chapters to examine alternative and far more ambitious conceptions of governing the globe, we should take three pluralist questions with us: First, even as we see more elaborate institutions and other forms of global governance, how are they related to the distribution of power,

---

[54] Andreas Osiander, 'Sovereignty, International Relations and the Westphalian Myth', *International Organization*, 55/2 (Spring 2001), 266.

whether balanced, hierarchical, or some combination of the two? Second, how strong and secure are the institutional mechanisms that will ensure that moves beyond pluralism will reflect the interests of the international community at large rather than simply those of a single state or group of states? And third, how do international law and society deal with the deep tension that exists between rules and institutions that seek to mediate amongst different values and those that seek to promote and enforce a single set of global or universal values?

3

State solidarism and global liberalism

If pluralism represents a long-standing tradition of reflection on international life, closely related to some of the dominant practices within the classical European state system, the view that pluralism would be rendered obsolete by economic and social changes and as a result of its moral failings has an equally long pedigree. Indeed both arguments were well established by the middle of the nineteenth century. In recent debates on global governance, much academic attention has focused on the implications of the end of the Cold War. Globalization and increasing economic and human interconnections between societies, the increasing seriousness of ecological challenges, democratization and changing notions of political legitimacy, the continued growth of transnational economic actors and the emergence of a dense and increasingly active transnational civil society, the decline in use of large-scale military force between major states together with the parallel expansion of many other forms of social violence, and the degree to which the state is under challenge as a legitimate and effective building-block of international order—all of these developments appeared to underpin and help explain the emergence of new forms of what increasingly came to be termed global governance, as well as to fuel demands for further change. But it is very important to see the developments of the 1990s from a broader context and to remember that such ideas came on top of a much longer-term change in the normative ambition of international society that had been gathering pace through the course of the twentieth century.

This chapter addresses three questions:

1. What are the main features of the liberal solidarist conception of international society?

2. What are the major forces and factors that explain the emergence of solidarist forms of international society as well as demands that international society move further in this direction?

3. In what ways has liberal solidarism complicated the search for legitimacy?

The features of liberal solidarism

The term solidarism has been used in various ways. For some, solidarism is about the enforcement of international norms and the possibility of war being waged on behalf of international society, especially within the context of collective security.[1] For others, the key feature of solidarism is the degree to which international society is normatively constructed around individuals rather than states.[2] Others again see solidarism in terms of the depth and breadth of institutionalization. 'Solidarism defines international societies with a relatively high, or wide, degree of shared norms, rules and institutions among states.'[3] Solidarism also refers to an important set of social ideas and doctrines, influential in late-nineteenth and early-twentieth-century France, whose influence on international law in France and whose stress on social interdependence highlight another strand in solidarist thinking. 'What united such diverse strands was their view of the State and of positive law as indicators or functions of the objective laws of the social realm, of economic and industrial development, division of labour, intellectual cultivation, the common good, and social solidarity.'[4]

In this chapter, I will build on these earlier usages, taking solidarism as a composite label for a qualitatively different kind of international society, in which four dimensions are especially important: the move to institutions and expansion of global rule-making; changes in the making, development, and justification of international law; the increasing emphasis placed on the enforcement of international norms and rules; and a changed understanding of the state and of state sovereignty.

---

[1] This is true of Bull whose view of solidarism can be traced back to his early reading of Grotius and to the influence of Lauterpacht's (dubious) interpretation of Grotius. See Hedley Bull, 'The Grotian Conception of International Society', reprinted in Kai Alderson and Andrew Hurrell (eds.), *Hedley Bull on International Society* (Basingstoke, UK: Macmillan, 2000); Hersch Lauterpacht, 'The Grotian Tradition in International Law', *British Yearbook of International Law* (1946), 1–53. Bull's understanding of this solidarist tradition was also heavily shaped by Walter Schiffer's book, *The Legal Community of Mankind* (New York, Columbia University Press, 1954). For an example of the idea that the revival of the UN and the 'renaissance of international law' in the 1990s constituted a neo-Grotian moment, see Boutros Boutros-Ghali, 'A Grotian Moment', *Fordham International Law Journal*, 18/5 (1995), 1609–16.

[2] See e.g. John Vincent, *Human Rights and International Relations* (Cambridge: Cambridge University Press, 1986); and Nicholas Wheeler, *Saving Strangers: Humanitarian Intervention in International Society* (Oxford: Oxford University Press, 2000). This view reflects Mayall's definition: 'By solidarism, I mean the view that humanity is one, and that the task of diplomacy is to translate the latent or immanent solidarity of interests and values into one'. James Mayall, *World Politics: Progress and Its Limits* (Cambridge: Polity Press, 2000), 14.

[3] Buzan (2004: 49).   [4] Koskenniemi (2002: ch. 4, esp. 282–3).

The focus on 'liberal solidarism' also requires a brief comment. The idea of a society of states united by a deeper set of common values or participating within a relatively strong set of institutions can take many forms, not limited to liberalism. The Holy Alliance provides a good example of a conservative or reactionary form of state solidarism, involving both shared principles of political legitimacy and extensive practices of intervention. Equally, although the relationship of Islam to the world of nation-states has been long and complex, one important strand of thought upholds what could broadly be described as an Islamic form of state solidarism: separate states exist but Islam underpins both the interstate law that binds states and the transnational law that binds all believers within the community of faith.[5] Moreover, even if the focus is on the forms of international society pressed by major Western states in the post-1945 and especially in the post-1990 period, the characterization of that society as 'liberal' still needs significant qualification. As we see, it certainly involved many core liberal themes (human rights, humanitarian intervention, collective security, economic liberalization, etc). But it also involved many practices whose liberal credentials are highly questionable, including the degree to which the prescriptive liberal multilateralism of the post–Cold War period rested on unequal power and coercion; on selectivity both in terms of which liberal values were taken up and how and when they were to be implemented; and on a persistent violation of one might call the epistemic conditions of liberalism: the liberal belief that human knowledge is always subject to questioning and revision and that open liberal institutions, including at the international level, are essential for that questioning and revision and for guarding against fundamentalisms of all kinds, including liberal fundamentalism.

The move to institutions and the expansion of global rule-making

Institutions can be defined as connected sets of norms and rules (transactional, regulative, and constitutive) embedded in stable and on-going social practices.[6] One measure of change can be gleaned from some indicative

---

[5] James Piscatori, *Islam in a World of Nation-States* (Cambridge: Cambridge University Press, 1986); and Sohail H. Hashmi, 'Political Boundaries and Moral Communities: Islamic Perspectives', in Allen Buchanan and Margaret Moore (eds.), *States, Nations and Borders: The Ethics of Making Boundaries* (Cambridge: Cambridge University Press, 2003), 181–213.

[6] In conscious opposition to the perceived formalism of earlier work, the resurgence of work on institutions in the early 1980s tended to focus on the very general and loose notion of 'regimes: 'explicit or implicit principles, norms, rules and decision-making procedures around which actors' expectations converge in a given area of international relations'. Since then there has been a renewed interest both in legal rules and in formal organization. On the former, see Judith L. Goldstein, Miles Kahler, Robert O. Keohane, and Anne-Marie Slaughter (eds.), *Legalization and World Politics* (Cambridge, MA: MIT Press, 2001); on the latter, see Kenneth W. Abbott and Duncan Snidal, 'Why States Act Through Formal International Organizations', *Journal of Conflict Resolution*, 42/1 (1998), 3–32; and Michael Barnett and

numbers. In 1909, there were 37 intergovernmental organizations (IGOs) and 176 international NGOs; by the late 1990s, this had increased to 260 IGOs and around 5,500 international NGOs.[7] Or, take this estimate of the increased pace of treaty-making: 3,000 between 1648 and 1814; 4,000 between 1815 and 1919; 5,000 between 1920 and 1945; 30,000 between 1945 and 1980; and 25,000 between 1980 and 1995.[8] Or, consider the complexity and density of such major international agreements as the NAFTA which runs to some 26,000 pages or the *acquis communitaire* of the EU which new members must adopt and which totals around 86,000 pages of legislation.

But this changing institutional dynamic is not just about numbers. It is also about change in the scope and ambition of global rule-making. In marked contrast to the pluralist concentration on a limited set of rules dealing with war, peace, and diplomacy, solidarist cooperation has sought to promote peace and security in new ways (involving increasing restrictions on the right of states to use force and a return of *jus ad bellum*, the enormous development in the law of armed conflict and humanitarian law, and broadening understandings of what constitutes a threat to peace and security and new forms of collective response). It has sought to solve common problems (such as tackling environmental challenges or managing an increasingly integrated global economy). It has also sought to sustain and promote common values (such as the promotion of self-determination, human rights, and political democracy). Rules are no longer about regulating state–state transactions but involve an ever-expanding range of 'beyond the border' issues that affect very deeply how societies are organized domestically. Increasingly, international agreements are addressed directly to private actors, reflecting the extent to which effective policies on economic development, environmental protection, human rights, the resolution of refugee crises, the fight against drugs, or the struggle against terrorism all require engagement with a wide range of domestic political, economic, and social players. International regulation is increasingly about positive obligations involving extensive domestic, legal, and administrative changes rather than limits or prohibitions on international behaviour. The move from the General Agreement on Tariffs and Trade (GATT) to the WTO, for example, and the inclusion of trade-related intellectual property rights and trade-related investment measures, took trade law well beyond tariff measures and into new areas of domestic legislation.

Martha Finnemore, *Rules for the World: International Organizations in Global Politics* (Ithaca, NY: Cornell University Press, 2001).

[7] David Held, Anthony McGrew, David Goldblatt, and Jonathan Perraton, *Global Transformations* (Stanford, CA: Stanford University Press, 1999), 53. See also David Armstrong, Lorna Lylod, and John Redmond, *International Organization*, 3rd edn. (Basingstoke, UK: Macmillan, 2004).

[8] Douglas M. Johnson, *Consent and Commitment in the World Community: The Classification and Analysis of International Instruments* (New York: Transnational, 1997), 8.

Changes in the character of international law

As was noted in Chapter 2, for the tradition-minded international lawyer, law is not best seen as an abstract or clearly defined system of rules. It is a practice that is closely connected with the messy world of power and politics. Indeed, the reality of international law comes precisely from that connection and from the way in which it helps solve concrete problems—rather than from some measure of the degree to which law 'wins out' over the myriad of other factors that determine state policy or from some theoretical notion of what it is that makes law binding.[9] Law is an activity not a body of knowledge.[10] Although this model continues to have a great deal of vitality in practice, international law has evolved into a far more complex set of rules, practices, and institutions that seek to structure and steer global governance.

The coverage of legal agreements has increased exponentially and there have been important changes in the forms that law has taken and in the types of legal agreements. Weiler, for example, has characterized these changes in terms of different layers of law and of law-making—from predominantly bilateral, contractual treaties to a much greater emphasis on multilateral agreements, to important constitutional treaties (such as the UN Charter), to an ever-thickening layer of administrative and regulatory rules.[11] The law-making process has become more complex in terms of the arenas and forums within which it is made (as with the increasing role of very large international conferences such as the 1992 UN Conference on Environment and Development (UNCED)) and in terms of the actors involved. Hence, there has been greater attention to the roles of NGOs and non-state actors and to transnational networks—for example, knowledge-based networks of economists, lawyers, or scientists; or transnational advocacy networks which act as channels for flows of money and material resources but, more critically, of information and ideas. Law, then, is no longer made and interpreted by a small community of international lawyers concentrated in and around foreign ministries but involves a much wider range of actors and broader and more diffuse interpretative community.

There has also been an easing of the degree to which states can only be bound by those rules to which they have given their explicit consent and a chipping away at the hard edge of state consent. The extent to which the model of law-making by state consent was ever precisely accurate is a subject of debate. But the question of giving or withholding consent is often not simply a matter of the unconstrained exercise of will, and in some cases may

---

[9] See e.g. Ian Brownlie, 'The Reality and Efficiency of International Law', *The British Yearbook of International Law 1981* (Oxford: Clarendon Press, 1982), 1–8.

[10] Vaughan Lowe, Inaugural Lecture, Oxford, 14 May 2001.

[11] Joseph Weiler, 'The Geology of International Law: Governance, Democracy, and Legitimacy', *Heidelberg Journal of International Law*, 64 (2004: 547–62).

not be a volitional act at all. This has followed partly from developments in practice and doctrine: restrictions on the right make reservations to treaties, changes in the identification of customary international law with the emergence of ideas of instant customary law, greater weight placed on general principles of law and on pre-emptory norms, the extent to which some international treaties can make 'generally accepted international standards' applicable to all parties even where they have not expressly accepted these standards, as with provisions on marine pollution in the 1982 Law of the Sea Convention. And it has followed partly from developments in the lawmaking process. In many areas, there has been a proliferation of multilateral treaty regimes, established around general principles which are then translated into detailed, and often highly technical, regulation by committees of specialists. International organizations are beginning to adopt decisionmaking procedures in which adoption of legal texts by majorities will bind all members (or, at least, all non-objectors). Decisions by majority vote in institutional bodies (whether executive, such as the UNSC, or plenary, such as the General Assembly) may establish legally authoritative rulings for all members, for example the interpretation of a treaty, the application of sanctions, and so on. Treaties are often negotiated as total packages, in which— if states wish to secure the benefits of becoming a party—they must accept all the burdens, as with the single undertaking in the WTO. Even where particular states formally withhold consent to an emerging rule, it may be difficult for one or two states to maintain opposition to a widely supported new rule of customary international law. Partly, then, in terms of doctrine and partly in terms of practice and politics, classic understandings of consent have been eroded (but not abolished) and the reality of 'effective exit' has been limited.

There has also been a steady expansion in the number of international courts and tribunals. These now number around 80, with 15 to 20 playing a significant role and some (such as the WTO dispute settlement mechanism) viewed as ushering in a new era of legal regulation.[12] International law has begun to shift from a horizontal, dyadic, self-help system towards a thickening triadic or multilateral structure with an expanding array of arbitration, courts, and panels. The growth of international adjudication has also involved a greater emphasis on general legal principles (as opposed to specific materials and sources relevant to a particular dispute) and on the idea that judges and those involved in international adjudication should be seen (and see themselves) as the agents of a global legal community rather than delegates of specific states. Finally, there has been a much greater degree of interpenetration between national and international law. International law has become

---

[12] See the project on international courts and tribunals, www.pict-picti.org

an increasingly important source of national law and is far more commonly used in the adjudication of law at the national level.

In contrast to the bilateralism and contractual character of traditional international law (and to the institutionalist focus on single issue areas and overt bargaining), international law has come more and more to be understood as an integrated set of practices and as an interconnected (but not necessarily unified) normative system in which historical development and the evolution of specific legal doctrines or concepts over time play a crucial role. The content of a norm and the degree of obligation that attaches to it are therefore related to its place within this broader normative order and, for many of those who teach and practice law, the idea of a global legal community assumes an increasing reality. This view has important implications for assessing the 'impact' of international law. Law, on this account, should not be viewed only in terms of formal treaty negotiation, ever more detailed legalization of agreements and institution-specific delegation of authority for dispute settlements. This picture misses the way in which the legal order as a whole contributes 'to legitimacy and obligation, and to the continuum of legality from informal to more formal norms', as well as its creative, generative, and constitutive influence on international political practice.[13]

Consensual solidarism to coercive solidarism

The third dimension has to do with the variety of attempts to move beyond the traditionally very 'soft' compliance mechanisms of international law and to give more effective teeth to the norms of this more ambitious society—a move from consensual solidarism to coercive solidarism. Traditionally, international law and institutions have rested mostly on 'soft' systems of implementation. In most areas of international law, sanctions for non-compliance have been weak, with few inescapable requirements that states resort to binding third-party procedures for settlement of disputes, let alone agreed systems of coercive enforcement—although countermeasures and collectively approved retaliatory action (as in the GATT/WTO context) have been important.

One part (but only a part) of the debate has concentrated on the possibility that the UN might be able to function as a collective security system able to enforce the decisions of the Security Council both in cases of formal interstate aggression and in cases of civil war or internal armed conflict which stretch the traditional notion of international peace and security. As is discussed in Chapter 7, there have been an ascending scale of multilateral actions on the part of both the UN and regional bodies: from non-recognition to

---

[13] Martha Finnemore and Stephen J. Toope, 'Alternatives to "Legalization": Richer Views of Law and Politics', *International Organization*, 55/3 (2001).

the application of economic sanctions, to conflict resolution and political reconstruction, to peacekeeping/peacemaking with a strong humanitarian component and a heavier emphasis on military force and coercion, to military intervention to restore an overthrown government, to international administrations under which sovereignty is suspended and the UN or other bodies take formal responsibility for government, and finally to large-scale collective enforcement action. It is also important to note the greater responsibility of UNSC for policing compliance with arms control regimes.

Yet such developments form only one part of a broader move towards coercive solidarism. One important example concerns the expansion of different forms of conditionality.[14] Although defining conditionality is complex, the core idea is clear enough: both individual states and multilateral institutions attach formal, specific, and institutionalized sets of conditions to the distribution of economic benefits in order to press other states to adopt particular kinds of domestic policy. Up to the mid-1980s, formal conditionality was mostly limited to IMF-style macroeconomic policy conditions. Since then, there has been a very significant expansion within the economic field towards detailed microeconomic reform conditions, and an even more significant extension beyond the economic field to include conditions designed to promote good governance, human rights, democracy, environmental goals and sustainable development, and limitations on the size and types of military spending. Here it is important to note, first, the crucial move away from conditionality as forming part of a specific economic bargain or contract; and second, the entrenchment of political and good governance conditionality within the international financial institutions and other international bodies such as the G8 or the Organisation for Economic Co-operation and Development (OECD) Development Assistance Committee.[15] A further important category of conditionality arises from the formalized establishment of criteria for admission to a particular economic or political grouping: the notion that membership of an alliance, economic bloc, or international institution depends on specific sets of membership criteria. Thus in both Europe and

---

[14] See Olav Stokke (ed.), *Aid and Political Conditionality* (London: Frank Cass, 1995); Tony Killick, *Aid and the Political Economy of Policy Change* (London: Routledge, 1998); and Vivien Collingwood, 'Assistance with Strings Attached: Good Governance Conditionality in International Society', D. Phil. thesis, Oxford University, 2003.

[15] Although the boundaries are fuzzy, it is an ongoing institutionalization that distinguishes conditionality from other forms of economic sanctions. These have also grown very significantly in the post-Cold War period, especially as a part of US foreign policy. Although clearly reflecting individual state interests, both the United States and the EU have applied sanctions in the name of the international community and justified sanctions as means to promote global norms and values, especially in relation to democratic government, weapons of mass destruction, and terrorism. See Kimberly Ann Elliott, Jeffrey J. Schott, and Gary Hufbauer, *Economic Sanctions Reconsidered*, 3rd edn. (Washington, DC: Institute for International Economics, 1999). On this count, of the 170 cases of economic sanctions imposed since the First World War, 55 were launched in the 1990s. Of these, 12 involved clear UN mandates.

the Americas, would-be members have to take their place in the queue. In order to move up the queue, aspiring governments have to adapt their domestic policies in order to meet the required standards. In the case of the EU, conditionality is central both to the process of accession and to all of its association agreements.

The conception of international law as a horizontal order of coordination is so deep-rooted that many international lawyers have felt, and still feel, uneasy with idea of enforcement. And yet the move towards coercive solidarism has been one of the most important developments within international society, often operating in penumbra around the formal heart of the legal order and raising awkward questions about the nature of 'state consent'.

Changes in the role and position of the state

Solidarism as a way of thinking about international order and as a normative system clearly involves very important changes in the idea of the sovereign state. International law and international institutions have increasingly sought to tame the right of states to resort to force other than for self-defence, to subject the relationship of citizens to their states to commonly agreed international standards, and to become deeply involved in the ways in which domestic society is organized economically. Sovereignty in sense of freedom to make choices as to economic, political, or social systems or external behaviour has been severely constrained. Sovereignty in the sense of the power of a state over its nationals has been eroded by human rights law and by the increased availability of variety of national courts and international tribunals. Hence we have seen the tendency to view sovereignty not as an absolute claim to independence or the sign of membership in a closed club of states but rather as a changing bundle of competences and as a status that signals a capacity to engage in an increasingly complex set of international transactions.

But behind these specific constraints lies a broader shift in the idea of the state as the principal agent of world order. Within the pluralist world, states could be understood as 'agents' simply in the sense of those acting or exerting power and of doing so for themselves: 'The law of nations is the law of sovereigns' as Vattel famously put it.[16] But the expanding normative agenda of solidarism has opened up a second and different meaning of agency—the idea of an agent as someone who acts for, or on behalf of, another. Within the solidarist order, states are no longer to act for themselves as sovereigns; but rather, first, as agents for the individuals, groups, and national communities that they are supposed to represent; and second, as agents or interpreters of some notion of an international public good and some set of core norms

[16] Emerich de Vattel, *The Law of Nations*, translated by Joseph Chitty (London: Steven and Sons, [1758] 1834), xvi.

against which state behaviour should be judged and evaluated. One of the most important aspects of solidarism is the idea that the norms that constitute what the state is, and what it is supposed to represent, become a formal part of the normative and legal order. The relationship between different understandings of what is meant by the term 'state', therefore, become far more consequential for international law and for the practices of international society: the state as the embodiment of a nation or people; the state as a territorially bounded polity; the state as an organizational unit, administering society, and extracting resources from it.[17] This trend is most clearly the case in terms of norms relating to human rights, self-determination, and, increasingly, political democracy. But regulatory rules can also have important constitutive effects. Thus, the increased density and intrusiveness of many regulatory rules in the global economy influence what it means to be a legitimate state and shape a state's capacity to act internationally.

However, it is precisely here that liberal solidarism confronts many of its most intractable problems, both within the legal order itself and still more in terms of the relationship between law and politics. Equally, although the principle of national self-determination has crept into the legal order, international society has been unable to devise any stable and coherent set of norms and rules for its implementation. Thus, although the logic of solidarism points towards the conditionality of sovereignty, movement in this direction has been, and continues to be, the subject of bitter contestation. Thus, although much global economic regulation does point towards harmonization and potential homogenization, the question of the legitimate scope for societal difference continues to engender political controversy.

Sceptics might acknowledge these four categories of change but nevertheless doubt the degree to which they represent a politically significant development. They point to the weakness of many institutions—the degree to which many international organizations are member-based without large and extensive secretariats or significant resources, the limits in most cases of formal supranational powers, and the capacity of large states to walk away and go it alone. Moreover, institutions themselves can be understood in terms of the response of government to the constraints of globalization and are about the *assertion* of state power rather than its *decline*.

To this there are two responses. The first says that, when taken in aggregate, institutional enmeshment is consequential even for the most powerful states in the system. Whilst it is not difficult to highlight the weakness of particular institutions, it is harder to deny the cumulative impact of institutional enmeshment across an ever-increasing range of subjects and sectors. Equally, institution-specific analyses of delegation cope badly both with the systemic

[17] On this broad theme, see Christian Reus-Smit, *The Moral Purpose of the State* (Princeton, NJ: Princeton University Press, 1999).

changes in the legal order and with the way in which the ongoing process of enmeshment within institutions over time can lead to significant changes in understandings of state interest, in the administrative organization of states, and in domestic legal practices. The degree to which the legal order has grown more complex and harder for even powerful states to control is one of the reasons why US frustration with international law has grown sharper, shifting the balance between law's power-cementing and legitimacy-creating advantages and its constraining and ensnaring costs.

The second response argues that it is precisely the variation in impact that is the most important point: increased institutional enmeshment has created new forms of global inequality and the vast majority of states are increasingly 'rule takers' over a whole range of issues that affect all aspects of social, economic, and political life. The dominant move in the post-Cold War era has therefore not been towards the end of sovereignty but rather a return to an earlier world of differentiated sovereignties. The changes in the character of institutionalization mean that that differentiation is not simply a matter of crude power, but is reflected in the character and operation of the international legal order itself. On the one side, the capacity to opt out of what was previously a largely consent-based legal system has declined. On the other, refusal to accept either non-derogable core legal norms or those norms that are particularly valued by the powerful runs the risk of being branded a 'rogue' or 'pariah'. Moves towards coercive solidarism have therefore brought back older, exclusivist conceptions of international society and remind us of the double-sided character of sovereignty within the classical state system: on the one hand, it was central to the constitutional and constitutive bargain amongst European states; on the other, it established a system of authority and complex rules to determine who was and was not to be accorded the status of a legitimate political community.

Explaining the development of liberal solidarism

There are three explanatory stories that dominate both political commentary and academic analysis: the first focuses on interests and incentives, the second on values and identity, and the third on power and coercion.

Interests

It is both an everyday intuition and the stuff of countless articles and speeches that interdependence and globalization create problems that can only be solved by stronger, deeper, and more effective forms of international cooperation. The rising costs of major war and the dangers posed by other forms of insecurity; the growth of economic, ecological, and social interdependence;

and the degree to which individual societies depend on each other have all dramatically increased the demand for international cooperation. On this view, the goal of a minimal international order has become ever less adequate. As noted in the Introduction, the expansion of institutions, regimes, and governance is frequently studied within a rationalist, interest-driven theoretical framework. From this perspective, norms and institutions are purposively generated solutions to the many different kinds of collective action problems generated by growing societal, ecological, and economic interdependence.

The proliferation of international institutions is therefore closely associated with globalization and with increased levels of transnational exchange and communication. Institutions are needed to deal with the evermore complex dilemmas of collective action that emerge in a globalized world. Norms, rules, and institutions are generated because they help states and other actors to deal with common problems and because they enhance welfare. In order to avoid the circularity of functional explanations, this work is heavily actor-centred.[18] The changed conditions of globalization and the problems and possibilities that result from globalization affect the interests and policy preferences of actors (states, societal interest groups, and private actors). Cooperation is not the same as harmony, nor is cooperation necessarily normatively positive.[19] The goal is rather to take self-interest as a given and to seek to explain the conditions under which governance develops and the different forms that it takes (for example, the degree of centralization, the balance between public and private regulation, or the extent of legalization). Interdependence creates huge scope for joint gains but cooperation under conditions of anarchy is difficult because of the difficulty of enforcing agreements and the temptations to cheat and freeride. Institutions make it easier for states to cooperate. They affect actor strategies (but not their underlying preferences) by reducing transaction costs, by securing stable conditions for multilateral negotiations, by identifying focal points for coordinated behaviour, by providing frameworks for productive issue linkage, and by increasing the value of reputation. Governments delegate to intergovernmental institutions in order to manage policy externalities, to assist collective decision-making, to provide more efficient dispute resolution, and to enhance domestic policy credibility. Moving beyond rationalism, cognitive approaches highlight the role of knowledge,

---

[18] Kahler and Lake provide a good example. See Miles Kahler and David A. Lake (eds.), *Governance in a Global Economy* (Princeton, NJ: Princeton University Press, 2003), ch. 1. For the most thorough application of these ideas to international law, see Goldstein et al. (2001). For one of the clearest critiques of agent-centred and choice-theoretic approaches, see Alexander Wendt and Raymond Duvall, 'Institutions and International Order', in Ersnt-Otto Cziempiel and James N. Rosenau (eds.), *Global Changes and Theoretical Challenges* (Lexington: Lexington Books, 1989), 51–73.

[19] See Robert O. Keohane, 'Governance in a Partially Governed World', in *Power and Governance in a Partially Globalized World* (London: Routledge, 2002), 245–71.

and especially of scientific or technical knowledge, in shifting state under-standings of interest in ways that foster cooperation.[20]

Values

The protest against the limitations, the cruelties, and the failures of a pluralist anarchical society are concurrent with its emergence. Here we could point to Kant's attacks on Grotius and Vattel as 'sorry comforters'; or to Rousseau's claim that, in taking all kinds of precautions against private wars we have kindled national wars 'a thousand times more terrible', and that 'in joining a particular group of men, we have really declared ourselves the enemies of the whole race'.[21] Those who saw war as a standing affront to any notion of morality or civilization grew in numbers and organization from the eigh-teenth century onwards. Their influence could be seen in peace movements, in the ideas of progressivist international lawyers, and in the programmes of an increasing number of liberal and socialist parties. And, of course, we also need to note the tremendous impact of the First World War on European views of the need to change and transform the anarchy of international relations and of the Second World War and of the Holocaust in pressing for a much more central role for human rights in the structure of international law and in the multilateral order built after 1945.

The idea of progressive change is itself a historical development. Take war: it is no doubt the case that human beings have always longed for, and dreamt of, the possibility of a true peace that goes beyond mere coexistence and that promises an end to violence, strife, and conflict. However, the notion that war and violence can be, and should be, eradicated as an element of social and political life is comparatively modern—certainly within European thought. As Ceadel explains, it is only in the course of the seventeenth and eighteenth centuries that the fatalistic acceptance of war as a natural and inevitable element of human affairs comes under sustained challenge, that peace becomes an imaginable political reality, and that religious and political movements come to be organized around this idea. Peace and a pacific theory of international relations had to be invented.[22]

---

[20] For a good account of these different approaches see Andreas Hasenclever, Peter Mayer, and Volker Rittberger, *Theories of International Regimes* (Cambridge: Cambridge University Press, 1997).

[21] J. J. Rousseau, 'Abstract and Judgement of Saint-Pierre's Project for Perpetual Peace', in Stanley Hoffmann and David Fidler (eds.), *Rousseau on International Relations* (Oxford: Clarendon Press, 1991), 54.

[22] Martin Ceadel, *The Origins of War Prevention: The British Peace Movement and International Relations, 1730–1854* (Oxford: Oxford University Press, 1996). On the modern construction of war, peace, and security, see Emma Rothschild, 'What Is Security?' *Daedalus*, 124/3 (1995), 53–98.

If the urge for moral change came partly as a response to the barbarities of war and conflict, it came also from the drive to universalize that is inherent in most of the world's most developed ethical systems—religious or secular. A limited 'order-privileging' system that has little or no place for justice is one that is hard to square with the teachings of any of the world's major religions. For others, again both religious and secular, the drive for justice has been tied to a belief that globalization and increased interdependence have given a greater reality to the previously abstract notion of sharing a single world and have helped to foster a cosmopolitan moral consciousness, however embryonic and fragile it may be. As we see, for many people, this cosmopolitan ethic demands that greater attention be paid to questions of individual and collective human rights and to the articulation and promotion of some notion of a global common good. It is a common intuition, and the subject of elaborate academic argument, that globalization and material interdependence may have at last provided a material basis for the kind of moral interdependence of which Kant wrote in 1795, namely, that 'The peoples of the earth have thus entered in varying degrees into a universal community, and it has developed to the point where a violation of rights in *one* part of the world is felt *everywhere*'.[23]

Analytically, the role of ideas, values, and identities presses in a broadly constructivist direction.[24] For constructivists, institutions matter because they do more than just reflect power (as neo-realists argue) or solve collective action problems (as institutionalists suggest). They also matter because they help to explain how new norms emerge and are diffused across the international system and how state interests change and evolve. Institutions play an important role in the diffusion of norms and in the patterns of socialization and internalization by which weaker actors come to absorb those norms. Institutions may be the forum where state officials are exposed to new norms; they may act as channels or conduits through which norms are transmitted (as with neoliberal economic ideas); or they may reinforce domestic changes that have already begun to take place (via state strategies of external 'lock-in' or via pressures exerted through transnational civil society). The 'strength' of institutions can therefore be understood in terms of how they shift actors' understandings of problems and of potential cooperative outcomes. Strength results from the way in which institutions create and embed processes of socialization by which norms and values are diffused

---

[23] Kant (1991: 107–8); cf. Robert Duncan's 1967 remark: 'The drama of our time is the coming of all men into one fate' quoted by Michael Ondaatje in *Anil's Ghost* (London: Picador, 2001), 203.

[24] See e.g. Martha Finnemore and Kathryn Sikkink, 'International Norm Dynamics and Political Change', *International Organization*, 52/4 (1998), 887–917; Martha Finnemore, *The Purposes of Intervention: Changing Beliefs about the Use of Force* (Ithaca, NY: Cornell University Press, 2003).

and internalized. Institutions are not about ways of helping actors achieve pregiven interests; rather interests and identities are shaped and reshaped by ongoing interaction, by institutional enmeshment, and by the processes of legal, administrative, and cognitive internalization to which this gives rise. Non-statist constructivists have emphasized similar processes of socialization, norm diffusion, and internalization; but have stressed transnational civil society as the most important arena for these processes and non-state actors as the most important agents involved.[25]

Power

As we see in many places in this book, changes in patterns of international law and patterns of governance have been closely linked with power and the distribution of power—not only within the state system but also within the global economy and transnational civil society. Power is important both for explaining the existence and character of particular institutions, and for its role in institutional choice. Even if institutions are about effective and efficient means of dealing with the externalities and negative spillovers associated with globalization, it is vital to ask which institutions are chosen and why. Power, not effectiveness or efficiency, is often the central determinant of that choice. Moreover, unilateralism can be compatible with the need for global regulation. For example, in many areas the United States has sought to avoid constraints of international law and instead to rely on the externalization or extraterritorial application of its own domestic law: through certification, unilateral sanctions, the use of US courts as international courts, and what Nico Krisch calls 'indirect governance' in areas that range from securities regulation and aviation standards to the development of the Internet.[26]

International Relations has often focused on the relationship between institutions and the distribution of power at the systemic level. Thus hegemonic stability theory grew out of the claim that only the existence of a hegemon could ensure the provision of important international public goods.[27] Power is often viewed in terms of the way in which the existence of a hegemon or dominant state provides the 'supply' conditions without which the 'demand' for cooperation will not be met. Thus, a hegemon is able to use a wide range of carrots and sticks to counter defection, cheating, and free-riding.

---

[25] See, in particular, Margaret E. Keck and Kathryn Sikkink, *Activists beyond Borders* (Ithaca, NY: Cornell University Press, 1998).

[26] Nico Krisch, 'More Equal Than the Rest? Hierarchy, Equality and US Predominance in International Law', in Michael Byers and Georg Nolte (eds.), *United States Hegemony and the Foundations of International Law* (Cambridge: Cambridge University Press, 2003), 135–75.

[27] Amongst a very large literature, see Robert Gilpin, *The Political Economy of International Relations* (Princeton, NJ: Princeton University Press, 1987), esp. 72–8; and Duncan Snidal, 'The Limits of Hegemonic Stability Theory', *International Organization*, 39 (1985), 579–614.

We can also look at the more specific power-political incentives for major states to engage in the creation and operation of international institutions. In the first place, institutions help project, cement, and stabilize power. They significantly affect the costs of rule, especially by reducing excessive reliance on direct and often risky and costly coercion, and by 'locking-in' preferred values and policies. States therefore use institutions to promote so-called milieu goals. In the case of the United States, they have served as 'a transmission mechanism in the effort to universalize American values, for example, the promotion of democratic and market reforms'.[28] Using institutions as platforms for the promotion of favoured values and for locking other states into particular policy choices is a good example of the so-called second face of power: the power to set agendas to 'decide what gets decided' and to mobilize bias.[29] But power is not simply about one state seeking to change or shape the actions of another—getting someone else to do what they would not otherwise have done. It cannot be reduced to the interactions of pregiven actors. It is also about the constitution of action and the material and discursive conditions for action. Such ideas can sometimes sound abstract and overly structural.[30] But they can have quite straightforward and very significant applications. Consider, for example, the way in which the market-liberal economic orthodoxy of the 1980s and 1990s and its implementation by the IFIs and the US Treasury quite literally constituted finance ministries and central bankers as the central actors, both in foreign economic policy and in most aspects of domestic economic management. Because of the way in which international and regional institutions operated, power shifted within governments: health and education policy came to be effectively controlled by finance ministers and central bankers who in turn were often closely integrated into particular international and transnational networks. It also involved a discourse of development and of foreign economic policy which delegitimized alternative values and voices.

A second category of power-related interest concerns the idea of strategic restraint and the role of institutions in signalling that strategic restraint. On this account, if a dominant power wishes to maintain its predominant

[28] Rosemary Foot, Neil MacFarlane, and Michael Mastanduno, 'Conclusion: Instrumental Multilateralism in US Foreign Policy', in Rosemary Foot, Neil MacFarlane, and Michael Mastanduno (eds.), *US Hegemony and International Organizations* (Oxford: Oxford Univeristy Press, 2003), 267.

[29] See Barnett and Duvall (2005: esp. ch. 1); and, more generally, Steven Lukes, *Power: A Radical Analysis* (London: Macmillan, 1974). On the power-cementing aspects of international law, see Pierre Klein, 'The Effects of US Predominance on the Elaboration of Treaty Regimes and on the Evolution of the Law of Treaties', in Michael Byers and Georg Nolte (eds.), *United States Hegemony and the Foundations of International Law* (Cambridge: Cambridge University Press, 2003), 363–91; and Nico Krisch, 'International Law in Times of Hegemony: Unequal Power and the Shaping of the International Legal Order', *European Journal of International Law*, 16/3 (June 2005), 369–408.

[30] Peter Digeser, 'The Fourth Face of Power', *Journal of Politics*, 54/4 (1992), 977–1007.

position, it should act with strategic restraint so as to prevent the emergence of potential rivals.[31] A rational hegemon will engage in a degree of self-restraint and institutional self-binding in order to undercut others' perceptions of threat.[32] A similar logic is stressed by those who believe that US goals will be best served by placing greater emphasis on its 'soft power'—the power represented by cultural emulation or ideological attractiveness.[33] Soft power focuses attention on the values expressed in culture, the extent to which a society can serve as a role model for others, and the capacity to promote a vision of international and global order.

Third, institutions may provide a 'legitimacy buffer' for specific aspects of foreign policy. For example, the 'legitimacy buffer' provided by international economic and financial institutions has been very important to the exercise of US power in many developing and transition economies. Imagine, counterfactually, a situation in which the promotion of economic liberalization and neoliberal reform in the 1980s and 1990s had had to depend exclusively on direct US pressure and on direct involvement, rather than being mediated through the policies and conditionalities of the Bank and Fund. Finally, as we see below, institutions are central to the broader legitimation of unequal power, whether this is approached from a classical realist, liberal, or neo-Gramscian perspective.

There are also important power-related interests that influence the policies of weaker states towards institutions. As one would expect, these help explain why weak states so often favour institutions as a means of levelling power and are willing to accept even hierarchically organized institutions. In the first place, institutions can provide important platforms for influence for weaker states by constraining the freedom of the most powerful through established rules and procedures. The most fundamental goal is to tie down Gulliver in as many ways as possible, however thin the individual institutional threads may be. Second, institutions open up 'voice opportunities' that allow relatively

---

[31] Although prominent in recent discussions of the United States, self-binding is an old idea. See e.g. Heinrich Triepel, *Die Hegemonie: Ein Buch von führenden Staaten* (Stuttgart: W. Kohlhammer, 1938). Triepel insisted on the distinction between leadership, hegemony, and domination; he argued that hegemony 'requires following by definition' and entails the integration of subordinated states within an order that seems beneficial to them. He talks explicitly about the need for strategic self-restraint (*Selbstbändigung des Machttriebs*, 131) and for the hegemon to exercise power in an indirect way that will lead subordinate states to emulate their behaviour and values. I am grateful to Miriam Prys for research assistance on this point.

[32] G. J. Ikenberry, 'American Grand Strategy in the Age of Terror', *Survival*, 43/4 (Winter 2001), 27; and Ikenberry (2001: ch. 3). Mastanduno gives a more realist version of this idea: Michael Mastanduno, 'Preserving the Unipolar Moment: Realist Theories and U.S. Grand Strategy after the Cold War', in Ethan B. Kapstein and Michael Mastanduno (eds.), *Unipolar Politics: Realism and State Strategies after the Cold War* (New York: Columbia University Press, 1999). See also the discussion in Chapter 11.

[33] On soft and co-optive power, see Joseph S. Nye, *Soft Power: The Means to Succeed in World Politics* (New York: Public Affairs, 2004).

weak states to make known their interests and to bid for political support in the broader marketplace of ideas. Third, and related, institutions provide opportunities for influence via what might be called 'insider-activism'. This involves working intensively within the institutions: being a catalyst for diplomatic efforts, doing a lot of the behind the scenes work in organizing meetings and promoting follow-up meetings; getting groups of experts together to push the agenda forward; exploiting what one might call the institutional platforms and the normative niches that create room for manoeuvre and shape how problems are understood.

Fourth, institutions provide political space to build new coalitions in order to try and affect emerging norms in ways that are congruent with their interests and to counterbalance or at least deflect the preferences and policies of the most powerful. And, fifth, there are the costs of exclusion. Weaker states may well enter a regime or institution even if it does not reflect their interests because the costs of remaining outside are simply too high. Yet, however much weaker states are attracted to the power-levelling potential of institutions, there are a number of serious and recurring dilemmas. If (as with the move from the GATT to the WTO) weaker states are trading concessions on substantive issues in return for a more legalized institutional process of dispute settlement, how confident can they be that the powerful state will stick to the rules and how effectively will they be able to muster the legal, financial, and technical resources to exploit the system of dispute settlement? At what point do the concessions on substantive issues outweigh any procedural or process advantages?

It is misleading to view the move to institutions and, still more, the process of normative expansion within and around institutions solely as a process of imposition by powerful states. The nature of power is seldom straightforward and the translation of crude material power into effective political action is complex. This is nowhere more true than when it comes to the creation and institutionalization of new norms and ideas. Thus, the revolt of the colonial world against Western dominance did involve a significant shift in many dominant legal and political norms, for example those relating to conquest and colonialism, non-intervention, self-determination, and racial equality. In addition, even at those moments when hegemonic imposition seems most clear-cut, the reality has turned out to be more complex with both freely accepted primacy and empire by invitation standing alongside cases of clear-cut hegemonic power. Most importantly, as the density and complexity of the international legal system increases, and as globalization opens up new channels of transnational political action, so the process of norm creation becomes harder for the powerful to control. Thus, apparently weak states have been able to use the institutional platforms and to exploit already established patterns of legal argument to promote new and often far-reaching legal rules and institutions. A good deal of the process of normative expansion has been driven by non-state groups and by transnational and trans-governmental coalitions, most conspicuously in the areas of human rights or the environment.

Nevertheless, the dense institutional core that formed the heart of really-existing liberal solidarism in the post-1945 period was intimately connected with the relationships that linked the United States with its Cold War allies and partners within the Greater West. This American-led system consisted of the transatlantic and trans-Pacific regional orders and alliance systems, involving a dense network of norms and institutions in the security, political, and economic fields, together with a set of multilateral economic agreements and institutions (the Bretton Woods institutions, the GATT, the OECD, and later the G7/G8), and an overarching multilateral political body in the form of the United Nations.[34] For a realist, the drive for the United States to engage in this intensive institution-building only makes sense given the perceived threat from the Soviet Union and the constraints of the Cold War (which is why realists expected the end of the Cold War to coincide with a fall-off in institutionalization and cooperation). On Ikenberry's 'liberal–realist' account, the realist side of this arrangement reflected the logic of the Cold War with a heavy emphasis on the maintenance of the balance of power, nuclear deterrence, and containment; whilst the more liberal side stressed binding security ties, open markets, and diffuse reciprocity. But whatever view one takes as to the exact character of this US-centred order, it is evidently the case that the origins of many multilateral institutions were bound up with the Cold War and that the development of liberal solidarism in the 1990s built on this inherited institutional core. It is also clear that the end of the Cold War ushered in a new distribution of power centred on the United States and the developed world, ending the challenges to Western conceptions of international society that had previously come from both the East and the South. The stability and legitimacy of liberal solidarism therefore cannot be divorced from the historical context of the highly unequal power relations from which it emerged.

Much of the explanation for the changing institutional dynamic of international society revolves around these three analytical stories. To these, however, must be added the profound transformation in the role of the state that gathered pace from the early years of the twentieth century—away from a narrow concern with the wealth and power of the sovereign and towards ever-deeper involvement in an increasing number of aspects of social, economic, and political life. This is crucial for understanding why *the politics of globalization* are very different today compared to earlier periods. A final

---

[34] On the creation of the post-war order, see Ikenberry (2001: ch. 6); Tony Judt, *Postwar: A History of Europe since 1945* (London: Heineman, 2005), part I; and Melvin Leffler, *A Preponderance of Power: National Security, the Truman Administration and the Cold War* (Stanford, CA: Stanford University Press, 2002).

factor pressing for the expanding range of international norms is also closely connected to the character of the state, but this time to state weakness or incapacity. For a state-centred conception of international order it is clearly of immense importance if a significant number of weak states are no longer able to provide the kinds of localized order that the statist model presumes. There is nothing new about weak states and the challenges they pose. Consider the contemporary resonance of the following nineteenth-century commentary:

All men are not in fact completely free, nor are all states completely sovereign. There may be States in name, which are not such in reality—Governments which labour under an incurable incapacity to govern, and which a makeshift policy keeps alive under an irregular and capricious tutelage, in order to avoid, on the one hand, the embarrassments which be occasioned by their fall, and to prevent, on the other, as far as possible, (for such efforts often come too late) atrocious barbarities and gross oppressions. To such cases the principle [of non-intervention] does not apply, and the hopeless infirmity which makes interference necessary is an evil that we have to deal with in the best way we can.[35]

There is also nothing new about weak states creating problems that affect the broader dynamics of international relations. From at least the Second Berlin Crisis, all of the major crises of the Cold War occurred within the developing world where unstable and fragile states both drew in superpower rivalry and were themselves undermined by the interventionism of the superpowers.[36]

State weakness has become a major theme of international politics in the post–Cold War period.[37] In many parts of the world, the old dichotomy between domestic 'order' and international 'anarchy' has been recast; an increasing number of states are perceived to be 'failing'; and the international community has faced increasing calls to act in order to prevent domestic problems from spilling over borders, to uphold humanitarian norms in the midst of widespread civil conflict, and to ensure the effective local implementation

---

[35] Montague Bernard, *On the Principle of Non-intervention* (Oxford: J.J. and J.A.S. Parker, 1860), 8. See also the famous words of the Roosevelt Corollary to the Monroe Doctrine: 'Brutal wrongdoing, or an impotence which results in a general loosening of the ties of civilized society, may finally require intervention by some civilized nation ....' On this question and on the crucial importance of this period in evolution of US foreign policy, see James R. Holmes, *Theodore Roosevelt and World Order: International Police Power in International Relations* (Washington, DC: Potomac Books, 2006); and Warren Zimmermann, *First Great Triumph: How Five Americans Made Their Country a World Power* (New York: Farrar, Straus and Giroux, 2002).

[36] See Odd Arne Westad, *The Global Cold War* (Cambridge: Cambridge University Press, 2005).

[37] According to one study, '[F]or the period 1955 to 1998, the State Failure Task Force identified 136 occurrences of state failure in countries with populations larger than 500,000.... In 1955 fewer than 6 percent of the countries were in failure. In the early 1990s the figure had risen to almost 30 percent, falling to about 20 percent in 1998, the last year of the study'. Stephen Krasner, 'Sharing Sovereignty: New Institutions for Collapsed and Failing States', *International Security*, 29/2 (Fall 2004), 91.

of policies that affect outsiders. The exact nature, scope, and implications of these issues will be picked up later. Here, it is important merely to note the extent to which the growing attention devoted to state incapacity and the emergence of the so-called 'new interventionism' has involved a further significant expansion of the normative ambition of international society, and one that unites both hard-headed pragmatists interested in order and security and progressive liberals interested in human security, human rights, and justice. The two most central consequences have been, first, the stimulus to new practices and norms of intervention and, second, the impact on global inequality—both of material condition in terms of those living in such states and of effective political agency given the extent to which state capacity remains a fundamental determinant of protecting and promoting interests in a globalized world.

Although the problems are real enough, the concept of 'state failure' needs to be treated with a degree of caution. In analysing relative state capacity, there is a common tendency to overstate the strength of states in earlier periods and to take the Weberian ideal-type as reflecting reality. Moreover, the language of state failure can easily lead to a view in which the problem lies 'there' with those inside the 'failed state', whilst the solution lies with 'us' residing in a fundamentally benevolent 'international community'. Such a view neglects the multiple vulnerabilities faced by weak states and, in particular, the problems caused by forces within the external environment. As Ayoob notes, the complex interplay of internal and external factors makes the task of state- and nation-building far harder in post-colonial and transition countries than it was in the case of Europe.[38] And finally, the language of state failure is sometimes associated with a still more misleading notion, namely states can be usefully classified across a premodern, modern, and postmodern spectrum.[39] However serious the challenges, the problems faced by weak states can only be understood as the product of modernity and analysed within the context of a globalized modern world.

Liberal solidarism and the dilemmas of legitimacy

In Chapter 2 I argued that materialist accounts of power-based orders were incomplete because they neglected the importance of legitimacy. This section unpacks the problem of legitimacy in more detail and considers some of the principal dilemmas raised by liberal solidarist conceptions of international society. These dilemmas are important not only because they highlight the

[38] Mohammed Ayoob, *The Third World Security Predicament: State Making, Regional Conflict, and the International System* (Boulder, CO: Lynne Rienner, 1995).

[39] For such a view, see Robert Cooper, *The Breaking of Nations: Order and Chaos in the 21st Century* (London: Atlantic Books, 2003).

deep tensions within solidarism but also because of the way in which they provide grist to the pluralist's mill: by seeking to achieve more, solidarists set themselves an impossible task and risk undermining the limited degree of consensus and order that has been achieved within the society of states.

Legitimacy is sometimes understood in a sociological or psychological sense—the tendency of individuals or groups to accept and follow the rules of a political order. However, the fact of actual acceptance or compliance is not enough and the study of legitimacy has for a long time focused on the beliefs of those who are complying and on the reasons why they come to accept a rule or a political order as appropriate and legitimate. Legitimacy, therefore, refers to a particular kind of rule-following or obedience, distinguishable from purely self-interested or instrumental behaviour on the one hand, and from straightforward imposed or coercive rule on the other.

It is true that legitimacy is often not easy to divorce from the calculation of interests. An international order that obtains in a given period may well be stable and considered legitimate to the degree that it reflects an agreed mutual satisfaction of interests. It has been common to argue that Great Power-dominated systems have been legitimate to the extent that the major powers take account of the views and interests of weaker states and formulate their own policies in such a manner that others see themselves as having a stake in the system. But if acceptance can be understood solely in terms of interests and the instrumental calculation of interests, it is unhelpful for the analyst to talk in terms of legitimacy, even if the actors themselves do so. Legitimacy implies a willingness to comply with rules or to accept a political order, even if this goes against specific interests at specific times.[40] We may also need to invoke notions or principles of legitimacy precisely in order to understand how the idea of mutual satisfaction of interests is understood and interpreted by the parties involved.

Power is also central. It is, after all, the existence of an international order reflecting unequal power and involving the use of coercive force that creates the need for legitimation in the first place. On the one side, the cultivation of legitimacy plays a vital role in the stabilization of an order built around hierarchy, hegemony, or empire: all major powers face the imperative of trying to turn a capacity for crude coercion into legitimate authority. On the other side, such power as the weak possess is often closely related to exploiting the arguments about legitimacy that have become embedded in international legal and political practice. There is undoubtedly a great deal of instrumentality in appeals to legitimacy, and nowhere more so than when weak states seek to strengthen legal and moral constraints against the use

---

[40] See Ian Hurd, 'Legitimacy and Authority in International Politics', *International Organization*, 32/2 (1999), 379–408.

of force by the strong. Legitimacy can therefore be seen as a strategic move in a political game and needs to be understood as much as a part of the messy world of politics as of the idealized world of legal or moral debate. The analyst needs to recognize the role of power and interest in the practice of legitimacy politics without falling into the trap of believing that understandings of power and interest can ever be fully grasped outside the conceptions of legitimacy that predominate in a particular historical period or cultural context.

Legitimacy, then, is not simply what people tend to accept in a sociological sense; it is what people accept because of some normative understanding or process of persuasion. Justification and reason-giving are fundamental. As the etymological origins of the concept suggest, this normative acceptance and the process of justification are often based on law. In many situations, legitimacy is often equated with lawfulness—lawfulness within the legal system itself, but also the lawfulness of a legally structured constitutional order within which day-to-day politics takes place. But the problem of legitimacy arises precisely because of the unstable and problematic relationship between law and morality on the one side and law and power on the other.

Legitimacy is an extremely slippery concept. Not all 'legitimacy talk' should be accepted at its face value and the interpretative study of subjective and intersubjective beliefs about legitimacy need to be set against more distanced accounts and explanations. Some have suggested that its very slipperiness means that the concept is best avoided or that it should be disaggregated into its component parts. However, as with sovereignty, the study of legitimacy takes us quickly into a site of contending claims that are so central to the analysis of political order that they cannot be easily ignored or avoided. Moreover, it is precisely the extent to which legitimacy represents an aggregate social quality (especially one attaching to a political order) that makes it valuable. Legitimacy and understandings of legitimacy are crucial if we are to understand the nature of state interests and how they change, the way in which the game of power-politics is structured, and the character of the pervasive conflict over values that so disrupts efforts to capture shared interests and to secure the stable management of unequal power. This is not the place to provide a detailed analysis of the concept of legitimacy,[41] nor of the role that it has played historically within international society.[42] My intention is rather to emphasize the many-sided character of legitimacy and the complex ways

---

[41] See especially David Beetham, *The Legitimation of Power* (Basingstoke, UK: Macmillan, 1991).

[42] See in particular Ian Clark, *Legitimacy in International Society* (Oxford: Oxford University Press, 2005); and Gelson Fonseca Jr, *A Legitimidade e Outras Questões Internacionais* (São Paulo: Paz e Terra, 1998).

in which the development of liberal solidarism has shifted and complicated the terms of the debate. Let me touch briefly on five dimensions of legitimacy.

The first dimension has to do with process and procedure. This is one aspect of what Fritz Scharpf labels 'input legitimacy'.[43] It involves the claim that an action or a rule is legitimate to the extent that it 'has come into being and operates in accordance with generally accepted principles of right process.'[44] Process-based conceptions of legitimacy meshed naturally with pluralist conceptions of international society. As we have seen, for the pluralist international society aims at the creation of certain minimalist rules, understandings, and institutions designed to limit the inevitable conflict that was to be expected within such a fragmented political system. These rules are to be built around the mutual recognition of states as independent and legally equal members of society, the unavoidable reliance on self-preservation and self-help, and the freedom of states to promote their own moral (or immoral) purposes subject to minimal external constraints. It is not difficult therefore to see why analysts of the pre-1914 European state system should so often view legitimacy in terms of shared procedural rules and practices—as with Bull's emphasis on the creation by common consent of rules and institutions by which clashes of interest and conflicting values can be mediated; or Kissinger's much-cited definition of legitimacy: '[I]t means no more than an international agreement about the nature of workable agreements and about the permissible aims and methods of foreign policy.'[45]

Whatever the exact character of legitimacy in the classical European state system, the crucial point is to underscore the ways in which understandings of process legitimacy have evolved and expanded. One strand points in a legal constitutionalist direction. Of particular importance has been the growth of those urging a form of international legal constitutionalism built around the UN Charter. As with all such constitutionalist designs, power, and especially coercive power, is to be thoroughly constrained by the exercise of constitutional authority. The goal is to close, or at least narrow, the gap between law and power both in terms of the collective enforcement of core norms and in terms of the effectiveness of legal constraints on the unilateral actions of the most powerful states. Proponents of this view tend naturally to stress the legal limits on the use of force, for example, in relation to humanitarian intervention or expanded understandings of self-defence, and to reject more

---

[43] Fritz Scharpf, *Governing Europe: Effective and Democratic?* (Oxford: Oxford University Press, 1999).

[44] Thomas M. Franck, *The Power of Legitimacy among Nations* (Oxford: Oxford University Press, 1990). For Franck, the compliance pull of international legal rules is related to the degree to which they meet tests of sources-pedigree, determinacy, perceived fairness, and coherence with the broader system of legal rules and principles.

[45] Bull (2003); Henry A. Kissinger, *A World Restored* (London: Weidenfeld and Nicolson, 1957), 1.

open readings that would allow the use of force to promote broad policy goals or allegedly shared moral values.[46]

Viewing the UN Charter in constitutionalist or quasi-constitutionalist terms can be seen as part of a broader trend towards the judicialization of international politics.[47] The EU is the obvious example at the regional level, whilst the WTO has been viewed both as performing constitutional functions (especially in terms of the scope and practices of its binding dispute settlement mechanism with its proclaimed triumph of law over politics) and representing an incipient global economic constitution.[48] On this account, then, legitimacy requires that the transfer of power to sites and arenas beyond the state be subject to new forms of constitutionalized governance that come to embody at least some of the features of domestic constitutionalism: that both the core principles and the underlying shared ideology are embodied in a canonical charter, treaty, or text; that there be a clear notion of legal hierarchy, including superiority over domestic law; that there be clear principles and effective processes of justiciability, including over time for private actors; and that the law be stable and entrenched and subject to change only by special procedures.

But the limits of a purely legal answer have led many to focus on a second liberal democratic strand. Here we see increasingly powerful demands that international institutions be subject to the same standards of political legitimacy that are applied within liberal democratic states. The core intuition is indeed a powerful one: that the exercise of all power in political life should be subject to appropriate standards (but not necessarily the same procedures) of democratic legitimacy; that the delegation of authority to international bodies has created increasingly serious 'democratic deficits' and 'crises of legitimacy'; and that these should be met by finding ways of implementing the values of representation, participation, transparency, and accountability at the international level. The perceived need to entrench global democracy is driven partly by the transfer of authority to sites and arenas beyond the state

[46] For an example of this tendency, see Bruno Simma (ed.), *The Charter of the United Nations: A Commentary*, 2nd edn. (Oxford: Oxford University Press, 2002). The emphasis on the need to 'constitutionalize international law' has also been visible amongst political theorists. Habermas, for example, has argued (with rather serious disregard to the way the UN actually functions) that 'The world organization ... has a veritable constitution, which sets forth procedures according to which international breaches of rules can be determined and punished. There have been, since, no more just and unjust wars, only legal or illegal ones, justified or unjustified under international law'. 'America and the World: A Conversation with Jürgen Habermas', *Logos*, 3/2 (Summer 2004), 14.

[47] See John Ferejohn, 'Judicializing Politics, Politicizing Law', *Law and Contemporary Problems*, 41 (Summer 2002).

[48] For a discussion (and critique) of these arguments, see Robert Howse and Kalypso Nicolaidis, 'Enhancing WTO Legitimacy: Constitutionalization or Global Subsidiarity?', *Governance* 16/1 (2003), 73–94. Special issue on Deliberately Democratizing Multilateral Organization.

and partly from the impact that both this transfer and the broader impact of globalization have had on the meaningfulness of democracy within the nation-state.[49] It is not just that states are heavily constrained by globalization; it is also that they are affected by an increasing volume of global rule-making in relation to which the traditional idea of 'state consent' has less and less reality. The problems appear clear enough. How can anyone expect the UNSC to be viewed as legitimate given the dominance of the P5, the often murky back-room diplomacy that characterizes the operation of the Security Council, and the non-representation or under-representation of important regions of the world? In a world where democratic values have gained such currency, how can the idea of representativeness not lead to legitimate demands for Security Council reform?[50]

But, whilst the problems may be clear enough, debates over potential solutions are characterized by deep contestation and the absence of agreement even on the terms of the debate. Why should giving a greater voice to the governments of undemocratic or dubiously democratic states or to unaccountable and unelected NGOs do anything to improve the democratic legitimacy of international institutions? In any case, is it even plausible to think of the idea of democracy beyond the state in the absence of a corresponding demos or people? And which conception of democracy should guide such a search? Many take it as obvious that democracy necessarily involves the representation and aggregation of individual preferences and conclude that majoritarian decision-making and directly representative institutions beyond the state are deeply problematic. But there are other important conceptions of democracy. Some, for example, stress the importance of deliberation and understand democracy in terms of the empowerment of public reason.[51] In this case, what matters most is participation and deliberation—bringing more voices and more groups to the international table, not as direct representatives of particular groups, but as bearers of arguments and values and as participants in a process of reasoned deliberation. Others, again, view democracy as a means of limiting domination and believe that the central focus should be on the interests of those affected by the exercise of public power. The aim of democracy should be 'to strengthen the hand of those whose basic interests are vulnerable in particular settings'.[52] These views might have far more purchase at the global level than straightforward majoritarian conceptions, but still carry with them far-reaching implications.

[49] See, in particular, David Held, *Democracy and Global Order: From the Modern State to Cosmopolitan Governance* (Cambridge: Polity Press, 1995).

[50] See David D. Caron, 'The Legitimacy of the Collective Authority of the Security Council', *American Journal of International Law*, 873 (1993), 552–88.

[51] See Philip Pettit, 'Democracy, Electoral and Contestatory', *Nomos*, 42 (2000), 105–44.

[52] Ian Shapiro, *The State of Democratic Theory* (Princeton, NJ: Princeton University Press, 2003), 147.

Given these difficulties, it is often suggested that we should focus less on democracy beyond the state and more on the problem of making international institutions more transparent and more accountable, in particular by strengthening the accountability of institutions to the states from which their authority is delegated.[53] But again the problems quickly become apparent. Why, for example, should we think of accountability in terms of the relationship between states as principals delegating authority to institutions as agents? What of the core liberal ideal that the autonomy-limiting and often coercive power of international institutions should be made accountable to those who are directly subject to them, rather than to those who already dominate them?

These problems have had important consequences for the functioning of existing institutions, whether as a result of neo-conservative attacks on the legitimacy-conferring role of the United Nations,[54] or from civil society groups enraged by the excessive secrecy and elitist and technocratic decision-making of the WTO, the Bank, or the IMF. As we see in Chapter 6, the spread of ideas about democratic legitimacy has also helped fuel demands for further moves towards making sovereignty conditional, towards the justification of intervention when governments fail in their responsibilities to their citizens, and towards the idea that democratic states should be granted a special role in the governance of international society. But the crucial point here is simply to stress that the spread of arguments about democratic legitimation has immeasurably complicated understandings of what process legitimacy does, or should, consist of.

The second dimension of legitimacy has to do with substantive values and, in particular, with a shared understanding of justice. In order for an institution or political arrangement to be legitimate, its core principles need to be justifiable on the basis of shared moral values. For natural lawyers of the sixteenth and seventeenth centuries, it was self-evident that the obligatory character of international law could not result simply from self-interest or some contractual arrangement based purely on bargaining. The authority of law stemmed from natural law—an ultimate norm of right and wrong that could be known through the exercise of right reason and was distinct from positive law. For Grotius the law of nature 'is the Rule and Dictate of Right

---

[53] On the different types of accountability, see Ruth Grant and Robert O. Keohane, 'Accountability and Abuses of Power in World Politics', *American Political Science Review*, 99/1 (February 2004), 29–43. See also Robert O. Keohane and Joseph S. Nye Jr, 'Redefining Accountability for Global Governance', in Miles Kahler and David A. Lake (eds.), *Governance in a Global Economy* (Princeton, NJ: Princeton University Press, 2003), 386–411.

[54] For example, see Henry R. Nau, 'The Truth about American Unilateralism', *The American Outlook* (Fall 2003); or John R. Bolton, ' "Legitimacy" in International Affairs: The American Perspecitve in Theory and Operation', Remarks to the Fedaralist Society, November 2003, http://www.state.gov/t/us/rm26143.htm accessed on 10.08.05. On this view, legitimacy should be based on domestic democratic consent and domestic constitutionalism, not on the agreement of others, nor on international law, nor on universal principles.

Reason'.[55] It could be proved either through reason alone or on the basis of reason as reflected in practice. 'The Proof by the former is by showing the necessary Fitness or Unfitness of any Thing, with a reasonable and sociable Nature. But the Proof by the latter is, when we cannot with absolute Certainty, yet with very great Probability, conclude that to be by the Law of Nature, which is generally believed to be so by all, or at least, the most civilized, Nations'.[56] Although Grotius was prepared to grant practice and custom some role in reflecting and validating natural law, others such as Locke and Pufendorf saw the exercise of reason and the necessary sanctioning power of law as secured directly by God. But for all of those writing within the natural law tradition, justice and morality form a necessary part of any legitimate legal order.

The return of natural law ideas has been a much noted feature of international law in the twentieth century. Alongside the old idea that actors create and uphold law out of self-interest, the post-1945 period has seen the emergence of a range of internationally agreed core principles—respect for fundamental human rights, prohibition of aggression, self-determination—which both provide a basis for evaluating specific rules and underpin some notion of a world common good. Doctrinally, some of these values are related to the emergence of the idea of peremptory norms of international law (*jus cogens*) 'accepted and recognised by the international community of states as a whole as a norm from which no derogation is permitted and which can be modified only by a subsequent norm of general international law having the same character'.[57] In terms of approaches to international law, natural law ideas are especially visible in the work of those influenced by the New Haven School with its emphasis on the values of human dignity and world order and on the legitimate role that they should play in the processes of legal decision-making.[58] Natural law ideas are also visible within idealist legal constructivism.[59]

Beyond law, there is, for many, a naturally close connection between the rise of liberal solidarism and justice. For some, this reflects a general belief in the inherent values of a global liberal order based on the rule of law, the

[55] Hugo Grotius, *The Rights of War*. Edited with an introduction by Richard Tuck (Philadelphia: Liberty Fund, [1625] 2005), book 1, ch. 1, 150. This on-line edition of the 1738 English translation is available at: http//oll.Libertyfund.org/Intros/Grotius.php/

[56] Ibid, 159.

[57] M. N. Shaw, *International Law*, 3rd edn. (Cambridge: Cambridge University Press, 1994), 98–9. The literature is enormous but on the question of universality and consent, see especially Jonathan I. Charney, 'Universal International Law', *American Journal of International Law*, 873 (1993), 528–51.

[58] See Robert J. Beck, Anthony Clark Arend, and Robert D. van der Lugt (eds.), *International Rules: Approaches from International Law and International Relations* (Oxford: Oxford University Press, 1996), ch. 5, The New Haven School, 110–43.

[59] See Philip Allott, *The Health of Nations: Society and Law Beyond the State* (Cambridge: Cambridge University Press, 2002).

market economy, and political democracy. For others, it can be seen in the consolidation of a more coherent agenda of global justice: the notion that individuals are the ultimate bearers of rights and that all individuals should receive the treatment that is proper or fitting to them; that states and other forms of difference and exclusion are only justified on the basis of general principles and only enjoy derivative moral standing; that international rights, duties, and entitlements should be respected and acted upon and that wrongdoing be punished wherever it occurs; and the still broader notion that the major international and global social, political, and economic institutions that determine the distribution of benefits and burdens should be organized and, if necessary, restructured in accordance with principles of global social justice.

Pogge suggests that there are three elements shared by all cosmopolitan positions: individualism (that the ultimate units of concern are human beings or persons), universality (that the status of ultimate unit of concern attaches to every living human being equally), and generality (that this special status has global force).[60] Most liberal solidarists accept some form of individualism and universality but raise questions about generality and global force. They argue that a world of separate states continues to provide the best means of supporting cosmopolitan principles and that there can be legitimate and non-arbitrary limits on the scope of these principles. Yet many of the most contested moral issues within liberal solidarism hinge on how this notion of 'having global force' is to be understood. Is it enough for it to be legitimate to engage in humanitarian intervention, or does morality require a responsibility or even a duty to protect distant strangers from the worst forms of harm and the denial of basic rights?

The law–morality relationship has been at the very heart of the great debates on legitimacy within both jurisprudence and political theory.[61] Can law and morality be separated as one central strand of legal positivism has argued? Should a law be obeyed if it manifestly violates moral standards or stands in the way of morally sanctioned action? These arguments remain central to the analysis of liberal solidarism in the contemporary world. In the first place, is it possible to ground principles of global justice on something other than express or explicit agreement? If so, what might that other something be? And

---

[60] Thomas Pogge, *World Poverty and Human Rights* (Cambridge: Polity Press, 2002), 169. See also Scheffler's useful distinction between cosmopolitanism as a doctrine about justice (opposed to the view that conceptions of justice apply as a matter of principle within states or other bounded groups) and cosmopolitanism as a doctrine about culture (opposed to the view that individuals' identity or capacity for effective human action depends on their membership of a particular cultural grouping). Samuel Scheffler, *Boundaries and Allegiances: Problems of Justice and Responsibility in Liberal Thought* (Oxford: Oxford University Press, 2001), 111–12.

[61] For an excellent analysis of these classical debates, see David Dyzenhaus, *Legality and Legitimacy: Carl Schmitt, Hans Kelsen and Herman Heller in Weimar* (Oxford: Oxford University Press, 1999).

what to do with those who deny the self-evident truths of liberal solidarist principles and who point, as earlier critics of natural law have so often done, to the continuing reality of value divergence and value conflict? And second, how should international society act when principles of procedural legitimacy come into conflict with established or emerging understandings of global justice? If we know what should be done—for example to engage in humanitarian intervention in order to save distant strangers from murder and oppression—why should we allow a legalistic or formalist concern with rules and institutions to get in the way?

The third dimension of legitimacy has to do with effectiveness, one crucial aspect of what Scharpf labels 'output legitimacy'. In many areas of global governance, especially concerning the global economy, it is routinely argued that the delegation of authority to international organizations, to regulatory networks, or to private systems of governance is legitimate to the extent to which such delegation provides effective solutions to shared problems. In many areas of international regulation, this appears relatively unproblematic. But where considerations of effectiveness appear to require hierarchical modes of management, and coercive action outside legal or institutional constraints, problems of legitimacy are clearly far harder to exclude. The question here is not the relationship between law and morality but rather the equally old and thorny question of how the legal order and the political order can be related and reconciled.

If it is effectiveness that really matters, surely both analytical attention and political priority should be focused on those political mechanisms and institutions that are most central to the emergence of international order. The Cold War order, for example, was one in which the balance of power, nuclear deterrence, and shared understandings of spheres of influence played a central role and did so in ways that were very hard to reconcile with legal norms relating to self-determination or the use of force. In more recent debates about terrorism and weapons of mass destruction (WMD), many have questioned why we should set such store by international institutions such as the UN when those institutions appear incapable of acting decisively and forcefully against challenges both to the security of individual states and to the broader security interests of international society as a whole. It is this line of argument that is central to those who are tempted by the possibilities of a power-political order built around empire and hegemony—the idea of an American Empire as the only possible provider of global security and other international public goods, as the only state with the capacity to undertake the interventionist and state-building tasks that the changing character of security has rendered so vital, and as the essential power-political pivot for the expansion of global liberalism.

But even if we continue to think that institutions and international law matter, we still need to place great weight on the relationship between the legal and political order. Thus, those who reject calls for a reform and expansion of the permanent membership of the Security Council often rest their arguments on the importance of effectiveness. Yes, reform might promote representation, but at what cost? If a Council of 25 or 26 is even less able to act effectively than the current arrangement, then how has this increased the legitimacy of the organization? Does not such reform carry with it the risk of repeating the very mistakes of the League that the founding fathers of the UN were so anxious to avoid? The Nuclear Non-Proliferation Treaty provides one of the clearest examples of where the need to promote effective order and to guard against the dangers of unchecked proliferation has been deemed by most states to justify a hierarchical and inherently discriminatory regime.

Legitimizing hierarchy in the name of effectiveness has a long history. A traditional defence of the role of the Great Powers within international society was that: 'The desire for some minimum order is so powerful and universal that there is a certain disposition to accept an order that embodies the values of existing great powers as preferable to a breakdown of order'.[62] Even as international society moved into the age of sovereign equality and as the number of international institutions expanded, the importance of order via hierarchy persisted, as did its justification on grounds of effectiveness. This trend was visible in the permanent membership of the Security Council and the veto, in the voting structure of the World Bank and IMF, and in the informal norms by which negotiations in the WTO are conducted. One of the most important functions of informal groupings within formal institutions is to provide a way of combining effectiveness and legitimacy.[63]

Underlying these positions is the nagging doubt as to whether coercive power can ever be wholly tied down within a legal constitutional order and that trying to do so might create insecurity and disorder. Realists, for example, have long argued that some agent has to possess the effective power to safeguard national security and some minimal international order when they come under challenge and when institutions are unable to act. The *locus classicus* of such arguments is Carl Schmitt: his critique of both domestic and international legal constitutionalism, and his argument that the essence of sovereignty is the capacity to decide on the exceptional situation when effective action is unavoidable.[64] Albeit in more moderate and restrained tones, one strand of international legal thinking has continued to stress the custodial role of major powers in general, and of the United States in particular, in upholding the international legal order and in linking it to a politically prior security order.

[62] Hedley Bull, 'The Great Irresponsibles? The United States, the Soviet Union and World Order', *International Journal*, XXV (1979–80), 439.
[63] See Jochen Prantl, 'Informal Groups of States and the UN Security Council', *International Organizaton*, 59/3 (2005), esp. 582–5.
[64] Schmitt (1976).

As the strongest power in the world community, the US is called upon to play an additional and unique role: that of the ultimate custodian of the fundamental goals of the multilateral institutions that it has helped to establish, when these institutions prove unable to act. And they often prove unable to act because one of the sad facts of international life is that multilateral institutions have certain inherent defects that arise from the very nature of international politics. ... As currently structured, the institutions often prove unable to act, whether because of a veto right or a requirement of consensus. But a change of procedure will not resolve the problem, for the obstacles to action are reflections of the international political process itself. So the alternatives for a state that is able to act unilaterally are to do nothing, because unilateral action would be 'against the law', to act alone, if necessary, to preserve the system.[65]

It is not difficult to see why such arguments create very serious problems of legitimacy, especially when the self-appointed custodial role involves the use of force, when so many aspects of governance involve deep intrusion into the domestic affairs of other societies, and when, as we see in Chapter 7, so much of the activity surrounding the UN takes place in a messy grey area that fits neither into a neat constitutionalized reading of the Charter nor into a pure world of power-politics (as when the UN wills a particular end but not the means to achieve that end, or when actual capacity to act depends necessarily on the power of a particular state).

The fourth component of legitimacy concerns specialized and specialist knowledge. Institutions and the norms and rules that they embody are legitimate to the degree that those centrally involved possess specialist knowledge or relevant expertise. Such arguments are of long standing—the idea that the conduct of international relations should be the specialized domain of skilled diplomats and a professional military and that 'democratizing' foreign policy would risk both endangering the particular state and disrupting international order. But the claims of technocratic legitimacy have grown far more central as governance has become more far-reaching and as the subject matter of governance has become more and more technical. The growth of international regulation of the environment, of the global financial system, of the Internet, and of countless other specialized areas requires that those involved in regulation possess the necessary technical skills. Hence we hear calls that only biologists have the necessary competence and technical skills to decide how tropical forests should be used, or that managing the complex dangers to global public health is 'obviously' a matter for experts and for the functional institutions or networks in which they operate.

Given this picture, analysts of institutions have devoted increasing attention to the roles played by epistemic communities ('respected guardians of policy-relevant knowledge in a world of ever-greater complexity' and 'a community of experts sharing a belief in a common set of cause-and-effect

[65] W. Michael Reisman, 'The United States and International Institutions', *Survival* 41/4 (1999–2000), 71–2.

relationships as well as common values to which policies governing these relationships will be applied').[66] Such communities are said to facilitate cooperation by promoting consensus on the scope and nature of the problem and by shifting understandings of state interest. Analysts of particular institutions such as the World Bank and the IMF have unravelled the ways in which their legitimacy and influence depend on claims to technical expertise, the control of information, and the possession of policy-relevant knowledge.[67] In addition to its explanatory role, there has long been a prescriptive and normative side to the emphasis given to technocracy. For the functionalist tradition, international cooperation is more likely to be achieved if the contentious issues of high politics are put aside, if attention is given to pragmatic progress on matters of low politics where common interests were most apparent, and if solutions grow out of the pragmatic solving of common problems rather than being based on grand schemes of constitutional redesign.

But the legitimacy issues are numerous and intractable. In the first place, it is difficult to prevent experts from becoming a special interest group of their own, unrepresentative of the states and societies whose interests they are supposedly guiding. Second, the idea of technical knowledge as purely technical and apolitical is often exaggerated. For example, the particular ways in which the technical knowledge of the Bank and Fund are linked to both political and bureaucratic interests (as well as the well-advertised policy failures that have resulted from their allegedly superior technical knowledge) mean that these institutions cannot be legitimized in purely technical terms. Moreover, as we see in Chapter 9, the environment is an area where the claims of science are bitterly contested and also confronted by powerful arguments that it is local knowledge that is environmentally most valuable. Third, the idea that controversies involving the scope for legitimate societal difference (as with the WTO cases on GMOs or beef hormones) could be legitimately resolved by a small group of specialized legal and technocratic experts within an untransparent institutional setting was bound to raise questions of democratic legitimacy and to spur demands for a more inclusive view of the constituencies entitled to participate in such decision-making. It is an important illustration of the power of legitimacy that even international institutions such as the Bank and Fund that have traditionally defined their role in terms of technocratic knowledge have been pressed to use the language of legitimacy and, in particular, to confront issues of transparency and accountability.

The fifth component of legitimacy has to do with giving reasons and with persuasion. In many ways, this is the most important element because it is here that the first four are brought together into an effective process of

---

[66] See Peter M. Haas (ed.), 'Knowledge, Power and International Policy Coordination', special issue of *International Organization*, 46/1 (1992).

[67] Ngaire Woods, *The Globalizers: The IMF, the World Bank, and their Borrowers* (Ithaca, NY: Cornell University Press, 2006).

legitimation. Even in the case of effectiveness, legitimacy has to rely on more than 'brute facts on the ground' and depends on a reasoned and accepted argument that an order or institution is legitimate because it provides an effective answer to common problems, it reflects shared values or rests on acceptable processes and procedures. Martin Shapiro has noted the tremendous significance of the apparently simple idea of giving reasons.[68] Political, legal, or moral debate necessarily involve providing reasons, and criticizing, debating, accepting, or discarding them. Legitimacy is about providing persuasive reasons as to why a course of action, a rule, or a political order is right and appropriate. Indeed the idea of an international society does not just involve the notion of being bound by a set of common rules. It also involves the assumption of a need to justify and explain policies in the light of principles that are held in common, including, and perhaps especially, when those principles are being extended, challenged, or violated. Three issues are of particular and persistent importance: audience, institutions, and language.

The first issue, then, concerns the audience. On a narrow Kissingerian view of legitimacy, it is reason-giving and acceptance within the club of Great Power that is politically crucial rather than consensus within some broader, and perhaps illusory, international community. At the other extreme, for many political theorists, the legitimization of power depends on reasoned deliberation within a committed public sphere constituted by domestic, international, and transnational civil society. Between these extremes we can recognize that the contemporary politics of legitimacy are played out to an increasing range of audiences, domestic, international, and transnational through an increasingly complex set of media and that one of the great political challenges of legitimacy politics is to speak to these multiple audiences and to manage their often sharply divergent demands. In addition, new technologies and the growth of connectivity are transforming patterns of communication, both reshaping and multiplying global 'audiences' and altering the ways in which individuals receive information about world politics and thereby develop understandings of legitimacy. The mediating role of states as shapers of notions of legitimate politics is thus under challenge. The geographical scope of the audience is also crucial. It is, for example, often argued that, in the global politics of legitimacy, endorsement of the use of force by a regional body is the next best thing to endorsement by the UN. And yet, in regions dominated by a hegemonic power (such as the Americas or the CIS), it is far from clear that the regional audience will see such legitimation in the same way. Asking which audience matters and why is therefore central to the analysis of legitimacy.

[68] Martin Shapiro, 'The Giving Reason Requirement', in Martin Shapiro and Alec Stone Sweet (eds.), *On Law, Politics and Judicialization* (Oxford: Oxford University Press, 2002), 228–57.

The second issue concerns the institutionalized setting within which attempts at persuasion and justification take place. In an age of global communication, appeals and arguments can be made outside any institutional structure. Yet attempts to legitimize policies are difficult to carry through in a sustained fashion if there are no institutions or institutionalized practices in which rules and norms can become embedded. The importance of the UN and, in particular, of the Security Council is not best understood in strict legal constitutionalist terms as the authoritative body that can rule on the legality or illegality of a particular action. It should rather be viewed as a deeply flawed and heavily politicized body in which arguments can be presented and policies defended because other, better, forums simply do not exist. For example, it has become very common to argue that a community of liberal democratic states should be the body that legitimizes the use of force in cases of humanitarian intervention or expanded self-defence. But this community has either no institutional embodiment or only a partial and deeply imperfect one (as in the claim that NATO as a military alliance should play such a role).

The third issue concerns language. In order to persuade and to justify, there has to be a shared language through which such claims can be articulated, addressed, and received. As noted in Chapter 2, diplomacy has long been seen as an important element of the procedural legitimacy of international society and international law has long sought to play a constitutive and communicative function. But although we can appeal to diplomacy and to international law, it is the difficulties of communication and of rational persuasion that need to be stressed. The politics of legitimacy is about asking difficult questions about who is included or excluded from these allegedly shared languages, and when, where, and why the gaps and breakdowns occur.

Conclusion

All political orders struggle with the trade-offs amongst these different dimensions of legitimacy. They dominate politics even within the most well-established example of governance beyond the state, namely in Europe. So it is hardly surprising that, within global politics more generally, the dilemmas of legitimacy are deep-rooted with these five dimensions often standing in stark contradiction.

For some, facing up to these tensions means that at some point global society will have to confront the issue of world government. Arguments about world government have tended to cluster around three themes. The first centres on necessity. Analogizing from the position of the Hobbesian individual in the state of nature, it is argued that the sheer dangers facing humankind will one day force states to give up their anarchical freedom within some global social contract. The dangers of the Cold War and the arrival of the atomic age made this argument prominent in the debates on world order of the late 1940s and 1950s. What is interesting here is the degree to which even hard-nosed realist thinkers accepted the structural failings of the state system. For Carr, the day of the nation-state was clearly over.[69] For Morgenthau, the failures of all previous attempts to tame the international anarchy pointed to the need for a world state. 'There can be no permanent international peace without a state coextensive with the confines of the political world. The question to which we now must direct our attention concerns the manner in which a world state can be created.'[70] More recent versions have stressed either nuclear one-worldism or environmental one-worldism.[71]

A second and related theme is functional and centres on the changing scale of political organization and the way in which the mismatch between political fragmentation and an increasingly integrated global society and global economy will gradually be resolved in favour of large political units.[72] And the third theme is normative. One strand of political theory has long found the messiness of existing international law intolerable. Kant is correctly seen as a theorist who rejected the 'positive idea of a world republic' in favour of 'a negative substitute in the shape of an enduring and gradually expanding federation likely to prevent war'.[73] He famously attacked both the 'soulless despotism' of large-scale government and viewed attempted world empires as monsters destined to break up and foment conflict. 'Yet this monster, in which laws gradually lose their force, after it has swallowed all its neighbours, finally dissolves of itself, and through rebellion and disunion breaks into many smaller states'.[74] But when considering the form that his preferred federation should take, he could not entirely escape from the idea that a

[69] On Carr and on the possible outline of post-Westphalian arrangements, see Andrew Linklater, *The Transformation of Political Community: Ethical Foundations of the Post-Westphalian Era* (Cambridge: Polity Press, 1998), 161–8.

[70] Hans J. Morgenthau, *Politics among Nations: The Struggle for Power and Peace*, 2nd edn. (New York: Alfred A. Knopf, 1959), 477. Especially noteworthy are the reasons that Morgenthau gives for the impossibility of such a move. There is very little discussion of power or the security dilemma. Instead, it is the power of existing national community and the absence of any broader political and moral community that are most crucial. The focus on community is also to be found in Niebuhr: 'Our problem is that technics have established a rudimentary world community but have not integrated it organically, morally or politically. They have created a community of mutual dependence, but not one of mutual trust and respect.' Reinhold Niebuhr, 'The Illusion of World Government', *Foreign Affairs*, 27 (1948–9), 379.

[71] On the former, see Daniel Deudney, 'Regrounding Realism', *Security Studies*, 10/1 (2000), 1–45; on the latter, see William Ophuls Jr, *Ecology and the Politics of Scarcity Revisited* (New York: W.H. Freeman, 1992), 278; and discussion in Chapter 9.

[72] See Christopher Chase-Dunn, 'World State Formation: Historical Processes and Emergent Necessity', *Political Geography Quarterly*, 9/2 (1996), 108–30.

[73] Kant (1991: 105).

[74] 'Religion with the Limits of Reason', in Carl Friedrich (ed.), *The Philosophy of Kant* (New York, 1949), 381.

law-governed external relationship required coercively enforced laws.[75] And this pattern recurs in at least one strand of cosmopolitan writing.[76]

What exactly is meant by world government is often unclear. Thus mid-twentieth century liberals tended to speak of international governance or cosmopolitan international government, highlighting the growth of internationalized administration, cosmopolitan lawmaking, and international standardization that was already occurring but arguing for a greater degree of centralized authority—one able, as Leonard Woolf put it, 'to coordinate the activities of regional and functional international organs and to deal promptly and authoritatively with any action or situation that may threaten the world's peace or prosperity'.[77] Contemporary believers in cosmopolitan democracy are rather coy about exactly what sort of changes they favour. But we move firmly in the direction of world government whenever we hear calls for a significant expansion of binding third-party dispute settlement; a functioning system of collective security both to enforce the settlement of disputes and to maintain international peace security; and sustained supranationalism involving both pooled and delegated sovereignty. This remains the case however much such calls may be glossed by ideas of subsidiarity or viewed in terms of a multilayered federal structure.[78]

If we compare the debates on world order of the 1940s and 1950s with the debates on global governance of the 1990s, the absence of discussion of world government is striking.[79] In the 1990s, although the objectives and scope of governance had expanded greatly, elaborate institutionalization was rejected. This no doubt reflected the obvious political obstacles and the preferences of the most powerful states in the system (above all the United States), the long-standing normative objections, mostly focused since Kant on the threat to freedom, and the logical problems (if the world is really as grim as is suggested, the move to world government is impossible; if it is not as grim, then such a move is unnecessary). But, this time around, the equivalent of Kant's 'negative substitute' was implicitly constituted not by a federation of states but by the effective centralization of power around the United States and a liberal Greater West. The idea of a hegemonic or imperial order, and the difficulties that it poses, is examined in Chapter 11.

---

[75] See Hurrell (1990: 186–94).

[76] See e.g. Kai Nielsen, 'World Government, Security and Global Justice', in Steven Luper-Foy (ed.), *Problems of International Justice* (Boulder, CO: Westview, 1988), 263–82.

[77] Quoted in Peter Wilson, *The International Theory of Leonard Woolf* (New York: Palgrave, 2003), 49.

[78] Pooled sovereignty involves governments agreeing to take future decisions other than by unanimity; delegated sovereignty occurs when supranational actors may take autonomous decisions. See Andrew Moravcsik, *The Choice for Europe: Social Purpose and State Power from Messina to Maastricht* (Ithaca, NY: Cornell University Press, 1998).

[79] For the most sophisticated exception, see Alexander Wendt, 'Why a World State Is Inevitable', *European Journal of International Relations*, 9/4 (2003), 491–542.

If all moves towards world government are rejected as both politically unviable and normatively undesirable, where else might we look? For a growing number of commentators, governance has already, as a matter of empirical record, moved substantively beyond the world of states and formal interstate institutions and there are very strong practical and normative reasons for believing that this multifaceted, multilayered, polycentric view of governance is the way of the future. It is to these views that Chapter 4 turns.

4

Complex governance beyond the state

If an old-fashioned anarchical society no longer reflects the way international relations has already changed and can no longer provide an adequate framework for global political order and if, at the same time, the possibilities of more elaborate international institutions are limited, where else should we look? It is here that the idea of 'governance' enters the picture. Definitions of both governance and global governance are often cast in highly general terms, building on the etymological origins of the word in the idea of 'steering' and on the wide range of processes by which social systems are coordinated and through which independent but interdependent actors are able to make decisions and to implement policies. According to one definition, global governance is 'the sum of the many ways individuals and institutions, public and private, manage their common affairs. It is the continuing process through which conflict or diverse interests may be accommodated and cooperative action may be taken'; or, on another much-cited definition, governance comprises 'the processes and institutions, both formal and informal, that guide and restrain the collective actions of a group.'[1]

A central feature of the recent usage of this term has been to differentiate governance from the Hobbesian idea of political order that relies on the hierarchical authority of the state and on 'command and control' methods of regulation.[2] Indeed governance is often defined in terms of horizontal interaction. From one side, this pushes outwards from the state and towards the variety of ways in which states interact with a wide range of social actors—through policy networks, public–private partnerships, and policy communities. From

[1] Commission on Global Governance, *Our Global Neighbourhood* (New York: Oxford University Press, 1995), 2; Robert O. Keohane and Joseph S. Nye, 'Introduction', in Joseph S. Nye and John D. Donahue (eds.), *Governance in a Globalising World* (Washington, DC: Brookings, 2000), 12. See also Chapter 1, footnote 13.

[2] For discussions of governance in its broader political context, see Jon Pierre and B. Guy Peters, *Governance, Politics and the State* (Basingstoke, UK: Macmillan, 2000); Jon Pierre, *Debating Governance: Authority, Steering and Democracy* (Oxford: Oxford University Press, 2000); and Andrew Jordan, Rüediger K. W. Wurzel, and Anthony Zito, 'The Rise of "New" Policy Instruments in Comparative Perspective: Has Governance Eclipsed Government?', *Political Studies*, 53 (2005), 477–96.

the other side, it pushes upwards from society and towards self-organization and decentralized coordination through civil society groups (NGOs, social movements, non-profit and voluntary organizations) and through market-based allocation and various forms of economic governance that do not involve formal state-based rules.

Such ideas are structurally modern in that they place a heavy emphasis on the impact of new technologies, especially the degree to which revolutionary developments in transport, travel, communication, and the processing and transmission of information have both enabled and empowered new forms of transnational political organization. Such ideas are contingently modern in that they reflect the power of global liberalism and the impact of liberal globalization over the last two decades of the twentieth century, the declining consensus on the value and viability of statist economic policies, the inability of states and state agencies to cope with high levels of administrative and regulatory demands, and a general belief that the prevalence of both state failures and market failures requires a broader understanding of what is involved in 'good' and 'effective' governance. But they are very definitely not modern in that they draw on long-standing elements of the Western liberal tradition, elements that emphasize the importance of market exchange, mutuality, and solidarity rather imperative hierarchical control.[3] This powerful liberal tradition stresses the complex patterns of social relations that exist and structure social life, often quite separate from the power and laws of the state.

This chapter considers these developments from three perspectives. In the first section, I look at the deepening of inter-state governance and suggest that, whilst the outward form of much institutionalization continues to have an inter-state character, the inner reality is changing in important ways. The second section looks at the many arguments that have been made about the increased role within global governance of civil society and transnational civil society. The third section turns to markets and asks what is involved in the idea of economic governance and how this contributes to the debate about global order. The concluding section raises four (open) questions about law, about power, about the state, and about legitimacy.

The deepening of interstate governance

Chapter 3 highlighted the expansion of inter-state governance in terms of the numbers of institutions, the volume of global rule-making, and the

[3] See Wolfgang Streeck and Philippe C. Schmitter, 'Community, Market, State—and Associations?' *European Sociological Review*, 1/2 (September 1985), 119–38. See also John Dryzek's useful discussion of the world's social choice mechanisms in *Rational Ecology* (Oxford: Blackwell, 1987), 63–184. See also Anthony Pagden, 'The Genesis of "Governance" and Enlightenment Conceptions of the Cosmopolitan World Order', *International Social Science Journal*, 155 (1998), 7–15.

increased complexity of the rule-making process. As these processes develop and deepen, their character becomes harder to classify: yes, the formal structure can still be viewed through statist lenses and related to 'inter-state' bodies. But what goes in and around those bodies becomes increasingly hard to understand in terms of states, inter-state bargaining, the formal delegation of authority, and state-based and consent-based conceptions of international law. Let us take three examples.

The first example concerns international tribunals. In complex legal institutions, norm development does not simply reflect periodic bargains amongst states. It often takes place internally through the practices of the institutions themselves: filling in gaps in treaties, developing answers to new problems, and developing relevant jurisprudence and establishing precedents (even where precedent is not formally admissible). These trends are strongly visible in the European Court of Justice and, to a lesser extent, in the WTO dispute settlement body (although decision-making and norm development in the WTO remain very state-led). More broadly, there is an inherent tendency for all normative systems (especially reasonably well-institutionalized judicial systems) to expand from within and to enmesh actors within certain patterns of discourse, reasoning, and argumentation. As Stone Sweet put it: '... norms ... develop in path-dependent, self-reinforcing ways, one mechanism of which is the ubiquity, and naturalness, of normative reasoning itself. Normative systems are inherently expansionary to the extent to which they enable people to reason from one situation to another, by way of analogy.'[4] In addition, as the development of European integration demonstrates, courts and judges become political actors with interests and agendas of their own.

A second example concerns the vast increase in the forms of trans-governmental regulation and administration. Within the EU, the European Council (made up of heads of government) and the Council of Ministers enact regular decisions but delegate detailed rule-making to committees made up of technical experts from member-states. In addition, a complex structure of advisory, regulatory, and management committees ('comitology') has grown up, linking the Commission with national administrations.[5] The result is that a great deal of detailed regulation and administration takes places in situations where formal delegation is at best attenuated and where the exact nature of 'decision-making' is complex and blurred. We can see similar developments in institutions such as the OECD which has created around 200 committees, working groups, and expert groups which link many thousands of senior

[4] Alec Stone Sweet, 'Judicialization and the Construction of Governance', *Comparative Political Studies*, 32/2 (April 1999), 147–84.

[5] See Desmond Dinan, *Ever Closer Union: An Introduction to European Union*, 2nd edn. (Basingstoke, UK: Palgrave, 1999), esp. 228–9; and Christian Joerges and Ellen Vos, *EU Committees: Social Regulation, Law and Politics* (Oxford: Hart, 1999).

officials in member-states and which produce rules governing money laundering, bribery, the environment and pollution, biotechnology, and transport.[6]

A third (and related) example is provided by trans-governmental regulatory networks. Slaughter argues that our understanding of governance has been hindered by an excessive concentration on states as the building blocks of global governance and on the image of states as unitary actors.

Seeing the world through the lens of disaggregated rather than unitary states allows leaders, policymakers, analysts, or simply concerned citizens to see features of the global political system that were previously hidden. Government networks suddenly pop up everywhere, from the Financial Action Task Force (FATF), a network of finance ministers and other financial regulators taking charge of pursuing money launderers and financiers of terrorism, to the Free Trade Commission, a network of trade ministers charged with interpreting NAFTA, to a network of ministers in charge of border controls working to create a new regime of safe borders in the wake of September 11. At the same time, it is possible to disaggregate international organizations as well, to see 'vertical networks' between national regulators and judges and their supranational counterparts.[7]

Networks contribute to the development, diffusion, and implementation of an increasing range of norms, rules, and regulations, covering issues which range from banking supervision to securities regulation, to antitrust regulations, and to health policy. Networks exchange information. They generate rules and principles, often filling in and expanding what has been negotiated at a formal inter-state level. Much of this is technical and takes the form of soft law or of memoranda of understanding.[8] Slaughter argues that these networks penetrate sovereignty very effectively and draw on a selective range of public and private actors. They are informal, fast, flexible, usually hidden from public view, and can adapt quickly to new problems and new situations. They avoid the cumbersome procedures of traditional inter-state negotiations and are effective because of the close links between norm development on the one hand and implementation and enforcement on the other. 'The actors who make the rules or formulate the principles guiding governmental networks are the same actors who have the power to enforce them.'[9]

---

[6] For further details and many other examples, see Benedict Kingsbury, Nico Krisch, and Richard B. Stewart, 'The Emergence of Global Administrative Law', *Law and Contemporary Problems*, 68/3 and 4 (2005), 15–62. See also John Braithwaite and Peter Drahos, *Global Business Regulation* (Cambridge: Cambridge University Press, 2000), esp. part I.

[7] Slaughter (2004: 5–6).

[8] For further examples of work in this broad area, see Wolfgang Reinecke, *Global Public Policy: Governing without Government?* (Washington, DC: Brookings, 1998); Thorsten Benner, Wolfgang H. Reinecke, and Jan Martin Witte, 'Multisectoral Networks in Global Governance: Towards a Pluralistic System of Accountability', *Government and Opposition*, 39/2 (2004), 191–210.

[9] Anne-Marie Slaughter, 'Governing the Global Economy through Government Networks', in Michael Byers (ed.), *The Role of Law in International Politics* (Oxford: Oxford University Press, 2000), 206.

I will come to questions of power and legitimacy later in the chapter, but here we should pause to note some of the analytical issues that arise. Given their 'elusive fluidity', how confident are we that we can in fact accurately delineate the nature, boundaries, and internal operation of many trans-governmental and policy networks?[10] More importantly, what exactly is involved in the idea of networked governance? Are networks models or metaphors? Are they actors or are they domains of action? If they are in some way influential, does the success have more to do with their efficiency in reducing transaction costs or with their capacity to generate shared norms of trustworthy behaviour, or some combination of the two? What explains the way in which policies are chosen—bargaining, deliberation, or argumentation?[11] If we talk of 'policy communities', what is the force, if any, of the idea of community?

Civil society

The increased attention devoted to civil society within International Relations has followed its importance in other areas of politics—for example, the part played by the 'resurrection of civil society' in the waves of democratization that took place in the 1970s and 1980s. As with market liberalism it has also followed ideological fashion, with support coming from both the political right (anxious to scale back the role of the state) and the left (keen to stress the potential for solidarity and emancipation inherent in civil society and social movements). It is also very closely tied to arguments about globalization and the degree to which globalization has created conditions for the development of global or transnational civil society as an increasingly important arena for political action. This has been facilitated partly by the ever-expanding infrastructure of increased interdependence (new systems of communication, data-processing, and transportation) and partly by the extent to which new technologies have made it increasingly difficult for governments to control flows of ideas and information. Globalization has facilitated the diffusion of values, knowledge, and ideas, and enhanced the ability of like-minded groups to organize across national boundaries.

[10] It is instructive that such problems are visible even in the relatively well-institutionalized world of the EU, see Hussein Kassim, 'Policy Networks, Networks and European Union Policy Making: A Sceptical View', *West European Politics*, 17/4 (1994), 15–27.

[11] For useful general discussions, see Joel M. Podolny and Karen L. Page, 'Network Forms of Organization', *Annual Review of Sociology*, 24 (1998), 57–76; Candace Jones, William S. Hesterly, and Stephen P. Borgatti, 'A General Theory of Network Governance: Exchange Conditions and Social Mechanisms', *The Academy of Management Review*, 22/4 (1997), 911–45. For a critique of the application of the concept to politics, see Keith Dowding, 'Model or Metaphor? A Critical Review of the Policy Network Approach', *Political Studies*, XLIII/1 (1995), 136–58. See also Braithwaite and Drahos (2000: ch. 23).

Transnational civil society refers to a domain and space in which self-organized intermediary groups that are relatively independent of both public authorities and private economic actors, that are capable of taking collective action in pursuit of their interests or values, and that act politically across state borders. Each of the three main stages in the historical emergence of the idea of civil society continues to shape contemporary usage: Locke's use of the term as a way of characterizing a legitimate political order; the emphasis in the late eighteenth century on the way in which the growth of commercial society was creating new solidarities, new forms of human association, and a new and potentially expanding domain of moral ties and affections; and, most influentially, Hegel's redefinition of civil society as a realm that was separate from the family on the one hand and from the state on the other, together with his view of civil society not as a sphere of instrumental needs and wants but also of human and social recognition.[12] There continues to be controversy as to how far market actors (including, for example, the media) should be included, with a common argument that the interests and values within civil society are not driven by motives of profit or individual gain. Some would wish to include in the definition a commitment to certain kinds of values (civility, willingness to engage in peaceful politics) or to see civil society as both an empirical reality and a regulative ideal or source of emancipatory values. Yet moves in this direction load the dice too heavily in favour of a particular view of how civil society and social order are linked, as well as excluding many of its most powerful, if distinctly uncivil elements (such as warlords, drug cartels or terrorist groups).

The global politics of civil society were dramatized by the large and increasing numbers attending the World Social Forums that began in Porto Alegre in 2001 and by the protests at the WTO ministerial conference in Seattle in 1999. There is a very general belief that NGOs have become more important and more influential. Numbers vary but point both to the overall increase and to the gathering pace of change in the 1990s.[13] On one estimate, around a quarter of the 13,000 INGOs (international NGOs) in existence were created after 1990.[14] On another, United Nations Development Programme estimated the number of INGOs to be around 44,000.[15] The literature

[12] See Sunil Khilnani, 'The Development of Civil Society', in Sudipta Kaviraj and Sunil Khilnani (eds.), *Civil Society: History and Possibilities* (Cambridge: Cambridge University Press, 2001), esp. 11–32. Amongst the massive literature, see also John Cohen and Andrew Arato, *Civil Society and Political Theory* (Cambridge, MA: MIT Press, 1992); and John Keane, *Democracy and Civil Society* (London: Verso, 1988).

[13] See Amrita Narlikar and Ngaire Woods, 'Governance and Accountability: The WTO, the IMF, and the World Bank', *International Social Science Journal*, 53/170 (2001), 569–83.

[14] Helmut Anheier, Marlies Glasius, and Mary Kaldor, 'Introducing Global Civil Society', *Global Civil Society 2001* (Oxford: Oxford University Press, 2001), 4.

[15] UNDP, Human Development Report 2000.

on transnational civil society has increased enormously,[16] and there has been much important work on the historical evolution of transnational civil society.[17]

For all the difficulties of definition, it is evident that NGOs, social movements, and transnational coalitions play a number of important roles in the changing constitution of international society: first, in the formal process of norm creation, standard-setting, and norm development, with particular attention being given to the gradual opening of formal institutions to NGOs and the role of civil society in the series of large UN conferences that became a prominent feature of the 1990s (as with those in Rio de Janeiro, Vienna, and Beijing); second, in the broader social process by which new norms emerge and find their way on to the international agenda; third, in the detailed functioning of many international institutions and in the processes of implementation and compliance; and finally, in direct participation in many governance activities (disbursing an increasing proportion of official aid, engaging in large-scale humanitarian relief, leading efforts at promoting democracy or post-conflict social and political reconstruction). The EU, for example, currently channels around one billion euros through NGOs mostly for development and humanitarian activities.

There is, however, little agreement on how we might evaluate or assess this importance, especially in relation to questions of order and governance. Let us look at four possible answers.

At one extreme, realists are clear in their dismissal. Writing in response to the 1970s wave of writing on transnationalism, Waltz put the matter thus:

When the crunch comes, states remake the rules by which other actors operate . . . a theory that denies the central role of states will be needed only if non-state actors develop to the point of rivalling or surpassing the great powers, not a few of the minor ones. They show no sign of doing that.[18]

Realists have long been attracted to the idea that the reality of international politics is revealed 'when the crunch comes', when 'push comes to shove', and in the 'exceptional situation'. Such a view does indeed highlight the extent to which non-state actors act within a political structure shaped by major power conflict (as with the idea that liberal transnationalism has been able to

[16] See e.g. Ronnie B. Lipshutz, 'Reconstructing World Politics: The Emergence of Global Civil Society', *Millennium*, 21 (1992), 389–420; Richard Falk, *On Humane Governance: Towards a New Global Politics* (Cambridge: Polity Press, 1995); and Anne Florini (ed.), *The Third Force: The Rise of Transnational Civil Society* (Washington, DC: Carnegie, 2000).

[17] See e.g. Akira Iriye, *Global Community: The Role of International Organizations in the Making of the Contemporary World* (Berkeley, CA: University of California Press, 2002). Iriye's broad historical sweep is especially useful in highlighting the importance of what we now call transnational civil society in the golden age of internationalism in the late nineteenth century, the role of transnational religious groups, and the shifting balance between public and private economic regulation.

[18] Waltz (1979: 94–5).

flourish precisely because of the space provided by the victory of the United States at the end of the Cold War). It also highlights the continued role of states as gatekeepers: NGOs have achieved greater access to some institutions but states can close doors as well as to open them. However, such a view tells us very little about many important areas of governance, and underplays the extent to which the changes in the density and integration of the system rather than in the distribution of power amongst discrete actors may be the most important indicator and source of systemic change.

A second position focuses on the influence of non-state groups on inter-state relations and the factors that explain the effectiveness of such influence, especially in terms of foreign policy and international institutions.[19] Here the focus is on the resources that NGOs can deploy;[20] their ability to utilize scientific knowledge and to harness causal ideas; their capacity to exploit the increasing number of institutional platforms and normative handholds within and around international institutions; their access to states via networks and policy communities; and their skill in engaging in the politics of symbolic action, the framing of problems, and the development of the dominant discourses that we use to interpret and make sense of issues. Within this context, Keck and Sikkink have influentially highlighted the roles of transnational advocacy networks. Especially in relation to issues such as human rights and the environment, these networks include not only NGOs but also churches, the media, and charitable foundations. Such networks are bound together by shared sets of principled ideas and values, and their activities are central to understanding the ways in which new norms are developed and achieve political salience—as, for example, in the landmines campaign, opposition to the Multilateral Agreement on Investment, changes in World Bank procedures and in the level of transparency within the IFIs more generally.[21]

A third view stresses the importance of what Paul Wapner has labelled 'world civic politics'.[22] Here the importance of, say, the global environmental movement does not lie in terms of the direct degree of influence that it has achieved, but rather in terms of deeper shifts in environmental

[19] See e.g. Thomas Risse-Kappen (ed.), *Bringing Transnational Relations Back in Non-State Actors, Domestic Structures, and International Institutions* (Cambridge: Cambridge University Press, 1995).

[20] In 2005, for example, the total budget for the UN Environment Programme totalled US$127 million compared to Greenpeace's worldwide budget of US$168 million and US$485 million for the WWF Network.

[21] See Keck and Sikkink (1998). Sydney Tarrow, *The New Transnational Activism* (Cambridge: Cambridge University Press, 2005).

[22] Paul Wapner, *Environmental Activism and World Civic Politics* (Albany, NY: State University of New York Press, 1996); and Ann Marie Clark, Elisabeth J. Friedman, and Kathryn Hochstetler, 'The Sovereign Limits of Global Civil Society. A Comparison of NGO Participation in UN World Conferences on the Environment, Human Rights and Women', *World Politics*, 51 (October 1998), 1–35.

consciousness, and in the creation of new political identities within new forms of transnational political space. The emergence and size of the World Social Forum is emblematic of this kind of transnational politics.[23] Under this heading we might also place George Soros's Open Society Network and the role that it has played in diffusing ideas and practices of democracy—and indeed ideas about the importance of civil society. Here, too, we might place the dramatically increased scale of private philanthropy. But this is, of course, a political space that is not occupied only by Western liberal groups and by the Gates, Turners, and Buffets. Islamic transnationalism is a particularly interesting example: first, because it demonstrates the historical continuity of 'global civil society', with the very long and rich Islamic tradition of traders, travelling elites, and scholars, judges, and officials; second, because it illustrates how the changes associated with globalization have given a greater intensity and reality to transnationalized Islam and stimulated pan-Islamic visions and values; and third, because of the tensions within Islam between aspirations to oneness and the continuity of difference and diversity—a tension that is visible in many areas of transnational civil society. The importance of all of these forms of politics is not in doubt. The difficulty is usually deciding what exactly is being claimed. They may be important in many ways but their relationship to issues of global political order is often asserted rather than carefully delineated.

A fourth way of evaluating the roles of groups within global civil society is to shift the focus from the empirical to the normative. Civil society matters because it is both a force for political change—resisting tyranny, building new understandings of sustainability, and humanizing global capitalism—and a regulative ideal. Very important claims have been made about the normative potentiality of global civil society as an arena of politics that is able to transcend the inside–outside character of traditional politics and to fashion and provide space for new forms of political community, solidarity, and identity. In debates about global democracy, the public quality of civil society is especially important and much of the discussion tends in a deliberative-democratic direction. Equally important are the roles that NGOs have played, or might play, in 'democratizing' global politics—in increasing the transparency and accountability of international institutions and in providing modes of representation to previously marginalized communities—for example, transnational cultural communities (such as women or indigenous peoples) and those affected stakeholders on whom, for example, the impact

---

[23] The numbers attending grew from 12,000 in 2001 to 80,000 in 2002 and the WSF has become part of a much broader anti-globalization network. See Teivo Teivainen, 'The World Social Forum and Global Democratization: Learning from Porto Alegre', *Third World Quarterly*, 23/4 (2002), 621–32; and Michael Hardt, 'Today's Bandung?', *New Left Review* (March–April 2002).

of globalization or environmental change falls most heavily.[24] Sometimes the emphasis is on global civil society as a relatively autonomous self-organized public sphere in which genuine deliberation amongst competing positions can take place and through which some notion of international public reason can be developed. In other cases, global civil society and its linked network of 'domestic' civil societies feed positively into state-based order through the provision of legitimacy and consent and into market-based order as the repository of the trust and other forms of social capital without which markets will not function. But on both views global civil society represents a pluralist and open arena for the negotiation of rules and norms based on genuine and unforced consent. It serves as a regulative ideal but one whose potential can be gauged from the changing real practices of world politics.

The market

We need to begin by looking briefly at the nature of economic order and, in particular, the relationship between markets and politically constructed norms and rules. The market, after all, embodies that aspect of social life in which the idea of a spontaneous order driven by notions of self-interest has long appeared most viable and most natural, and in which coopera-tion is based on reciprocity and mutual advantage, rather than on political hierarchy or shared values. There is a long tradition within both Christian and secular natural law that asserts that a right to travel and to engage in peaceful commerce is a fundamental tenet of natural law, reflecting either the inherent nature of human sociability or a dictate of right reason. By the late eighteenth century in Europe, and especially in the writings of Smith and Hume, two ideas had begun to take root: first, that states should not be viewed in terms of the relationship between the sovereign and his subjects but rather as a community of individuals seeking multiple private interests; and second, that the emergence of commercial society and distinctly modern modes of economic exchange opened up new possibilities for social order and for the promotion of public welfare.

It is no doubt true that markets draw on universal impulses and imperatives. Nevertheless, the emergence of the modern conceptions of exchange relations and of a modern liberal individualist society was historically contingent. Here, we should note the emergence of modern distinctions between different forms of exchange relations,[25] the crystallization of notions of interest and

---

[24] For the fullest defence of the democratic roles of NGOs, see Terry Macdonald, ' "We the Peoples": NGOS and Democratic Representation in Global Politics' DPhil thesis, Oxford University Press, 2005.

[25] See Natalie Zemon Davis, *The Gift in Sixteenth-Century France* (Oxford: Oxford University Press, 2000).

self-interest,[26] and the ever more common equation of human nature with the liberal individualized self. Building on these foundations but subject to much critique and contestation, many within the tradition of modern liberalism have argued that international order would be furthered by allowing the pacific and cooperative character of market exchange to be given greater scope: partly because the spirit of commerce is inherently antithetical to the spirit of war (St Simon), partly because, although conflict will still exist, high levels of exchange and interdependence will make the costs of war wholly disproportionate to any likely benefit (Cobden and Angell), and partly because of the idea that an increasingly dense and integrated cosmopolitan society will form the basis for a cosmopolitan moral order (Kant).

It is important to distinguish between the market as itself constituting a mechanism for allocation of resources and the resolution of social conflicts on the one hand, and the rules and institutions that are necessary for markets to function on the other. As noted above, an important element in the move from government to governance has been increased reliance on markets. For some, increased attention to the role of markets in governance debates over the past twenty years reflects straightforward normative preference: markets as guarantors of freedom, as instruments for democratic change, or as paths to international peace. For others, markets are simply the most efficient solution to shared problems, whether dealing with climate change, promoting economic development, or harmonizing societal differences. For the hard-line free-marketeer, even if there are market failures, state intervention and the rent-seeking behaviour of state officials are almost always likely to make things worse rather than better. For still others, the focus on markets follows from the extent to which globalization has as a matter of hard fact eclipsed the once-central role of the state. On this (exaggerated) view (which is examined in Chapter 8), globalization has itself driven a significant shift of power from states to markets. Even if partially driven by state power and state policies, it has created a dynamic that is increasingly difficult to reverse or control.

But despite Hayekian ideas about spontaneous order and despite Cobdenite calls for 'as little intercourse between the Governments, as much connexion as possible between the Nations of the world', all markets require political ordering. Dixit suggests that 'Economic governance consists of the processes that support economic activity and economic transactions by protecting property rights, enforcing contracts, and taking collective action to provide appropriate physical and organizational infrastructure. These processes are carried out within institutions, formal and informal.'[27] The issue, then, concerns the

---

[26] See Albert O. Hirschman, *The Passions and the Interests: Political Arguments for Capitalism before Its Triumph* (Princeton, NJ: Princeton University Press, 1977).

[27] Avinash Dixit, 'Economic Governance', in *The New Palgrave Dictionary of Economics*, 2nd edn. (London: Palgrave, 2006). See also Avinash Dixit, 'On Modes of Economic Governance',

form of economic governance in global society and the foundations of that governance. We can distinguish four broad models.

The first model is statist but based on only limited formal agreements amongst states. One of the stranger claims about 'Westphalia' is that it was a system characterized by tightly patrolled borders and by limited economic interdependence. This is strange because the high point of the sovereignty-based order in the nineteenth century coincided with an era of globalization and cross-border exchange which on many dimensions was more extensive and more far-reaching than that of the late twentieth century. It is perfectly possible to conceive of an international economic order emerging with only minimal agreed rules. Each state decides how it will conduct its international economic relations, and the ways in which it will regulate cross-border transactions; and it does so primarily on the basis of its own interests and objectives. Insofar as many different states share similar views and similar economic beliefs, a common pattern of behaviour is likely to emerge. Although these shared objectives may find expression in various institutions, it is the uniformity and regularity of state policy which is most important in constituting an economic order. Moreover, this is likely to be particularly true of a liberal economic order, characterized by the promotion of openness across three categories of international transactions: goods and services; finance and investment; and the movement of individuals. Each state would practice free trade, reduce or abolish exchange controls, and permit free movement. Independent jurisdictions would exist but, in the economic domain, their relevance would be minimized.[28]

Even in such circumstances, some collaborative action would be needed. First, the existence of independent states and of separate national jurisdictions creates problems for the conduct of international transactions. As a result in the period from around 1830, we see the practical and doctrinal construction of public international law and private international law as distinct realms and professions. Private international law is concerned with which legal system should govern a transaction and how disputes should be resolved. In this period, every major country developed national laws for the regulation and conduct of international trade and the period saw the development of classic doctrines within private international law for managing conflict: principles of jurisdiction; mechanisms for dealing with conflicts over jurisdiction or over

Econometrica, 71/2 (March 2003), 449–81; and Oliver E. Williamson, *The Economic Institutions of Capitalism: Firms, Markets, Relational Contracting* (New York: Free Press, 1985).

[28] This section draws on A. G. Kenwood and A. L. Lougheed, *The Growth of the International Economy, 1820–1980* (London: Unwin, 1988): 73–89. See also Kevin H. O'Rourke and Jeffrey G. Williamson, *Globalization and History: The Evolution of a Nineteenth Century Atlantic Economy* (Cambridge: MIT Press, 2000); Martin Wolf, *Why Globalization Works* (Yale: Yale University Press, 2004), chs. 7 and 8; and Paul Hirst and Graham Thompson, *Globalization in Question* (Cambridge: Polity, 1996), ch. 2.

which law should apply, especially conventions of comity (deference shown by one state's courts to decisions of another); rules on application of foreign judgements or awards, and state immunities.[29] Second, the effective functioning of a liberal system will be improved if states enter into a variety of formal commitments to define the system more clearly, and increase the consistency, regularity, and predictability of its operations—facilitating agreements (travel, communications, weights, and measures); and explicit free trade agreements (because the benefits of unilateral free trade have always been hard to sell politically).[30] Although far from contemporary practice, there remain those who favour the restoration of such an economic order.[31]

The second model of economic ordering is imperial. This was the other central feature of the pre-1914 'liberal' global economy. On the one side, imperial powers sought colonial possessions as a means of exploiting gains from trade; applied metropolitan systems of law, property rights, and contract to their territories; and provided the physical infrastructure for the expansion of economic exchange. On the other side, and more interesting, was the role played by collective political action in defence of an open global economy. This included the collective coercive enforcement of debt (as against the Ottoman Empire), unequal treaties to enforce openness and low tariffs (as with China), the use of naval power to open markets (as in British policy towards Latin America), the collective suppression of piracy, and the establishment of extraterritorial jurisdiction through consular, merchant, and admiralty courts scattered across the globe. Taken together they provide a very good example of how a sovereignty-based legal order sought to regulate transnational spaces. The idea of imperial ordering has returned in the contemporary period. Examples include: first, the role that was played by the power of the United States in the liberalizing agenda of trade negotiations and the expanded scope of the WTO; second, the use of direct coercive power to open foreign markets (as in the succession of 301 and Super-301 trade actions); third, the extraterritorial application of US law and the externalizing of US domestic law and domestic regulatory practices as one route to global

---

[29] On the historical relationship between public and private international law, see Stefano Mannoni, *Potenza e Ragione: La Scienza del Diritto Internazionale nella Crisi Dell'Equlibrio Europeo (1870–1914)* (Milan: Editore Guiffre, 1999). The relationship of different bodies of law to the question of international governance appears to have received little explicit attention, but see David Kennedy, 'New Approaches to Comparative Law: Comparativism and International Governance', *Utah Law Review* (1997), 545–637. Kennedy identifies two modes of operation and underscores the tensions between them: first, law as a means of managing difference between national legal systems, and second, law as a means of harmonization and the diffusion of 'best practice'.

[30] See Craig Murphy, *International Organizations and Industrial Change* (Oxford: Oxford University Press, 1994).

[31] Deepak Lal, for example, argues for the dismantling of the Bank, Fund, and WTO. See Deepak Lal, *Reviving the Invisible Hand: The Case for Classical Liberalism in the 21st Century* (Princeton, NJ: Princeton University Press, 2006), esp. 85–90 and 122–6.

regulation; and fourth, the increased adoption of the dollar as the national currency in a number of countries in the western hemisphere.

The third model is also statist but involves far more extensive and intrusive regulation of the global economy. This is the model that grew in importance after 1945, reflecting the broad factors discussed in Chapter 3 and the specific forces associated with the changing role of the state and with the intensification of globalization that will be discussed in Chapter 8. But the fourth model involves private ordering and it is this that brings us directly back to the question of governance beyond the state.[32]

The idea of the private ordering of economic transactions has important historical antecedents—the most commonly cited of which is the *lex mercatoria* of early modern Europe that comprised the customary practices and norms that grew up amongst merchants and traders. In recent years, private ordering has become the focus of a growing body of literature.[33] One example concerns the growth of private arbitration, with the number of arbitration houses growing from 10 in 1919 to over 100 in 1985 and with the creeping codification of international commercial law in the form of the UNIDROIT (International Institute for the Unification of Private Law) Principles of International Commercial Contracts.[34] A second example concerns the role of credit rating agencies whose role builds on the crucial importance of information in systems of private ordering. A third example concerns private structures of rule generation, diffusion, and implementation—for example, in the area of accounting standards or product standards. Mattli and Büthe, for example, examine the role of private sector standards developing organizations such

[32] A fifth potential model, global centralism or world government, is notable by its absence in this debate. Compared to security and the environment, there has been little impetus behind the idea that an integrated global economy requires greater political centralization. It is true that functionalist writing has implied that the imperatives of managing will push inevitably beyond the nation-state. It is also true that, for all their vagueness as to the nature of a post-capitalist world, Marx and Engels did think in terms of what they described as 'the conscious organization of production on a global scale'. But arguments about moving to more centralized governance above the state have been rare—partly because the most powerful promoter of economic liberalism has been so resolutely opposed to supranationalism, and partly because the thrust of economic liberalism itself is inimical to centralized, top–down economic management.

[33] For example, Thomas J. Biersteker and Rodney Bruce Hall (eds.), *The Emergence of Private Authority in Global Governance* (Cambridge: Cambridge University Press, 2002); A Claire Cutler, Virginia Hauffler, and Tony Porter (eds.), *Private Authority and International Affairs* (Albany, NY: State University of New York Press, 1999); Gunther Teubner (ed.), *Global Law Without a State* (Aldershot, UK: Dartmouth, 1997); Karsten Ronit and Volker Schneider, 'Global Governance through Private Organizations', *Governance*, 12/3 (1999), 243–66. The role of private and market-based coercive power (via mafias and mercenaries) is examined in Chapter 7.

[34] See Walter Mattli, 'Private Justice in a Global Economy: From Litigation to Arbitration', *International Organization*, 55 (2001), 919–47; Alec Stone Sweet, 'Islands of Transnational Governance', in Guiseppe de Palma and Christopher Ansell (eds.), *Restructuring Territoriality: Europe and the United States Compared* (Cambridge: Cambridge University Press, 2004), 122–49; Hans-Joachim Mertens, 'Lex Mercatoria: A Self-Applying System Beyond National Law', in Gunther Teubner (ed.), *Global Law without a State* (Aldershot, UK: Dartmouth, 1997), 31–43.

as the International Organization for Standardization whose work is carried out by a dense network of 180 technical committees, 550 subcommittees, and 2,000 working groups.[35] In other cases, the focus is on non-profit actors, for example the Forest Stewardship Council which develops rules for sustainable forest use and for the certification of products (as do a range of other NGOs concerned with fair trade). And finally, there are hybrid public–private forms of regulation and administration such as the Internet Corporation for Assigned Names and Numbers, or the Codex Alimentarius Commission which develops standards on food safety, which includes business and NGOs, and whose standards have formal status under the Sanitary and Phytosanitary Agreement (SPS) Agreement within the WTO.[36]

An important element of 'governance beyond the state' therefore consists of private authority structures that have some autonomy from the framework of both municipal and international law, private systems of arbitration and dispute settlement, privatized rule production resulting from technical standardization or the development of internal regulations within transnational firms, and private regimes governing particular sectors of the global economy. From this perspective, globalization is leading to a range of different ways in which norms emerge and converge: partly through traditional inter-state negotiations but involving an increasing range of non-governmental actors, partly through processes of societal convergence, involving both market pressures and broad social changes, and partly by non-state actors acting more or less autonomously.

Theoretically, there are three principal explanatory stories. The first is interest driven, with the core intuition well expressed by Ellickson: 'Hobbes apparently saw no possibility that some non-legal systems of control—such as the decentralized enforcement of norms—might bring about at least a modicum of order even under conditions of anarchy [ie lack of government] ... he was too quick to assume that foundational rules must be established by a state'.[37] The second is more macrosociological and traces the emergence of convergent state norms and forms of 'world law' that develop not through explicit or formalized inter-state bargaining but rather through regulatory competition, pressure from international bodies, or mimesis.[38] And the third is power-based, stressing either the impact of sanctions and enforcement or simply the adoption by weaker actors of the rules and norms of the most powerful

---

[35] Walter Mattli and Tim Büethe, 'Setting International Standards: Technological Rationality or the Primacy of Power', *World Politics*, 56 (1993), 1–42.

[36] See Kingsbury, Krisch, and Stewart (2005: 22–3).

[37] Robert C. Ellickson, *Order without Law: How Neighbours Settle Disputes* (Cambridge: Cambridge University Press, 1991), 131.

[38] John W. Meyer, John Boli, George M. Thomas, and Francisco O. Ramirez, 'World Society and the Nation-State', *American Journal of Sociology*, 103/1 (1997), 144–81; and Gili S. Drori, John W. Meyer, and Hokyu Hwan (eds.), *Globalization and Organization: World Society and Organizational Change* (Oxford: Oxford University Press, 2006).

state or grouping of states (e.g. the United States in the Americas or the EU and its periphery) because there is no practical alternative—emulate or else face exclusion.

As with NGOs, the task is not so much to describe these varied forms of economic governance but rather to find a set of criteria for judging their significance. First, in what ways have their roles changed? Sassen argues that 'There is a new set of intermediary strategic agents that contribute to the management and coordination of the global economy.'[39] But much depends on the extent of that 'contribution'. If the claim turns out to be that non-state actors need to be 'taken into account' or 'have a bearing on' our understanding the nature of international society and global governance, then the claim is less dramatic and certainly not very new.[40] Second, insofar as their roles have expanded, are we talking about a simple shift in power or the creation of new sites of authority? Authority, after all, implies a particular kind of social control that is closely bound up with the idea of legitimacy. And third, to what extent are many of these different forms of 'governance beyond the state' dependent on states: dependent on enforcement within national legal systems or at least possibility of that option, dependent on structures of national law, or dependent on the political bargains between and amongst state actors.

Four open questions

Any contemporary analysis of international society needs to take these claims very seriously. We know all too little about social order but what we do know suggests that all three arenas matter and that much hinges on the often delicate balance amongst them. Moreover, although it is useful to talk analytically of three arenas, it is the linkages that are most interesting and most important—for example, the way in which civil society feeds positively into state-based order through the provision of legitimacy and into market-based order as the repository of the trust and other forms of social capital without which markets will not function.

We can draw out some of the implications of these changes by highlighting four questions: about law, about power, about the state, and about legitimacy.

About law

All of these changes have diluted and clouded the idea of international law as a state-privileging system and have unsettled the concept of sovereignty that

---

[39] Saskia Sassen, 'Embedding the Global in the National', in David A. Smith, Dorothy J. Solinger, and Stephen C. Topik (eds.), *States and Sovereignty in the Global Economy* (London: Routledge, 1999), 159.

[40] See, e.g., the definition of global governance in Held et al. (1999: 50).

lay at the heart of the inherited legal order.[41] We increasingly find a variety of different kinds of rules, norms, and principles, developed through the actions of a wide variety of actors, in a wide variety of national, international, and transnational settings, and diffused, internalized, and enforced through a variety of material and symbolic incentives. As a result, the interpretative community involved in law creation and implementation is broadened very significantly—regulating states but no longer wholly dependent on states for its existence, content, or implementation. This picture of international law is therefore very different from the traditional idea of international law as the preserve of foreign offices and dominated by the issues of war, peace, and diplomacy. But it is also different from the law of a solidarist society of states. For all the changes in the nature of law-making outlined in Chapter 3 and for all the tensions that have resulted, law was to remain firmly anchored within a constitutional structure in which states continue to play a dominant role.

The trends discussed in this chapter illustrate the erosion of distinctions between public and private international law and between municipal and international law. More importantly, they are increasingly difficult to reconcile with a theory of law which places significant weight on state consent. The complexity, the fluidity, and the secrecy of the networks within which many norms and rules are generated sit very uneasily with the idea of consent. Such developments feed into accounts of what has come to be called transnational legal process: 'the theory and practice of how public and private actors including nation-states, international organizations, multinational enterprises, NGOs, and private individuals, interact in a variety of public and private, domestic and international fora, to make, interpret, internalize, and enforce rules of transnational law'.[42] They feed into managerial notions of compliance that stress ongoing interaction and negotiation rather than the hard enforcement of clear rules.[43] And they suggest a view of law that stresses policy, pragmatism, and problem-solving. This, in turn, reflects a specific set of US legal traditions, especially legal realism which emphasizes the role of policy in reaching legal decisions, and the New Haven School which rejects the idea of law as a body of rules in favour of a view of law as an ongoing process of authoritative decision-making serving the interests of world public order.

---

[41] For an analysis of how the legal order is shifting, see Benedict Kingsbury, 'The International Legal Order', in Peter Cane and Makr Tushnet (eds.), *Oxford Handbook of Legal Studies* (Oxford: Oxford University Press, 2003), 271–97.

[42] Harold Koh, 'Why Do Nations Obey International Law?', *Yale Law Journal*, 106/8 (1997), 2626.

[43] Abram Chayes and Antonia H. Chayes, *The New Sovereignty: Compliance with International Regulatory Agreements* (Cambridge, MA: Harvard University Press, 1995).

We might question whether existing approaches provide a theory of law capable of both capturing the changing empirical reality of law-making and regulation and explaining the generation of some notion of legal normativity. We might also conclude that this is really a problem for lawyers and legal theorists. To do this, however, is to overlook the importance of consensus not on any specific aspect of international law but also on the underlying foundations of the legal order. This is particularly the case because of the possibility that flexibility, pragmatism, and problem-solving work to the advantage of the strong. There is a tremendous difference between the utility (and acceptability) of legal theories that stress problems, power, and process within the context of a functioning domestic constitutional order and appealing to those same ideas within the context of weakly institutionalized and highly unequal international society. I will return to this point in the Conclusion.

About power

Where does power lie within the forms of governance discussed in this chapter? Let us look at networks. There is very little reason for believing that all states are able to operate effectively within the sorts of networks discussed in this chapter. The extent of the relevant expertise and resources possessed by the United States increases the likelihood that its norms, values, and preferences will win out. Slaughter recognizes the 'ineradicability' of power and the extent to which the particular trans-governmental networks that she examines are dominated by officials of the industrialized world, its bureaucracies, and its industries. But the issue receives relatively little treatment.[44] None of this is to deny the importance of networks and networked governance, nor is it to deny that many of the processes of norm development and diffusion may involve liberal notions of learning, emulation, persuasion, and socialization. But they also involve power and structurally unlevel playing fields. Again, to make the point in more general terms: technocratic approaches to governance tend to ask which organizational forms are best suited to which governance functions. The more important political question, however, involves asking whose interests are being served by which governance mechanisms, and whose values protected and promoted.

There is a similar neglect of power in much of the liberal writing on transnational civil society. First, state power. State action may be shaped by NGO lobbying but it is often state action that is crucial in fostering the emergence of civil society in the first place and in providing the institutional framework that enables it to flourish. In some cases, the links with states are direct. In trade, for example, governments play a crucial role in facilitating (and often financing) the activities of NGOs and in shaping the actions and agendas

[44] Slaughter (2004: 228–9).

of the insider networks associated with both the WTO and such regional processes as the Free Trade Area of the Americas (FTAA) negotiations.[45] In human rights, as Chinkin notes, '[A]lthough NGOs have made significant inroads, States retain a tight grip on the formal law-making processes while apparently ceding ground'.[46] State power is also increasingly determined by the ability of governments to work successfully within civil society and to exploit transnational and trans-governmental coalitions for their own purposes. Thus, we need to note the very different capacity of countries to operate within these arenas. Countries accustomed to pluralist politics adapt easily to such changes. Many developing countries have found it much harder to navigate in this kind of world, perhaps due to domestic political sensitivities or to inherited traditions of very statist foreign policymaking.

Second, power within weaker societies. Transnational social action will often work to tilt the political, social, and economic playing field within weaker societies. Funding one group rather than another and legitimizing one set of claims rather than another (say indigenous peoples in the Amazon rather than small farmers) affect national political processes and may almost certainly undermine the authenticity of democracy. Whether or not this is legitimate, it is an important aspect of the power of transnational civil society. Third, power within transnational civil society. There is nothing normatively special or sacred about civil society. It is an arena of politics like any other in which the good and thoroughly awful coexist, in which the pervasive claims made by social movements and NGOs to authenticity and representativeness need to be tested and challenged, and in which outcomes may be just as subject to direct manipulation by powerful actors as in the world of inter-state politics. If this is true domestically, it is, given the myriad forms of inequality in world politics, far more true globally. And finally, power and particular parts of the international system.[47] Here, we have to face the argument that existing NGO influence already works to favour the values and interests of Northern states and societies, and that moves to expand such influence as part of attempts to democratize international institutions would magnify still further the power of the already powerful. As Woods puts it, transnational NGOs '... magnify Northern views—both outside governments and through

---

[45] The 'North/South' character of the FTAA make it an especially interesting example, see Roberto Patricio Koreniewiecz and William C. Smith, 'Transnational Social Movements Elite Projects, and Collective Action from Below in the Americas', in Louise Fawcett and Monica Serrano (eds.), *Regionalism and Governance in the Americas* (Basingstoke, UK: Palgrave, 2005).

[46] Christine Chinkin, 'Human Rights and the Politics of Representation', in Michael Byers (ed.), *The Role of Law in International Politics* (Oxford: Oxford University Press, 2000), 140.

[47] Liberal constructivist writing tended to focus on the diffusion of Western norms and on NGOs (and IOs) as teachers of norms. The interaction between these and local and regional norms has been neglected. See Amitav Acharya, 'How Ideas Spread: Whose Norms Matter? Norm Localization and Institutional Change in Asian Regionalism', *International Organization*, 58 (Spring 2004), 239–75. Equally, more and more empirical work on transnational civil society has underscored the scale of divergences between Northern and Southern NGOs.

governments—in the international organizations, adding yet another channel of influence to those peoples and governments who are already powerfully represented'. Around 87 per cent of the 738 NGOs that were accredited at the Seattle Ministerial were based in the industrialized countries.[48] In the case of human rights, Hopgood notes the picture of Amnesty's membership and activism: in 2005, there were 1,157,939 members in North America and Western Europe, compared to 56,195 in Asia-Pacific and 4,201 in Africa.[49]

About the state

The approaches to governance considered in the chapter clearly involve a very different view of the state. Instead of seeing the state simply either as a sovereign or as an agent acting on behalf of different groups, the dominant tendency is to disaggregate the state. This builds on well-established analytical trends within liberalism.[50] On the one hand, this view gives ontological primacy to individuals and groups within the state: what states are and how they act internationally is based on the character of state–society relations. On the other, the growth of globalization means that more and more politically salient transactions will involve different parts of the state acting together with private actors, with firms, and with parts of other states across borders.

Normatively this view presses in a functional-contractual direction. From this perspective, institutions, including state institutions, should not be seen as representatives of sovereign power or as embodiments of a particular community, but rather as functional bodies that compete with one another to provide efficient solutions to governance problems. There is no prior normative preference as to what governance functions should be undertaken at what level, by what kinds of actors, or by what social mechanism (state, market, and civil society). State functions are substitutable and may be assumed by

---

[48] Ngaire Woods and Amrita Narlikar, 'Governance and Accountability: The WTO, the IMF and the World Bank', *International Social Science Journal*, 53/170 (December 2001), 569–83.

[49] Stephen Hopgood, *Keepers of the Flame: Understanding Amnesty International* (Ithaca, NY: Cornell University Press, 2006), 172, and ch. 6.

[50] See Andrew Moravcsik, 'Liberal International Relations Theory: A Scientific Assessment', in Colin Elman and Miriam Fendius Elman (eds.), *Progress in International Relations Theory* (Cambridge, MA: MIT Press, 2002). For Moravcsik, '[T]he first assumption [of liberal theory] is that the fundamental actors in international politics are rational individuals and private groups, who organize and exchange to promote their interests. Liberal theory rests on a "bottom-up" view of politics, in which the demands of individuals and societal groups are treated as exogenous causes of the interests underlying state behaviour...The second assumption of liberal theory is that states (or other political institutions) represent some subset of domestic society, whose weighted preferences constitute the underlying goals ("state preferences") that rational state officials pursue via foreign policy. Representative institutions thereby constitute a critical "transmission belt" by which the preferences and social power of individuals and groups in civil society enter the political realm and are eventually translated into state policy' (pp. 161–3).

external agencies, by private companies, and by a range of transnational actors. States still exist but the status and the protection conferred by the norm of sovereignty would disappear. Sovereignty would become overtly contractual.

I will come back to the broad arguments about the fate of the state in an era of globalization in Chapter 8. However, we should note here the importance and the complexity of the links between states and non-state actors and the extent to which a great deal that happens in relation to governance beyond the state depends, either directly or indirectly, on state power and state policies. Braithwaite and Drahos, for example, find a good deal of evidence for a generally realist interpretation. 'Notwithstanding the complex plurality of actors we have shown to be involved in global regulatory games, if we ask the crude question, "which is type of actor that has had the greatest influence?", the answer is fairly clear: the nation-state. If we ask which single actor has had the greatest influence, that answer is even clearer—the US state.'[51] But they add three extremely important provisos: first, 'what we find to be crucial is how state and non-state actors are linked'; second, that '[W]hat has changed is the nature of state power'; and third, that the complexity of governance means that there is considerable variation in the ability of weaker states to improve their position.[52]

We should also note the empirical doubts about the extent and significance of the changes that have taken place and how we should understand them. In the financial crises of the 1990s, for example, one might argue that trans-governmental regulatory networks were indeed able to manage the crises effectively—that is without recourse to too much governmental action or to a new round of institution-building. But this 'success' can be seen as reflecting the power of private economic interests anxious to protect their own freedom of action and to resist the restrictions that more formal international regulation would bring with it. This freedom of action is, in turn, related to their domestic political power within the United States and the importance of the financial services sector to the US economy. To put the point more generally: a liberal theory of transnational governance cannot simply stress the importance of societal interests. There has to be some judgement as to the nature and impact of the power that is aggregated either directly within networks or policy communities, or in the links between those networks and the states and private actors with which they are closely involved.

Finally, even if we reject the Weberian notion that legitimate political order is necessarily dependent on the coercive power of the state, there is still a sense in which many of the liberal ideas about governance via market and

---

[51] Braithwaite and Drahos (2000: 475 and ch. 20 'Contests of Actors').
[52] Ibid. 475 and 504.

via civil society are about governance in good times and in nice places. One of the most important limits of such approaches is that, by concentrating on the problem of capturing shared or potentially shared interests, they leave a series of difficult questions to one side. For example, in his excellent elaboration of the institutions needed for economic governance, Dixit states that 'We might also consider a fourth category, namely the deep institutions that are essential to avoid serious cleavages or alienation that threatens the cohesion of the society itself. But this has not been studied in this context so far.'[53] Internationally, however, it is precisely the absence or weakness of such 'deep institutions' that places the most serious limits on the effectiveness of global economic governance. Or, put another way around, the viability of many of the modes of governance considered in this chapter are significantly dependent on the prior political order provided by the relations between and amongst the major players.

About legitimacy

The individual aspects of governance examined in this chapter each raise particular issues of legitimacy. Trans-governmental networks, for example, draw potential legitimacy partly from claims to technical knowledge, partly from the delegation of authority from states, and partly from the claims to effectiveness and efficiency. Yet the problems of legitimacy are clear: how to prevent such networks from being dominated by a small, self-selected, and unaccountable elite?[54] Equally, there has been a great deal of criticism made in relation to NGOs and attacks on their claims to representativeness and authenticity and about their own internal structures of representation and accountability. But there is also a larger and more intractable set of questions.

As I suggested, questions of legitimacy emerge whenever power is exercised in the context of competing interests and conflicting values. Principles of political legitimacy are sustained in part by the strategic purpose of placing effective constraints on the use and abuse of power, and in part by the specifically liberal goal of seeking to do so in ways that further particular values such as individual autonomy or equality via such mechanisms as transparency, accountability, or representation. But before we can debate the exact nature of these principles, we need to decide upon the subject of legitimacy. Traditionally, the argument has been that it is the state and, by extension, inter-state institutions that should be the proper subjects of political legitimacy. Hence we hear many arguments about the need to increase the accountability of already-existing bodies such as the World Bank or the WTO. This, in turn, reflects a strong trend in Western liberal thought to emphasize

[53] Dixit (2006).
[54] See e.g. Philip Alston, 'The Myopia of the Handmaidens: International Lawyers and Globalization', *European Journal of International Law*, 3 (1997), 435–48.

divisions between the public and private realms and between public and private power. However the changes sketched in this chapter suggest that states are clearly no longer the sole wielders of decision-making power, that many areas of governance are characterized by both private and public actors and by hybrid forms of governance, and that non-state actors such as NGOs are both themselves involved in the exercise of global public power and as well as being the agents that play an important role in the legitimation of that power. In so far as governance beyond the state is developing, there will be a corresponding need to re-think the principles of political legitimacy that are most appropriate for the emergence of new forms of global public power.

Part II

Issues

5

Nationalism and the politics of identity

Hannah Arendt has written of the 'haunting obscurity' of all attempts to explain the variety of human societies:

The only trait that all these various forms and shapes of human plurality have in common is the simple fact of their genesis, that is, that at some moment in time and for some reason a group of people must have come to think of themselves as a "We". No matter how this "We" is first experienced and articulated, it seems that it always needs a beginning, and nothing seems so shrouded in mystery as that "In the beginning", not only of the human species as distinguished from other living organisms, but also of the enormous variety of indubitably human societies.[1]

This chapter concentrates on the most powerful modern expression of this idea of 'we', namely political nationalism. Nationalism and national self-determination are fundamental to the problem of global order because they speak to the issue of who the dominant political agents of order are to be (empires? states? nations? nation-states? peoples?), because so much conflict and disorder have resulted from the complexities and ambiguities of the relationship between nation and state, and because attempts to apply the principle of national self-determination expose so clearly the deep tensions that arise amongst the conceptions of international society outlined in the previous chapters. Moreover, many of the 'ethically constitutive stories' that play such an important role in the politics of peoplehood are themselves stories about the world as a whole, about where particular groups fit into the world, and about the values that underpin the relationship between the inside and the outside, the one world and the many worlds.[2]

If state sovereignty has provided the basic institutional framework of the society of states, it was national self-determination that came ever more to provide the political power and the moral meaning to the idea of an international society. The assumed naturalness of living in a world of states derives

---

[1] Hannah Arendt, *The Life of the Mind* (San Diego, CA: Harcourt, 1978), 202.
[2] Rogers M. Smith, *Stories of Peoplehood: The Politics and Morals of Political Membership* (Cambridge: Cambridge University Press, 2003).

in large part from the notion that nation-states represent meaningful political communities. The process by which national self-determination moved from being a political principle to an international political norm, and then to an international legal norm, was complex and contested. And yet it has become crucial to debates about the legitimacy of international political arrangements and about the legitimacy and moral purpose of political groupings. It is a fundamental feature of the discourse by which claims to political authority and to the control of territory are articulated and justified. And it is this norm that, more than any other, ties the inside and the outside: what the units are to be, who their members are, and how their boundaries are to be determined.

Political nationalism has been the most persistent and pervasive ideology of the modern state system, not least because of its capacity to meld and mesh with other ideological systems, whether fascist (think of Hitler's Germany), socialist (think of Soviet Russia), liberal (think of the United States), or religious (think of post-revolution Iran). It has been intimately implicated in the exercise of immense political power—the power to redraw boundaries, to bring down empires, and to complicate all attempts at post-imperial coercive control. This power derives not only from its international legitimacy but also from the processes of group mobilization and identification that underpin effective social power. National self-determination has worked to reinforce the state system by providing such a politically and morally powerful justification for living in a world made up of states; and there is a long tradition of thought that argues that the road to a better and more stable international order necessarily involves the recognition and satisfaction of nationalist demands. But, on the other side, national self-determination has also represented a profound challenge to the society of states: by generating new sources of conflict, by empowering and legitimizing nationalist and ethnic movements to challenge both existing states and established political orders within states, and by undermining the mechanisms and institutions that were central to old-style pluralism.[3]

This chapter addresses five questions:

1. What do we mean by the doctrine of national self-determination and what are the main stages of its emergence within international society?
2. What has been the impact of national self-determination on international order?
3. What have been the major strategies for managing or containing the problems created by national self-determination?
4. To what extent are the problems becoming evermore serious? To what extent are they changing in character?

[3] On this dual impact, see James Mayall, *Nationalism and International Society* (Cambridge: Cambridge University Press, 1990).

5. To what extent do nationalism and the politics of identity push beyond the pluralist–solidarist divide?

National self-determination

The focus of this chapter is on political nationalism. This involves some combination of the following ideas or claims: that humanity is divided naturally into nations; that each nation has a particular character defined in terms of common territory, customs, laws, beliefs, language, artistic, and religious expression; that the character of individuals is shaped by and cannot be understood apart from the national group; that loyalties to the nation override all other loyalties; and, finally, that the nation can only be protected, fulfilled, and developed within its state. It is this last claim that underpins the principle of national self-determination: that nations and states should be coextensive in their boundaries, that the nation should have a state corresponding to it, and that any state that does not express a nation or national idea is potentially illegitimate. It is this stress on the need for political expression (including but not limited to statehood) that distinguishes political nationalism from more general kinds of national sentiment, group cohesion, or sense of collective identity which are far older and are embodied both in many historic nations and in many other forms of human association.

Nationalists often simply assert that nations constitute the building blocks of humanity. This is clearly untrue. Many nations have very little collective history and, as is often noted, that history has to be invented, imagined, or mythologized. Some see nationalism as but one expression of an essential and overwhelming need to belong to a group and to assert a collective identity. But such primordial or essentialist accounts cannot explain the many different forms that such feelings have taken, and the specific historical conditions under which modern political nationalism emerged and developed. Hence, others see nationalism as bound up with modernity, with capitalist development, and with social change. Nationalism is necessarily connected to the emergence of industrial society and to such changes as increased literacy, a national high culture, and increased equality and mobility within society.[4] There is much in such explanations. But they can suffer from a circular, functionalist reasoning; they tend to underplay the normative and psychological appeal of particular national ideas and doctrines; and their economistic bias seems hard to reconcile with the extraordinary tenacity of nationalist beliefs and programmes in such a wide range of societies. More recently, the trend has been to focus on construction and choice—to analyse the political and/or social processes by which nations are constructed, and to

[4] See e.g. Ernest Gellner, *Nations and Nationalism* (Oxford: Basil Blackwell, 1983).

123

adopt a more agent-centred view which looks at how changing economic or political conditions create incentives for elites and individuals to promote and exploit nationalist ideas, programmes, and stories as a means of developing or maintaining the social trust and political legitimacy necessary to achieve specific sets of goals.[5]

The literature on nationalism is enormous and I cannot engage here with its complexities. But two points need to be highlighted: the role of the international system and the modernity of political nationalism. Even more compelling than the links between war and state-formation are those between geopolitical conflict and the emergence and diffusion of political nationalism, with images of the collective 'national self' and 'foreign other' flourishing on the battlefield as nowhere else and the central place of wars and massacres in the mythology of so many nationalisms. But the role of international factors is more fundamental than this. The very need for a cohesive national community arose both from the rejection of empire and from the imperative of survival in what was increasingly identified as an international state of war—either by making conquest by others unviable (as Rousseau argued to the Poles) or by yourself becoming a more effective conqueror of others. The search for recognition, standing, and status that are so fundamental to nationalist programmes cannot be understood outside the context of the one world of international relations characterized by increasingly higher levels of war and by the emergence of exclusivist conceptions of territorial sovereignty which raised the stakes in the battle for political power.[6]

As against all the talk of history, political nationalism and the demand for national self-determination are recent phenomena that have been fully developed only in the last two centuries with the coming together of two distinct sets of developments. First, changes in notions of political legitimacy and the growth of the idea of popular sovereignty meant that since kings were to cease governing, the 'people' were to take their place. But the people, the new sovereign, necessarily had to be defined, to be given a personality. For some, the identity of the people was seen in abstract, civic terms: the citizen and the general will. But it came to seem increasingly obvious that what mattered was not just any people, but a particular people with a particular history and sense

---

[5] For a wide-ranging collection of different views, see John Hutchinson and Anthony D. Smith, *Nationalism* (Oxford: Oxford University Press, 1994). For an overview of recent debates, see Lars-Erik Cederman, 'Nationalism and Ethnicity', in Walter Carlsnaes, Thomas Risse, and Beth Simmons (eds.), *Handbook of International Relations* (London: Sage, 2002), ch. 21. For especially important works, see Rogers Brubaker, *Nationalism Reformed: Nationhood and the National Question in the New Europe* (Cambridge: Cambridge University Press, 1996); and David Laitin, *Identity Formation: The Russian Speaking Populations in the Near Abroad* (Ithaca, NY: Cornell University Press, 1998).

[6] On the need to give greater importance to the international state of war in our understanding of nationalism, see Erica Benner, 'Is There a Core National Doctrine?', *Nations and Nationalism*, 7/2 (2001), 155–74.

of themselves. Hence the replacement of the emotionally inert idea of popular sovereignty with the emotionally powerful idea of the nation—the nation as a body of subjects that endures across generations; that exists separately from particular governments or even forms of government; and that expresses a will that is more than the simple aggregation of individual preferences at a particular point in time.

Second, there was the growth of cultural and linguistic nationalism in Europe in general and in Germany in particular. Again, this had complex roots and diffuse effects: the reaction against the cosmopolitanism of the Enlightenment; the idea that what was valuable was not what was universal but what was unique and particular; the pre-Romantic idea that moral value lay in individual feeling and sentiment, not universal reason or fixed and universal aesthetic laws; and a new approach to time and to history. What emerges in writers such as Herder is a way of thinking about human society that comes to have an enormous impact on the subsequent nationalist thinking and practice: the belief that each people is unique with its own history, culture, and traditions; that individuals are shaped by this particular and unique environment; and that language, myth, and religion play a particularly important constitutive role.

These two sets of developments are important not only because of the role that they played in the historical development of political nationalism but also because they feed into the almost universal tendency to distinguish between two types of nationalism: on the one hand, the liberal, civic, or voluntarist idea of the nation as resulting from the free choice of individuals and as a community of equal citizens united around a shared set of political values and practices; on the other hand, the culturalist or historicist idea of nationalism which understands the nation in terms of pre-political cultural identities and as an entity (often an organism) which stands above the individual and has a life and purpose of its own. As I will come to argue later, these sorts of distinctions are considerably more complex than suggested by those who seek to deploy them either analytically or politically.

The place of national self-determination within the evolution of international society is complex and contested. It can be seen, first of all, as a *political ideology* asserting that the nation can be distinguished from the state, that nations and states should be coextensive in their boundaries, that every nation should have a state corresponding to it, and that any state that does not express a nation or national idea is potentially illegitimate. This ideology clearly represented a major challenge to the earlier (if always rather stylized) image of international relations as the relations of ruling princes and their dynastic houses—a world in which sovereignty over people and territory belonged to rulers; in which people or territory were exchanged from one ruler to another on the basis of inheritance, marriage, or conquest without the consent of the people or any attention to issues of nationality or ethnicity;

and in which political loyalties were assumed to be to dynastic rulers and states.

National self-determination can also be seen as *an international political norm* which confers political and moral rights on national groups or on those speaking in their name and which encourages and legitimizes demands for the redrawing of state boundaries. As a norm influencing political action, this was already well established by the mid-nineteenth century. This was a period which saw the emergence of national liberation groups commanding loyalty and able to challenge the state's monopoly of legitimate force, the ascription to such movements of moral rights, and the development of a doctrine of national liberation. As a norm shaping the institutional structure of international society, the events of 1918–19 and the roles of Lenin and Wilson remain crucial despite the simplifications.[7]

Its application as a political norm has always been uneven and highly selective for all of the well-known reasons: the difficulties of identifying the 'self' given incompatible definitions and conflicting claims, the importance of other criteria in redrawing boundaries (economic/strategic viability, etc.), and, above all, the intrusion of political imperatives and the special interests of the powerful. Nevertheless, despite the ambiguities, national self-determination has been implicated in almost all of the great redrawing of maps of the past 150 years—the four great waves of decolonization, the unification of Germany, and the breakup of Yugoslavia. The idea and the practice of national self-determination were also central to the extension of the state system to the non-European world and to the globalization of international society. Once in control of a state, anti-colonial nationalists were of course extremely unwilling to allow others to use self-determination to threaten their own power—hence the decision of the Organization of African Unity (OAU) in Cairo in July 1964 to recognize the legitimacy of colonial frontiers and to

---

[7] See Wilson's four principles speech: 'There shall be no annexations, no contributions, no punitive damages. Peoples are not to be handed about from one sovereignty to another by an international conference or an understanding between rivals and antagonists. National aspirations must be respected: peoples may now be dominated and governed only by their own consent.' Woodrow Wilson, *The Public Papers of Woodrow Wilson, Volume I. War and Peace: Presidential Messages, Addresses and Public Papers 1917–1924*, edited by R. S. Baker and W. E. Dodd (London and New York: Harper and Brothers, 1927), 180. That peoples and provinces were 'not to be bartered from sovereignty to sovereignty as if they were mere chattels and pawns in a game' (ibid. 182) was clear to Wilson. But note that Wilson both reflected and gave impetus to the frequent confusion between national self-determination as an extension of democratic self-government and national self-determination as embodying a clear right of national groups to create their own states. Note, too, that he often referred to the 'interests' and 'benefits' of peoples rather than their wishes, and to 'autonomous development' rather than any right to statehood. For a classic account of the problems, see Alfred Cobban, *The Nation State and National Self-determination* (London: Collins, [1945] 1969, originally published in 1945). For a recent account of Wilson's travails, Margaret Macmillan, *Paris 1919* (New York: Random House, 2003).

rule out any further application of the principle of self-determination on the African continent.

International lawyers have always treated self-determination extremely cautiously and its emergence as *international legal norm* has been gradual and highly qualified. For a long time, it was common to see it only as a political principle which might have some legal implications. However, the political power of the principle, especially in the context of decolonization, and its close association with ideas of the emerging solidarist norms of human rights and democracy, meant that it could not be kept out of the legal order. As a result the strategy of denial gradually gave way to a strategy of limitation and it came to be seen, first, as a general principle against which individual rules and state actions could be judged and, second, as a set of more specific rules which sought to contain the concept of self-determination along two crucial dimensions: to narrow as far as possible the 'units' to which self-determination may be held to apply, and to limit understandings of the meaning of self-determination so as to inflict as little damage as possible to the core features of the pluralist order: state sovereignty and territorial integrity. Yet the ambiguities have remained, as have the need for extreme caution in speaking of anything approaching a 'right' of national self-determination.[8]

What has been the impact on international order?

There is a powerful tradition of thought that sees national self-determination as a necessary element in a stable and legitimate international order. In the first place, as we have noted, national self-determination has added powerful justification for the existence of separate nation-states and for obligations owed to them rather than to humankind in general. States, now nation-states in aspiration and in the ideology of the system, are deemed legitimate because they embody the exercise of political self-determination; because they allow groups of individuals to give expression to their values, their culture, and their sense of themselves; and because they offer protection to groups who would otherwise be extremely vulnerable. Hence state boundaries become both politically and morally far more important. They are, after all, the lines that demarcate not just abstract units of administration but communities that are supposed to share both an identity and a legitimate political purpose. The system of nation-states therefore guards against the tyranny of the world state or universal empire, allows for the diversity of human values and cultures, and can be justified in Mill's terms as a way of safeguarding a plurality of 'experiments in living'. Mill's successors have also seen the value

[8] For an accessible introduction to the legal issues, see Rosalyn Higgins, *Problems and Process: International Law and How We Use It* (Oxford: Oxford University Press, 1994), ch. 7.

of political nationalism in instrumental terms as providing the social cement and cohesion necessary for active citizenship and social welfare.[9] And anti-colonial nationalists have valued nationalism as providing the solidarity and collective political agency necessary for effective resistance and the defeat of the colonizers, and as a means of restoring a sense of collective purpose and self-respect to colonized peoples who had been humiliated, marginalized, and often brutalized in the pursuit and maintenance of empire.

Second, from this perspective, the stability of a world made up of a plurality of political units cannot depend on the crude ordering mechanisms of the balance of power and Great Power management. It must depend also on the degree to which those units have a stable identity through time. All forms of nationalism posit the idea of the nation as a trans-generational collective that can be distinguished from other such groups and that has a reasonably stable set of norms for distinguishing those who belong to it from those who do not. More importantly, the suppression of claims to self-determination has been a major cause of violent conflict both within and amongst states. As Wilson put it, 'No peace can last, or ought to last, which does not recognize and accept the principle that governments derive all their just powers from the consent of the governed, and that no right anywhere exists to hand peoples about from sovereignty to sovereignty as if they were property.'[10] This has remained a central element in much liberal thinking, especially in the United States, from the Fourteen Points to the Atlantic Charter and beyond. It is a position that has been strongly argued by Michael Walzer who talks of the internationalist claim, '[t]hat we and our fellows and others like us, are disturbers of the peace only insofar as we are denied the protective and expressive powers of sovereignty. Hence the vindication of this critical principal, for every nation its own state, would open the way to an international settlement.' He recognizes the dangers and difficulties but argues that the direction of policy is clear:

> The way itself is bloody enough, and there probably are cases where people from different nations are so radically entangled on the same piece of territory that a "good border" is virtually inconceiveable. Still, the completion of the state system is a reform worth pursuing.[11]

It has always been easy to scoff at Wilson and to find examples of liberals either downplaying the problems or being ignorant of the complexities involved in trying to apply the principle. But Wilson, for all his faults, could

---

[9] Most notably Miller (1995).

[10] Woodrow Wilson, 'Address to the United States Senate, 22 January 1917', in Arthur S. Link (ed.), *The Papers of Woodrow Wilson*, vol. 40 (Princeton, NJ: Princeton University Press, 1982), 536–7.

[11] Michael Walzer, 'The Reform of the International System', in Øyvind Østerud (ed.), *Studies in War and Peace* (Oslo: Norwegian University Press, 1986), 229.

see more clearly than many of his opponents that the nationalist genie could not be put back into the bottle and that there was no going back to the idealized world of nineteenth-century diplomacy.

Finally, many nationalists have denied that there is an incompatibility between their nationalism and cosmopolitan claims and allegiances. For Mazzini, the nation was the 'cradle of humanity'. Zimmern believed that 'the road to Internationalism lies through Nationalism, not through levelling men down to a grey indistinctive cosmopolitanism but by appealing to the best element in the corporate inheritance of each nation. A good world means a world of good men and women. A good international world means a world of nations living at their best.'[12] However difficult it may be, a balance must be struck between the need for cultural and communal rootedness on the one hand and commitments to humanity on the other.

Against this, however, are the many arguments of those who argue that nationalism added a powerful element of conflict and divisiveness to the already dangerous and unstable world of interstate anarchy. Lansing's famous prophecy has proved correct: 'The phrase is simply loaded with dynamite. It will raise hopes that can never be realized.'[13] Again, we can unpack various more specific claims. In the first place, national self-determination represents a force for destabilization and disintegration. It provides both a criterion and a moral imperative by which the boundaries of existing political units can be redrawn to reflect the aspirations of national groups and it empowers and legitimizes national groups as actors in their own right. In the nineteenth century, nationalism was often seen as reducing the number of states, for example, through the absorption of many smaller units into the new united nation-states of Germany and Italy. But, in general, national self-determination came to be viewed as a disintegrating force, taking existing structures and breaking them into smaller units. This has been visible in each of the four great waves of decolonization—the independence of Spanish and Portuguese America in early nineteenth century; the breakup of Austro-Hungarian, Tsarist, and Ottoman empires after the First World War; the dismantling of the European overseas empires between 1918 and 1974; and the disintegration of the Soviet Empire and states associated with that empire.

Pluralist-minded lawyers saw this as a direct challenge to the stability of state-based international order. As a classic statement put it:

To concede to minorities, either of language or religion, or to any fractions of a population the right of withdrawing from the community to which they belong, because it is their wish or their good pleasure, would be to destroy order and stability within

---

[12] Alfred E. Zimmern, *Nationalism and Government* (London: Chatto and Windus, 1923), 85. See also Alfred E. Zimmern, 'Nationalism and Internationalism', *Foreign Affairs*, 1/4 (1923), 115–26.

[13] Robert Lansing, *The Peace Negotiations: A Personal Narrative* (Boston, MA: Houghton Mifflin, 1921), 97–8.

States and to inaugurate anarchy in international life; it would be to uphold a theory incompatible with the very idea of the State as a territorial and political unity.[14]

In fact national self-determination runs directly counter to a world of stable borders and the stable identity of the units through time. It also threatens other elements of the pluralist legal order, for example constraints on the use of force. In the nineteenth century, the growth of national liberation struggles was closely associated with the development insurrection and guerrilla warfare. As Mazzini put it: 'Insurrection—by means of guerrilla bands—is the true method of warfare for all nations desirous of emancipating themselves from a foreign yoke'.[15] In the twentieth century, the anti-colonial movement argued that colonialism constituted permanent aggression and that force was justified by peoples struggling against colonial or racist rule.

Realist-inclined politicians have stressed the many ways in which national self-determination threatens disorder: through the creation of an increasing number of weak and unviable states that would become a focus of external intervention and geopolitical competition, whether in East Central Europe in the 1930s or in the developing world in the 1950s and 1960s; and through the 'nationalization' of foreign policy in which the emotive impact of nationalism and the democratization of foreign policy would lead states to pursue their interests more ruthlessly and tempt them towards excessive intervention. Most worryingly from a pluralist perspective, national self-determination complicated the harder-edged mechanisms for order connected with the balance of power. The balance of power clearly depended on dividing or transferring territory either out of calculations of power or because of perceptions of stability and equity. Little or no account was taken of the interests of the peoples concerned, which was, of course, one of the major reasons why liberals such as Wilson so distrusted the balance of power. The difficulties of trying to mesh national self-determination with the balance of power were plainly visible in the interwar period. On the one hand, any sustained balance of power against Germany was weakened by the application of national self-determination to the Austro-Hungarian and Russian empires and by the creation of a series of weak states in Central Europe. On the other, the trumpeting of the principle gave legitimacy to Germany's own revisionist demands against Czechoslovakia, Austria, and Poland. Hence, the classic double-bind: the norm cannot be applied consistently because of its impact on the balance of power; but not applying it consistently would breed resentment and antagonism both in Germany and amongst the other revisionist states.

[14] *The Aaland Islands Question.* Report presented to the Council of the League by the Commission of Rapporteurs, League of Nations Doc.B.7.21/68/106, 1921, 28.

[15] Cited in Michael Howard, *War and the Liberal Conscience* (Oxford: Oxford University Press, 1989), 49–50.

In the post-1945 period, we find tensions of a different but equally potent kind. On the one hand, many saw the stability of the long Cold War peace as premised on the division of Germany and the acceptance of spheres of influence. Dividing countries (Germany, Korea, and Vietnam) might be regrettable but that was the tragic nature of what a stable power-political order was all about. On the other side, the notion that 'stability' could rest on the denial of the democratic rights and national aspirations of subject people was rejected as unsustainable and resting on an outdated view of international relations—a view that of course proved correct. And the tensions remain: as in the argument that a stable power-political relationship with Russia involves an acceptance of a Russian sphere of influence and a denial of the right of self-determination, in Chechnya most conspicuously.

Third, these problems were increased because of the inherent difficulties of implementing the principle and of reaching consensus as to what national self-determination involved and how it was to be acted upon. The list of problems is long and familiar: the impossibility of drawing frontiers that respected the principle of nationality without leaving minorities that would then become a source of both domestic instability and interstate conflict; the conflicts caused by more than one people fighting for the same piece of land; and the extent which each application of the principle created new potential sources of conflict—through demands for secession from within the new states, through the disruptive role of national irredentist movements focused around the historic lands and national groups excluded from the 'nation', and through the human misery and political instability caused by the large-scale population movements and the proliferation of ethnic cleansing.[16] The dangers are partly the result of direct spillovers and partly the impact of contagion or demonstration effects—if we allow Yugoslavia to break up, this will stimulate similar movements in Russia; if we allow the breakup of Iraq, this will threaten the stability of other regional states, including through further demands for Kurdish self-determination. The cases can be varied but the logic remains the same.

However, the critics pointed at difficulties beyond simple implementation. They highlighted the way in which many of the most divisive conflicts reflected the impossibility of reconciling the different strands of the nationalist tradition. The 'free choice of the people' may say one thing; the 'objective facts of history' say another. For the Serbian nationalist, Kosovo is part of the historic heartland of the Serbian nation, whatever those who happen to live there at one point in time might wish. Moreover, who is to count as the 'people', particularly in cases of expulsion or large-scale population

[16] For an account of the evolution of the concept and an indication of the numbers involved, see Jennifer Jackson Preece, 'Ethnic Cleansing as an Instrument of Nation-State Creation: Changing State Practices and Evolving Legal Norms', *Human Rights Quarterly*, 20/4 (1998), 817–42.

movement? How can the will of the Palestinian people be limited to the choices of those living in Gaza and the West Bank rather than including those living in refugee camps and in the broader Palestinian diaspora? And, most problematically, who decides who is to count as a people? As Ivor Jennings wrote in 1956: 'On the surface it sounded reasonable: let the people decide. In fact it was ridiculous because the people cannot decide until somebody decides who are the people.'[17]

Finally, national self-determination is a problem for overtly liberal understandings of order and, in particular, for democratic peace theory (DPT)—to be discussed in Chapter 6. On one reading, national self-determination enters the analysis as a destabilizing external or indirect element in the equation. Disputes over the character of the political community, over the boundaries of that community, and over membership of that community all serve to make successful democratization far harder. Although fully consolidated democracies may well be peaceful, problematic democratization feeds into a propensity for violent conflict, both internally and internationally. These problems are real enough. But the difficulty runs much deeper. National self-determination cannot be seen as something purely external to the idea of democracy. It cannot, as Bruce Russett implies, be simply associated with ethnic conflict.[18] National self-determination is not something external to democratic theory but is a theoretically and historically fundamental aspect of it. As we have seen, one of the well-springs of national self-determination was precisely the demand that the now-sovereign citizens should have the right to constitute their own state—to determine its boundaries and its membership as well as its internal arrangements. Certainly, this foundational connection was obvious to many classic liberals such as Mill. As Hobsbawm notes: 'We observe without surprise that Mill discusses the idea of nationality not in a separate publication as such but, characteristically—and briefly—in the context of his little treatise on Representative Government, or democracy.'[19]

How have these contradictory pressures been managed?

What emerged in the course of the twentieth century has been a deep structural tension between the imperatives of stable boundaries, stable identities, and the legal structures of the older pluralist world on the one hand, and the

[17] Cited in Lee C. Buchheit, *Secession: The Legitimacy of Self-determination* (New Haven, CT: Yale University Press, 1978), 9.

[18] Bruce Russett, *Grasping the Democratic Peace: Principles for a Post-Cold War World* (Princeton, NJ: Princeton University Press, 1993), 133–4.

[19] E. J. Hobsbawm, *Nations and Nationalism since 1870: Programme, Myth, Reality* (Cambridge: Cambridge University Press, 1992), 19.

dynamic character of self-determination as both a political and legal norm on the other. International society and international law navigated constantly between the growing legitimacy of the principle and its disintegrative potential. The answer has been an expanding range of strategies aimed either at limiting the disruptive potential of self-determination or at meeting aspirations for self-determination in ways that would hopefully undercut secessionist demands. Five such strategies can be noted.[20]

The first has been to restrict the range of 'units' to which self-determination should apply. Thus, after the First World War, self-determination was to apply to (at least parts of) the defeated European empires and, very indirectly, to mandated territories. After the Second World War, it would apply to peoples under European colonial domination, and then to peoples under alien occupation or under racist regimes (such as South Africa under apartheid). In each case, law followed and adjusted to political developments and reflected powerful pluralist imperatives at the obvious cost of normative coherence.

The idea that self-determination applied only to places separated by water from the mother country, while depending on a manifestly unjustified distinction, at least had a certain clarity. It also served a policy that was easy to understand: namely, that it was time to stop breaking up larger state entities into ever smaller ones.[21]

Second, within the context of decolonization, international law generally took the UN Charter idea of the 'equal rights and self-determination of peoples' to mean the peoples of established territories who should enjoy a one-off choice (although not necessarily to form an independent state). So many state borders derived either from boundaries between imperial powers or from domestic boundaries within imperial polities. Those boundaries were to remain sacrosanct unless all of the people within those boundaries agreed to alter them by dividing the state or integrating with another. And, after this one-off moment of self-determination had passed, the principle of territorial integrity would be resolutely upheld and, of course, all further secessionist claims would be resisted. Hence the continued importance in all four waves of decolonization of the principle of *uti possidetis*. Once more the pluralist impulse persisted and, whenever there was any doubt, the default position lent towards territorial integrity or the reliance on some pre-existing boundaries.

These first two strategies are reflected in the doubletalk of the classic decolonization statements on self-determination: statements that seek to uphold both self-determination as a basic norm of the system and the territorial

---

[20] See, in particular, Antonio Cassese, *Self-Determination of Peoples: A Legal Reappraisal* (Cambridge: Cambridge University Press, 1995).

[21] Thomas M. Franck, *Fairness in International Law and Institutions* (Oxford: Clarendon Press, 1995), 155.

integrity of states. They reflect the tremendously powerful impulse towards stable frontiers and the finality of borders. This instinct persists, for example, in the case of the former Yugoslavia where all of the Western states decided from 1991 that the former internal borders of its constituent republics would remain sacrosanct.

A third strategy has been to try and distinguish between different types of nationalism. Hegel, Marx, and Mill all sought to do just this, evaluating nationalist movements and ranking them in terms of their potential to act in historically progressive ways. As we have seen, one of the most common moves to distinguish has been between liberal civic nationalism on the one hand, and historicist and ethnic nationalism on the other, and to suggest that it is ethnic nationalism that constitutes the most serious challenge to international order. Although there is some reason to believe that conflicts involving liberal nationalisms are more amenable to political resolution, such distinctions are slippery and very hard to operationalize in the form of agreed international rules. On the one side, 'ethnic' is used in many ways. Sometimes it refers narrowly to racial groupings, but often it refers to all ascriptive (birth-based) identities of race, religion, tribe, or caste whether they are real or imagined.[22] On the other side, civic nationalism must depend on the idea of a shared pre-political identity; some community that exists separate from any particular set of political arrangements. If this were not the case, it would be impossible to separate it from patriotism.

Nor can we make firm distinctions on the basis of the goals sought or the means employed. It is sometimes argued, for example, that it is only ethnic nationalism that is deeply wedded to a morality of heroic sacrifice and to the justification of violence against the enemies of the nation.[23] But the mystique of heroic sacrifice is also powerful within civic nationalism (as a visit to the Arlington National Cemetery; or Les Invalides would reveal) and even developed liberal nations are capable of dehumanizing their enemies and justifying horrendous violence against the barbarian 'other' (as the so-called war on terrorism has reminded us once more). More importantly, liberal nationalists have tended to concentrate on the positive value that national feeling has *within* domestic society; they have tended to assume a stable international environment and to detach their arguments from questions of international order, or rather the lack of it.[24] If we reconnect the internal and external,

---

[22] Varshney (2003: 86–7). For writers such as Smith, it is crucial to focus on the 'durable constitutive features of ethnic communities', 'not the more ephemeral dimensions of collective will, attitude, even sentiment, which make up the day-to-day fabric of ethnic consciousness, but the more permanent cultural attributes of memory, value, myth, and symbolism'. Anthony D. Smith, *The Ethnic Origins of Nations* (Oxford: Basil Blackwell, 1986), 3.

[23] See e.g. Michael Ignatieff, *Blood and Belonging* (London: Vintage Books, 1993), esp. 3–7.

[24] See Erica Benner, 'The Liberal Limits to Republican Nationalism', in Daniel A. Bell and Avner de-Shalit (eds.), *Forms of Justice* (Lanham, MD: Rowan and Littlefield, 2003), 205–25.

the picture may appear less reassuring and it is Rousseau rather than Mill who is the better guide.[25] In addition, labelling your opponent as an ethnic nationalist is a political rather than an analytical move and there can be few more misleading notions than the claim that '[E]mpirically, it is relatively easy to determine which conflict is an ethnic one: one knows them when one sees them'.[26] But the most important point here is that, even if it were analytically possible to differentiate between different forms of nationalism, there has been no movement towards the embodiment of these differences into stable rules, nor any reason to believe that such a development would be possible.

A fourth strategy is to reduce the problem by unpacking sovereignty. Inside the state this may involve a wide variety of federal, consociational, non-territorial rights and protections, and power-sharing models. But it may also involve rethinking the international position of the state. As noted earlier, the problems of self-determination have at least as much to do with the triumph of a hard notion of sovereignty as it does with nationalism. In any case nationalism is obdurate despite the prophecies of the modernists and anti-essentialists. So let us seek a solution in which we unpack sovereignty and promote forms of multilevel governance in which state responsibilities are dispatched to various sites of power and the diversification of human loyalties is encouraged. Conflict will be lessened if there is no longer one single site of power and authority to be fought over and captured, or if there is a broader political framework for the management of nationalist conflicts. This is an old idea. It lay behind the arguments of many imperialists that questions of 'government' should be separated from questions of 'nationality' and that empires could provide different forms of autonomy and political space that would facilitate the accommodation of a wide range of communal attachments.[27] In the contemporary system, such views are widely propounded in the context of regional groupings: a multilevel and neo-medieval Europe is precisely the sort of polity that can accommodate substate and transnational nationalisms. There is clearly a great deal of good sense in these kinds of arguments. But there is also a good deal of romanticization of the possibilities of such a

[25] Rousseau could see the tensions. On one side, it was only by limiting sympathy and compassion within a cohesive community that what he calls the 'sentiment de l'humanité' could become meaningful. But on the other side, and unlike many optimistic liberal nationalists, he recognizes that 'le patriotisme et l'humanité sont, par exemple, deux vertus incompatibles dans leur énergie, et surtout chez un peuple entier', and that this adds a destructive twist to the logic of anarchy which he analyses so powerfully in L'Etat de Guerre. The quotation is from Lettres de la Montagne in C. E. Vaughan (ed.), The Political Writings of Jean Jacques Roussea (Cambridge: Cambridge University Press, 1915), vol. II. Available at: http://oll.Libertyfund.org/Texts/Rousseau0284/PoliticalWritings/HTMLs/0065-2_pt03_Passages.html.

[26] Stefan Wolff, Ethnic Conflict: A Global Perspective (Oxford: Oxford University Press, 2006), 2.

[27] See Kedourie's attack on nationalism in the developing world and his nostalgia for the Ottoman Empire. Elie Kedourie, Nationalism, 4th edn. (Oxford: Blackwell, 1993).

post-Westphalian order in which it is assumed that the fundamental problem of legitimate political order remains intact whilst sovereignty is reparcelled out in this way. It is instructive that the limits to this view should visible even in the very favourable conditions of Europe. It is also true that the management of conflicts may be assisted by the return of semi-sovereign territories and internationally administered protectorates (as in Bosnia and Kosovo). But this depends on the effectiveness of a broader system of collective security.

The fifth, and in many ways most important, strategy is to seek to undercut the problem via the promotion of different forms of political self-determination, especially in the area of human rights and democracy. The basic intuition is that in thinking about national self-determination, the 'national' should be decoupled from the idea of 'self-determination'. In part this has been a response to the abuses committed by regimes that have achieved external self-determination. But in part it reflects the belief that, if we can get internal self-determination right and if we can provide an alternative framework for self-determination, we can then reduce demands for external self-determination and the redrawing of boundaries. This is the dominant way in which solidarist international law has sought to deal with the issue. It is visible most notably in the dominant tendency within international law to reinterpret self-determination from the mid-1960s onwards as part of the international human rights regime.

The discussion of human rights and democracy will have to wait until Chapter 6. But three points are relevant here. First, for all the liberal good sense of this approach, it is not clear that internal and external self-determination are in fact transposable in this way. Resistance to what is perceived as 'alien rule' may have a political power that even relatively successful internal self-determination cannot dislodge. Second, the most relevant element on the human rights agenda, namely group rights and minority rights, is precisely that element that states have been most reluctant to develop. The failures and dangers of the interwar minority rights treaties meant that the post-1945 view of human rights was exclusively to be a matter of protecting individuals. The pressure of many of the forces described in this chapter has helped to bring minority rights back into the picture—but serious political and legal tensions remain. And, third, other points of contact between human rights and national self-determination remain problematic. For example, attempts to link secession to human rights and democracy appear an obvious way of squaring at least some part of the circle. Secessionist movements might be recognized where the putative new state is willing to sign up to international human or minority rights agreements. But effective implementation has been limited and the difficulties remain as to who has the legitimacy to speak and act on behalf of a particular group.

The result of these strategies and of their limitations has been a notable process of normative expansion combined with a significant element of moral hazard. *If* international society is unwilling to accept the forcible redrawing of boundaries; *if* it is also unwilling to sanction the movement of peoples into ethnically more homogeneous entities; and *if* it also unwilling to accept the denial of self-determination and the atrocities that denial may often lead to, there can be logically no other route except to deeper and deeper involvement in the restructuring and internal administration of states. Yet, as I discuss elsewhere, international institutions remain weak and, where there has been a significant degree of success (as in the EU's approach to member-state-building), this has depended both on a well-established set of regional and other institutions and on a willingness to engage in an expensive and long-term engagement (as in the Balkans). But, these limited cases apart, it is morally troubling that many countries, including many leading Western countries, proclaim something approaching a 'right' to self-determination but are able to do so little to provide for its consistent or effective implementation.

An ever-worsening problem?

The post–Cold War period witnessed recurrent arguments that conflicts involving national self-determination were proliferating and that international society was also faced by an explosion of ethnic conflicts, involving violent and large-scale intragroup conflict within states over territory, resources, and political power.[28] As Ignatieff put it: 'The key narrative of world order is the disintegration of nation states into ethnic civil war; the key architects of that order are warlords and the key language of our age is ethnic nationalisms.'[29]

One strand of this pessimism stressed the dangers of ever greater fragmentation. As in previous rounds of imperial disintegration, many predicted that each successful claim for national self-determination would lead to a further process of fragmentation and to a world with an increasing number of weak, unviable, and failing states. As Boutros-Ghali put it in 1994: 'Yet if every ethnic, religious or linguistic group claimed statehood, there would be no limit to fragmentation, and peace, security and economic well-being for all would become evermore difficult to achieve.'[30] Given that there are around 15,000 cultural groups in the world, the idea of statehood as the primary vehicle for cultural recognition seems clearly incompatible with any stable

[28] Gurr suggests that the post-Cold War period did see an upsurge in ethnic conflict but this was the continuation of a trend that began in the 1960s. Ted Robert Gurr, 'Peoples against States: Ethnopolitical Conflict and the Changing World System', *International Studies Quarterly*, 38/3 (1994), 347–77.

[29] Ignatieff (1993: 2).

[30] 'Agenda for Peace', 31 January 1992, reprinted in Adam Roberts and Benedict Kingsbury (eds.), *United Nations, Divided World: The UN's Roles in International Relations*, 2nd edn. (Oxford: Oxford University Press, 1993), 474.

international order. A second old argument was the idea that nationalism provided a basis for coherence, comfort, and a sense of belonging in societies undergoing wrenching change. This idea of nationalism as a response of the disinherited to the rootlessness of the modern world has been a persistent theme of modern political consciousness.[31] But it was given a new twist by those who viewed the assertion of particularist identities as a response to the dislocations caused by the collapse of communism, the failures of economic modernization, and the challenges of globalization. And third, it was argued that democratization as a transnational political force, as an international norm, and as a principle of the foreign policy of major states had opened space for intensified demands for self-determination. On the one side, the external environment had become more permissive; on the other, elites in countries undergoing democratization had increased incentives to use nationalism as a source of political power and legitimacy.

However, it is also important to note the factors that press in the other direction. First, we have already noted the complexity of so-called ethnic conflicts. The thesis that conflicts can be understood as the product of 'tribalism' or 'ancient hatreds' has been thorough debunked. The mere existence of ethnic identity, even of conflicting ethnic identities, cannot on its own explain conflict—think of the many ethnic dogs that do not bark or the peaceful resolution of potential conflicts (as in the Velvet Divorce within the former Czechoslovakia). In addition, the breathless rush to novelty has undoubtedly exaggerated the globalized character of many supposedly ethnic conflicts. The Chiapas conflict in southern Mexico, for example, has attracted a great deal of attention as a postmodern war and as a reaction to NAFTA and to globalization; but it also forms part of a well-established pattern of regional and indigenous violence that has very deep roots in Mexican history.

It is also unclear whether the system has in fact become more permissive. During the 1990s, some commentators suggested that the combination of extreme internal state weakness or even collapse, devastating regional conflicts, and the emergence of new conceptions of sovereignty in the 1990s created the need to demonstrate that there was 'at least some fluidity in the state system'; to propose regional solutions 'without regard to country boundaries'; to accept the possibility of recognizing new sovereign states; and even to 'decertify failed states'.[32] But, the striking feature of even such a conflict-ridden region as Central Africa has been the absence of any such 'less dogmatic approach to sovereignty', and certainly not in the sense of seeing security other than in terms of rebuilding or reconstructing existing

---

[31] As Rilke put it in the early 1920s: 'Each torpid turn of the world has such disinherited children, those for whom the former has ceased, the next hasn't yet come, to belong.' Rainer Maria Rilke, seventh elegy, *Duino Elegies* (London: Hogarth Press, 1968), 73.

[32] Jeffrey Herbst, 'Responding to State Failure in Africa', *International Security*, 21/3 (Winter 1996–7), 120–44.

states, whatever the oddities or illogicalities of their historical emergence or their unpromising potential for stable development. There is also a broader question concerning state capacity. Historically, states have often been able to engage in successful nation-building, whether through coercion or co-option, often out of exceedingly unpromising materials. The puzzle is to account for relative success both in aggregate and in individual cases (think of India), rather than to concentrate on the failures. One of the most important open questions is how far the bases of that success have been eroded by the unravelling of statist economic policies which allowed bargains to be struck and goods to be distributed across different groups.

To what extent are we dealing with an ever-changing problem? If the key narrative of the 1990s was ethnic conflict, today it is religious terrorism. Many see the 'new wave' of transnational religious terrorism as representing a decisive break in the evolution of terrorism undertaken by non-state groups. It is certainly the case that much is indeed new in terms of the conditions, means of operation, and, in some cases, goals and objectives. But nationalism, national self-determination, and the broader resistance to alien rule have all been long-standing and prominent features of terrorism and remain so.[33] This was evidently the case in the role that terrorist acts played in the anti-colonial struggle and in the creation of states such as Ireland, Israel, Kenya, and Algeria. Although many radical movements in the 1970s spoke the language of internationalism, nationalist goals remained prominent, as with the Basques, Irish, and Palestinians; and the movement against United States and Western imperialism was closely tied to the idea of national liberation and to resistance to alien rule and domination. In the so-called religious wave that developed from the late 1970s, the link between religious and ethnic identity is often close, as is the relationship between terrorist violence and the goal of self-determination and resistance to alien rule—as with Sikh demands for a religious state, the Islamist goal of a Palestinian state, and the conflicts in Kashmir, Sri Lanka, and Chechnya. From this perspective, truly transnational religious terrorist movements are the outliers.

Conclusion: beyond pluralism/solidarism?

All debates about global political order are necessarily concerned with the usually unstable and often conflictual relationship between political structures on the one hand and understandings of community, peoplehood, and group-belonging on the other. This chapter has concentrated on nationalism and national self-determination. The resilience of nationalism is one of the

[33] See David C. Rapoport, 'The Four Waves of Modern Terrorism', in Audrey Kurth Cronin and James M. Ludes (eds.), *Attacking Terrorism: Elements of Grand Strategy* (Washington, DC: Georgetown University Press, 2004), 46–73.

core planks of the pluralist view of international relations: that we continue to live in a world of nation-states and that it is good that we should continue to do so. Nationalism shows few signs of receding as a major feature of major powers such as Russia, China, and India. Moreover, although disguised by its own ideology of civic patriotism, the United States has long been a strongly nationalist society and, in the face of the external challenge from terrorism and a domestic political shift to the right, this element has become still more prominent.[34]

Yet, whilst reinforcing the apparent naturalness of living in a world of states, the idea and the practice of national self-determination has proved a major source of conflict and opened up a series of unresolved dilemmas. The seriousness of these problems has pushed international society in a generally solidarist direction and led to a range of strategies of mediation: attempts to acknowledge both the political power and moral claims of national self-determination but in ways that minimize its damage to international society. The most important of these involve attempts to restrict the application of the principle, to unpack the link between nationalism, state sovereignty, and self-determination, and to manage cooperatively the conflicts that inevitably arise. The question of national self-determination therefore provides one of the purest examples of where returning to a world of old-fashioned pluralism is impossible for both moral and pragmatic reasons, but where there is insufficient consensus either to agree on clear and applicable rules or to secure sufficiently robust forms of international cooperation necessary for the effective management of the ensuing conflicts and tensions.

But neither the problem nor potential solutions can be captured solely within the pluralist–solidarist divide. The reason is clear. Solidarism for all its greater attention to moral claims and to human rights remains resolutely statist and this statism is in tension with the variety of communities, memberships, and identities that characterize global society. Within the solidarist image, there is a consolidation and hardening of the boundary that separates political communities from each other and citizens from non-citizens. There may be a degree of greater space for other arrangements (protectorates, confederations, condominia, and not-quite federal unions), but territorial states remain central. The statism of this model also narrows the range of options through which self-determination can be pursued—if not through one's own state then through the structure of rights and institutions created by, and around, states. Many of today's successful states were constructed through the internal and often violent suppression of difference and diversity and the

---

[34] Interestingly, recent conservative writing on US nationalism sees the civic ideals embodied in the flag and the constitution as being closely tied to what is effectively a common ethnic core that is white, English-speaking, Anglo-Saxon, and Protestant. See Samuel Huntington, *Who Are We? America's Great Debate* (New York: Free Press, 2004). US nationalism, then, is not so very different from other people's, despite exceptionalist claims.

enforced creation of a homogeneous national culture and identity. Think, for example, of the success of English imperialism in the construction of Britain, of the suppression of the Vendée during the French Revolution, or of the annihilation of indigenous peoples and the mass slaughter of the Civil War in the emergence of the United States. For the post-colonial world, 'emancipation' and entering into the society of states meant coming to terms with a one-dimensional relationship between political form and political community in place of the far greater complexity of both political structures and communities that had previously existed. And, for groups such as indigenous peoples, there is a troubling paradox in the idea that international protection involves fitting into a set of political categories (such as human rights and self-determination) that may be in deep tension with their own traditions.

Many of the features and dynamics of contemporary global politics have sharpened the politics of identity. The causes of this intensification are contested but are very often related to the dislocations and disruptions associated with globalization, to the massive movements of peoples and ideas, and to the increased intrusiveness and interventionism of both outside states and international institutions. The much acclaimed age of globalization is also an age of cultural division and diversity. The forms that these struggles for recognition have taken are varied. For Tully the politics of recognition include the claims of national groups either for their own state or for a change in the political structure of existing states; the demands of the world's 250 million indigenous peoples that their culture and ways of life be protected; the demands of cultural minorities, migrants, and refugees for recognition of their language and traditions; and the claims of cultural feminists for equality within the constitutional and legal order of states.[35] In addition, we might wish to add the continued power of pan-regional ideas and civilizational groupings, the revival of transnational religious identities, and the existence of internationalist commitments that took the classic form of political internationalism (as with the communist international) but which can be seen in many aspects of contemporary political transnationalism within global civil society.

Politically, these movements and the ideas that they represent press towards new forms of non-territorially based political identity and new mechanisms of political organization and action that go beyond the nation-state and which challenge the hegemony of statist world politics. For cosmopolitan liberals, such developments should also press us towards different kinds of complex governance beyond the state: meshing non-exclusive constitutionalism within states with the transnationalization of a culture of human rights that includes the rights of groups and different sorts of transnational constituencies. Such a move takes the rights of individuals and groups that have

[35] James Tully, *Strange Multiplicity: Constitutionalism in an Age of Diversity* (Cambridge: Cambridge University Press, 1995), 1–15.

already been developed within the solidarist legal order, but pushes them harder and further. In part this involves an expanded range of international norms seeking to govern the domestic arrangements of states (from human rights to rights to democratic government). But it gives higher priority to the rights and identity claims of peoples. These rights should not be constrained by the concepts and clusters of rules that states have developed, and often manipulated for their own purposes. Self-determination should not be understood solely in terms of a right to form a territorially defined state or to enjoy individual political rights within such a state. Rather such arrangements should be open to reassessment and re-evaluation particularly on the part of those groups that have found it hardest to find a secure place within the traditional interstate order.

6

Human rights and democracy

The greatly increased normative ambition of international society is nowhere more visible than in the field of human rights and democracy—in the idea that the relationship between ruler and ruled, state and citizen, should be a subject of legitimate international concern; that the ill treatment of citizens should trigger international action; and that the external legitimacy of a state should depend increasingly on how domestic societies are ordered politically. The first part of this chapter sketches some of the main features of this process of expansion; it then considers the ways in which this expansion has pushed beyond a state-based liberal solidarism, both conceptually and in terms of an increasingly strong element of transnational legal and political practice. Finally, it examines both the gaps in the process of expansion and the limits to that process.

Liberal solidarist and cosmopolitan claims in relation to human rights and democracy have long attracted a high degree of scepticism. The changed global security climate and the challenges to human rights resulting from the so-called war on terrorism have served only to sharpen that scepticism. They have reinforced the sense that liberal solidarist ambition has become ever-more disconnected from power-political realities and that human rights and democracy have become stark symbols of division and confrontation rather than well-institutionalized reflections of a shared humanity. The second part of the chapter therefore looks at three sets of problems: first, the impact of the changing character of threats to human rights and democratization; second, the tensions that exist within the liberal agenda: between human rights and democracy and between democracy and peace; and third, the deeply problematic relationship between human rights and democracy on the one hand and the political and security interests of major states on the other.

The expanding agenda of human rights and democracy

According to the textbook narratives of human rights, international human rights were born with the Universal Declaration on Human Rights in 1948. To see the place of human rights in this way is to underplay the role played by liberal ideas of human rights in the evolution of thinking and practice within international society, especially from the end of the eighteenth century.[1] But what is true is that the post-1948 period (and especially the period from the mid-1970s) saw a far more determined attempt to cement norms relating to human rights much more securely within the formal rules of international law and the practices of international society; and that the post–Cold War period witnessed a powerful move to make democracy a more dominant international norm.

Human rights and international society

Normative expansion has been most obviously visible in the increasing number of international human rights agreements, encompassing civil and political rights, social and economic rights, as well as more recent claims to so-called 'third generation' or 'solidarity rights' (rights to development, peace, clean environment, cultural identity).[2] Other aspects of this normative expansion have included moves to apply the laws of war and humanitarian law to 'internal' conflicts and civil wars, and the revival of ideas of internationally recognized and protected minority rights—as in the recognition process in the former Yugoslavia or the creation of a Commissioner on Nation Minorities within the OSCE.

One set of pressures for this expansion came from within the human rights system itself. Although its origins were intimately bound up with the power, interests and values of the United States and other Western states in the immediate post-war period, once created the human rights regime provided both institutional platforms and normative handholds for weaker actors (both states and non-state groups) to press their interests. The programmatic use of soft law, the space provided for experts and working groups, and the broader role of NGOs helped to open up the process of norm creation and development. State control over this process was diluted and a degree of political space was created for the elaboration and promotion of a new range of rights

---

[1] For a still very valuable broad perspective, see Vincent (1986).

[2] For overviews of the development of human rights, see David P. Forsythe, *Human Rights in International Relations* (Cambridge: Cambridge University Press, 2000); Jack Donnelly, *Universal Human Rights in Theory and Practice* (Ithaca, NY: Cornell University Press, 1989); and Rosemary Foot, *Rights Beyond Borders: The Global Community and the Struggle over Human Rights in China* (Oxford: Oxford University Press, 2000), ch. 2. Also useful is Rhona K. M. Smith and Christien van den Anker (eds.), *The Essentials of Human Rights* (London: Hodder Arnold, 2005).

(e.g. rights of future generations, rights related to the status of women, rights to cultural identity, rights to development and a clean environment).[3] Expansion was also been closely bound up with arguments concerning the interdependency and indivisibility of rights. At one level this was driven by politics: no bargain would have been possible between East and West and North and South that did not accept international recognition of both civil and political, and economic and social rights. Yet indivisibility works also at a deeper and more substantive level. For example, when pressed hard, the attempt to draw clear-cut distinctions between civil and political rights and economic and social rights, or between rights that demand state abstention, and then positive action breaks down and becomes untenable.[4]

But the expansion of the normative agenda has also been driven by pressures and developments from outside the human rights system, most obviously as a result of the end of the Cold War and the pervasive sense within major Western countries that liberal ideas had indeed conquered the world and that all good things could go together—not only human rights and democracy, but also democracy and peace and democracy and economic development. Those who press in this direction argue that there can be no neutral definition of human rights and that human rights cannot be logically disengaged from comprehensive notions of what constitutes a good society. Cut-off points between different clusters of rights will inevitably be arbitrary. On what basis (other than an unargued—for judgement as to what his well-ordered non-liberal societies will in practice accept) does Rawls include the right to life and the prohibition of slavery in his list of actionable international human rights but exclude freedom of press or of association, or the right to education?[5] In addition, the expansionists argue that we should keep pushing out the normative boat and keep asserting important sets of rights even if the chances of effective or consistent implementation remain slim—that is, after all, what having a normative agenda is all about.

If we move from the scope of rights towards questions about their implementation, there has been a move away from soft systems of implementation and towards attempts at stronger enforcement. The implementation of human rights standards under many existing international human rights regimes has been based largely on enquiry and exposure, involving the creation of supervision bodies under major global and regional treaties, the submission of reports by states, the establishment of working groups, and the

[3] For a discussion and critique of the expansion of rights, see Philip Alston, 'Conjuring up New Human Rights: A Proposal for Quality Control', *American Journal of International Law*, 78 78/3 (July 1984), 607–21.

[4] On this point see, in particular, Henry Shue, *Basic Rights: Subsistence, Affluence and US Foreign Policy* (Princeton, NJ: Princeton University Press, 1980).

[5] John Rawls, 'The Law of Peoples', in Stephen Shute and Susan Hurley (eds.), *On Human Rights* (New York: Basic Books, 1993).

creation of theme and country rapporteurs and fact finding missions. Civil and political rights are generally the most strongly protected, with the 1966 UN Covenant establishing a body of experts, the Human Rights Committee, to receive and examine periodic reports from states, and with an optional procedure allowing the investigation of complaints brought by states alleging a violation, and to investigate complaints by or on behalf of individual victims. In both the Latin American and European regional human rights system, individuals are empowered to bring suit in order to challenge the domestic activities of their own government. An independent court and commission are invested with the respective mandates to respond to individual claims by judging whether the application of domestic rules or legislation violates international commitments.

Even within this world of soft implementation, it is, of course, very clear that governments have fought hard to preserve their dominant position, to maintain control over the implementation procedures, to restrict the scope for individual action, and to control the political process within which regional courts and commissions operate. It is equally clear just how difficult it has been to insulate the system from cross-cutting foreign policy goals and the ability of major powers to exempt themselves from scrutiny. Yet it is also important to note a number of positive developments: the gradual increase in the range of states subjected to external monitoring and in the intrusiveness of the procedures; the achievement of a greater degree of distance from direct political pressures, even within the UN system; the enormous expansion in the availability of information on human rights conditions (produced and disseminated by national governments, by the NGO community, and by international institutions); and the extent to which state-based regimes have provided the political platform for ever-greater NGO involvement. On one level, the system seeks to protect human rights through the mobilization of shame and by increasing the costs to a state's reputation (the extent to which China has been prepared to cajole votes in support of no-action motions at the UN Commission on Human Rights provides some indication that reputational concerns do have some political impact). At another, and probably more important level, there is the role played by international norms in strengthening and empowering groups struggling domestically, and in creating both material incentives and normative pressures for the internalization of such norms into domestic legal and political systems (see below).

The move towards stronger systems of implementation has involved four areas. The first can be seen in the marked, and normatively highly significant, shift towards individual criminal responsibility for grave rights violations. This has been evident in the development of international courts and tribunals, most notably the tribunals established for the former Yugoslavia (International Criminal Tribunal for Yugoslavia) and Rwanda (International Criminal Tribunal for Rwanda) and the creation of the International Criminal

Court; and in the increased number of domestic trials (as with the trials that have taken place in Spain for abuses of human rights in Latin America).[6] The second area has been the growth of human rights and democratic conditionalities—that is the institutionalized application of human rights or pro-democracy conditionality to interstate flows of economic resources as a means of inducing domestic policy change. The third has been the move towards coercive humanitarian intervention on the part of the UN and other international bodies. The final category concerns the unilateral actions by powerful states employing a range of positive and negative sanctions. In the case of the United States, the general issue of human rights has become relatively firmly established in both the foreign policy process and in political consciousness, with significant elements of continuity in the period since the mid-1970s and a much greater degree of institutionalization of human rights within the foreign policy bureaucracy.[7]

A final feature of the process of expansion has been the role of human rights NGOs. These have carved out very important roles, four of which may be briefly noted: (*a*) information gathering and facilitating flow of information from those directly affected to international human rights groups and monitoring bodies. This has been critical in opening up knowledge of human rights abuses in remote areas where national media might be uninterested assessment and evaluations of individual countries records given the failings of formal implementing bodies to do this; (*b*) the 'hue and cry' function of such groups in using that information both to mobilize shame and to pressure specific cases and to extract from governments the need for new areas of rights; (*c*) NGOs and community organizations as a vital conduit for external assistance on human rights and for creating social structures within which external assistance can be effectively used, especially when state structures have been weakened or destroyed; (*d*) as a transmission belt for changes in attitudes and values where the focus of attention is not direct influence on governments, but rather broader social changes. The role of human rights NGOs and advocacy groups has also been central to constructivist explanations of how the international human rights system has developed. This view sees the origins of human rights regimes in terms of norm mobilization by norm entrepreneurs; their evolution in terms of processes of transnational socialization and the creation of a norm cascade; and their dominant mode of action not in terms of a logic of domination and adaptation as realists would suggest, nor in terms of the logic of consequences and interests as

---

[6] See Bruce Broomhall, *International Justice and the International Criminal Court* (Oxford: Oxford University Press, 2003); and Ellen Luz and Kathryn Sikkink, The Justice Cascade: 'The Evolution and Impact of Human Rights Trials in Latin America', *Chicago Journal of International Law*, 2/1 (2001), 1–34.

[7] See Kathyrn Sikkink, *Mixed Signals: U.S. Human Rights Policy Towards Latin America* (Ithaca, NY: Cornell University Press, 2004).

institutionalists argue, but rather in terms of a logic of appropriateness in which argument and persuasion play crucial roles.

Human rights beyond solidarism

Although central to a liberal solidarist vision of international society, the expansion and consolidation of human rights press hard against the statist limits of that conception. Take, first, the question of sources. The liberal solidarist wishes to argue that the status of human rights rests on the degree to which they are embodied in legally binding international treaties and conventions and to which their rights are recognized by international law, with its doctrines of sources and its rules of recognition. The human rights lawyer wants to establish the *legal* status of rights, partly to limit the extent to which rights can be manipulated for political purposes and partly to take advantage of the institutional potential for implementation and enforcement. Human rights are not just 'soft' moral principles but 'hard law'. Yet this attempt is caught in a narrow and extremely problematic space between the limits of a positivist doctrine of sources on the one hand and the difficulties of appealing directly to a traditional idea of natural law on the other. It is deeply implausible to argue that torture and genocide are simply legally wrong because a certain number of states have signed and ratified a particular convention. But, if this is not the case, on what basis can they be legally justified?

One solution is to go down the route of customary international law.[8] But, in the case of human rights, the brutal realities of what states routinely do to their citizens means that the balance between state practice and *opinion juris* has to be tilted heavily towards the latter: of course many states still torture but it is the constant evocation of the normative unacceptability of torture that allows the international lawyer to claim the stability and embeddedness of the norm. This is one of the reasons why the retreat from even such an apparently accepted and fundamental norm as the proscription of torture in the context of counterterrorism is theoretically as well as morally so serious and so threatening. Another solution is to appeal implicitly to some notion of natural law, perhaps built around an understanding of the fundamental necessities of social life, or around an account of human flourishing or self-development, or perhaps around an argument about the nature of meaningful human agency. But such arguments will always take us outside the narrow reaches of the legal order itself. Rights always assume a prior set of values; and their role is to protect, promote, and prioritize those values. As Griffin argues, legal debates that seek to pin down an idea as central but as open-ended as

[8] See Martti Koskenniemi, 'The Pull of the Mainstream', review of Theodor Meron, *Human Rights and Humanitarian Norms as Customary Law, Michigan Law Review*, 88 (1989–90), 1946–62.

the 'dignity of the person' will necessarily appeal to some broader argument as to what the relevant right should be and how it can be related to justice.[9]

A third common solution seeks to develop an underlying cross-cultural consensus in which there is a convergence of certain norms of conduct but where these norms continue to rest on a wide variety of different value systems and political and moral languages. The problem is that this is rarely a sufficient or stable answer. As Taylor argues, reaching agreement in practical contexts requires more than a broad consensus; it also requires that we reach agreement on the priority of rights, and on their detailed content; this, in turn, necessitates a 'fine grained understanding of what moves the other' and a continued willingness to negotiate the particular disagreements that will inevitably arise. 'Consequently the bare consensus must strive to go on towards a fusion of horizons'.[10]

The development of human rights also presses up against the inherited statism of the system in terms of how it operates. Sovereignty in the sense of power of the state over its nationals has been eroded by human rights law and by the increased availability to groups and individuals of a range of national courts and international tribunals. But it is important not to overlook the extent to which international human rights regimes in the post-1945 period continued to be marked by statism and sovereignty—not just in terms of the capacity of states to resist the transfer of effective authority but also in terms of how the system itself was conceived. As Louis Henkin noted:

In our international system of nation-states, human rights are to be enjoyed in national societies as rights under national law. The purpose of international law is to influence states to recognize and accept human rights, to reflect these rights in their national constitutions and laws, to respect and ensure their enjoyment through national institutions, and to incorporate them into national ways of life.[11]

States, then, are the source of the system, the locus of responsibility, and the focus for pressure. The road to a common humanity lies through national sovereignty. This perspective suggests that we should think of international human rights regimes as affecting political actors primarily on an interstate level and in terms of the dynamics of the interstate system. For some, human rights only come to 'matter' when big and powerful states take them up and seek to use their own power to enforce human rights standards. On this view,

[9] James Griffin, 'Discrepancies between the Best Philosophical Account of Human Rights and International Law of Human Rights', *Proceedings of the Aristotelian Society*, 101 (2000), 21–2.

[10] Charles Taylor, 'Conditions of an Unforced Consensus on Human Rights', in Joanne R. Bauer and Daniel A. Bell (eds.), *The East Asian Challenge for Human Rights* (Cambridge: Cambridge University Press, 1999), 137–8.

[11] Louis Henkin, 'International Human Rights and Rights in the United States', in Theodor Meron (ed.), *Human Rights in International Law: Legal and Policy Issues* (Oxford: Oxford University Press, 1989), 25.

149

human rights institutions are of only marginal importance. On this view, too, the role of NGOs and advocacy groups is principally to publicize human rights violations in order to sway public opinion within the political system of powerful states, especially in the United States and Europe. For others, human rights regimes matter but primarily because of what they can do to shift the incentives facing member-states—by generating publicity, by naming and shaming, by creating positive or negative linkages with other issues, or by providing external lock-in especially for fragile regimes in newly democratized countries.[12]

This way of thinking, however, seriously underplays the increasingly transnational character of the human rights regime—in terms of the transnational political spaces that have been created; and in terms of the increased dialogue and interaction between national legal orders and international and regional constitutionalism. The human rights system therefore displays significant elements of the sorts of complex governance beyond the state that was described in Chapter 4. The development of regional courts and commissions has led to the generation of an increasingly complex human rights jurisprudence. Thinking of human rights in transnational terms focuses attention on the interaction between international human rights developments and national-level political and legal debates. In many states human rights have been 'constitutionalized', although there is widespread variation not just in the effective enforcement of international human rights within domestic legal systems, but also in the willingness of judges to engage in the transnational legal culture of human rights. Understanding the sources of this variation (e.g. divergent national legal traditions, patterns of legal education, different sorts of engagement with the transnational legal community, and so on) plays an important role in understanding the ways in which international human rights regimes may, or may not, affect political outcomes.

Viewing international human rights in transnational terms also suggests a number of important questions in terms of the way in which international human rights may affect domestic political actors and also where the major constraints lie—for example, how integration and interaction with the international regime may affect the relative power of sections of the bureaucracy dealing with human rights, or may lead to processes of socialization on the part of those state officials involved. And, finally, it is important to understand the capacity of transnational civil society groups to engage directly with human rights regimes. As political actors increasingly operate across state borders, it becomes increasingly important to identify the linkages (and tensions) that exist between the 'inside' and the 'outside' of domestic political action. The transnationalization of human rights and democracy has provided

---

[12] On this last point, see Andrew Moravcsik, 'The Origins of Human Rights Regimes: Democratic Delegation in Postwar Europe', *International Organization*, 54/2 (2000), 217–52.

domestic actors with new political and legal opportunities to pursue their interests. Here we need to understand why NGOs in some states are more active transnationally and how human rights regimes interact with country-specific patterns of political democratization.

Democracy and international society

Democracy as a norm and the promotion of democracy as an activity have become far more deeply embedded within international society in various ways. In the first place, there has been an enormous expansion in the involvement of the UN and regional organization in elections.[13] Electoral assistance has become an established part of UN activities and has also led to the development of a broad transnational and trans-governmental network of electoral assistance, party support, and monitoring.[14] Second, external actors have routinely become involved in democracy promotion as a result of the expansion in the number and scope of peacekeeping operations, whose multidimensional character came in many places to include human rights and democracy as well as demilitarization, refugee protection and state-building. In cases of the direct international administration of territory (as in Cambodia, Bosnia, Eastern Slavonia, Kosovo, and East Timor), the assumption of the sovereign power involved both transitional administration and also democratic regime-building. Third, democratic membership criteria have been established in two regions (Europe and the Americas), and, in the case of Europe, democracy, human rights, and minority rights have all played a central part of the process of EU enlargement, the conditionality policies of the EU, and its extensive programme of member-state building. Finally, an increasing body of academic writing has opened up the idea of a legal right to democratic governance.[15]

In part, this expansion has an internal logic. Surely, if we want to protect human rights on a sustainable long-term basis, should not we also work to foster systems of government which are most conducive to that end? But the normative expansion of international society to include democracy was also driven by political factors. Although there are references to 'democratic' rights in the UN Declaration, the conditions of the Cold War meant that formal incorporation of political democracy into the human rights system was politically impossible. This changed as a result of the wave of transitions

[13] See Gregory H. Fox, 'Democratization', in David M. Malone (ed.), *The UN Security Council: From the Cold War to the 21st Century* (Boulder, CO: Lynne Rienner, 2004), 69–84; Christopher C. Joyner, 'The United Nations and Democracy', *Global Governance*, 5/3 (1999), 333–57.

[14] Thomas Carothers, *Aiding Democracy Abroad: The Learning Curve* (Washington, DC: Carnegie Endowment for International Peace, 1999).

[15] See Thomas Franck, 'The Emerging Right to Democratic Governance', *American Journal of International Law*, 86/1 (January 1992), 46–91; James Crawford, 'Democracy and International Law', *British Yearbook of International Law*, 64 (1993), 113–33; and Gregory H. Fox and Brad R. Roth, 'Democracy and International Law', *Review of International Studies*, 27 (2001), 327–52.

from authoritarian rule in Southern Europe and the developing world in the late 1970s and 1980s; and the fall of communism in Eastern Europe and the Soviet Union; by the liberal self-confidence that followed the ending of Cold War and the belief that liberal democracy and free markets were sweeping the world; and the consolidation of the place of democracy in US foreign policy.

Two broader shifts need to be highlighted, both of which link academic analysis and political perceptions. The first concerns the progress of democratic change and the possibilities of democratization. During the Cold War, Western governments were suspicious that political change would be destabilizing, bringing to power either those who would ally themselves with the Soviet Union or who would challenge Western economic interests. Democratization, then, clearly carried with it a significant counter-hegemonic potential. It was also widely held in Western capitals and amongst the private sector that authoritarian governments were most suited to promoting economic development. Many academics argued that, in any case, democracy required a wide range of 'prerequisites' that were lacking in many post-colonial societies. The wave of transitions that began in Southern Europe and Latin America in the late 1970s ushered in a striking reassessment:[16] democratization becomes the norm rather than the exception; the expectation is of a generally forward movement; and democratization appears to be easier and less problematic than had been previously believed. A post–Cold War world meant that unstable and potentially oppositional regimes could no longer look to the Soviet Union. And a globalized world meant that economic nationalism was no longer an option. The trade-offs between uncertain democratization, security interests, and economic preferences were apparently easing and a strong sense of the difficulties of democracy gave way to an increased sense of 'possibilism'. The conversion by the mid-1980s of US neoconservatives to the viability and possibility of democracy promotion provides a striking indication of the changes that had occurred. And it is against this background that the history of US foreign policy was retold through a different lens that stressed the country's historic mission to extend and promote democracy.[17]

The other important shift in thinking reflected the allegedly 'proven' link between democracy and peace.[18] Democratic peace theory builds on a long tradition in liberal writing on international relations, often associated with

[16] See Samuel P. Huntington, *The Third Wave: Democratization in the Late Twentieth Century* (Norman, OK: University of Oklahoma Press, 1991).

[17] Tony Smith, *America's Mission: The United States and the Worldwide Struggle for Democracy in the Twentieth Century* (Princeton, NJ: Princeton University Press, 1994).

[18] See Michael Doyle, 'Kant, Liberal Legacies and Foreign Affairs', *Philosophy and Public Affairs*, 12/3 and 4 (Summer and Fall, 1983), 205–35, 323–53. Michael Brown, Sean Lynn-Jones, and Steven Miller (eds.), *Debating the Democratic Peace* (Cambridge, MA: Cambridge University Press, 1996); Russett (1993).

Kant (hence references to 'Kantian peace'). However, it only formed one (and not the most central) part of Kant's political thought and had already become a liberal commonplace by the end of the eighteenth century. Other precursors of modern DPT include Karl Deutsch's writing in the 1950s on security communities—groups of states (such as North America, Scandinavia, and Western Europe) in which there is real assurance that the members of that community will not fight each other physically but will settle their disputes in some other way. Overlooked or neglected by many studies of war causation, it became a major theme both of academic writing on international relations and of political and public debate on the nature of the post–Cold War international order (as in the Clinton administration's policy of democratic enlargement or in the justifications for EU and NATO expansion).

Theorists argue that two sets of causal factors are important in explaining the democratic peace. In the first place, the structural constraints of democratic institutions and of democratic politics make it difficult or even impossible for war-prone leaders to drag their states into wars. They also stress the joint effect of these democratic constraints, together with the greater openness and transparency of liberal democracies. If both sides are governed by cautious, cost-sensitive politicians that only use force defensively, then conflict is far less likely to occur. Second, democratic peace theorists highlight the importance of normative mechanisms. Liberal and democratic norms involve shared understandings of appropriate behaviour, stabilize expectations of the future, and are embedded in both institutions and political culture. Rule-governed change is a basic principle; the use of coercive force outside the structure of rules is proscribed; and trust and reciprocity, rule of law are at the heart of democratic politics. From this view, then, the democratic peace is produced by the way in which democracies externalize their domestic political norms of tolerance and compromise into their foreign relations, thus making war with others like them unlikely.

The democratic peace hypothesis rests on two claims: (a) that democracies almost never fight each other and very rarely consider the use of force in their mutual relations and (b) that other types of relations are much more conflictual including democracies' interactions with non-democracies. The claim is almost always made in probabilistic terms. Few claim that it is a determinstic law. It is not a general theory since it is agnostic or at least much less certain about the relationship between democracies and non-democracies. But it provides some grounds for liberal optimism, even if only within the democratic zone. If true, it holds out the possibility that the homogenization of domestic political systems could transform global political order—in marked contrast both to traditional realist accounts of world politics and pluralist accounts of international society. The main debates surrounding the democratic peace and the main issues raised by critics and sceptics include: (a) the reliability of the statistical evidence for the democratic peace, especially in the pre-1945 period; (*b*) the existence of alternative causal logics, especially in explaining regional clusters of peaceful states as in Western Europe or the Americas; (*c*) the difficulties of defining key terms in the theory, especially war and democracy; (*d*) and the problems raised by democratization processes and the evidence that, whilst fully consolidated democracies may be peaceful, democratizing states, especially in unstable regions, may be more conflict-prone than authoritarian regimes.

Gaps and limits

It is tempting to paint a post–Cold War picture in which there is a constant expansion of the human rights agenda with Western liberal states consistently leading the way. But even in the 1990s, there were important gaps. The most important of these concerns refugees and those seeking asylum—precisely those individuals and groups those who have consistently fallen between the cracks of the society of states. Here we can note: the erosion of the core idea of non-voluntary return, the very limited progress towards the provision of material assistance towards those societies in the South most burdened by refugees (in 2001, around 75% of the world's 20 million refugees were in developing countries); the political blindness and institutional failures in terms of the protection of human rights of the estimated 6 million refugees living in camps; and increasing calls for the replacement of the core of the international refugee regime, the 1951 Convention.

What are the limits to this process of normative expansion? The thrust of the changes sketched out above has been to make sovereignty conditional and contingent. States are only legitimate to the extent that they act on behalf of their citizens and do not abuse their rights. One important area of debate (and contestation) has focused on humanitarian intervention. Although the issue is a very old one, the post–Cold War period saw a clear increase in the willingness of states to use force for humanitarian purpose.[19] As we shall see in Chapter 7, humanitarian motivations played an important role in the way in which understandings of what might constitute a threat to international peace and security have been broadened. For some, there has been a clear normative shift towards an acceptance of a norm of humanitarian intervention.[20] This shift can also be clearly seen in the increased attention that has been given to the notion of sovereignty as responsibility and a responsibility to protect. As the International Commission on Intervention and State Sovereignty put it in 2001: 'It is acknowledged that sovereignty implies a dual

---

[19] See J. L. Holzgrefe and Robert Keohane (eds.), *Humanitarian Intervention: Ethical, Legal and Political Dilemmas* (Cambridge: Cambridge University Press, 2004); Jennifer Welsh (ed.), *Humanitarian Intervention and International Relations* (Oxford: Oxford University Press, 2004).

[20] For example, Wheeler (2000).

responsibility: externally, to respect the sovereignty of other states, and internally, to respect the dignity and basic rights of all the people within the state'.[21] The adoption by the General Assembly of the idea of a responsibility to protect at the UN World Summit in September 2005 has been viewed as evidence of change in the normative climate and, perhaps, in the structure of legal rules. These moves clearly expand the normative ambition of international society—by permitting coercive intervention without the consent of the affected state, by shifting the burden of responsibility from those seeking to intervene to the state said to be in breach of its responsibility to protect, and by leading to further 'natural' expansion in goals. If there is a responsibility to intervene, then surely there should also be a responsibility to rebuild and to engage in post-conflict democratization and reconstruction.

On the other side, there remain serious doubts as to whether a legal norm of humanitarian intervention has in fact crystallized, with sceptics stressing the limited number of cases of classically defined humanitarian intervention (Iraq, Somalia, Haiti, and Kosovo) and arguing that interventions without explicit UN authorization (most notably Kosovo) cannot be considered as legal.[22] Even where we have seen some movement towards the acceptance of the norm of humanitarian intervention (including on the part of several major developing countries), this has been accompanied by a reassertion of the need for explicit authorization. The Report of the UN High Level Panel on Threats, Challenges and Change, issued in December 2004, identified five 'basic criteria for legitimacy' before the use of force should be authorized: seriousness of the threat, proper purpose, last resort, proportionate means, and the balance of consequences. The problem, however, is that the Security Council already has considerable freedom to interpret the meaning of 'threats to international peace and security and there is nothing that stands in the way of authorizing more expansive notions of preventive or pre-emptive self-defence. The Panel therefore evaded the crucial issue: what status are these 'criteria for legitimacy' supposed to have in precisely those difficult cases when the Council is unable to act?[23] On this there remains little sign of agreement.

A second limit concerns coercive democratization and regime change. Again, this lies in the space beyond any existing legal consensus but forms a major part of contemporary political debate. This question has, of course, attracted a great deal of attention in the context of the war in Iraq but was a subject of legal controversy with respect to the conservative crusading of

---

[21] ICISS, *The Responsibility to Protect: Report of the International Commission on Intervention and State Sovereignty* (Ottawa: IRDC, 2001), 8.

[22] See e.g. Michael Byers and Simon Chesterman, 'Changing the Rules about Rules? Unilateral Humanitarian Intervention and the Future of International Law', in J. L. Holzgrefe and Robert Keohane (eds.), *Humanitarian Intervention: Ethical, Legal and Political Dilemmas* (Cambridge: Cambridge University Press, 2004). See also Adam Roberts, 'The So-called "Right" of Humanitarian Intervention', *Yearbook of International Humanitarian Law*, 3 (2000), 3–51.

[23] *A More Secure World: Our Shared Responsibility*, paras. 204–9.

the Reagan administration in the 1980s. A standard pattern of argument is to stress the fundamental purposes of the UN Charter—not just upholding peace but also promoting states that respect human rights and fundamental freedoms. Restraints on the use of force have therefore to be interpreted within the context of this broader purpose. Those on the other side argue that to endorse a particular end is not the same as to endorse all sorts of means to achieve those ends and, in particular, that legal restraints on the unauthorized use of force cannot, and should not, be overturned in the pursuit of democratic interventionism. It remains the case that forcible regime change cannot provide a valid legal justification for going to war.

The third area of debate is the idea that only liberal democratic states should be full members of international society or that a grouping of democratic states should have a special place within the normative structure of international society. From this perspective democratic states should have a privileged role in the provision of international legitimacy, especially in cases of intervention and the use of force. Non-democracies would lose their sovereign rights, for example, in terms of the right to possess weapons of mass destruction. Such arguments are justified partly because of the allegedly greater danger that such states pose to the international community but also because of the view that it is only democracy that can morally justify a government placing its citizens in the sort of hostage situations that nuclear weapons involve. As with regime change, these arguments have considerable political vitality, especially in the United States; but there is very little sign of their reflecting any political or legal consensus within international society as a whole.

Doubts, problems, and challenges

The changing character of the problem

The first challenge comes from the changing character of human rights violations. In a depressingly large number of countries, the human rights agenda remains concerned with the direct abuses of human rights by governments on their citizens. In many other cases, it is concerned with the legacies of authoritarianism and issues of transitional justice (amnesty laws, proper compensation, and the right to know about details of past violations). But, in addition to these 'traditional' human rights violations perpetrated by state agents as part of a deliberate policy, increasing attention has had to be given to violations that involve challenges to the rule of law (access to justice and due process), and to the rights of vulnerable groups (especially the rights of indigenous peoples in relation to land ownership and access to healthcare, the rights of women, and the rights of children). Across many parts of the developing world, sustained and 'structural' human rights violations occur on a large scale and include low-level police brutality, the murder of street children, rural violence, and continued discrimination of indigenous peoples. In many cases, the role of state authorities may be difficult to demonstrate, or may indeed be entirely absent. The causes do not lie in the exercise of arbitrary state power but are often the consequences of state weakness and failure to act. The capacity of weak and inefficient state institutions to address such violations may be extremely limited, especially in situations characterized by multiple forms of violence, and the blurred character of relations between public and private power.

These trends pose major challenges for a regional human rights system that is geared towards the protection of individuals against actions of the state, built around legal notions of state responsibility, and that assumes, politically, that pressure can be exerted on states which, in turn, possess the levers necessary to improve the situation—in other words, that states which are part of the problem can also be part of the solution. It also challenges those notions of human rights (especially deriving from the US tradition) that place almost their entire weight on the relationship between the individual and a potentially threatening state. And finally, especially when considering situations of protracted conflict and violence, 'traditional' human rights law comes into an inherently closer relationship with other bodies of law, including international humanitarian law. Even assuming widespread goodwill, these changes pose major challenges for the mechanisms of the international human rights system.

A closely related challenge concerns the changing character of democratization. Even if the big-picture narratives about democratic waves captured the widespread move away from authoritarianism that was taking place in the 1980s and early 1990s, many countries have been undergoing complex and uncertain processes of democratization in which the nature of the challenge to democracy has shifted. There are multiple ways in which power obtained through democratic means may be exercised undemocratically and illiberally. If democratic backsliding were simply a matter of military coups and the failure to hold clean elections, an international consensus might be relatively easy to sustain. But contemporary challenges to democracy often have far more to do with the murky erosion of democratic systems ('authoritarian inclinations in democratic day-dress'), near-coup crises, and the erosion of the social and economic fabric and interpersonal trust that sustains democratic institutions. Moreover, the divergences between the formal and procedural characteristics of political democracy and the perceptions and experiences of those living under democratic regimes vary enormously. There is increased contestation as to the nature of democracy, increasing expectations as to what democratic systems should deliver, and increasing discontent with the gap between inflated expectations and delivered outcomes. Hence, there is

157

renewed debate about the adequacy of minimalist and procedural conception of democracy and, indeed, about the meaning of democracy itself. 'Democracy' turns out to have an inherently contested and unstable meaning.[24] As with 'self-determination', this inevitably raises serious problems as to the status of democracy as a core constitutive norm of contemporary international society. The very uneven and uncertain process of democratization also raises serious doubts as to whether democratization should be viewed as a forward process in which setbacks and problems are merely temporary aberrations.

Tensions within the liberal agenda

All good liberal things do not go easily together. There are, for example, significant tensions in the relationship between political democracy and the promotion of human rights.[25] This is true theoretically. Thus both Berlin and Elster have underlined the extent to which formal political democracy can entrench murderous majorities of all kinds—both murderous ethnic majorities and religiously sanctioned intolerance.[26] Rights are conceptually distinct from democracy. They are designed to protect their bearers from actions or conditions that threaten individual autonomy or well-being. The whole point of rights is to ring-fence certain activities from the decisions of day-to-day democratic politics and to insulate certain areas of politics from the control of others, and to set limits as to what may be legislated. The values protected by rights are more basic than the values of democracy. For the rights purist, rights are 'trumps'. This is the particular appeal and power of rights. But it can also be a central source of weakness—especially in periods when the security or identity of a state is held to be at stake.[27] Moreover, it can be an important underlying barrier to the idea of universality. The apparently apolitical quality of rights is itself the product of political struggles and compromises that naturally vary greatly across time and across space. Even within Western liberal world, think of the very different construction placed on rights to

[24] On the vexed meaning of democracy, see Laurence Whitehead, *Democratization: Theory and Experience* (Oxford: Oxford University Press, 2002), ch. 1.

[25] We should also note the common elision between rights and justice. 'There is no inference from something being a matter of justice or fairness to it being a matter of rights.... Some write as if the domain of justice and of human rights were identical. But they are clearly not. Human rights do not exhaust the whole domain of justice or fairness.' Griffin (2000: 14).

[26] Isaiah Berlin, 'Two Concepts of Liberty', in *Four Essays on Liberty* (Oxford: Oxford University Press, 1969), 165–9; Jon Elster, 'Majoritarian Rule and Individual Rights', in Stephen Shute and Susan Hurley (eds.), *On Human Rights: The Oxford Amnesty Lectures* (New York: Basic Books, 1993), 111–34.

[27] For a powerful critique of excessive 'rights purism' but one which involves a problematic argument in favour of greater pragmatism, see David Kennedy, *The Dark Sides of Virtue: Reassessing International Humanitarianism* (Princeton, NJ: Princeton University Press, 2004).

free speech and how these varying constructions are unintelligible outside the particular political histories of the countries involved.

In practice, there may be an elective affinity between human rights and democracy and many aspects of the human rights agenda are important for a well-functioning democracy. And yet very large numbers of democratic states commit violations of human rights, especially highly unequal and stressed societies. Looking over the past twenty years (i.e. beyond the recent focus on counterterrorism), nearly one in three institutional democracies have committed significant human rights violations.[28]

What of the much acclaimed link between democracy and peace? This is not the place to provide a full evaluation of democratic peace theory. But two points can be made. The first picks up on the idea that the externalization of domestic norms of tolerance and compromise is one of most important causal mechanisms that might explain the existence of the democratic peace. For the critics this idea of externalization is very hard to reconcile with the behaviour of liberal democratic states both in their imperial wars and in their interventions against other democracies.[29] The second concerns the links between peace and the often messy processes of democratization. Although end-state, consolidated democracies may be wonderfully peaceful, but the messy processes of transition and consolidation can be very destabilizing. This is the force of the arguments of Snyder and Mansfield: democratizing states, especially when they are in politically or geopolitically, rough neighbourhoods, are more likely to engage in conflict than either fully democratic or stable authoritarian governments. They point to the use of aggressive foreign policies as a means of cementing domestic support and, especially, to the use of strongly nationalist foreign policies as a basis for political legitimacy.[30]

What, finally, of the links between human rights and economic development? As the ongoing debates about Chinese development (and about a possible Chinese 'model') suggest, the relationship between successful economic development and political democracy/human rights turn out to be far more complex and ambiguous than the Western triumphalism of the 1990s would pretend. Moreover, whatever the aggregate data on the actual nature of the relationship, the political appeal of a developmentalism that stresses the imperatives of state-building and development above human rights and democracy has certainly not disappeared. Ayoob, for example, has argued that we need to recognize that the historic successes of today's liberal and

[28] Emilie Hafner-Burton and Kiyotera Tsutsui, 'Human Rights in a Globalizing World: The Paradox of Empty Promises', *American Journal of Sociology* (2004), 1373–411.

[29] See Sebastian Rosato, 'The Flawed Logic of Democratic Peace Theory', *American Political Science Review*, 97/4 (2003), 585–602; and Steve Chan, 'In Search of Democratic Peace: Problems and Promise', *Mershon International Studies Review*, 41/1 (1997), 59–91.

[30] Edward D. Mansfield and Jack Snyder, 'Democratization and the Danger of War', *International Security*, 20 (1995), 5–38.

democratic states were built on a great deal of blood, coercion, and conquest; that developing countries face a far harder task than their European counterparts; and that increasing external demands from international society make the task harder still.

One wonders if West European and North American States would have successfully completed their state-building endeavours and eventually emerged as liberal, democratic states, if they had the UN Human Rights Commission, Amnesty International and now the UNSC breathing down their necks during the crucial early phases of their state making endeavours.[31]

Although morally problematic, such arguments continue to have considerable political appeal in many parts of developing world.

Human rights, democracy, and political interest

Pluralists have always laid great emphasis on the problems that arise when foreign policy is driven by concerns for human rights and democracy. In terms of individual states, they feared that this would lead to immoderate foreign policies, to crusading and to the uncontrolled, and maybe uncontrollable, expansion of goals. The result would be an unstable foreign policy that would oscillate between excessive engagement and interventionism on the one hand and disillusion and retreat on the other. In terms of the system, the coherence of a solidarist liberal order would always be undermined by the problems of double standards, of self-serving behaviour cloaked in idealistic clothes, and countries picking only those cases of humanitarian distress and human rights violations that served other political, economic, or security interests. The paradox of universalism has always been that the successful promotion of 'universal' or 'global' values would usually depend on the willingness of particularly powerful states to promote them and that their successful promotion will work to reinforce the already marked inequality of power and status.

The end of the Cold War, it was argued, allowed for a broader definition of 'national interests' and greater room for the promotion of genuinely liberal goals. But, even in the 1990s, the problems of selectivity and of cross-cutting pressures did not disappear. Whilst increased coercive pressure in pursuit of human rights and democratic governance was applied in a number of cases where the costs were relatively low (e.g. Kenya or Malawi), the rhetoric of democratic enlargement was often at odds with broader foreign policy goals (as with the absence of firm action or even of mild criticism in respect of, say, Russia or Saudi Arabia).

---

[31] Mohammed Ayoob, 'Humanitarian Intervention and State Sovereignty', *International Journal of Human Rights*, 6/1 (2002), 93.

The return of these traditional problems has been sharpened immensely by the changed security environment created by the attacks on the United States of 9/11 and by the unfolding of the so-called long war on global terrorism.[32] The repercussions on human rights have been clear, and clearly negative— in terms of the human rights violations committed by the United States and its major allies; in terms of the cynicism engendered by the mismatch between US words and US deeds; and in terms of the incentives and political space for other groups in many regions to emulate Washington's rhetoric and behaviour. The war on terrorism has been viewed by the United States as a struggle in which, to quote George Bush, 'there are no rules' and where it is justified to 'to deny protection to people who do not deserve protection'. The existence of legal black holes and sites of so-called secret rendition, the creeping practice of extrajudicial killings of terrorist suspects, the curtailing of civil liberties within many Western democracies, and the return of arguments justifying torture have had a deep and negative impact on the international human rights landscape.

The impact of the so-called war on terror on democratic norms and on democracy promotion is more complex, but no less problematic. On the one side, the idea of promoting democratic regime change in the Middle East grew in importance as the other rationales for the war in Iraq faded. Equally, the role of democracy as a core value has been constantly reasserted as part of the need to justify the 'war on terrorism' and the broader need to legitimize US policy in the world. Moreover, as the policy failures have increased, so has the need to blame those failures on the enemies of democracy and to cast the fight against terrorism as a Manichean global struggle being fought on behalf of democratic civilization. But, on the other side, the possibility of acting consistently in support of democracy becomes much harder as a long list of democratically dubious states are enlisted and supported as core allies—from Pakistan, to Saudi Arabia, to Uzbekistan—and as counterterrorism reshapes the tone of US policy towards major regional states. The United States and its allies are faced with an ever-widening gap between the rhetoric of promoting democracy and the failures in Iraq and the instability engendered elsewhere across the Middle East. In such circumstances, it becomes politically harder to accept that democracy and democratization are inherently open-ended and uncertain processes that have regularly shown themselves to be destabilizing, disorderly, and often violent. This means that, however much they may be valuable long-term objectives, they are very difficult to mesh with short-term and specific foreign policy goals—as evidenced in the Palestinian territories or in Lebanon, or Venezuela. As we have seen, part of the increased willingness to 'take the risk' of democracy promotion came from the idea

---

[32] See Rosemary Foot, 'Human Rights and Counterterrorism in Global Governance: Reputation and Resistance', *Global Governance*, 11/3 (2005), 291–310.

that there was greater space to accept whatever democracy might throw up. But this has been challenged, not just by the cross-cutting demands of counterterrorism; but also by the problem of managing nuclear proliferation (as with Iran) and by the return of economic nationalism (as in Venezuela or Bolivia).

Conclusions

The legal and normative developments charted in the first part of this chapter have made it possible to believe that a real change has taken place in the normative structure of international society and in a remarkably short period. In the first place, international society has seen the hardening of an impressive normative structure and agreed standards built around a commitment to universality. The human rights regime that emerged in the period since the Second World War is global in at least two senses: first, that the individual and collective rights defined in the increasing number of international legal instruments are indeed held to apply to all human beings; and second, that the UN has played a central role in the process of standard setting, promotion, and (to a clearly far less satisfactory extent) protection of human rights. Moreover, on most core rights the scope for governments to exempt themselves or to raise the old claim of unlimited sovereignty has gone, or has been very heavily constrained. By the end of the 1990s, there was widespread agreement that, although precise lines remained blurred, sovereignty was indeed bound up with the way in which governments treated their own citizens; and, compared to the 1970s, the number of people who reject the very idea of human rights and their role in foreign policy had declined very significantly.

Second, the international and transnational culture of human rights involves a widely shared common language, an inclusive moral vocabulary, and an authoritative and well-developed normative structure from which fewer groups are prepared to try and exempt themselves. This shared discourse implies a general acceptance of certain general principles and processes, and of a particular kind of rationality and argumentation. It limits the range of permissible justifications and motivations; it empowers particular groups and particular institutions; and it helps create incentives for socialization and internalization; and it has become embedded in concrete political practices and specific institutional structures. It is, of course, shaped by its historical origins within a particular culture; but it is open, dynamic, and resistant to permanent capture by a particular interest or power-political grouping. However varied the philosophical, political, or cultural backgrounds from which it is approached, the emergence and spread of this transnational moral and legal discourse represent a major historical development.

Third, this consensus may be said to reflect a shared and widespread apprehension in the face of cruelty, barbarism, and oppression, and a shared awareness of the reality of human suffering. Suffering is a brute fact of social life whose significance is widely shared across cultures and religions. Of course, such apprehension does not stand wholly outside historical circumstances. Nor is it universal. It is not shared by the torturers, nor by all of those who justify cruelty and oppression in the name of some overriding political, economic, or religious cause. But it remains the most resilient bridge between the objective position of impartiality and detachment that is central to all moral judgement and the subjective commitment to particular affections, local circumstances, and individual histories that is central to all moral passion and purpose.[33] As Carlos Santiago Niño has argued so powerfully, the project of human rights is above all a conscious and artificial construction designed to uphold human dignity and to prevent suffering in the face of persistent human bestiality.[34]

These three aspects of the international culture of human rights marked many of the positive changes of the 1990s and can be seen in much of the unfolding resistance to the far darker situation of the world since 2001.

Even within the human rights system itself, there are two major tensions. The first has to do with expansion of the normative agenda and the need to maintain the scope for legitimate difference and for the possibility of authentic democratic politics. Although the precise line may be very hard to draw, there has to be a difference in a world of cultural, religious, and social diversity between proscribing and preventing manifest violations of human rights and externally seeking to dictate the ways in which societies organize themselves and determine their priorities and values. The international community has a legitimate role in ensuring that governmental power is not abused, in setting human rights standards, and in reviewing compliance with those standards. If external involvement is extended beyond this into the detailed ways in which policies are chosen and implemented, the central liberal principals of representation, of accountability, of pluralism and the respect for diversity will be undermined. This is one of the reasons for believing that a core list of human rights should form the basis for international action rather than the aim of promoting democracy. There is also the tension between the possibility of success via imposition of coercion and the long-term process of regime building. Attempts to move too rapidly towards the enforcement of international norms undermine the importance of consensus and the need for self-enforcement on which most international legal regulation will continue to be based. Too strong an emphasis on enforcement may hinder the hardening of existing human rights institutions and make states unwilling even to

[33] See Thomas Nagel, *The View from Nowhere* (Oxford: Oxford University Press, 1986).
[34] Carlos Santiago Nino, *The Ethics of Human Rights* (Oxford: Clarendon Press, 1991).

sign up to loose agreements or sets of principles for fear that they might be used to legitimize coercive intervention. Recent interventions provide a good illustration of the trade-off between short-term effectiveness and a long-term erosion of legitimacy

The dilemmas grow sharper still when we consider the relationship between aspirations towards human rights and democracy and the reality of international political structures within which those aspirations are embedded. There are certainly powerful arguments why sovereignty should be made conditional on the ability and willingness of a state to protect the rights and welfare of its citizens and for the development of a responsibility to protect. The difficulty is that this responsibility has not devolved to a politically and normative coherent set of institutions but rather to an 'international community' whose actions continue to depend on the power, interest, and preferences of its most powerful members. In those cases where humanitarian needs are most acute, interests have pointed, and will often continue to point, towards inaction (as in Dafur). In other cases actions are marked by a denial of human rights, by selectivity and by cross-cutting security and economic goals.

Scepticism, however, does not result solely from the practical difficulties of implementation; nor from the existence of cross-cutting pressures and the inevitability of tensions and trade-offs. Both of these are not only to be expected but are inherent in any likely form of imaginable politics and perhaps even in most realistic utopias. The most serious challenge comes from the extent to which, despite the universalization of agreements and of the language and idiom of human rights, internalization remains both shallow and all too easily reversible. The essence of international society is embodied in the idea of actors being bound by shared rules and cooperating in the operation of shared institutions. This core idea has been challenged in many ways by the resurgence of terrorism and by the responses of government to it. Terrorism itself clearly involves both a violation of the rights of the victims and a challenge to the core norms of international society. From the side of those responding to terrorism, the problem is not merely the specific violation of human rights that have occurred in the course of the so-called war against terrorism—the sanctioning of torture, the arbitrary arrests, the active support of dubious allies. It is rather the erosion of the very idea of there being a shared framework of rules to which all are committed, in all times, and in all places.

7

War, violence, and collective security

The idea of collective security and the drive to increase the collective element in the management of violence and insecurity have long been fundamental elements of the liberal solidarist conception of international society. It was around the expansion of the role of the UN in the field of international security and the emergence of the 'new interventionism' of the 1990s that strong claims were advanced about the erosion of 'Westphalian sovereignty'. Many saw a clear advance of solidarism in the increased role of the UN, in emerging practices of humanitarian intervention, in the potential for the international community to act against the illegal use of force, and in the acceptance and legitimacy of coercive intervention to promote a much broader interpretation of threats to international peace and security and to uphold important rules and prohibitions in the field of arms control. Central to such thinking is the hope that the power of the international community can be harnessed for a common social purpose. The incentives pressing states towards more collective and institutionalized forms of security management have been partly practical and instrumental. But they have also been driven by power of the Kantian moral imperative that 'there shall be no war' in a century in which around 160 million human beings died in war and other forms of violent conflict.[1]

The urgency of debates about collective security comes, on the one side, from the many different forms of war, violence, and insecurity. But it also comes from the continued rationality of war and of the utility of coercive force. In the case of states, war remains a central instrument of government policy. Indeed, there is an important sense in which the end of the Cold War and the reduction in the dangers of nuclear confrontation increased the acceptability of war and broadened the range of goals for which military power could legally and legitimately be used. This has been especially the case for the United States and the United Kingdom. In addition to the traditional objective of hard security, coercive force has come to play an important role

[1] Even during the much acclaimed 'long peace' of the Cold War, there were around 120 wars in which over 25 million people were killed and 75 million seriously injured.

in dealing with non-traditional security threats (such as terrorism) and as a means of promoting liberal goals (as with humanitarian intervention). In addition to the on-going importance of coercive diplomacy, contemporary security challenges have provided new justifications for the use of force and for new forms of interventionism. The character of war has continued to change, as have the forms in which militaries are organized and deployed and their relationship to society. But if by 'Clausewitzian' we mean the controlled and rational use of coercive force designed to achieve political goals, it is abundantly clear that we continue to live in a 'Clausewitzian' age.[2]

At the level of international society, war was viewed within the pluralist conception as a means for the self-enforcement of basic rights, above all the right of self-defence; for the safeguarding of the balance of power; and for effecting change in the structure of the system when the pressure for change could no longer be contained nor achieved via peaceful means (such as the co-option or appeasement of rising powers). It was in this sense that war could be said to constitute an 'institution' of international society. As liberal solidarist hopes grew in the wake of the end of the Cold War, so did the neo-Grotian belief that war could be legitimately and effectively used to further the shared purposes of the 'international community' and to promote common values.[3] The collective enforcement of the decisions of the UNSC became a central element of coercive soldarism.

Finally, for many non-state groups, violence has been a rational means of achieving their objectives. This was true of the use of force by non-state political actors in the struggle for decolonization and the creation of new states and national homelands (from the African National Congress to the Zionist movement), and it remains true of many contemporary nationalist movements and many terrorist groups. In addition, in cases where the state is unable to protect property rights, to enforce contracts, and to provide security, private groups often emerge to perform these functions for a profit—hence, the provision of private contract enforcement by mafias, the economic logics to many civil wars, and the expansion of privately provided security.[4]

This chapter approaches the problem of violence and conflict from the perspective of collective security. There is sometimes a strangely detached quality to writing on collective security. Of course the failings of collective security are well recognized, and the many weaknesses of the UN are sagely and sadly acknowledged. But most of the criticism of pluralist answers to

[2] For a discussion of the end of the 'Clausewitzian age', see Martin van Creveld, *The Transformation of War* (Basingstoke, UK: Macmillan, 1991).

[3] On the evolution of the concept of the international community, see Andreas Paulus, *Die internationale Gemeinschaft im Völkerrecht* (Munich: Beck, 2001).

[4] On the former, see Diego Gambetta, *The Sicilian Mafia: The Business of Private Protection* (Cambridge, MA: Harvard University Press, 1993); on the latter, see Mats Berdal and David M. Malone (eds.), *Greed and Grievance: Economic Agendas and Civil Wars* (Boulder, CO: Lynne Rienner, 2000). On private security firms, see fn. 5 below.

security problems and still more of hegemonic or imperial answers depends on belief—often simply asserted or assumed—that a 'better' multilateral alternative can exist. A very great deal therefore depends on the recurring dilemmas of collective security and on the way in which the changing security agenda may have eased, or worsened, those dilemmas.

The chapter addresses three questions:

1. What do we mean by collective security and what has been the place of collective security in international society?

2. How have changes in the agenda of international security complicated the challenges facing international society?

3. What are the principal dilemmas that arise in relation to the practice of collective security in contemporary collective security?

The meaning of collective security

If any concept has an important conceptual history, then it is that of collective security. The phrase itself only seems to have come into general use in the 1930s, but the key ideas which underpin it have a much older history and can be found in many of the proposals for the reduction or abolition of war that have been elaborated since the sixteenth century. Five questions recur.

First, what kind of security is embodied in the phrase 'collective security'?[5] As it developed in the late nineteenth and early twentieth centuries, collective security was conceived as a response to the dangers of formal inter-state violence and, in particular, to the problem of the aggressive use of force by states. At its heart was the idea that states should either proscribe the aggressive use of force by states (or at least severely curtail the right to use armed force) and that they should take collective measures to enforce that proscription. The desire for conquest and expansion might not be easily eradicated, but, faced with the united opposition of the international community, states would come to accept that aggression simply could not pay. Yet it is important to realize that such a view of security has never exhausted the range of possibilities. Early proposals for collective action to maintain peace sought to counter both interstate violence and domestic disorder. Saint-Pierre's *Project for Settling an Everlasting Peace in Europe* of 1713 sought to protect sovereigns both against secessionist movements and 'against the ambition of irresponsible and iniquitous Pretenders and the revolts of rebellious subjects.'[6] Equally, one strand of

[5] For two classical discussions, see Inis L. Claude, *Power and International Relations* (New York: Random House, 1962), esp. ch. 4; and Maurice Bourquin (ed.), *Collective Security: A Record of the Seventh and Eighth International Studies Conference, Paris 1934–London 1935* (Paris: International Institute of Intellectual Cooperation, 1936).

[6] Quoted in F. H. Hinsley, *Power and the Pursuit of Peace* (Cambridge: Cambridge University Press, 1980), 53.

criticism of the League of Nations stressed the insufficient attention that had been given to the non-military aspects of security. And, as we shall see, central to debates in the post–Cold War period has been the argument that collective action must be developed around a much broader definition of security.

Second, security for whom? It follows from the above that the dominant conception of collective security in the twentieth century had been intended to strengthen the rights of states to independence and to reinforce an international legal order built around the concepts of sovereignty and non-intervention. According to the Wilsonian view, one of its chief attractions was that it guaranteed the independence of all states, including small and weak states. Yet the stress on reinforcing the rights of states and the sanctity of established borders against forcible change gave rise to two enduring dilemmas: first, how to accommodate change and how to avoid a collective security organization becoming an instrument for maintaining the status quo; and second, how to deal with the many sources of instability whose origin lies within the borders of states.

Third, which collectivity is involved in 'collective security'? There have always been strong arguments for the broadest possible membership of a collective security system—partly to ensure that the power of the collectivity is sufficient to deter aggression and, if necessary, to enforce its decisions; and partly to reduce the danger that collective security will merely provide a framework within which power-political competition and alliance politics are played out under a different guise. Rousseau could see all too clearly that, whilst leagues and federations of states might create peace between their members, they might also serve to reinforce and to exacerbate broader patterns of conflict. Indeed, the misuse of the term to describe alliance politics has been a recurring feature of the debate.[7] On the other hand, there have also been repeated arguments that an effective collective security system requires leadership and that the collectivity that matters will consist of a smaller group of like-minded states with the effective (as opposed to theoretical) power to enforce its decisions. Similarly, it is often argued that the notion of a global community of states will always remain an illusory goal and that regionally based collective security systems are most likely to prove effective: because such groupings have a greater understanding of the causes and nature of security problems affecting the region; because the incentives for managing conflict are likely to be higher; and because there will be a greater degree of consensus over basic values.

Fourth, what form of collectivity? It is important to disentangle two approaches to thinking about collective security systems. On one view, the

---

[7] See e.g. the comments of Aldous Huxley in 1937: 'In the actual circumstances of the present day, "collective security" means a system of military alliances opposed to another system of military alliances.' *Ends and Means* (London: Chatto & Windus, 1937), IX/109. The same could be said of the way in which the term was used during much of the Cold War.

dominant one in the recent past, collective security is understood as a means of enforcing order between independent political communities, and of achieving a degree of centralization that does not radically threaten the independence and autonomy of states. Despite some of the language in the UN Charter and some expectations to the contrary, the UN system was essentially a limited organization that was built around state and state sovereignty and a frank acceptance of hierarchical power. It was a mixture of idealism and realism. An alternative, and historically deep-rooted, conception has viewed moves towards the collective management of armed force as part of a broader process of reorganizing the political system. Many early peace proposals were aimed not solely, or even principally, at peace but rather at the reconstruction of a single political structure. Equally, much discussion of collective security in the twentieth century was closely bound up with proposals for federalism, either within Europe or on a wider scale.

And finally, what forms of collective action are envisaged in a collective security system? Collective security involves a shared understanding of what kinds of force have been proscribed and also a shared acceptance that a threat to the peace threatens the interests of all states. It also involves a shared willingness to act effectively to enforce the law and to protect those interests. Enforcement has very often been seen as critical, but not always. Much nineteenth-century liberal thought, for example, believed fervently in international law but did not see enforcement as the key. What was needed was a clear elaboration of the law and mechanisms for the fair and efficient adjudication of disputes. Rationality and understanding of one's true interests would ensure compliance. In his *Plan for a Universal and Perpetual Peace* in 1789, Bentham stressed that 'between the interests of nations there is nowhere any real conflict, if they appear repugnant anywhere it is only in proportion as they are misunderstood.'[8] Or, if rationality was not quite enough, governments would be pressed by enlightened public opinion. The arguments for effective enforcement, whether by economic sanctions or armed coercion, were given greater force by the First World War. As Wilson put it: 'In the last analysis the peace of society is obtained by force... If you say "We shall not have any war", you have to have the force to make that "shall" bite.'[9] At the same time, however, these older liberal views (or illusions) never entirely fade and there remains the hope that the paradox of war for peace can be avoided. Indeed, one of the recurring problems facing collective security has been that its most natural supporters are those least willing to make timely and credible threats to uphold the purposes and values of the collective security system.

---

[8] Jeremy Bentham, *A Plan for a Universal and Perpetual Peace* (London: Grotius Society Publications, 1927), proposition XIV.
[9] Quoted in Claude (1962: 95).

That the Cold War bears a heavy responsibility for the failure of the UN to function as it was envisaged by its creators is beyond doubt. The UN was by no means a 'pure' collective security system, particularly in relation to the existence of the veto and the special role accorded to the five permanent members of the Security Council. But there were powerful elements of collective security in the Charter, in terms of the clear prohibition of aggressive force in Article 2,4 and in the far-reaching responsibility of the Security Council for the maintenance of international peace and security, including the authorization of mandatory sanctions and military action. Whilst the phrase 'collective security' carried too many gloomy overtones of the failures of the 1930s, there was, as Michael Howard points out, a clear invocation of collective security as a basic objective of the organization in the call 'to unite our strength to maintain international peace and security'.[10]

The Cold War undermined this objective in numerous ways that have been well documented. The intensity of the confrontation between the United States and the Soviet Union undermined a system that was premised on the existence of Great Power consensus as to the nature of unacceptable aggression and on Great Power cooperation in enforcing the peace. This premise was visible, above all, in the veto given to the five permanent members. This was made necessary not solely because of the Cold War itself but because of the concentration of military power (and especially nuclear weapons) in the hands of superpowers. In such a situation, collective action could only be threatened against either of them at the risk of provoking a devastating conflict. Thus, in contrast to the neat assumptions of the collective security model, there were states that simply could not be coerced even by the united will and power of the rest of the international community. The veto highlighted, then, the clear and shared recognition that the collective security system could not deal with threats to peace emanating from the superpowers or affecting their vital interests. Contingencies in that domain would have to be dealt with by the traditional right of individual and collective self-defence as reiterated in Article 51.

The system of Cold War alliances meant that idea of an isolated aggressor was also illusory. The globalization of the Cold War, particularly after the outbreak of the Korean War, and the density of the Cold War alliance systems meant that the majority of the most serious conflicts and crises came to involve the interests of one or other of the superpowers or its allies. On the one hand, this meant that there would a friendly superpower willing to use its veto to block UN action. On the other, the intensity of the Cold War meant that loyalty to the Cold War alliance would tend to predominate over loyalty

[10] Michael Howard, 'The United Nations and International Security', in Adam Roberts and Benedict Kingsbury (eds.), *United Nations, Divided World*, 2nd edn. (Oxford: Oxford University Press, 1993), 64–5; and Paul Kennedy, *The Parliament of Man: The United Nations and the Quest for World Government* (London: Allen Lane, 2006).

to the international community. Thus, the UN proved to be, at best, of only marginal importance in any actual use or threat of force that occurred in the backyards of the superpowers (Hungary, Czechoslovakia, Afghanistan, Central America, and the Caribbean). Similarly, its role in the major crises of the Cold War was either limited (e.g. the first Berlin crisis or the Cuban missile crisis, and Afghanistan) or negligible (e.g. the second Berlin crisis, Suez, or the war in Vietnam).

It is true that resolutions were adopted under Chapter VII. But with the single exception of the Korean War, these either entailed no enforcement measures (the 1948 demand for ceasefire in Palestine, the call for Argentina to withdraw from the Falklands/Malvinas, the call for a ceasefire in the Iran–Iraq War), or enforcement was strictly limited to the imposition of economic sanctions (mandatory sanctions against Rhodesia, sanctions on weapons sales to South Africa). Because of this, the thrust of UN activity in the field of international security was concentrated on activities that were either not considered as fundamental by the drafters or not considered at all: on conciliation (supervising troop withdrawal, direct/indirect mediation); on preventative action (keeping sides apart); or on encouragement of peaceful change (decolonization, South Africa).

It is important not to exaggerate the extent to which all the problems facing the UN were simply a product of the Cold War itself. Take, for example, the changing patterns of conflict. The model of collective security assumes that there can be a clear consensus as to what precisely the unlawful use of force means and what constitutes an unlawful act of aggression. For the founding fathers at San Francisco, the kind of conflict to be proscribed, deterred, and, if necessary, collectively opposed was quite naturally a reflection of experience: clear breaches of the peace between clearly recognizable armies crossing clear and internationally accepted frontiers. Yet in the post-1945 period most violent conflict took place on the territory of one state with the international dimension being most frequently a matter of covert intervention, proxy wars, or externally supported insurgencies. In many of these cases there was a great deal of scope for debate as to whether an act of aggression or a breach of international peace and security had occurred and who was to blame. This difficulty was compounded by the heterogeneity of the international system: certainly by the ideological confrontation between East and West but also by the divide between North and South, where the struggle for decolonization was played out in what the colonial powers considered to be their internal affairs and where consensus over what constituted aggression and justified force was strained—at times to near breaking point.

The end of the Cold War seemed to many to presage a neo-Grotian moment in which increased agreement amongst the major powers, the systemic dominance of the United States and its liberal democratic allies, and the increased salience of a new range of security challenges would open the door both to a renaissance of the UN and to a broader increase in the collective element in the management of security. Events such as the 1993 Vienna Human Rights Conference and Gorbachev's 1988 speech to the General Assembly on Global Human Values seemed to open up a new era of consensus. The number of Security Council resolutions had averaged 15 per year during the Cold War but increased to an average of around 60 per year through the 1990s in the period from 1946 to 1987 only 13 resolutions had been adopted under Chapter VII; in the period from 1988 to 1997 this increased to 112. By the end of the 1990s, the UN had established 42 peacekeeping operations, the great majority taking place in the post–Cold War period and involving internal conflicts and civil wars (as in Angola, Cambodia, El Salvador, Mozambique, Rwanda, Somalia, the former Yugoslavia, and Haiti). Peacekeeping evolved in novel and significant ways, away from classic peacekeeping characterized by host state consent, the non-use of force, and impartiality, and towards so-called wider peacekeeping and robust peacekeeping as well as an increasing range of peace support and peace stabilization operations. The scope, the scale, and the range of tasks undertaken under Chapter VI operations increased dramatically. The 1990s saw the imposition by the UN of numerous economic sanctions, of both a general and more limited and targeted kind. The UN authorized the use of force by states and regional bodies, including in the cases of Iraq–Kuwait, Somalia, Haiti, Bosnia, Sierra Leone, and Liberia. Finally, in a number of cases (Eastern Slavonia, Kosovo, East Timor, and Afghanistan), the UN established international administrations which involved the effective suspension of sovereignty and the day-to-day administration of all aspects of political and economic life in the territory concerned.[11]

A changing security agenda

The period since the end of the Cold War has seen an enormous literature on the changing character of security and the changing dynamics of the global security landscape: the fading into the background of the old agenda of major power rivalry and conflict; the emergence of a wide range of new security challenges connected with civil wars, domestic social conflict, ethnic strife, refugee crises, and humanitarian disasters; intensified concern over weapons of mass destruction and over the adequacy of existing multilateral constraints on nuclear proliferation; and, of course, the way in which new weapons technologies and the infrastructure of globalization have interacted with both new and on-going forms of non-state terrorism. In many cases, these new security threats derive not from state strength, military power,

[11] The case of Bosnia-Hercegovina can be added although its authority stems from the Dayton Accords.

and geopolitical ambition, but rather from state weakness and the absence of political legitimacy, from the failure of states to provide minimal conditions of public order within their borders, from the way in which domestic instability and internal violence can spill into the international arena, and from the incapacity of weak states to form viable building blocks of a stable regional order and to contribute towards the resolution of broader common purposes.

One feature of these arguments concerns the obsolescence of the 'old' agenda.[12] The centrality of power politics and of an inescapable and ineluctable security dilemma driven by unequal power amongst states is difficult to reconcile with many features of contemporary international society. In the first place, despite the urgings of neo-realist theorists, emerging 'Great Powers' such as Germany and Japan do not seem very keen to take on the military trappings of their traditional forebears. In both cases, the balance between welfare and security goals has shifted and both see all sorts of other ways to promote their interests and objectives. Profound domestic changes and altered external circumstances have led to very different definitions of interest and, more fundamentally of identity. A second argument in this direction suggests that major war has itself become obsolete. On this view, military capacity is unnecessary given the declining role of territorial control and conquest in the definition of state power. It is irrelevant to the success and prosperity of individual states and to the management of the economic, social, and environmental problems that are characteristic of globalization. For some this is due to the nuclear revolution and the increased totality of total war which have undermined the rationality and controllability of force that was central to the pluralist world. On this view, the unthinkability of major modern conflict means that war must be seen as the breakdown of policy and politics, rather than as its servant. The costs of major conflict and political tolerance of those costs have increased exponentially—because of the high levels of economic interdependence and the impact of globalization, because of the rise in Third World nationalism and social mobilization, which has rendered old-style imperial or neo-imperial control unviable, and, finally, because of the increasingly accepted illegality and illegitimacy of the use of force and the increased unwillingness on the part of citizens in developed countries to bear the economic and human costs of war.

On the one hand, then, the classical imperatives, whether of material gain, of security and fear, or of doctrine and ideology, that produced the major wars of the nineteenth and twentieth centuries and the need for military power appear to have receded. Mercantilist impulses may well persist but these are not readily susceptible to the use of military power, nor do they obviously

---

[12] Particularly useful overviews are Robert Jervis, 'Theories of War in an Era of Leading-Power Peace', *American Political Science Review*, 96/1 (March 2002), 1–14; and Azar Gat, *War in Human Civilization* (Oxford: Oxford University Press, 2006), ch. 16.

threaten to create military conflict. On the other, modern developed societies are supposed to have learnt that major war is 'rationally unthinkable'[13]—a view that draws on the deep-rooted liberal belief that '... physical force is a constantly diminishing factor in human affairs', as Norman Angell put it in 1910.[14]

More convincingly, the force of these changes is acknowledged but placed within their regional context. In a number of regions (Western Europe, Scandinavia, North America, and parts of South America), international relations have been characterized as a reasonably well-established security community—a group of states in which 'there is real assurance that the members of that community will not fight each other physically, but will settle their disputes in some other way.'[15] Within such a community, there are dependable expectations of peaceful change, with military force gradually disappearing as a conceivable instrument of statecraft. Inequality of power takes on a very different character. Security communities may be built around a powerful core to which outside states no longer respond by balancing behaviour, but rather view as a zone of peace and security in which membership is valued.[16]

Even within and amongst these zones of relative regional pacification, liberal optimism has led to an exaggerated sense of ease that forgets its own precariousness, for example regarding the potential political impact of severe economic dislocation; the crises of identity provoked by globalization and interdependence; and the coexistence of inter-state peace with domestic violence or civil war. Indeed the often close juxtaposition of high levels of economic prosperity and successful democratic consolidation with civil war, terrorist violence, marginality, and human rights abuses strains the view that the post–Cold War world could be neatly divided into zones of peace and conflict.[17]

In many other regions, however, a much more traditional picture persists, made worse by the weaknesses and instabilities of many of the states involved. In South Asia and the Middle East, power and the dynamics of unequal power continue to play a powerful role in regional security—for example between India and Pakistan, Iran and its neighbours, or Israel and Syria.

[13] John Mueller, *Retreat from Doomsday: The Obsolescence of Major War* (New York: Basic Books, 1990).

[14] Norman Angell, *The Great Illusion: A Study of the Relation of Military Power in Nations to the Economoic and Social Advantage* (London: Heinemann, 1910), 129.

[15] Karl W. Deutsch, Sidney A. Burrell, and Robert A. Kann, *Political Community in the North Atlantic Area* (Princeton, NJ: Princeton University Press, 1957), 5.

[16] For a contemporary application of Deutsch's arguments, see Emanuel Adler and Michael Barnett (eds.), *Governing Anarchy: Security Communities in Theory, History and Comparison* (Cambridge: Cambridge University Press, 1998).

[17] Max Singer and Aaron Wildavsky, *The Real World Order: Zones of Peace/Zones of Turmoil* (Chatham, NJ, 1993).

Even discounting the alleged inevitability of geopolitical rivalry in East Asia, inequalities of power and status remain all too visible. Finally, military force has remained as relevant to many very traditional categories of conflict: border conflicts (e.g. Peru/Ecuador), securing economic advantage (e.g. the wars against Iraq or China and Sprately Islands), the promotion of ideological values whether religious (as in Iran) or secular (as with Western attempts to promote human rights and democracy), securing regime change (e.g. Angola in the Central African Republic, or the United States in Haiti or Iraq), or, finally, in the widespread use of military power to reinforce diplomacy. Of the traditional drivers for conflict, it is around resources (oil and water most notably) that much future concern is likely to revolve.

If the 'old' agenda of war and peace has receded, academic and policy debates over the past ten years have been dominated by arguments concerning the emergence of a new security agenda. According to this view, our understanding of security needs to be broadened and expanded away from the traditionalist emphasis on military power and national security—security understood fundamentally in terms of external military threats to the state. Expansionists make three core arguments.[18] In the first place, that the critical question 'whose security?' can no longer be adequately answered exclusively in terms of the state—in other words the referent object of security should include, below the state, individuals and other collectivities (minorities, ethnic groups, and indigenous peoples) and, above the state, humanity at large (people in general and not just the citizens of a particular state) and also the biosphere on which human survival depends. Second, that any meaningful analysis of security must consider the importance of a much wider range of 'existential' threats, including those whose origin lies in environmental destruction, economic vulnerability, and the breakdown of social cohesion. And third, that responsibility for the provision of security rests not just on the state but on international institutions, on NGOs and civil society operating within an increasingly active transnational civil society, and on an increasingly influential range of private actors.

Just as there is a wide-ranging debate on the meaning of security, so there is also extensive debate over the claim that the 'new' wars of the post–Cold War era represent a qualitatively new phenomenon.[19] On this view, wars are new in terms of their goals (with the far greater importance of identity politics in contrast with the geopolitical or ideological goals of earlier wars); in terms of methods of warfare (whereas old wars attempted to capture territory by

---

[18] For three influential examples, see Richard H. Ullman, 'Redefining Security', *International Security*, 8 (Summer 1983), 129–53; Jessica Tuchman Matthews, 'Redefining Security', *Foreign Affairs*, 68 (Spring 1989), 162–77; and Rothschild (Summer 1995).

[19] See e.g. Mary Kaldor, *New and Old Wars: Organized Violence in a Global Era* (Cambridge: Polity Press, 2002); see also Michael Clarke, 'War in the New International Order', *International Affairs*, 77/3 (2001), 663–71.

military means, new wars tend to avoid battles and aim to control territory through the political control of the population, with violence being directed primarily against non-combatants), and in terms of methods of financing (whilst old war economies were centralized, totalizing, and autarchic, new war economies are decentralized and heavily dependent on external resources, often involving diasporas and illegal transnational networks). Rogers makes a distinction between 'epilogue wars' which allegedly flow from past trends (as with wars of decolonization and liberation) and 'prologue wars' which are increasingly taking the form of anti-elite rebellions in the context of migratory pressures, resource scarcity, and a growing divide between rich and poor.[20] Especially in the context of terrorism, still others have stressed the role of new forms of communications and connectivity in facilitating new forms of political and military mobilization and new forms of networked violence.

These claims for novelty are contested by those who argue that, quantitatively, there has been no clear increase in the number of internal or non-traditional wars or that the crucial shift occurred in the 1960s, not in 1989;[21] and by those who deny that qualitative shift has occurred. Civil wars are not a unique feature of the post–Cold War world; the distinction between public and private violence was a feature of much historical conflict, particularly that associated with the process of state-formation; and diasporas and networks have been important in previous conflicts both ideologically (as in the Spanish Civil War) and in decolonization struggles. What is new is the salience of many internal conflicts, rather than any qualitative shift.[22] Nor is it the case that globalization makes certain sorts of violence 'naturally' more internationalized. It is the invisibility and political unimportance of many very violent conflicts that is often most striking. Nor is there any simple relationship between globalization and the role of state. Indeed, many 'new wars' have led many to reconsider the importance of state strength and to see solutions in very old-fashioned terms: how to reconstruct and remake viable nation-states as the building blocks of local or regional order. And, of course, other conflicts have seen a reassertion of state capacity (militarily and in terms of the control of borders and citizens) and of traditional ideas of national interest and national sovereignty.

---

[20] Paul F. Rogers, 'Politics in the Next 50 Years: The Changing Nature of International Conflict', October 2000, http://www.brad.ac.uk/peace/pubs/pspl1.pdf

[21] Wallensteen and Sollenberg contest the claim that the end of the Cold War saw an increase in the number of armed conflicts and, commenting on the period 1989–99, argue that of the 27 major armed conflicts active in 1999, at least 17 dated back to the period before 1989. Peter Wallensteen and Margareta Sollenberg, 'Armed Conflict, 1989–99', *Journal of Peace Research*, 37/5 (2000), 638 and 640.

[22] Mats Berdal, 'How "New" Are "New Wars"?', *Global Governance*, 9/4 (2003), 477–502; see also Stathis N. Kalyvas, ' "New" and "Old" Civil Wars: A Valid Distinction', *World Politics*, 54 (2001), 99–118.

Whatever the precise answers to these questions, there are a number of important implications which both feed into the overarching themes of this book and which complicate attempts at collective security.

In the first place, the management of many forms of contemporary insecurity is highly likely to require deep intrusion and often persistent and continuing intervention. In common with many other aspects of contemporary global governance, security is clearly a 'beyond the border' issue. Given the embeddedness of norms relating to non-intervention and to self-determination, it is hardly surprising that this both creates significant problems of legitimacy and generates nationalist resistance.

Second, a great deal of contemporary insecurity is characterized by inherent complexity and by a multiplicity of different forms of violence which overlap and are superimposed on one another. These forms of violence shift from place to place and from one period to another. It is common to distinguish between political violence on the one hand (that is violence that is planned, deliberate, carried out by organized groups of society against other groups) and individual violence on the other (purposeless, random, and individual violence).[23] Yet such a dichotomy misses out far too much and we clearly need further categories and distinctions, for example between *political violence* (civil wars and struggles between civilian and military groups, armed insurrection and revolutionary movements, and terrorism), *entrepreneurial violence* (criminal organizations whose key characteristic is the capacity to supply private protection or to use violence for profit), *community violence* (responses to lack of effective state power by communities to enforce social norms, most notably in the growth of vigilantism), *religiously sanctioned or religiously inspired violence*, and *everyday individual-level criminal violence*. Particular conceptualizations of violence can have a great impact on how violence is understood and on the policy responses that are called for. Equally clearly, there is nothing neutral in these classifications. How a particular incidence of violence is understood depends on one's political perspective. For example, one of the most important policy issues facing governments is whether to legitimize an outbreak of social violence by treating it as a political act and attempting to draw its leaders into open political dialogue. Terrorism has added a new and politically divisive twist to these long-standing dilemmas. The complexity of many new threats means that even those who share common interests and common values will often and quite legitimately differ as to the precise nature of threat, the most adequate response, or the role of use of force in that response. If old style military threats pressed alliances together, new threats

---

[23] For an overview, see Keane (1996). For the most thorough recent analysis of collective violence, see Stathis N. Kalyvas, *The Logic of Violence in Civil War* (Cambridge: Cambridge University Press, 2006), esp. 16–31.

are inherently more likely to divide than to unite. And it is entirely natural that national positions will reflect fundamentally different perspectives.

A third implication concerns the range of actors involved. In addition to the roles that NGOs have come to play in many conflict zones, there has been a significant increase in the use of coercive force on the part of private actors. The declining capacity of the state to enforce legitimate order has led in many parts of the world to the privatization of violence as diverse social groups are increasingly able to mobilize armed force, and to the privatization of security as individuals seek to protect themselves, whether through the growth of vigilantism, the formation of paramilitary groups, or the purchase of security within an expanding commercial marketplace. The move to the market and the increased role of private security firms is especially important: because of the substantive importance of PMCs in many conflict zones; because of the serious regulatory deficits that are emerging; and because of their implications for the legal categories that have played such an important role within international society (the notion of 'war' as a distinct social and legal category, the distinction between public and private violence, and the decline in the monopolization of legitimate coercion on the part of the state).[24] A war involves violence by organized groups (whether states or of other kinds) for political purposes. It is a clash between agents of political groups. This is one of the ways in which public war was to be distinguished from private violence against which there was a common purpose—hence the characterization of the pirate and the terrorist as the enemies of all humankind, *hostis humani generi*. Speaking in terms of a war therefore legitimizes a particular conflict as having a political character and as involving political actors. Given the weakness of many states, the distinctions between public and private war and the state's monopoly over legitimate violence—both of which marked the emergence of the classical state system—have been eroded with the empowering of other war-making groups and the widespread privatization of both violence and security.

Fourth, and following from the above, the changing character of the security agenda has led to a blurring of the legal categories around which the use of force has been legally, politically, and morally structured. For example, the specific challenges posed by terrorism and weapons of mass destruction (and by the threat of their coming together) have led to calls for a rethinking of the categories of pre-emptive and preventive self-defence. The US attempt to enunciate such a doctrine has been the focus of a great deal of criticism, and for good reason. As with unsanctioned humanitarian intervention, the dangers of predation and abuse appear to be unacceptably high, and the idea

---

[24] See Deborah Avant, *The Market for Force* (Cambridge: Cambridge University Press, 2005); Peter Singer, *Corporate Warriors* (Cornell, NY: Cornell University Press, 2003); and Sarah Percy, *Regulating the Private Security Industry*, Adelphi Paper 384 (London: IISS, 2007).

that a state can unilaterally decide to use force against a long-term and remote threat represents a fundamental challenge to accepted legal understandings. However, the need to engage in such rethinking has been acknowledged both in the security strategies of other states and in the UN's 2004 High Level Report. The problem is therefore a real one even if the US 'solution' is rejected. Equally, the struggle against terrorism has involved both waging war and pursuing criminals and a great deal of political contestation has resulted from differences in the balance to be accorded to the two strategies and from the tensions between them.[25] Again, the particular policies adopted by the United States, especially in relation to the treatment of detainees, have been the subject of much well-deserved criticism. But it is important to note that the structural characteristics of the struggle against terrorism make increased tensions amongst different bodies of law inevitable. These are tensions that the current international legal order is singularly ill-equipped to deal with.

Fifth, there is the important and relatively neglected role of inequality.[26] For most developing countries and states elites, the security threats that matter most are internal and are rooted in their lack of development and the uncertain and often conflictual processes of state building. Inequality enters here as part of the broader problems of underdevelopment. Inequality also needs to be seen much more directly as a central cause of many forms of social violence, ethnic conflict, and civil wars. Poverty and immiseration, overpopulation, resource scarcity, and environmental degradation foster social conflict and are thereby deeply implicated in discussions of collapsing states, the generation of refugee flows, and the background conditions which influence the degree of support for terrorist movements. Inequality (especially understood in terms of aggregate levels of deprivation) does not cause conflict in any straightforward sense. Social conflict can take many forms and cannot be reduced to any simple set of causal explanations. There is little academic consensus on exactly how inequality is related to social violence.[27] Nevertheless, most conflict studies have viewed inequality as a potentially important factor, especially when taken together with the destabilizing effects of globalization on state strength and the increased openness of societies and communities to external forces.

---

[25] For further details, see Andrew Hurrell, ' "There are no rules" (George W. Bush): International Order after September 11', *International Relations*, 16/2 (2002), 186–93.

[26] For a powerfully argued view of how the already strong link between inequality and insecurity is likely to be exacerbated by on-going environmental change, see Paul Hirst, *War and Power in the 21st Century* (Cambridge: Polity Press, 2001).

[27] For reviews, see March Irving Lichbach, 'An Evaluation of "Does Economic Inequality Breed Political Conflict?" Studies', *World Politics*, 41/4 (July 1989), 431–70; and Jenk W. Houweling, 'Destabilizing Consequences of Sequential Development', in Luc van de Goor, Kumar Rupesinghe, and Paul Sciarone (eds.), *Between Development and Destruction: An Enquiry into the Causes of Conflict in Post-Colonial States* (Basingstoke, UK: Macmillan, 1996), 143–69.

Inequality and the environment interact in potentially destabilizing ways. Homer-Dixon, for example, has highlighted the role of environmental scarcity in driving the poverty, refugee flows, ethnic tensions, and weak state institutions that are implicated in so much social conflict in the developing world.[28] Indeed inequality is more central than Homer-Dixon himself allows given that his rather natural-sounding category of 'environmental scarcity' conflates resource scarcity, population growth, and the *unequal social distribution of resources*. Inequality is also central to critical and feminist critiques which view traditional, approaches to security as having ignored the security of women, the marginal, the poor, and the voiceless. The security of these groups has been marginalized because of the narrowness and ethnocentrism of the definition of what constitutes security.[29]

Finally, and most importantly, the changing nature of the global security agenda underscores the essential contestability of security. Whose security is to be protected and promoted? Against what kinds of threats? And through the use of what sorts of instruments? Some seek to answer these questions in objective and material terms, assessing the material dangers involved, evaluating the numbers killed or threatened, and measuring the negative security externalities caused by differing forms of interdependence. In the 1990s, many aspects of the new security agenda were seen as important to 'international security', but only where drugs, social upheaval, political violence, or environmental destruction directly affected outsiders or had the potential to do so. Globalization, mass communications, and the liberalization of economic exchanges are problematic for the new security agenda because of the way in which they facilitate illicit flows of drugs, weapons, or mass migration. Seen in this way, terrorism is becoming objectively more important because of the rise of religious terrorism which increases the willingness to bear costs and to reject legal and moral constraints, because the number and lethality of terrorist attacks have increased, and because globalization and technological change has provided groups with new forms of global reach, new means of recruitment and propaganda, and new forms of financing.

And yet there is no uncontested and objective way of deciding what matters or is 'really' important. Although embodied in institutions and material forces that take on a high degree of concreteness and reality, security and securitization are intersubjective processes that are socially constructed, not objectively given, and, as such, inevitably reflect both inequalities in social

[28] For example, Thomas Homer-Dixon, 'Environmental Scarcities and Violent Conflict: Evidence from Cases', *International Security*, 19/1 (1994), 5–40. See also Chapter 9, fn 8.

[29] Keith Krause and Michael Williams (eds.), *Critical Security Studies* (Minneapolis, MN: University of Minnesota Press, 1998); J. Ann Tickner, 'Re-visioning Security', in Ken Booth and Steve Smith (eds.), *International Political Theory Today* (Cambridge: Polity Press, 1995), 175–97.

power and diversity of values. To understand what is meant by 'new security challenges' we have to open up the politics of security: understanding the political process by which issues come to be defined in terms of threats, identifying the actors that are involved in the process of securitization, and being alert to whose interests are being served by treating issues as security issues.[30] An issue becomes a security issue because a particular group (whether a state, an international organization, an NGO, a terrorist group, or the media) has successfully forced it onto the security agenda, not because it is in some objective sense important or threatening. The process of threat creation (the 'how') is therefore a central part of the explanation (the 'why'). There is no need to adopt an extreme constructivist position and to deny that certain sorts of security threats pose very broad dangers (as with a potential nuclear conflict in East or South Asia); nor to deny that there can be a strong and broadly shared interest in combating particular dangers (as with many forms of terrorist violence). There also remains a great deal of truth in the pluralist argument that a stable structure of relations amongst major powers provides the necessary political structure within which other forms of insecurity can be managed, including by multilateral institutions. Nevertheless, critical theorists and constructivists correctly alert us to the political and contested character of security and to the crucial role of unequal power in explaining whose security counts.

Others seek to answer these questions in moral terms. For advocates of human security, morality dictates that security is fundamentally about the promotion of human security in the face of all kinds of existential threats. Human security should include safety from hunger and disease as well as from all forms of violence.[31] For nationalists and communitarians, the answer is equally simple but very different. From this perspective there is no such thing as international security any more than there exists an international community. The only security that matters is the security of one's own state or community. Limited costs may be incurred to safeguard the security of other groups or to promote a more benign international environment. But such efforts must be subject to a test of national interest not merely because of the legitimate political imperatives faced by the leaders of states but also because of a particular view of what morality requires.

A great deal of the divisiveness over when it is legitimate to use force in the interest of security follows inevitably from the essentially contested character of the concept of security and from the intensely and unavoidably political character of contemporary processes of securitization. It is this which explains why an organization such as the UN will always be susceptible to the charge

---

[30] See Barry Buzan, Ole Waever, and Jaap de Wilde, *Security: A New Framework for Analysis* (Boulder, CO: Lynne Rienner, 1998).

[31] See S. Neil MacFarlane and Yuen Foong Khong, *Human Security and the UN: A Critical History* (Bloomington, MN: Indiana University Press, 2006).

of turning 'collective security' into 'selective security'. There is nothing self-evident about the statement that the greatest threat to peace and security comes from international terrorism. Indeed, from a variety of contexts, moral positions, and analytical perspectives, such a statement is manifestly wrong.

The recurring dilemmas of collective security

Building on the earlier discussion, it is helpful to distinguish between strong and weak understandings of collective security. On a strong view, every state accepts that the security of one is the concern of all and agrees to join in a collective response to threats to international peace and security. The focus is on the system as a whole and on the collective and organized efforts by states to reduce insecurity by punishing members that violate the norms of the system.[32] On the weaker view, states commit themselves to developing and enforcing generally accepted rules, norms, and principles in the area of international peace and security, and doing so through action that has been authorized by international institutions. Both versions, however, have faced four recurring dilemmas.

The dilemma of stabilizing core norms

One of the most important roles of the UN (and to a lesser extent other non-global and regional institutions) is as a site for the negotiation, evolution, and implementation of norms related to security and as a focal point for normative expectations. Central to the Charter System was, of course, the return of the old notion of *jus ad bellum* and the view that the use of force was only to be justified in case of self-defence or as authorized by the UN. In the post-Cold War period there has been a great deal of normative development in the areas of human security, humanitarian intervention, and the responsibility to protect. These developments can be analysed under three headings.

First of all, the UN became increasingly involved not simply in cases of interstate aggression (as with Iraq–Kuwait in 1990) but also in a increasingly broad range of internal matters: the protection of human rights and countering large-scale humanitarian emergencies, threats to civilians and NGOs by armed groups, dealing with refugee issues, restoring democracy, the policing of safe areas and protection zones, and the implementation of

---

[32] It is noteworthy that the UN High Level Panel spoke explicitly of the need for a collective security system, despite all of the problems associated with the concept and despite failing to address those problems. See especially Part II(D): Elements of a credible collective security system. *A More Secure World: Our Shared Responsibility*. Report of the Secretary-General's High Level Panel on Threats, Challenges and Change. United Nations (December 2004).

disarmament and arms control measures.[33] As has been widely noted, the practice of the UNSC has been to define threats to international peace and security in novel and far broader ways—although we should also note that the language of resolutions has often been cautious, balancing new goals (such as humanitarianism and democracy) with more traditional concerns (such as the loss of effective government control or the international impact of internal conflicts), and stressing the unique circumstances of the particular case.

Second, such measures were to be enforced rather than undertaken with the consent of the parties concerned (as with traditional peacekeeping but also in line with a great deal of traditional international legal practice). The erosion of consent has been most obviously apparent in direct enforcement actions involving economic sanctions or military operations and in the establishment of international administrations. But it could also be seen in the far-reaching forms of interventionism embodied in many Chapter VI operations which ranged from demilitarization to the provision of law and order, to electoral assistance and democracy;[34] in the peacekeeping operations that fell in the grey area between Chapters VI and VII; and in cases such as East Timor where 'consent' was effectively coerced. And third, these moves increasingly came, both implicitly and explicitly, to be built around an understanding of human security—the idea that human beings represent the morally fundamental referent object of security and that the sovereignty of states is, at least to some degree, contingent upon the fulfilment by their governments of their responsibilities to their citizens to refrain from at least the most serious violations of the rights of their citizens. This normative shift can be traced both in the language and negotiation of resolutions and in the broader set of practices involved in multilateral operations and in the various UN reports, statements, and proposals.[35]

However, the emergence and embeddedness of these new norms does not end contestation. As I suggested in Chapter 1, it is not helpful to juxtapose power and interests on the one side and law and norms on the other. Norms are important because of their role in shaping the ends and goals of policy and the means to secure those ends, rather than in establishing a clear set of regulatory rules that dictate what states should do. New norms open up new questions. How far, for example, did UN Charter law in relation to the use of force replace established custom? What are the circumstances that

---

[33] Terrorism has led to a further expansion, involving attempts at controlling transnational flows of terrorist financing and the assertion of far more direct authority over individuals.

[34] See Michael Doyle, Ian Johnstone, and Robert Orr (eds.), *Keeping the Peace: Multidimensional UN Operations in Cambodia and El Salvador* (Cambridge: Cambridge University Press, 1997).

[35] See MacFarlane and Khong (2006: chs. 5 and 6); ICISS (2001); *A More Secure World: Our Shared Responsibility*. Report of the Secretary-General's High Level Panel on Threats, Challenges and Change. United Nations (December 2004), especially para. 199–203; references to the literature on humanitarian intervention are given in Chapter 6.

constitute legitimate self-defence, especially in the context of recent debates on anticipatory self-defence? Moreover, many core issues remain beyond agreement. There is no agreed definition of 'aggression', just as there has been movement but no closure in reaching an agreed definition of terrorism. Equally, norms related to human security and to humanitarian intervention open up many further questions (what precisely is to count as the trigger for humanitarian intervention?); they also have to be applied to the facts of often very murky cases; and the reasons have to be debated and argued over (the so-called jurying function of the UN). As is clearly the case with humanitarian intervention, there is no settled consensus on what to do in the event that agreement within the Security Council cannot be reached. Finally, although normative debate may be narrowed, the essentially contested character of security discussed in the previous section remains, especially given the return of much harder and more traditional understandings of security in the context of the post-September 11 world.

The dilemma of containment

The second issue in the debate about collective security concerns the question of the restraints on the scope and extent of conflict. The critics of collective security have long argued that enforcement action could actually make conflict more divisive and harder to manage because of the way in which it undermines both geographical limits on the scope of conflict (above all in the concept of neutrality) and legal limits on the kinds of military force that could be employed (international humanitarian law). In the model of collective security, all states must be prepared to act against *any* state that commits a breach of the peace. In Rousseau's terms, the general will of the community must prevail over sectional interests. The moral and political imperative for the just side to win would tempt it to use whatever force was necessary to achieve that goal—irrespective of whether such force undercut internationally agreed constraints based on mutual interest and the fact that they applied equally to both sides. Collective security would also lead naturally to crusading and to couching conflicts in terms of a struggle between good and evil and this would, in turn, undermine the constraints on the form of conflict and erode the effectiveness of diplomatic and political accommodation. For Carl Schmitt: 'The Geneva League of Nations does not eliminate the possibility of war, just as it does not abolish states. It introduces new possibilities for wars, permits wars to take place, sanctions coalition war, and by legitimizing and sanctioning certain kinds of wars, it sweeps away many obstacles to war.'[36]

The notion that collective security works in a straightforward fashion against restraint is too simple. Although its implementation is often

[36] Schmitt (1976: 56).

problematic, international humanitarian law has not been abandoned or overthrown. Indeed, its importance has been consistently stressed in UNSC resolutions. In addition, all recent peacekeeping operations have protection mandates and human rights mandates. There are, nevertheless, two ways in which the theory and practice of collective security works to expand the scope of international action and involvement. The first concerns justice and punishment. In its classic forms collective security understands war in terms of an aggressor who can be identified and punished. In addition, the expansion in the 1990s of the range of threats to international peace and security came to involve many activities of an international criminal character (genocide, crimes against humanity, and transitional justice). Moving in this way towards the so-called 'domestic analogy' raises very difficult questions— about the balance between the political and the legal in the operation of the Security Council, about how just punishment is to be related to the impartiality required of traditional peacekeeping, and about the relation of justice to the often crude political deal-making around which many conflicts have traditionally been resolved. But the general move has been clearly in a politically and legally expansionist direction. The second trend towards expansion is related to the perceived necessity to engage in state-building and post-conflict reconstruction in order to secure longer-term solutions. For all the talk in the 1990 of moving beyond Westphalia, most international responses to insecurity have been conducted in a rather traditional manner: progress is to be achieved by reconstructing countries as viable nation-states, even in the most unpromising of circumstances, and maintaining the borders of existing states, even in cases where state breakdown and regional conflict have been intense.[37]

The dilemma of preponderant power

In theory collective security offers the purest solution to the dilemma of preponderance. Inequality is not to be feared, opposed, or balanced against, but is, instead, to be harnessed to the legitimate collective purposes of international society. In practice the situation is more complex. First, the veto reflects the reality of a power distribution in which attempts to coerce the major powers of the system could only be achieved at great risk and high, and in

[37] During the 1990s some commentators suggested that the combination of extreme internal state weakness or even collapse, serious sub-regional conflicts, and the emergence of new conceptions of sovereignty created the need to demonstrate that there was 'at least some fluidity in the state system', to propose regional solutions 'without regard to country boundaries', to accept the possibility of recognizing new sovereign states, and even to 'decertify failed states'. Herbst (Winter 1996–7: 120–44). Yet, although different forms of interventionism have certainly increased in number and scope, there has been very little sign of any such 'less dogmatic approach to sovereignty' in the sense of permitting or encouraging the reconstitution of states. See also Chapter 4 on national self-determination.

an era of nuclear weapons, potentially disastrous, costs. For all the illogicality of the present composition of the P5 (the permanent members of the UNSC), this remains a basic feature of the system, which reform is unlikely to alter. Second, unable to command substantial military forces in the ways envisaged by the Charter, UN enforcement action has operated by means of authorizing the use of force by member-states (as with US-led coalitions as in Iraq–Kuwait in 1990, Somalia in 1992, Haiti in 1994, or NATO in Bosnia in 1995).[38] UN authorization of limited use of force has also become the common method of enforcing sanctions, air exclusion zones, and other restrictions on particular states and their activities. This situation is always likely to create problems of effective delegation and control.[39] But these have been made worse when resolutions of the UNSC have laid out objectives to be achieved and values to be protected but have failed to specify or provide for the means by which these are to be achieved.[40]

Third, dealing with even relatively small-scale threats to peace and security requires military capacities and economic resources of a kind possessed by a relatively small group of states. It may well be the case that the rapid deployment of a small but effective 'international police force' could make a difference in particular situations (as perhaps in Rwanda in 1994). However, situations such as the Iraq–Kuwait war and in former Yugoslavia demonstrated the need for the sorts of coercive power that can only be deployed by major states and the military alliances in which they act. Equally, both the relatively successful cases of post-conflict stabilization and state-building (Namibia, Cambodia, Mozambique, El Salvador, and Timor) and the failures (as in Rwanda, Angola, Liberia, and Somalia) suggest that multidimensional peace-building cannot be achieved without a major commitment of resources.[41] A collectively drawn force in a balanced way from a wide variety of states, able

[38] The high-flown language of global governance always needs to be set against the extremely limited administrative, bureaucratic, and financial resources of those bodies purporting to govern the globe.

[39] See Danesh Sarooshi, *The United Nations and the Development of Collective Security: The Delegation by the UN Security Council of Its Chapter VII Powers* (Oxford: Oxford University Press, 1999).

[40] The space between willed ends and provided-for means was characteristic of the bombing of Iraq in December 1998 and of the NATO air attacks in March 1999. The United States and the United Kingdom sought legal justification for the use of force against Iraq in March 2003 on the basis that previous UNSC resolutions provided 'continuing authority'. Whilst there are very good legal reasons for disputing such claims, the general point remains valid. If international society is capable only of such actions in the field of international security built around the authorization of individual states or groups of states to act on its behalf, what sense does it make to deny those states the autonomy to carry through the agreed goals? See Adam Roberts, 'Willing the End but not the Means', *The World Today* (May 1999), 8–12; and 'Legal Controversies in the War on Terror', keynote address, US Pacific Command, International Military Operations and Law Conference, Singapore, 21–4 March 2005, 4–5.

[41] Michael Doyle and Nicholas Sambanis, 'International Peacebuilding: A Theoretical and Quantitative Analysis', *American Political Science Review*, 94/4 (2000), 778–801.

to act effectively and not dominated by any single power, is unlikely in most imaginable situations. But the particular distribution of power in the post–Cold War world and the military predominance of the United States have made this problem far more acute.

The effectiveness of collective action has therefore continued to depend on restricting decision-making and action to a small number of powerful states that have both capability and willingness to act. On the one side, this leads naturally to the risk of selectivity in terms of which security issues are to be addressed and to the all-too-evident danger that the collective will of the 'international community' will be contaminated by the special interests and preferences of particular states. In addition, since the mid-1980s more and more business has been conducted in informal yet structured negotiations and consultations amongst the P5.[42] The Security Council thus appears as an instrument in the hands of the most powerful. On the other, major states, and especially but by no means only the United States, remain resistant to having their hands tied by a multilateral body. The Security Council is an unwelcome constraint that stands in the way of both national interest and the actions necessary to safeguard international security. It is partly because of these divergent pulls that the proliferation of formal multilateral institutions has been accompanied by the continuing importance of informal groupings of states—contact groups, core groups, groups of friends—that act in and around formal bodies.[43]

The dilemma of common interest

The final issue concerns the relationship between law and principle on the one hand and state interest on the other. The model of collective security assumes that each member of international society be prepared to see an aggression anywhere as a threat to the peace and to view an attack on one as an attack on all. Peace, in other words, must be seen as indivisible. In addition, the model assumes that states be prepared to act decisively on this recognition even if such action is costly and goes against their more immediate short-term interests. For the self-styled realist critics of the 1940s, these assumptions were simply fallacious and inherently flawed. It might be that a state's political interests coincided with opposition to a particular aggression. But this could never be an absolute or automatic conclusion. Whether a state responded to a particular act of aggression would be determined by the overall pattern of its foreign policy interests. As Morgenthau put it:

---

[42] See especially David Malone, *The International Struggle over Iraq: Politics in the UN Security Council, 1980–2005* (Oxford: Oxford University Press, 2006).

[43] See Prantl (2005: 559–92).

The only question collective security is allowed to ask is: 'Who has committed aggression?' Foreign policy cannot help asking: 'What interest do I have in opposing this particular aggressor and what power with which to oppose him?'[44]

In an anarchical world of conflict and power competition, the responsibility of the statesman was to his own community and to the national interests of that community. In such a world, no overarching moral imperative to oppose unjust aggression and to defend all states against such aggression could be allowed to prevail over a state's own national interest. Why not? Partly because the moral responsibility of the statesman was necessarily and justifiably to his national community, and partly because the logic of collective security rested on an erroneous understanding of the nature of international order. Collective security envisaged order in terms of law and international legal structures. For the realists, such precarious order as obtained in international life was a function not of law but of power. It rested on the inequality of states, on the balance of power between states, and the manipulation and management of that balance by skilled diplomatists. Moreover, the problem was not simply that collective security did not work; it was that the illusion of trying to make collective security work would undermine the functioning of more limited but more realistic means to promote both national interest and at least a degree of international order. This was the real failing of the League in the 1930s.

The events that led from September 11 to the resort to war in 2003 against Iraq without the authorization of the Security Council saw a resurgence of many of these old arguments. For many they reinforced the obvious truth of the Schimittian position, namely that, in times of war, it is for the state to decide for itself when exceptional measures have to be taken, irrespective of what international law or institutions might say. More broadly, they reinforced the belief that attempts to subject the use of force to the rule of law were doomed to fail and, if law is to enter the picture at all, it can only be by staying close to the realities of power. During the Cold War attempts to subject the use of force to the rule of law had been undermined by the intensity of the bipolar confrontation between the superpowers. In the post–Cold War world, they are undermined by the scale and extent of US power.[45]

The black and white view of both the traditional realist critics and the more recent doubters overstates the nature of the choice and fails to specify

---

[44] Hans J. Morgenthau, *Politics among Nations*, 5th edn. (New York: Alfred A. Knopf, 1978), 420; see also Henry Kissinger, *Diplomacy* (London: Simon and Schuster, 1994), 249; and John J. Mearsheimer, 'The False Promise of International Institutions', *International Institutions*, 19/3 (Winter 1994–5), 5–49.

[45] See e.g. Michael J. Glennon, 'Why the Security Council Failed', *Foreign Affairs* 82/3(May–June 2003), 16–35. Compare with Hans Morgenthau's famous article of 1940, 'Positivism, Functionalism and International Law', *American Journal of International Law*, 34 (1940), 261–84.

the conditions under which the limits and constraints bite most deeply. In the first place, neither interests nor identities are fixed for all time. Hence, the defenders of the logic of collective security in the UN High Level Panel Report argue that state interests are changing, and will continue to change, because of increasing interconnectivity, mutual vulnerability, and the impossibility of unilateral defence; and that these changes will increase the incentives for cooperation.[46] As we have already noted, international institutions have helped to embed new legal understandings of human security and the responsibility to protect in ways which do not determine state policy but which shape how state interests are understood and how the costs and benefits of different policy choices are debated and sold politically.

Second, there are many instances of insecurity in which some practical or moral interest is engaged, but of a limited character. In such cases, the realist critique that to act collectively is necessarily to put core national interests at risk is overblown. In these cases, the burden-sharing and the legitimacy benefits provided by multilateralism are considerable and help explain why in 2004 there were some 60,000 troops from 96 states participating in UN operations, in addition to the roles of the EU in Macedonia and Eastern Congo; NATO in Kosovo; Afghanistan and Bosnia; and Economic Community of West African States (ECOWAS) in Liberia. But even on matters of major importance, the incentives pressing states towards engagement with multilateral institutions remain considerable, above all because of the problems of legitimacy. These problems have been increased by the changing character of security challenges, particularly in terms of their non-state, intrastate, and transnational characters which inevitably raise politically difficult questions of selectivity, moral contestability, and unavoidably deep intrusion into the organization of domestic society. For all of the failures associated with the UN, its defenders argue powerfully, and correctly, that interest and institutional engagement can coincide even for the strong: partly because of the burden-sharing opportunities created by effective multilateralism, partly because the multilateralism has a rather better record in the immensely difficult task of state and nation-building, but most especially, because of the unique role of the UN as the source of collective legitimation for the use of force and the forum within the norms surrounding the use of force are maintained, developed, and interpreted.[47] The importance of mobilization, justification,

---

[46] The idea that there is a shared interest in a peaceful and stable world has often been linked to the growth of interdependence. As Alain Plaunt put it in 1934: 'The idea of collective security springs out of the economic and scientific interdependence of the modern world', in Maurice Bourquin, *Collective Security: A Record of the Seventh and Eighth International Studies Conference, Paris 1934—London 1935* (Paris: International Institute of Intellectual Cooperation, 1936), 133.

[47] The classic statement is from Inis Claude, 'Collective Legitimation as a Political Function of the United Nations', *International Organization*, XX/3 (1966), 367–79; see, more recently,

and legitimation in the context of the so-called 'long war against global terror' has been evident, as have the high costs of unilateral action that was both widely perceived as illegitimate and which made the subsequent task of burden-sharing and on-going cooperation much harder.

And yet, although the collective *element* in security management has increased, we remain as far away as ever from anything approaching a functioning *system* of collective security. Peace is not indivisible, and states and their citizens remain unwilling to bear the costs of collective action in complex and dangerous conflicts in which their direct interests are only weakly engaged. It may well be that the horrors of the Rwanda genocide prompted increased normative momentum in the areas of human security and the responsibility to protect. But the continued failure of outside states to undertake effective action in Dafur highlights the continuity of the problem. The problem is not just one of initial unwillingness to act; just as serious is the reluctance of member-states to follow up on their post-conflict peace-building (even in cases such as Afghanistan where substantial national interests would appear to be at stake). The UN is a site for interstate diplomatic activity, as well as a stage for important forms of political theatre and symbolic politics.[48] But it is also a dustbin into which leaders seek to throw problems that they cannot solve and the capacity of the organization to 'act' remains extremely limited. Its many failures are overwhelmingly the failures of individual states rather than of the organization.

Nor is it the case that the problem of collective security can be understood simply as a problem of capturing a well-understood common interest and being able to overcome the well-known problems of defection and freeriding.[49] Although defection and freeriding are certainly severe problems, this is a hopelessly over-optimistic way of characterizing the problem. Circumstances, contexts, and values mean that there can be no easily shared answer to the question of whose security or against which threats that security is to be promoted. International order is not an easily agreed commodity in which everyone has an equal stake. States are unlikely to defend the status quo unless they are convinced that it embodies their own interests, their own values, and their own conceptions of social justice. Northedge's comment on the 1930s remains all too relevant: 'Seen through the eyes of different states, the world may seem to one group a familiar and perhaps acceptable place, which suits

Mats Berdal, 'The UN Security Council: Ineffective but Indispensable', *Survival*, 45/2 (2003), 7–30.

[48] See what continues to be one of the best books on the UN, Conor Cruise O'Brien, *The United Nations: Sacred Drama* (London: Hutchinson, 1968).

[49] See e.g. George W. Downs (ed.), *Collective Security Beyond the Cold War* (Ann Arbor, MI: University of Michigan Press, 1994), especially part I.

their interests and accords with their sort of game; to another group it may seem the very incarnation of wrong?'[50]

Conclusion

In terms of security—as with so many of the other issues discussed in this book—our understanding of what it is legitimate, indeed perhaps necessary, to expect from the international political system has grown enormously. These expectations lead inevitably away from a pluralist security order built around minimalist norms of coexistence and in which the balance of power played a central role, and towards a security order that both seeks much tighter control over the use of force and reaches deep into the ways in which domestic societies are organized. The normative ambitions of international society in relation to security have therefore come to include: progressively tighter limits on legitimate justifications for the use of force by states, more effective control over the development and proliferation of weapons of mass destruction, and increased concern for the security of an expanded range of social groups against an expanded range of threats.

This greatly increased normative ambition has been driven in part by moral concerns. However uneven and inconsistent such concerns may be, major states have been unable to define their interests solely in narrow instrumental or power-political terms. But it has also been driven by this pragmatic pressures which have increasingly linked the security of the rich with the insecurity of the poor. For those affected by state breakdown or large-scale social violence, security and the provision of public order remains a precondition for sustained and equitable development. For those in the developed world, the dangers of diffusion and spillover remain very real. However difficult it may be to measure and assess particular linkages, it is highly implausible to believe that, over the medium term, those living in the richest parts of the world will be able to insulate themselves from the instability and insecurity of the rest. Nor can the countries of the North do without the political support of major developing countries if collective and cooperative solutions are to be found to global problems.

Clearly, many contemporary security problems, including not only terrorism but also threats related to civil violence, migration, and environmental degradation are not readily susceptible to military responses, or to military responses alone. There is a widely shared sense that new security issues need to be tackled within the context of economic and political

[50] F. S. Northedge, *The League of Nations* (Leicester, UK: Leicester University Press, 1986), 289.

191

development because of the resistance of new security challenges to resolution via traditional security instruments. The interpenetration of security and development issues is illustrated by the way in which regional and international financial institutions have increasingly had to grapple with political and security issues, adding 'peace conditionalities' to the ever-growing list of non-economic factors that influence their lending policies.[51] It is also the case that responsibility for the provision of security has shifted away from the state to include groups within civil society, private military companies and international organizations. Yet it is states and states alone that command the legitimate military power to promote both individual state interest and the common goals (such as collective security or humanitarian intervention) that require coercive capacity and socialized power.

To a much greater extent than realists acknowledge, states need multilateral security institutions both to share the material and political burdens of security management and to gain the authority and legitimacy that the possession of crude power can never on its own secure. If we think of the architecture of global security, different forms of collective security have come to bear a modestly greater weight, whilst the evolving legal rules in relation to the use of force and the broader security-related norms of the UN have come to influence both the construction and functioning of many other parts of the building. However, major aspects of the structure continue to have little or nothing to do with formal institutions, still less with the idea of collective security. They remain firmly rooted in the pluralist world.

During the Cold War, the central elements of the global security architecture were built (often dangerously and precariously) around nuclear deterrence, the alliance systems developed around the two superpowers, and a set of loose pluralist institutions (involving norms and practices of crisis management, arms control, and spheres of influence). In the post-Cold War world, many aspects of the system have continued to play a decisive role, most notably in the US-led alliance systems that reach across the Atlantic and Pacific. Although major power relations are in a state of flux as unipolarity fades, the balance of military power and the character of security relations amongst the major powers continue to play their traditional role as important determinants of the overall structure. Equally in many regions the security order is structured around balanced or hierarchical power. This may be supplemented by a range of institutions, but, with the exception Europe, these are institutions whose scope and impact remains limited. Finally, the renewed

---

[51] This chapter has concentrated on the UN's roles in relation to peace and security. There are many complex issues relating to the UN 'system' more generally, to the problems of many agencies, and to the way in which they relate, or not, to each other. For an overview of the UN's roles, see Roberts and Kingsbury (1993: ch. 1). For a critical view, see Rosemary Richter, *Utopia Lost: The United Nations and World Order* (New York: Twentieth Century Fund, 1995).

centrality of nuclear weapons suggests that deterrence will continue to play a major role in global security. The renewed importance of nuclear power and nuclear weapons reflects many factors but has resulted in the erosion of an important element of collective management of security, namely the Nuclear Non-Proliferation Treaty. If such trends continue, they will lead to a further diffusion of effective power, something that cannot but weaken the prospects for collective security in the future.

This chapter has sought to trace the role of collective security in contemporary international society and the recurring dilemmas to which it gives rise. It has also sought to highlight and explain the vast gulf that continues to exist between the normative ambitions of international society in the field of security and the power-political structures on which effective responses have depended; and between the increased demands for security from a growing range of subjects against a growing range of threats and the very modest degree of protection that is all too often available.

8

Economic globalization in an unequal world

More than any other single idea globalization has become a central part of the rhetoric of contemporary world politics and the subject of increasing volumes of academic analysis. It is the most common term to capture the sense of radical and increasing change in the character of global politics. It resists any single or simple definition but the many strands within the globalization debate are fundamental to the analysis of the changing character of international society and the emergence of new ideas about global governance. Although often associated with claims that the present world system is undergoing a structural transformation, it is an old idea. This chapter addresses four questions:

1. What is globalization?
2. What has been the impact of globalization on the state?
3. What is the relationship between globalization and inequality and in what ways has this influenced the question of legitimacy?
4. How far has globalization reinforced the element of consensus in international society and, in particular, consensus behind a liberal solidarist conception of international society?

Globalization

There is a long tradition of writers emphasizing the external economic constraints that act upon nation-states and the transforming impact of global economic processes. By the mid-nineteenth century, it was widely held that the industrial revolution and the development of capitalism were transforming world politics. As Marx and Engels famously suggested:

The need of a constantly expanding market for its products chases the bourgeoisie over the whole surface of the globe. It must nestle everywhere, settle everywhere,

194

establish connections everywhere.... The bourgeoisie has through its exploitation of the world market given a cosmopolitan character to production and consumption in every country. ... In place of the old wants, satisfied by the productions of the country, we find new wants, requiring for their satisfaction the products of distant lands and climes. In place of the old local and national seclusion and self-sufficiency, we have intercourse in every direction, universal interdependence of nations.[1]

In 1910, Norman Angell argued that 'the very complexity of the division of labour tends to set up cooperation in groups which right athwart political frontiers, so that the political no longer limits or coincides with the economic... in a thousand respects association cuts across state boundaries, which are purely conventional, and render the biological division of mankind into independent and warring states a scientific ineptitude'.[2] Such beliefs reflected the dramatic expansion in the scale and globalizing character of economic relations that had taken place during the golden age of internationalism in the period from 1850 to 1914—the revolution in transport and communication (steamships, railways, the telegraph, and refrigeration); the mass migration of peoples and the intense activism of transnational civil society; and the extent to which private economic actors were able to exercise immense influence over the fortunes and fate of both colonial societies and formally independent states—think for instance of the impact of British banks, finance houses, insurance companies, and public utilities in nineteenth-century Latin America or Asia.[3]

Such themes were revived in the late 1960s and early 1970s when writers on interdependence and modernization argued that the rapid expansion of international trade and investment, the increased awareness of ecological interdependence, the declining utility of military power, and the increasing power of non-state actors (transnational corporations [TNCs] but also religious organizations and terrorist groups) constituted a systemic shift that would increasingly undermine the traditional role and primacy of nation-states.[4] The 1970s literature on interdependence faded under pressure from two sources. First, the reappearance of superpower confrontation and the second Cold War appeared to justify those who took a more Hobbesian view of international life, dominated by military and ideological confrontation rather than by economic exchange. Second, within academia, statists and realists

---

[1] David McLellan (ed.), *Karl Marx: Selected Writings* (Oxford: Oxford University Press, 1977), 224. Many of Marx's most powerful statements on the global expansion of capitalism can be found in Shlomo Avineri (ed.), *Karl Marx on Colonisation and Modernisation* (New York: Doubleday, 1968).

[2] Norman Angell, *The Great Illusion: A Study of the Relation of Military Power in Nations to their Economic and Social Advantage* (London: Heinemann, 1910), 157.

[3] See O'Rourke and Williamson (1999). For an excellent overview of the historical background to present debates, see Wolf (2004: chs. 7 and 8).

[4] See e.g. Richard Cooper, *The Economics of Interdependence: Economic Policy in the Atlantic Community* (New York: McGraw-Hill, 1968).

responded vigorously, arguing, for example, that TNCs were closely tied to states and to patterns of interstate politics (Robert Gilpin); that the state was still the most important institution of international order (Hedley Bull); that military power had not declined in its utility (Robert Art); and, most important of all, that the international political system with its dominant logic of power balancing remained the most important element of any theory of international politics (Kenneth Waltz, Stephen Krasner).

However, with the end of the Cold War, academic interest shifted back to the role of external or global economic factors, this time under the broad banner of 'globalization'. Globalization has become a very powerful metaphor for the sense that the world is becoming increasingly integrated and interconnected. The prevailing image of globalization is one of a global flood of money, people, images, values, and ideas overflowing the old system of national barriers that sought to preserve state autonomy and control. Indeed, globalization has been increasingly seen as the most important external influence on both the character of societies and dominant patterns of governance. It is far from easy to gather the wide variety of meanings attached to the term globalization.[5]

At one level it appears simple. Globalization is about the universal process or set of processes which generate a multiplicity of linkages and interconnections which transcend the states and societies which make up the modern world system. It involves a dramatic increase in the density and depth of economic, ecological, and societal interdependence, with 'density' referring to the increased number, range, and scope of cross-border transactions; and 'depth' to the degree to which that interdependence affects, and is affected by, the ways in which societies are organized domestically.[6] We can also think about globalization as having three 'faces'. One face concerns 'who is observing what': the way in which an increase in transactions and interconnectedness amongst (especially OECD and selected other) states can be 'observed' by scholars, economists, and other onlookers. The second face of globalization is about 'who is experiencing what', and the understandings, meanings, and constructions of globalization as it is experienced by actors in very different positions across the globe. Some capture this latter face of globalization by describing it as a mode of thought, an emerging change in identity and

[5] The literature is vast. For useful places to start, see the following: Ngaire Woods (ed.), *The Political Economy of Globalization* (Basingstoke, UK: Macmillan, 2000); Held et al. (1999); Jan Art Scholte, *Globalization: A Critical Introduction*, 2nd edn. (Basingstoke, UK: Palgrave, 2005); David Held and Anthony McGrew (eds.), *The Global Transformations Reader*, 2nd edn. (Cambridge: Polity Press, 2003); Joseph S. Nye and Robert O. Keohane, 'Globalization: What's New? And What's Not? (And So What?)', *Foreign Policy*, 118 (2000), 104–12; and Michael Zürn, 'From Interdependence to Globalization', in Walter Carlsnaes, Thomas Risse, and Beth Simmons (eds.), *Handbook of International Relations* (London: Sage, 2002), 255–74.

[6] See Andrew Hurrell and Ngaire Woods, 'Globalisation and Inequality', *Millennium*, 24/3 (1995), 447–70.

discourse or an intensification of consciousness of the world as a whole. And the third face of globalization involves seeing it in terms of changes in the mode of operation of major international actors—the organizational forms that firms develop for new global production networks or the extent to which NGOs have come to think globally and to develop global strategies for their operations and their advocacy.[7]

In reality, much of the muddle and inconclusiveness of the debates on globalization stems from the ambiguities of the concept. Globalization is sometimes presented as a causal theory: certain sorts of global processes are held to cause certain kinds of outcomes. Sometimes, it is a collection of concepts, mapping (but not explaining) how the changing global system is to be understood. And sometimes it is understood as a particular kind of discourse or ideology (often associated with neo-liberalism). There are also an important distinction between economistic readings of globalization (that stress increased inter-state transactions and flows of capital, labour, goods and services) and social and political readings (that stress the emergence of new forms of governance and authority, new arenas of political action ['deterritoralization' or the 'reconfiguration of social space'], or new understandings of identity or community).[8] Within economistic readings, there are also distinctions between a traditional focus on inter-state economic transactions and the argument that the most significant changes are to be found in the emergence of new highly integrated transnational production-structures and new forms of de-territorialized markets. Distinctions are also drawn between globalization, internationalization, Westernization, and modernization. And there is the important distinction between the claim that globalization should be seen as the continuation of a deep-rooted set of historical processes and the view that contemporary globalization represents a critical breakpoint or fundamental discontinuity in world politics.

Globalization and the state

The alleged demise of the territorial, sovereign state has been a persistent feature of writing on economic globalization. This was true in the early years of the twentieth century, in the late 1960s, and again in the 1990s.[9]

---

[7] See Thomas J. Biersteker, 'Globalization as a Mode of Thinking in Major Institutonal Actors', in Ngaire Woods (ed.), *The Political Economy of Globalization* (Basingstoke, UK: Macmillan, 2000), 147–72.

[8] Highlighting a particular aspect of globalization determines the way its history is understood. In economic terms, for example, it is clear that the period 1918–45 saw a dramatic decline in the openness and integration of the global economy. But the influenza epidemic of 1918 was also a manifestation of globalized connections (especially in terms of the movement of servicemen). It killed twice as many people as the First World War and foreshadowed our present concern with the transnational character of infectious diseases.

[9] Compare: 'The state is about through as an economic unit' (Charles Kindleberger, 1966); 'For the first time in 400 years, the territorial political unit and the economic unit are no

Perhaps the most important single idea concerns the growing disjuncture between the notion of a sovereign state directing its own future, the dynamics of the contemporary global economy, and the increasing complexity of world society. Indeed, globalization breathed new life into many of the core liberal claims about the changing character of world politics: the multiple and ever-increasing links that exist between societies, many of which are either beyond the direct control of governments or can only be controlled with tremendous difficulty; the consolidation (if not novelty) of the role of many more actors, both corporations and NGOs; the increasing irrelevance of military power for solving the key issues on the international agenda, whether promoting global financial stability or tackling climate change. This view has been particularly strongly held by those who see economic globalization as driven by technological development. New technologies, especially when allied to powerful market forces, constantly create new challenges even for those states that are keenest to assert their control (e.g. Chinese attempts to control the Internet) or for the most powerful states (the vulnerability of the United States to those who seek to use the technologies of globalization as part of a campaign of terrorism). There is a dialectical relationship between globalization challenges and state responses. But, on this view, it is technologically driven globalization that is faster and smarter.

Earlier chapters have already considered several of the general arguments—the degree to which globalization has created the conditions for an ever more intense and activist transnational civil society that challenges the state as the dominant locus of identity and as the primary site of political mobilization; and the extent to which states have become far more deeply enmeshed in a web of international institutions. To these we should add the more specific arguments about the impact of economic globalization on state capacity and state autonomy. Hence it is widely argued that certain sets of economic policy tools have ceased to be viable and that states face ever-increasing pressures to adopt increasingly similar pro-market policies. Because of the increasing power of financial markets, governments are forced into pursuing macro-economic policies that meet with the approval of these markets. As Garrett puts it in reviewing this literature, governments 'are held to ransom by the markets, the price is high, and punishment for non-compliance is swift'.[10] Increasing trade also places governments under pressure to adopt pro-market

---

longer congruent' (Peter Drucker, 1969); the state is a 'a very old fashioned idea and badly adapted to serve the needs of our present complex world' (George Ball, 1969); 'The nation state has become an unnatural, even dysfunctional, unit for organizing human activity and managing economic endeavor in a borderless world. It represents no genuine, shared community of economic interest; it defines no meaningful flows of economic activity' (Kenichi Ohmae, 1993).

[10] Geoffrey Garrett, 'Global Markets and National Politics: Collision Course or Virtuous Circle', *International Organization*, 52/4 (1998), 793.

policies, avoiding policies which would imply the need to harm business by taxation, or to raise interest rates as a consequence of increased borrowing. They find themselves forced to cut back the role of the public sector in order to attract inward investment from increasingly footloose multinational companies quick to punish governments who stray from the path of economic righteousness by exercising their exit option. Consequently, the range of policy options open to governments is claimed to be dramatically reduced. Social democratic parties in particular have had to adjust their policy pro-posals, as traditional left-of-centre economic programmes, focused on active government involvement in economic activity, along with generous welfare state provisions, will simply trigger the wrath of both the multinationals and the markets.

Against such claims, a number of powerful arguments have been made. First, and most generally, it is extremely unhelpful to see states and markets as necessarily in opposition. As we have seen already complex global markets depend on a dense set of rules and norms, on secure systems of property rights and of contract, and on civil order that only states can provide. Financial mar-kets can impose huge costs on states, but the operation of the global financial system depends on an institutionalized interstate order with well-respected rules and national economies that are under the control of reasonably well-functioning states.[11]

Second, there are empirical grounds for scepticism concerning the more exaggerated claims made for the impact of external pressures, both in terms of the reality of the systemic phenomena themselves, and also their effects on nation-states. They point to the mounting empirical grounds for doubt, for example: that levels of globalization are not higher or more intense than in earlier periods (especially the period before the First World War); and that there is no clear evidence of state retreat, of welfare states being cut back because of globalization pressures, of transnational capital standing in automatic opposition to social welfare, or of globalization being the most important factor in explaining levels of inequality in OECD countries. It is impossible to survey what is a large and ever-expanding literature in any detail here. Nor is it necessary to side with the arch-sceptics who deny that globalization matters at all. It is only necessary to stress that, whilst many of the changes and challenges of globalization are very real, they do not point in a single direction and certainly do not provide secure grounds for accepting the claim that some sort of deep change or fundamental transformation is under way.

Third, the critics point out that globalization has not been driven by some unstoppable logic of technological innovation but by specific sets of

---

[11] Peter Evans, 'The Eclipse of the State? Reflections on Stateness in an Era of Globalization', *World Politics*, 50/1 (1997), 62–87.

state policies, backed by specific political coalitions. This suggests that states themselves are not passive players and that the impact of globalization will often depend on national-level political and institutional factors. Equally, even where liberalizing effects can be attributed to globalization, it is not always the case that this implies state retreat—as in the process whereby privatization and deregulation at the domestic level have involved re-regulation at the level above the state. Nor does globalization inevitably push governments towards declining state activism. It can, on the contrary, lead to increased pressure on government to provide protection against the economic and social dislocations, as well as security challenges that arise from increased liberalization and external vulnerability.

Fourth, the critics remain deeply unconvinced by the argument that states in general (as opposed to particular states) have become irredeemably enmeshed in new structures of global governance, highlighting the degree to which international institutions are created by states for particular purposes and the evident capacity of powerful states to resist or even abandon such institutions. It is precisely in the area of global economic governance that institutionalist theory has produced some of its most penetrating analysis. Increasing integration and the high mobility of actors create many negative externalities and a strong demand for the production of international public goods. States create institutions and delegate (limited) authority to them precisely in order to manage those externalities, to capture the benefits of collective decision-making and institutionalized dispute resolution, and enhance domestic policy commitments and 'lock-in' particular sets of domestic economic policies. Many who press this line of argument suggest that institutions can be profitably analysed in terms of the controlled and limited delegation of certain functions by states in order to achieve certain limited purposes. In other words states remain firmly in the driving seat.[12]

Fifth, the degree and nature of state control of the economy is closely linked to security concerns. Thus the move to economic multilateralism is very hard to understand except against the background of the Second World War and the Cold War. Equally, a dominant theme of world politics since 2001 has been the attempt to reassert state control over transnational flows— of people, of ideas, of military technology, and of money. Moreover, again as in the Cold War, military power is not only important within the security sphere but also because of the way in which the security dependence of other states on the United States allows Washington to attain influence over economic matters. This leads to a final and more general argument about the relationship between politics and economics. It is after all politics and

---

[12] This is why the idea of delegation and the application of principal–agent models have become so influential. See e.g. Daniel L. Nielson and Michael J. Tierney, 'Delegation to International Organizations: Agency Theory and World Bank Environmental Reform', *International Organizaton*, 57 (2003), 241–76; and, more generally, Kahler and Lake (2003).

power that make political economy political. Marx wrote brilliantly about the expansive, transforming, and universalizing power of global capitalism and about the tensions that recur as the transforming development of technology and productive relations grates and grinds against the rigidities of political and social structures. His great blind spot, shared by many technologically obsessed liberals, was his belief that, in the end, economic structures are all-determining and his inability to grasp the autonomous logic of security and power-political competition—whether we are talking about the response of states to new security challenges or the continued role of balance of power logics amongst major states.

It is clear, then, that globalization has not led to the demise of the state. However, these black and white arguments for and against 'the state' do not take us very far. It is not enough to say that, because states have freely chosen to embark on liberalization, they are in control. There are certainly important examples of where changes in the operation of markets have made regulation intrinsically harder. Global finance provides a clear example. Global financial markets are more open, more liquid, and more internationally integrated than ever before with an increased number of market actors and an ever-increasing range of market operations. It is highly misleading to view power as a lump that can be carved up: more power for me means less power for you. Indeed, there are good reasons for arguing that globalization has resulted in a general diffusion of power and an international and global system that is much harder for anyone to control or govern.

Equally, the continued role of states does not mean that either individually or collectively states have been, or will be, able to create the sorts of effective institutions necessary to provide effective and legitimate economic governance. After all, a major criticism of functionalism is that the functional demand for institutions is in many cases not met because it does not mesh with the interests and incentives of powerful political and economic agents. In addition, the ideology of globalization may itself be part of the problem. As Evans puts it: 'The fact that private transnational actors need competent, capable states more than their own ideology admits does not eliminate the possibility of eclipse. The calculations of even sophisticated managers are biased by their own ideology. Bent on maximizing its room for maneuver, transnational capital could easily become an accomplice in the destruction of the infrastructure of public institutions on which its profits depend'.[13]

Analysing the relationship between 'globalization' and the 'state' presses us to think about the profound transformation in the role of the state that gathered pace from the early years of the twentieth century—away from a narrow concern with the wealth and power of the sovereign and towards ever-

---

[13] Evans (1997: 72).

deeper involvement in an increasing number of aspects of social, economic, and political life. In this process, the legitimacy of governments (democratic and authoritarian) came to depend on their capacity to meet a vastly increased range of needs, claims, and demands. In part this involved increased expectations of the role of the state in economic management, something that remains substantially true even in an era of deregulation, privatization, and globalization. In part it reflected changed notions of political legitimacy and broadened understandings of self-determination, of human rights, and of citizenship rights. In the case of the developed world, we saw the emergence of an embedded liberal bargain in which the commitment to open markets externally was balanced both by limits on external openness (most especially through the control of capital markets) and, more importantly, by an activist state able to promote social and economic stability.[14] In the case of the post-colonial and developing world, we saw the emergence of national-developmental states implementing policies of import-substitution industrial-ization (ISI) and balancing the twin goals of development and autonomy. The emergence of the welfare state, the regulatory state, and the developmental state is crucial for understanding why *the politics of globalization* in the late twentieth and early twenty-first century are so very different from a century earlier when interactions and interdependencies of different kinds were at a similarly high, or even higher, level.

The causes of this transformation are beyond the scope of this chapter. But they cannot be simply viewed as 'domestic-level factors'. What states are, what purposes they seek to promote, and their capacity to promote them, has long been shaped by one-world forces and factors, and by the changing patterns of political and economic power and dominance in the international system. In the twentieth century, many of the most important changes in the character of states were driven by developments in the international system. Thus the vast expansion of European state power and state functions was closely bound up with the geopolitical conflicts of the period from 1870 to 1989 and with the transnational ideological confrontation between liberalism, fascism, and communism. War and transnational ideological conflict drove the expansion of the state: with the advent of total war, the range of state agencies and ministries increased, budgets and levels of taxation soared, and the scope and range of legislation expanded.[15] It is only within the context of these systemic pressures that we can understand the shifting boundaries between politics and the market and between the public and private spheres, as well as the emergence of new understandings of the responsibilities of the state to its citizens as reflected in both an expanded conception of social rights and,

---

[14] John Ruggie (1998).
[15] On the increasing economic role of the state, see Vito Tanzi and Ludger Schuknecht, *Public Spending in the 20th Century* (Cambridge: Cambridge University Press, 2000).

of course, the rise of the welfare state. As Michael Howard puts it: 'war and welfare went hand in hand'.[16]

In addition, although it may be true, as realists tell us, that the international system tames and socializes revolutionary regimes, it is also true that each of the great social revolutions of the modern era has left an indelible mark on the dominant norms of international society.[17] Within International Relations there is a tendency to distinguish too sharply between 'thick' domestic norms and 'thin' international norms. Many international norms (national self-determination, economic liberalism, and sustainable development) are powerful precisely because of the way in which they relate to the transnational structures within which all states are embedded and to the broad social forces that have transformed the character of states and altered the dynamics of the state system.

Does this mean that we can identify the emergence of a new kind of state? It is certainly the case that the development of welfare states and changing understandings of political legitimacy had profound implications for the kinds of economic regulation to be undertaken at the international level. It is also the case that the specific forms of regulation and administration embodied in the domestic expansion of the state have influenced the scope and character of international and transnational regulation today.[18] But this is very different from claiming that globalization is both associated with and reflects a new kind of state either in some archetypal or essentialist sense.

In his impressive account of the evolution of international order, Philip Bobbit traces the development of many different varieties of state before arguing that the nation-state has given way to the market-state.[19] This was a plausible account of the direction of some aspects of change in the developed world in the mid-1990s. But, as a general account, it neglects the continued role of nationalism in state legitimation, as well as the continued vitality of the nation-state as a powerfully felt community of fate. In the case of the developed world, it underplays the continued high levels of state involvement in the economy and society, even in an age of state retrenchment and deregulation, and exaggerates the shift from welfare to an emphasis on markets and the private sector. In the crucial case of the United States, it represents, at best, only one side of the story. Yes, certain aspects of domestic and foreign policy certainly fit the picture of the market-state. But there are many aspects

---

[16] Michael Howard, *The Lessons of History* (Oxford: Oxford University Press, 1991), 156.

[17] See David Armstrong, *Revolutions and World Order* (Oxford: Oxford University Press, 1993); and Fred Halliday, *Revolution and World Politics: The Rise and Fall of the Sixth Great Power* (Basingstoke, UK: Macmillan, 1999).

[18] See e.g. the work of Giandomenico Majone on the European regulatory state. 'From the Positive to the Regulatory State: Causes and Consequences of Changes in the Mode of Governance', *Journal of Public Policy*, 17 (1997).

[19] Philip Bobbitt, *The Sword of Achilles: War, Peace and the Course of History* (London: Penguin, 2003), esp. ch. 10.

that do not, including the role of nationalism, ideology, and security as major factors in shaping foreign policy, and the continuity of military force in the implementation of that foreign policy. In the case of the developing world, variation of state-type has been a crucial feature of patterns of development;[20] and, however much understandings of the road to power and plenty may have changed, the nationalist developmental state is alive and well.

Globalization and inequality

There are three aspects to the relationship between globalization and inequality. The first focuses on economic outcomes, measured and assessed along various dimensions. The arguments here are complex and contested. Those in favour of economic liberalization and greater economic integration argue that globalization has reduced both poverty and inequality, and that the 'globalizers' have done better than the 'laggards'.[21] Others dispute such findings.[22] It is not possible to go into these arguments in any depth. I would only note that the political reality has been clearly influenced by three developments: first, the failure of large parts of the world to share in the benefits of globalization (Africa most notably); second, the situation in other parts of the world in which the adoption of liberal economic reform has not been associated with economic improvement (as in many parts of Latin America); third, the widening gap between the richest and poorest and the extent to which, whatever the story of international inequality, the period of increased globalization has seen a rise in income disparities within many individual countries. Given the extent of persistent inequality, it is hardly surprising that many remain sceptical about claims that globalization is making the world a more equal place.

Whatever globalization's effects on economic measures of inequality, it has had a profound impact on global political equality in two ways: first, through the differential capacity of societies and states to adapt to globalization; and, second, through uneven influence on the institutions and evermore intrusive rules through which globalization is governed. The impact of globalization is mediated by national-level institutions and the life-chances and welfare of individuals are very strongly shaped by whether they live in a politically stable and administratively capable state. But the crucial question here is

[20] See Peter Evans, *Embedded Autonomy: States and Industrial Transformation* (Princeton, NJ: Princeton University Press, 1995), especially chs. 1–3; and Robert Wade, *Governing the Market: Economic Theory and the Role of Government in East Asian Industrialization* (Princeton, NJ: Princeton University Press, 1990).

[21] For example, Wolf (2004: ch. 9); David Dollar and Aart Kraay, 'Spreading the Wealth', *Foreign Affairs*, 81/1 (2002), 120–33.

[22] Branko Milanovic, 'The Two Faces of Globalization: Against Globalization as We Know It', *World Development*, 4/4 (2003), 667–83; Robert Wade, 'Is Globalization Reducing Poverty and Inequality?', *World Development*, 32/4 (2004), 567–89.

whether there is a link between globalization and state weakness. In the 1960s and 1970s, states were commonly viewed as creatures and creations of the global capitalist system. Dependency theory stressed the global pattern of dominance and dependence and the continued external control by the core capitalist states of the destinies of the periphery.[23] Early theorists viewed dependency theory in terms of a rigid law of underdevelopment and argued that participation in the international economy served only to perpetuate inequality and underdevelopment. Others developed a more case-specific 'historical structural' approach which accepted the fact of economic development but which nonetheless argued that the character of that development would remain indelibly marked (and distorted) by the dependent status of the region. The focus therefore shifted from the notion of the 'development of underdevelopment' to the analysis of 'dependent development'. But the dependent character of the state remained a central element in the analysis. By the early 1980s, such views had come under sustained attack. The core refrain of the critics was that states should be viewed not as potential engines for development but as highly inefficient and costly structures that were always likely to be captured by rent-seeking elites. The basic message was that the problems of inequality and underdevelopment lie within domestic societies rather than with the international system.

Such an argument, however, replaced one implausibly extreme view with another. It clearly underplays the vulnerability of developing societies to global markets, a situation which economic liberalization, whatever its benefits, has inevitably increased. It neglects the degree to which the emergence over time of the unfavourable conditions which afflict poor societies are as much to do with external and global factors as with internal ones. And it ignores the extent to which national economic policy choices are shaped by international economic institutions and powerful states and, indeed, the extent to which economic institutions have come to prevent states from adopting the very sorts of economic policies that rich countries had themselves used in their own development.[24] Economic liberalization has had a profound impact on the role and position of the state in many developing societies, often undermining the political bargains (across class, region, or sector) on which politics had previously been built. One might not like the patrimonial or clientilist states that grew up in the era of ISI; but the burden of proof seems to lie with those who believe that economic liberalization and

---

[23] See Fernando Henrique Cardoso and Enzo Faletto, *Dependency and Development in Latin America* (Beverly Hills, CA: University of California Press, 1979); Peter Evans, *Dependent Development: The Alliance of Multinational, State and Local Capital in Brazil* (Princeton, NJ: Princeton University Press, 1981); and Gabriel Palma, 'Dependency and Development: A Critical Overview', in Dudley Seers (ed.), *Dependency Theory: A Critical Reassessment* (London: Pinter, 1981), 20–78.

[24] H. Chang, *Kicking Away the Ladder: Development Strategies in Historical Perspective* (London: Anthem Press, 2002).

greater openness will somehow naturally serve to produce better, leaner, and more efficient states. In many countries, the problem is not one of economic models: it is rather about how the state can form the basis of a new social and political pact. Without moving back to first-generation dependency theorists who unconvincingly placed all responsibility on the external, there is enough evidence of the importance of external influences and of the impact of the global system to suggest, analytically, that state strength has to be understood both in terms of the one world and the many; and, normatively, that the idea of co-responsibility should act as the overall guiding principle in judging who is responsible for present ills.

The third aspect of inequality concerns the ways in which the structures of global economic governance both reflect and reinforce unequal political power. Hierarchical ordering is central to existing institutions. In the case of the Bank and Fund, unequal power is reflected in their voting systems and governance structures as well as in the closeness of the institutions to the United States. The WTO reflects unequal power in numerous ways.[25] Negotiating power depends on market size. Although the dispute settlement mechanism does represent a levelling of the playing field, making use of the mechanism requires financial resources and technical expertise that only the largest developing countries possess. In addition, the dispute settlement mechanism is built around sanctioned decentralized enforcement, in which, again, market power counts. The WTO is a member-driven organization in which participation depends on the technical and diplomatic capacities of member-states, and in which much decision-making takes places within closed or semi-closed groups and invitation-only meetings. Last, inequality is reflected in the process of accession in which new members are made to sign on to higher levels of rules and disciplines ('WTO plus') and in which the costs of late entry are high, even for very large states such as China.

Hierarchy is still more evident in weakly institutionalized groupings, most notably the G7/G8. The Group of Seven (G8), now the G8, is a club of advanced industrialized states that meets annually to discuss important economic, financial, and political issues. G8 summits are also used to set international priorities, to identify and define issues, to set up new regimes and reinvigorate existing ones, and to provide guidance to international organizations. Unlike the UN or the Bretton Woods institutions, the G8 has no charter, formal rules, or permanent secretariat. The G8 reaches 'understandings' rather than resolutions, and relies on consensus formation rather than formal voting. Whereas at the outset it was little more than an informal club, the G8

[25] Amongst a large and complex literature, see Amrita Narlikar, *The World Trade Organization: A Very Short Introduction* (Oxford: Oxford University Press, 2005); and Bernard Hoekman and Michel M. Kostecki, *The Political Economy of the World Trading System*, 2nd edn. (Oxford: Oxford University Press, 2001).

may now be described as a *system* consisting of complex, multilevelled bodies. Since the 1980s, G8 working groups and task forces have addressed specific problems such as nuclear proliferation, organized crime, terrorism, and the global environment.

Finally, as we have noted, inequality is visible in the composition and operation of networks involved in global economic governance, in the ability of major states to control the degree of access for NGOs (and in the far lower levels of NGO involvement in global economic governance compared, say, to human rights and the environment); and in their ability to choose different forms of governance. Major states will always have more options: to determine which issues get negotiated via formal interstate bodies and which are, for example, managed via market mechanisms; to shape social, political, and economic processes through which new international norms evolve; to influence both the rules of the bargaining game and what is allowed onto the agenda; to deploy a wide range of sticks and carrots in the bargaining process, including the threat of direct coercion; to navigate more successfully within global civil society, including through transnational and trans-governmental coalitions; and, finally, to walk away from any institution that becomes too constraining.

How do these three dimensions of inequality relate to the discussion of legitimacy developed in Chapter 3? Let us begin with process and procedural legitimacy. It is true that the transparency of international economic institutions has increased, as indicated by a degree of openness to civil society groups and by the number of mechanisms for evaluation (such as the World Bank Inspection Panels). Yet serious problems of process legitimacy clearly remain—especially if we think of political legitimacy in terms of how those adversely affected by the exercise of power are able to achieve redress (or even voice) and whether an institution is able to set some meaningful limits on the exercise of power on the part of its dominant members.

If procedural legitimacy remains problematic, what of legitimacy built around claims to technocratic and specialist knowledge? It has been common to view the Bank and Fund as technocratic agencies generating and disseminating sophisticated technical knowledge. It has also been common to argue that these claims have been severely dented by specific failures—for example in relation to the unintended consequences of economic reform in Russia, or of the Polonoroeste projects in the Amazon. And more important than debates over specific cases is the issue of how universal technical knowledge is to be applied and by whom. Trumpeting the victory and the superiority of economic liberalism after the end of the Cold War led in many cases to a top-down and institutionally closed approach to the operation of the IFIs, which violated the core epistemic conditions of liberalism. In the Conclusion, I suggest that the application of general moral rules needs to be context-rich and interpretative, involving dialogue with interlocutors from different regions and recognizing aspects of social phenomena that can easily go unnoticed from one's own familiar perspective. A similar argument can be made about the erosion of the technocratic legitimacy of the IFIs and the extent to which this has resulted precisely from the difficulties of applying universal technical knowledge, however sophisticated, to the complex facts and widely differing circumstances of a particular case—whether we are talking about how political and economic reforms are to be 'sequenced' in very different contexts or the impact of market reform on the mechanisms by which social trust is generated and sustained.

But the core, and most problematic dimension, concerns legitimacy based on the effective promotion of shared values that are, in turn, debated in an accessible and shared language. If we look back over the evolution of global economic governance, we can see how power has served to undermine or distort purposes which had been, at least to some degree, shared. The original objectives of the IMF, for example, included the maintenance of a stable system of exchange rates, the management of balance of payments and financial crises, and the promotion of balanced growth across countries and within countries. But, as Woods has argued, a great deal of its actual operation and much of its success lay in its role as a 'globalizer', using institutional, ideational, political, and market power to integrate a large number of countries evermore deeply into the global economy.[26] In the case of the Fund, a crucial change took place when it ceased to be an institution on which a wide range of states might potentially come to depend (as with Britain in the 1970s) and instead became an institution whose operations were overwhelmingly targeted at a particular group of states.

Power has also been deployed to limit the discussion of shared values and shared purposes. One prominent aim of this book has been to trace the dramatic growth in the normative ambition of international society, even if those aspirations and ambitions have remained more rhetorical than real. Yet there are some telling silences, and nowhere more important than in relation to economic rights and distributive justice. By the end of the 1970s, the developed world had effectively defeated demands for a New International Economic Order which, whatever the inadequacy of its policy prescriptions, did embody a set of claims to economic justice. It is true that economic and social rights have come to form part of human rights system. Yet the argument that these are not 'real rights' is routinely heard in major Western countries and these rights have rarely shaped government policy. Equally, all of the high-income countries have been extremely vigilant in resisting

---

[26] Woods (2006: 186): 'To date they [the Bank and Fund] have successfully magnified and accelerated the expansion of global commerce. Yet they were created to help manage and balance globalization, not simply to accelerate it'.

anything that might be interpreted as a formal commitment to economic justice.[27]

If we turn to the present, the most striking feature of global economic governance is the disarray of existing institutions and the absence of consensus on the values and purposes for which new and improved institutions might be needed. Negotiations on the future of the WTO are deadlocked; the role of the IMF has become evermore marginal; and, although the aid debate has swung back in favour of increasing levels of aid, there is very little agreement on what the 'aid regime' should look like.

There remain powerful arguments that global economic governance should be about the provision of international public goods such as financial stability or clear and well-enforced rules for international trade. The devastation wrought on particular societies by financial crises and the dangers to the system of contagion create incentives for the effective regulation of financial markets. And, as I argue in more detail in the Conclusion, there is good reason for believing that threats to systemic stability are likely to rise. But the extent to which such goods are produced has far more to do with the power and interests of particular actors than with any functional logic of governance. The contrast between the extremely high levels of banking regulation domestically and the very low level of the regulation of global financial markets provides the clearest example. In the case of trade, many of the purposes and values embodied in the WTO system have come under sustained challenge. On the one side, existing purposes have been subverted by the power of dominant states and powerful private actors (as with the enforcement of openness on weak countries whilst refusing to implement promised liberalization themselves, most obviously in agriculture). On the other side, there are renewed demands that economic efficiency needs to be balanced by norms that protect the legitimate scope of societal difference (e.g. in relation to attitudes to risk, to the valuing of environmental goods, and to cultural production); and that the dislocations inevitably produced by globalized markets have to be accompanied by shared rules as to how those dislocations are managed within states.

---

[27] See e.g. the US reservations entered to the Declaration and Programme of Action of the 1995 Copenhagen Summit. On the US view, these are 'not legally binding and ... consist of recommendations concerning how States can and should promote social development'. It is also important to remember that the United States has never ratified the International Covenant on Economic, Social, and Cultural Rights and that, as Forsythe puts it, '[W]hen the USA talks about its support for the Universal Declaration of Human Rights, it simply omits any reference to those articles endorsing fundamental rights to adequate standards of food, clothing, shelter, health care and social security'. (Forsythe 2000: 145) In 2000, Canada and the EU proposed a draft declaration to the 2000 Geneva World Summit for Social Development which speaks of 'our determination and duty to eradicate poverty'; but this duty is only loosely specified ('we will strive to fulfil the yet to be attained internationally agreed target of 0.7% of GNP of developed countries for overall ODA as soon as possible') and even such good global citizens rejected the G77 draft which argued for 'equitable distribution of wealth within and among nations'.

Globalization and consensus

Almost all discussions of globalization recognize that its impact is highly uneven, as some parts of the world are incorporated into ever-denser networks of interdependence whilst other regions are left on, or beyond, the margins. In the 1990s, much analysis concentrated on a stark dichotomy between fusion and fragmentation or between convergence and revolt. Countless commentators have stressed the extent to which globalizing forces are producing fragmentation, reaction, or backlash, involving at least very different kinds of groups: first, the anti-globalization movement with its shifting coalitions of NGOs and CSOs;[28] second, those terrorist groups whose violence might be in some form linked to the disruptions and alienation produced by globalization; and third, those governments which have come to power on the back of broad popular rejection of the market-liberal policies pursued in the region in the 1990s (as with Chavez in Venezuela or Morales in Bolivia).

The most obvious challenges may well come from backlash movements and the most pressing difficulties may well occur in parts of the world that have missed out most in terms of stable government and prosperity. But meeting those challenges and building a stable and legitimate order will depend on the broader solidity of consensus amongst major developing states, especially in relation to the common rules, values and institutions of international society.[29] It is also particularly important to focus on the views and policies of what was called the Third World and has now come to be called the Global South because of the historic role of these countries as challengers to Western conceptions of international society. In the 1960s and 1970s this challenge was embodied in calls for a New International Economic Order, backed by what appeared to be a solidifying coalition of developing countries in the form of the G77 and the Non-Aligned Movement. This challenge took various forms, from the (at least rhetorical) revolutionism of China, to the hard revisionism of countries such as India and Indonesia, to the soft revisionism of countries such as Brazil. Yet these demands were, as Bull argued, part of a broader and historically more deep-rooted challenge to the Western-dominated international society that had reached its apogee around the turn

[28] See e.g. Emma Bircham and John Charlton (eds.), *Anti-Capitalism: A Guide to the Movement* (London: Bookmark, 2001).

[29] There are clearly other important ways of considering these questions. One is to follow the world society theorists and to trace the extent to which globalization is demanding or facilitating the organizational reconstruction of social life. See Drori, Meyer, and Hwan (2006: esp. chs. 1 and 2). Another is to consider consensus at the level of ideological systems, as with Fukuyama. Francis Fukuyama, *The End of History and the Last Man* (London: Penguin, 1992). A further way is to identify shifts in both mass and elite attitudes—either towards special aspects of the liberal solidarist agenda or as an indicator of the emergence of a broader culture of modernity that might at some point spill upwards and outwards, influencing understandings of order and global governance.

of the twentieth century. Earlier phases of this challenge had included the struggle for equal sovereignty, the anti-colonial revolution, and the struggle for racial equality.[30]

The early 1990s seemed to mark a decisive shift in the development of international society, not simply because of the collapse of the Soviet Union but also because of the transformation that was taking place in North–South relations and in the foreign and foreign economic policies of developing countries. With the end of the Cold War and the intensification of globalization, many developing country governments seemed to be abandoning the Third World orthodoxies that had shaped and inspired policy for the previous half century. These policy reversals were perhaps most apparent in the international political economy, when traditional bloc-type coalitions began to fragment, and hard-line demands for a revision of dominant international economic norms began to give way to an emphasis on liberalization and participation. Developing countries began to restructure their domestic economies in line with the prescriptions of the IMF and the World Bank. As members of the GATT, they took on deeper commitments in traditional areas such as goods and began to adhere to new disciplines in the areas of services, Trade Related Intellectual Property Rights (TRIPs), and Trade Related Investment Measures (TRIMs). Meanwhile, non-members seemed to be falling over each other in their attempt to acquire membership of the WTO. The GATT at the start of the Uruguay Round in 1986 had 92 members; this membership had increased to 128 by the end of the Uruguay Round in 1994, and 147 by 2003. For many commentators, these shifts followed naturally from the changes that were taking place in the economic policy of developing countries—away from the economic models based on ISI, high tariffs and a large role for the state, and towards market liberalism and greater emphasis on integration in world markets. Finally, changes in development policy appeared to be going hand in hand with a willingness to sign-up to many aspects of the liberal multilateralism of the 1990s and to join, or at least less actively oppose, a wide range of specific regimes, including those dealing with the environment, human rights and humanitarian intervention, and nuclear proliferation and arms control.

The importance of these changes has increased because of the extent to which globalization has already produced significant shifts in the global balance of economic power—with the high levels of growth of China and India and the broader shift in the location of manufacturing from the developed to the developing world. To what extent, then, have the emerging powers of the early twenty-first century become socialized into a liberal solidarist

[30] Bull was clear both that power had shifted away from the West in the course of this 'revolt' and that the element of consensus in international society had declined significantly. See Hedley Bull, 'The Revolt Against Western Dominance', in *The Hagey Lectures* (Waterloo: University of Waterloo, 1984).

international society? Against the apparently straightforward notion of convergence and consensus, three points need to be noted.

In the first place, it is important to look critically at the manner in which changes in the developing world took place. Liberals tell a story of progressive enmeshment. This develops the Kantian notion of a gradual but progressive diffusion of liberal values, partly as a result of liberal economics and increased economic interdependence, partly as a liberal legal order comes to sustain the autonomy of a global civil society, and partly as a result of the successful example set by the multifaceted liberal capitalist system of states. The dynamics here are provided by notions of emulation, learning, normative persuasion, and technical knowledge. Yet this image glosses far too quickly over the roles played by coercion and conditionality and skirts far too delicately around the importance of power hierarchies and asymmetries. The adaptation of developing countries to the post–Cold War international system took many forms which range from progressive enmeshment at one end of the scale to straightforward hegemonic imposition at the other. In many cases, the mixture of consensus and coercion can be captured by the idea of coercive socialization. Coercive socialization describes the ways in which interaction within a highly unequal international system leads to the adoption and incorporation of external ideas, norms, and practices. As part of the process of internalization, historically embedded conceptions of interest shift, actors re-evaluate their political options, organizational structures are revised, and a changing institutional context provides the framework for an evolving set of bargains between state and society. Socialization certainly involves material forces, incentives, and constraints that result from interstate political competition and from market competition within the global economy. But it is also heavily influenced by the ideas, norms, and shared understandings that define and give meaning to both of these material structures, and by the institutions in which they are embodied. These processes have certainly involved very significant changes in the policies of many Southern countries, often reinforced by the changing patterns of domestic interests created by the process of liberalization. But there have also been important elements of continuity and, to the extent that change was coerced, we would expect changing external circumstances to lead to a reassertion of earlier ideas and preferences.

In many recent accounts of globalization, the adoption of market-liberal policies by the Brazilian President Fernando Henrique Cardoso is viewed as the perfect example of the rationality of global liberalism and the bankruptcy of the dependency theories of which he himself had been one of the leading academic exponents. Yet changes in the position of the South can be seen as the result of the changing dynamics of capitalism in a manner that is consistent with important strands in dependency theory. As Cardoso himself put it:

We are dealing, effectively, with a far more cruel phenomenon [than earlier forms of dependency]: Either the South (or a part of it) enters into the democratic-technological-scientific race, invests heavily in research and development, and supports the transformation into an 'information economy', or it will become unimportant, unexploited and unexploitable. The South finds itself under a double threat: apparently incapable of integrating itself, seeking its own interests, but equally incapable of avoiding 'being integrated' as the servant of the richer economies. Those countries (or parts of them) incapable of repeating the revolution of the contemporary world, will end up in the 'worst of all possible worlds'. They will not be worth the trouble of being exploited and will become irrelevant, without any interest to the developing global economy.[31]

Second, for all the talk about the imperatives of globalization and the pressure to adapt to those imperatives, it is the continued variation of the trajectories of political and economic development that is more striking. Globalization has certainly involved very powerful external pressures for change. But these have come up against very deep-rooted sets of domestic social, political, and economic structures and very distinctive national traditions, leading to developmental trajectories that continue to vary very significantly. Although the systemic pressures associated with globalization are very powerful, it is crucial to unpack and deconstruct the complex process of breakdown and adaptation that are occurring within individual societies, especially large and complex societies. The result is that the intuitively powerful idea of homogenization breaks down, as it becomes clear that outcomes conform neither to anything resembling a simple liberal 'model', nor to a simple rejection of that model.

In the post–Cold War period, a great deal of the analysis of globalization was built around binary categories of fusion and fragmentation, homogenization, or revolt. On the one hand, we have an expanding political world of liberal states, gradually socializing others into its pacific and cooperation realm and a dynamic capitalist economy that is making the world 'flatter'. On the other, we have a world of rogue states, of religious tyrannies which refuse to respect the will of their people or which demand blind submission, and of regions characterized by chaos and anarchy. These polarities do capture important parts of the picture, but they also illustrate the twin dangers of false similarity on the one hand and excessive difference on the other.[32]

Third, although inwardly oriented development models were strongly associated with nationalist foreign policies during the post-1945 period, the move towards economic liberalization and greater integration in the global economy does not necessarily mesh with an acceptance of the broader liberal

---

[31] Fernando Henrique Cardoso, 'Relações Norte-Sul no Contexto Atual: Uma Nova Dependência', in Renato Baumann (ed.), *O Brasil e a Economia Global* (Rio de Janeiro: Editora Campus, 1996), 12.

[32] On the first, see Thomas L. Friedman, *The World Is Flat: A Brief History of the Twenty-First Century* (New York: Farrar, Straus and Goroux, 2005); on the second, see Robert D. Kaplan, *The Coming Anarchy: Shattering the Dreams of the Post-Cold War World* (New York: Vintage, 2001).

213

order. Even within the context of continued market-liberal economic reform within a mostly market-liberal global economy, the scope for real clashes of interest and values remains very wide. Who gets how much? Who sets the rules of the global economy? Whose values are embodied in those rules? More generally, all states, but especially large states with a sense of their historical entitlement and their aspirations for the future, balance the pursuit of economic welfare and development with considerations of power—to promote security and autonomy; to strengthen regional influence or even predominance; and, especially, to gain recognition as major and legitimate players in the system. The goals of power and plenty have always been closely intertwined. Indeed, for important groups within China and India globalization and economic integration was chosen precisely because it appeared to offer the most promising route to national power. Success is arguably what matters most and a willingness to challenge comes from the renewed confidence that economic success brings. In their different ways, both India and China also indicate how nationalism and economic liberalization can co-exist—whether spontaneously or as a result of active cultivation on the part of government. And, as with past modernizers such as Russia or Japan, there is a continued tension between the need and desire to appropriate successful models, on the one hand, and to maintain cultural distinctiveness on the other.

To argue in this way does not imply acceptance of the neo-realist belief that all economic power ends up inevitably in a military challenge and an intensification of balance of power politics. The demand for recognition both as a legitimate major power and as the representative of a particular set of values has been the most common feature of rising powers. Moreover, a future challenge to liberal solidarism may take the form not of a radical rejection of global liberal values but of demands for their differential application—demands that are already visible in the renewed activism of developing country trade coalitions such as the G20; or in calls for the reform of international institutions to reflect better the balance of world population and the changing balance of world power (as in calls for reform of the UNSC or of the voting rights within the IMF). Or it may take the form of demands that further hardening of the enforcement of human rights or democratic norms be conditional on effective constraints on the ability of the currently powerful to decide how and when this enforcement is to take place. Consensus on substantive values can coexist with deep dissensus over the procedural values by which a group of states organizes itself and through which shared values are acted upon.

Classical liberals had a far more subtle awareness of the relationship between power and plenty than many contemporary liberal commentators on globalization. Thus, the optimistic, individualist, and cosmopolitan side of Adam Smith was balanced by an emphasis on the importance of national power and security. His book, after all, is entitled the *Wealth of Nations* and he was clear that '[T]he great object of the political economy of every country is to increase the riches and power of that country'. Not only was defence the first duty of the sovereign, but economic interdependence with neighbouring states could constitute a danger; wealthy states were more liable to be attacked; commercial society undermined the martial spirit, a problematic development given Smith's view that war was 'the noblest of the arts'; and, although commerce had the potential to foster 'a bond of union and friendship' amongst nations, Smith's realism led him to conclude that 'the violence and injustice of the rulers of mankind is an ancient evil, for which I am afraid, the nature of human affairs can scarce admit a remedy'. [33]

The evolution of economic globalization will have a crucial impact on the balance of power in the twenty-first century and thereby on the forms of international society and global governance that emerge. We can conclude this chapter with a further quotation from Smith that highlights the relationship between power and trade and that also looks forward to the arguments about power and justice developed in the Conclusion of this book.

At the particular time when these discoveries were made, the superiority of force happened to be so great on the side of the Europeans, that they were enabled to commit with impunity every sort of injustice in those remote countries. Hereafter, perhaps, the natives of those countries may grow stronger, or those of Europe may grow weaker, and the inhabitants of all the different quarters of the world may arrive at that equality of courage and force which, by inspiring mutual fear, can alone overawe the injustice of independent nations into some sort of respect for the rights of one another. But nothing seems more likely to establish this equality of force than that mutual communication of knowledge and of all sorts of improvements which an extensive commerce from all countries to all countries naturally, or rather necessarily, carries along with it.[34]

---

[33] Adam Smith, *An inquiry into the Nature and Causes of the Wealth of Nations* (Chicago: University of Chicago Press, [1775] 1976): although Cobden was far more of a liberal cosmopolitan than Smith and famously attacked the balance of power as a 'chimera' and a 'foul idol', at least part of his argument was that traditional interventionist balance of power politics had been overtaken by the changes brought about by the industrial revolution. Power still mattered. The problem was that leaders were playing the wrong sort of power game. See Richard Cobden, *Political Writings of Richard Cobden* (London: Routledge/Thoemmes Press, [1867] 1995), 79 and 147–8. See also Ceadel (1996: 110–11).

[34] Smith, 1976: book IV, ch. VII, p. 141). I thank Sankar Muthu for drawing this passage to my attention.

9

The ecological challenge

The increased seriousness of many environmental problems provides one of the most intuitively plausible reasons for believing that the traditional forms of international society are inadequate and that the nation-state and the system of states may be heading towards a crisis. Running through much of the writing on the subject is the sense—sometimes explicit, more often implicit—that the state and the fragmented system of sovereign states are less and less able to guarantee the effective and equitable management of an interdependent world in general, and of the global environment in particular.[1] Environmental issues (and especially 'global' environmental issues) present states and the state system with new challenges of unprecedented complexity. The state is widely seen to be both too big and too small for dealing with these challenges: too big for the task of devising viable strategies of sustainable development which can only be developed from the bottom up; and too small for the effective management of global problems such as combating global climate change or protecting biodiversity which by their nature demand increasingly wide-ranging forms of international cooperation.

There are three principal arguments concern the inability of international society to meet the ecological challenge.[2] The first concerns the state system as a whole. From this perspective, the system of nation-states may be said to be in crisis or to be dysfunctional because it can no longer provide a viable political framework for the collective management of the global environment.

[1] See e.g. Joseph A. Camillieri and Jim Falk who argue that '...First, the principle of sovereignty is an impediment to action designed to ameliorate critical ecological dilemmas. Second, it is itself a major contributing cause of the environmental problems which confront humanity', in *The End of Sovereignty? The Politics of a Shrinking and Fragmenting World* (London: Edward Elgar, 1992), 179.

[2] Much of the literature makes a distinction between environmental and ecological. On one account: '*environmentalism* argues for a managerial approach to environmental problems, secure in the belief that they can be solved without fundamental changes in present values or patterns of production and consumption.... *ecologism* holds that a sustainable and fulfilling existence presupposes radical changes in our relationship with the non-human natural world, and in our mode of social and political life.' See Andrew Dobson, *Green Political Theory*, 3rd edn. (London: Routledge, 2000), 2.

Although there is little agreement on alternative paths, there appears to many to be a basic contradiction between a single integrated, enormously complex, and deeply interdependent ecosystem and our still dominant form of global political organization: a fragmented system of sovereign states, normatively built around mutual recognition of sovereignty, and politically forming an anarchical system in which cooperation has been historically limited and in which war and conflict a deeply rooted, and for many, an inherent feature. As the Brundtland Report put it: 'Our Earth is one, our world is not'. Or, as Lynton Caldwell suggested: 'By this time, experience should have taught us that a complex planetary biosphere cannot be addressed effectively for protection or for rational management by a fragmented and uncoordinated political order.'[3]

A second argument is that an increasing number of individual nation-states are no longer able to provide localized order and an adequate degree of environmental management within their own borders. The weakness of many states and state structures is all too evident. What is harder to discern is the degree and significance of this weakness. For some, the environmental failings of many weak states are merely suggestive of a crisis of particular policies, or, at worst, a crisis of particular political or economic institutions. But for others, something altogether more far reaching is under way. Lipschutz and Conca, for example, believe that we are witnessing 'the emergence of a fundamental new social dynamic, with which governments, their critics, and their observers may be poorly equipped to deal'. Global ecological interdependence is leading both to 'tighter systemic binding among actors in the prevailing international system, and the simultaneous decay and fragmentation of the traditional authority structures of world politics'.[4] Of these authority structures, the position of the state is particularly shaky and they speak of 'the fundamental incapacity of governments to control the destructive processes involved'.[5]

The third argument moves beyond the state's practical capacity to deal effectively with new challenges. On this view, environmental problems are eroding the normative appeal of the state and the idea of the nation-state as the primary, if not exclusive, focus for human loyalties. In part, this loss of legitimacy derives from the domestic environmental shortcomings of many states. But in part, it results from the extent to which increased awareness of global environmental problems and of the deep and unavoidable

[3] Lynton Keith Caldwell, *Between Two Worlds: Science, the Environmental Movement and Policy Choice* (Cambridge: Cambridge University Press, 1992), 151.

[4] Ken Conca and Ronnie D. Lipschutz, 'A Tale of Two Forests', in Ronnie D. Lipschutz and Ken Conca (eds.), *The State and Social Power in Global Environmental Politics* (New York: Columbia University Press, 1993), 9.

[5] Ronnie D. Lipschutz and Ken Conca, 'The Implications of Global Ecological Interdependence', in Ronnie D. Lipschutz and Ken Conca (eds.), *The State and Social Power in Global Environmental Politics* (New York: Columbia University Press, 1993), 332.

reality of environmental interdependence has created a new sense of planetary consciousness which is leading to new forms of non-territorially based political identity. Moreover, this sense of planetary consciousness is embodied concretely in the increasing mobilization of new social actors around environmental issues. Undoubtedly tied to other processes of globalization, the consolidation of what is loosely termed the global environmental movement is seen as one of the most significant and substantial pillars of an emerging transnational civil society. On this view, we are therefore witnessing the emergence of new forms of non-territorially based political identity and new mechanisms of political organization and action that go beyond the nation-state and which challenge the hegemony of statist world politics.

The ecological challenge is so important and so profound because of the way in which it calls into question both the practical viability and the moral adequacy of this pluralist conception of a state-based global order; and because of the way in which responding to the ecological challenge has pushed states towards new forms of international law and global governance. The chapter is divided into three sections. The first examines the nature and extent of the challenge posed. The second section sets the responses to the ecological challenge within the context of the changing constitutional structure of international society—the move towards a solidarist state system on the one hand and the emergence of increasing elements of transnational governance on the other. The third section draws out the way in which unequal power and value conflict have complicated the capturing of what would appear to be the obvious common interest in promoting environmental cooperation.

The ecological challenge

There are four principal aspects to the ecological challenge. The first derives from increased awareness of the material limits to the kinds of progress and development around which Western understandings of political order have traditionally been constructed, and from the real possibility that our dominant forms of political organization may be inadequate to manage the relationship between humankind and the natural environment on a lasting and sustainable basis. The international political salience of environmental issues has increased enormously as a result of accelerating rates of environmental degradation, increased scientific knowledge, and heightened popular awareness of the seriousness of the ecological challenges facing humanity. Dominant understandings of the most pressing environmental problems moved from the discussions of the 1970s about the impact of localized pollution and the limits to natural resources (the focus on population and natural resources, the emergence of the idea of 'limits to growth', the shock of Organization of

Petroleum Exporting Countries, etc.) to an increased emphasis on the notion of 'global environmental change' and on the limited capacity of the planet to absorb the wastes produced by economic activity: in shorthand, a shift from 'resource limits' to 'sink limits'.[6] Although much of the picture remains contested and obscure, there is increasing evidence that human social and economic activity is placing excessive strains on the physical limits of the ecosphere and that, in a crude but real sense, we are filling up the ecological space available to us.[7]

The second aspect of the challenge concerns the increasingly global character of contemporary environmental issues. There are three senses in which the environment has become a global issue. First, and most obviously, humanity is now faced by a range of environmental problems that are global in the strong sense that they affect everyone and can only be effectively managed on the basis of cooperation between all, or at least a very high percentage, of the states of the world: controlling climate change and the emission of greenhouse gases, the protection of the ozone layer, safeguarding biodiversity, protecting special regions such as Antarctica or the Amazon, the management of the seabed, and the protection of the high seas are amongst the principal examples. In the case of climate change, we are dealing with a global, uncertain, and long-term process that carries with it a significant risk of large-scale and irreversible change that could transform the physical geography of the world and undermine existing patterns of social and economic organization.

Second, the increasing scale of many originally regional or local environmental problems, such as extensive urban degradation, deforestation, desertification, salination, denudation, or water or fuel-wood scarcity, now threaten broader international repercussions: by undermining the economic base and social fabric of weak and poor states, by generating or exacerbating intraor interstate tensions and conflicts, and by stimulating increased flows of refugees.[8] Moreover, although many such problems are 'localized' in that

---

[6] For a useful overview of the issues and responses, see Elizabeth R. DeSombre, *The Global Environment and World Politics* (London: Continuum, 2002).

[7] Ideas about 'carrying capacity' are highly contested. For one view, see Joel E. Cohen, *How Many People Can the Earth Support?* (New York: W.W. Norton, 2004).

[8] There is an extensive literature on environmentally related security issues. One strand focused on the way in which environmental stress was related to violent conflict. The aim here was to move beyond very general arguments about the environment as the 'ultimate security issue' (as in Norman Myers, *Ultimate Security: The Environmental Basis of Political Security* (New York: W.W. Norton, 1993), and, instead, to identify the conditions under which environmental degradation was implicated in violent conflict. See e.g. Homer-Dixon (1994: 5–40). Important features of the debate include the argument that it is the existence of natural resources (timber, diamonds, and oil) that fuel violent conflict rather than their absence and the importance of the interaction between environmental stress and political inequality. For a good analysis, see Paul F. Diehl and Nils Petter Gleditsch (eds.), *Environmental Conflict* (Boulder, CO: Westview, 2001). For critiques, see Marc Levy, 'Is the Environment a National Security Issue?', *International Security*, 20/2 (1995), 35–62; and Nils Pieter Gleditsch, 'Armed Conflict and the Environment: A Critique of the Literature', *Journal of Peace Research*,

their *effects* are felt locally, their *causes* often lie far beyond national borders, as local ecosystems are tied into transnational structures of production and exchange.

The third aspect of increased globalization derives from the complex but close relationship between the generation of environmental problems and the workings of the now effectively globalized world economy. On the one hand, there is the range of environmental problems caused by the *affluence* of the industrialized countries; by the extent to which this affluence has been built upon high and unsustainable levels of energy consumption and natural resource depletion; and by the 'ecological shadow' cast by these economies across the economic system. On the other, there is the widely recognized linkage between *poverty*, population pressure, and environmental degradation. Sustainable development is an inherently global issue both because of the high levels of economic interdependence that exist within many parts of the world economy and because it raises fundamental questions concerning the distribution of wealth, power, and resources between rich and poor. To talk of the environment as a global issue is not to imply that all environmental problems have global repercussions, still less to argue that all problems need to be managed on a global basis. Rather it is to argue that the material foundations of political and social order are necessarily limited by the carrying capacity of the earth as a whole and that the ways in which politics is organized globally have become a critical factor influencing the long-term sustainability of the relationship between human beings and the natural world.

The third aspect of the challenge concerns the character of cooperation that is required to deal with environmental problems. The management of globalization necessarily involves the creation of deeply intrusive rules and institutions and debate on how different societies are to be organized domestically. This is a structural challenge. Grubb describes the problem of climate change as a 'quintessentially' global problem '. . . since the location of emissions is irrelevant to the outcome, and it involves direct interaction between, on the one hand, two of the most basic activities associated with economic development—energy consumption and land use—and, on the other, two of the fundamental driving forces of the biosphere—the carbon cycle (in the form of CO_2 and methane) and the radiative properties of the atmosphere'.[9] Effective international policies on the environment therefore

35 (1998), 381–400. See also Chapter 7, fn. 28. The second strand focused on the idea of 'resource wars' and on interstate conflicts generated by competition for water and energy resources. Here the earlier conventional wisdom suggested that such conflicts were unlikely to be a major feature of future conflicts, a view that has subsequently come under challenge. See e.g. Michael T. Klare, *Resource Wars: The New Landscape of Global Conflict* (Place: Henry Holt, 2002).

[9] Michael Grubb, 'Seeking Fair Weather: Ethics and the International Debate on Climate Change', *International Affairs*, 71/3 (1995), 465–6.

necessarily involve engagement with a complex array of international and transnational actors and interaction between central governments and a much wider range of domestic players and with debates about the domestic organization of society. George Bush Sr said at the Rio Conference in 1992 that the American way of life was not up for debate. Global environmental governance necessarily involves debate about everyone's way of life.

The fourth aspect of the challenge concerns the increasing number of individual nation-states that are no longer able to provide localized order and an adequate degree of environmental management within their own borders. Many of the most serious obstacles to sustainability have to do with the domestic weaknesses of particular states and state structures. In some cases, these stem from the limits of economic development: the fragility, inefficiency, and corruption of government bureaucracies; the absence of appropriate human, financial, and technological resources; the prevalence of deep-rooted economic problems; and the increasing susceptibility to international and transnational economic forces. But in many cases the problems are directly political: the opposition of powerful political interests that benefit from unsustainable forms of development and the difficulties of the state in regulating both itself and the many areas of economic life in which it is directly involved.

Clearly these problems are most severe in many of the weakest states, such as Haiti, El Salvador or many parts of Africa. But, even in states that have not in any sense 'failed', the capacity of governments to control or manage access to natural resources is often far from clear. The story of the Brazilian Amazon provides a parable of how a strong developmentalist state came to grief: an extensive state-led development programme built around a powerful ideology of national integration and national development; the attempt to achieve direct centralized control, displacing traditional local elites and replacing them with new bureaucratic structures of control; and the gradual erosion of the capacity of the state to control the powerful and contradictory forces that have been unleashed. Moreover, the Brazilian case does not stand alone, as shown by the role played by environmental degradation and environmental protest in the collapse of communist regimes in the Soviet Union and Eastern Europe. And there are worrying signs that China's shaky environmental foundations may yet force a dramatic reassessment of the much vaunted 'Chinese miracle' and of the image of China as a strong state.[10]

These challenges would be serious even if we were to see the state as an environmentally neutral form of social organization. For many ecological theorists, however, the state is anything but neutral.[11] In the first place,

---

[10] Judith Shapiro, *Mao's War against Nature: Politics and the Environment in Revolutionary China* (Cambridge: Cambridge University Press, 2001).

[11] See John Barry and Robyn Eckersley (eds.), *The State and the Global Ecological Crisis* (Cambridge, MA: MIT Press, 2005).

ecological thinking is necessarily about relationships, interconnections, and community. The state can, at best, form only one part of this broader whole. Second, green political theory has long suspected that the bureaucratic logic of Weberian state-machines is deeply antithetical to viewing nature in anything other than the narrowest of instrumental terms. Third, as it has emerged historically, the state has been very closely connected with the development of capitalism and hence with the productivism, expansionism, and emphasis on ever-higher levels of material consumption that is such a central target of the ecological critique. And finally, for many ecologists the anarchical character of interstate politics generates a recurrent logic of security competition that leads to violent conflicts with their attendant environmentally destructive effects; that presses political leaders to look to their short-term interests and to their power position relative to other states; and that reinforces narrow and exclusivist conceptions of national community.

There is a wide spectrum of opinion as to the seriousness of many environmental problems and a great deal of scope for legitimate uncertainty. For the environmental optimists the ecological challenge is not nearly as severe as suggested above and both technology and continued economic development will allow human societies to achieve higher levels of sustainability and to adapt successfully to the environmental changes that will inevitably occur.[12] The environmentalist pessimist's response is to argue that human capacity to control the natural environment has been greatly and consistently overestimated, in particular because of insufficient attention to complexity, non-linearity, and unpredictability. In the case of climate change, it is the cumulative destabilizing dynamics that are of central importance. Moreover, even taking a rosy view of the problems and even assuming that the costs of adaptation are less than the costs of structural change, a very great deal of the optimism depends on there being a well-functioning set of political institutions capable of achieving historically unprecedented levels of cooperation. Maybe technology will solve many problems, but that technology has to be applied and distributed to where it is needed. Maybe the world is capable of dealing with particular kinds of scarcity in aggregate. But for this to be a meaningful solution, there has to be a global mechanism for distribution and allocation and one that is able to take into account both efficiency and equity. To a much greater extent than they acknowledge, it is the environmental optimists who are most dependent on answers to some of the most intractable political problems facing international relations. Whatever view one takes about the state itself, the ecological challenge has undoubtedly served to call into question both the practical viability and the moral acceptability of state-based pluralist international order.

---

[12] See Bjørn Lomborg, *The Skeptical Environmentalist. Measuring the Real State of the World* (Cambridge: Cambridge University Press, 2001).

Responses

The seriousness of the ecological challenge and suspicion of the state have led some to look to radical political solutions. At one end of the spectrum this has involved arguments either for world government or for strong global centralism of a kind that would certainly change the role of the state and the character of international society. '[T]he need for a world government with enough coercive powers over fractious nation states to achieve what reasonable people would regard as the planetary common interest has become overwhelming.'[13] However, arguments in favour of world government have always faced very powerful objections, most importantly that any effective concentration of power would pose a severe threat to liberty. After all, if one of the purposes of a well-functioning political system is to reflect and promote some conception of the common good, the other is to limit, or at least minimize, domination. In addition, there are many solid ecological arguments against any form of global centralism, above all the critical importance of diversity—both of forms of interaction with nature but also of ecological ideas, possibilities, and ways of thinking.

At the other end of the scale, ecological thinking has long stressed the value of decentralization.[14] The empowerment of both individuals and communities, combined with a strong emphasis on decentralized forms of political organization, has become a major theme of ecological writing. Decentralization and empowerment facilitate sustainability in various ways: by bringing consumption and production closer together; by strengthening local democracy and focusing public opposition to the seriousness of existing environmental problems; and by building on the extent to which local groups and communities possess special knowledge of sustainable forms of development and provide the social organizations within which that knowledge can be effectively implemented. And yet, however valuable these arguments may be, the global nature of the ecological challenge necessitates a significant degree of coordination, regulation, and long-term planning. Even if decentralized or more regionally or locally based communities were to replace the state, some pattern of external or global political relations and institutions would need to be created or recreated. It is hard to see how these could entirely avoid replicating many of the features of contemporary state-based governance, both in terms of its positive possibilities and its recurring dilemmas.

It is certainly the case that very important processes of adaptation to the ecological challenge have occurred within individual states: through the 'greening' of domestic politics; through the increased emphasis on

---

[13] Ophuls (1992: 278).

[14] See Dobson (2000: chs. 3 and 4); and Robert E. Goodin, *Green Political Theory* (Cambridge: Polity Press, 1992), ch. 4.

environmental issues within state administrations; through varied processes of ecological modernization; and through the different ways in which the environment has been connected to the problem of state legitimacy.[15] Perhaps surprisingly, given the insistent cries of the need for change, one also finds important strands of statist and nationalist thinking in terms of environmental management. The statist strand argues that the powerful pressures towards globalization and integration need to be reversed and the world economy needs to be 'brought back under control'.[16] The nationalist strand argues that meaningful sustainability needs to reflect the values and traditions of particular national communities. This often takes the form of a soft Burkean conservatism.[17] But this position can shade into exclusivist and anti-immigrant nationalism which remind us of the historically close relationship that has existed between environmentalism and several variants of European fascism.

However, it has always been problematic to look at the state as an isolated, discrete institution, and nowhere more so than in relations to the environment.[18] As we have already seen, there are very good reasons as to why so much discussion of the ecological challenge is couched in terms of a move 'beyond sovereignty'—either in terms of the changes that have already occurred or in terms of the changes that need to take place if the ecological challenge is to be met. Given the seriousness of the challenge, much ecological thinking and almost all environmental practice has tended to follow the two principal dimensions along which the normative structure of international society has evolved: the move towards more solidarist forms of interstate cooperation on the one hand, and the emergence of new forms of governance beyond the state on the other.

Solidarist cooperation

Cries of despair need not be taken at face value. Indeed, it is perfectly possible to provide an optimistic reading of the evolution of global environmental governance. On this view, international society has begun to tackle emerging environmental problems, albeit fitfully and perhaps belatedly, by building on

[15] For a recent comparative study of these changes, see J. S. Dryzeck, D. Downes, C. Hunold, and D. Scholsberg (eds.), *Green States and Social Movements: Environmental Movements in the United States, United Kingdom, Germany and Norway* (Oxford: Oxford University Press, 2003).

[16] See e.g. Herman E. Daly and John B. Cobb, *For the Common Good* (London: Earthscan, 1990).

[17] See e.g. Roger Scruton, 'Conservatism', in Andrew Dobson and Robyn Eckersely (eds.), *Political Theory and the Ecological Challenge* (Cambridge: Cambridge University Press, 2006), 7–19.

[18] See, Karen T. Litfin (ed.), *The Greening of Sovereignty in World Politics* (Cambridge, MA: MIT Press, 1998).

the common interests, common rules, and common institutions of international society.[19]

In the first place, optimists can point to the emergence of an increasingly complex structure of global environmental governance and to the increased attention given by policymakers and politicians to international environmental issues. However varied the level of concern, it is now very difficult to imagine environmental concerns disappearing completely from the agendas of governments. Not only has there been a mushrooming of environmental regimes but the time taken from recognition of a problem to international action has decreased (compare, e.g., the Law of Sea negotiations with the emergence of the ozone regime and both with the signature at UNCED of the framework conventions on biodiversity and climate change). Here we could also note the 500 or so multilateral environmental agreements that form the heart of the structure of global environmental governance—60 per cent of which have been negotiated since 1972 Stockholm Conference, and 85 per cent of which cover domestic (as opposed to trans-border) activities.[20]

Second, international society has seen the emergence of a wide variety of new international legal concepts with which to deal with environmental problems. Legal duties to prevent environmental harm, liability for environmental harm, duties to inform and to consult, duties to undertake environmental assessments have all become firmly established. Moreover, quite radical principles have appeared on the international scene, albeit usually in a 'softer' form: for example, the precautionary principle, the principle of intergenerational equity; ideas of common heritage, of shared resources, and of common concern; and the recognition by the industrial countries of a duty to help secure sustainability in the developing world through the transfer of funds and technology. Such a normative shift is undoubtedly important and needs to be seen as part of a broader shift in international legal understandings of sovereignty: away from an emphasis on the rights of states and towards a far greater stress on both duties and common interests. Such developments also bring home the extent to which sovereignty needs to be understood not as a single discrete claims based solely on state power, but rather as a historically constituted 'bundle of competences' whose exact

[19] Amongst the large literature on international environmental cooperation, see Ronald B. Mitchell, 'International Environment', in Walter Carlsnaes, Thomas Risse, and Beth Simmons (eds.), *Handbook of International Relations* (London: Sage, 2002), 500–16; Michael Zuern, 'The Rise of International Environmental Research: A Review of Current Research', *World Politics*, 50/4 (1998), 617–49; Matthew Paterson, 'Interpreting Trends in Global Environmental Governance', *International Affairs*, 75/4 (1999), 793–802; Peter M. Haas, Robert O. Keohane, and Mark Levy (eds.), *Institutions for the Earth* (Cambridge, MA: MIT Press, 1993); and Oran R. Young (ed.), *Global Governance: Drawing Insights from the Environmental Experience* (Cambridge, MA: MIT Press, 1997).

[20] Peter M. Haas, 'Social Constructivism and the Evolution of Multilateral Environmental Governance', in Aseem Prakash and Jeffrey A. Hart (eds.), *Globalization and Governance* (New York: Routledge, 1999), 109.

definition depends on the changing constitution of the international legal order as a whole.[21] Environmental governance has therefore come to include an increasing number of formal institutions, specific legal rules and principles, and broad political norms. In the context of North/South relations the most potentially significant of these political norms is the idea of 'common but differentiated responsibilities—recognition of shared interests but recognition too that the distribution of costs has to be differentiated according to a state's level of development, its ability to pay, and (less clearly) some notion of historic justice.

Third, optimists stress the extent to which environmental regimes need to be understood and evaluated as part of an ongoing process of management and negotiation. For the optimists it is wrong to make excessive play on the failures and loopholes of a particular agreement. Rather, the effectiveness of environmental regimes derives from the extent to which states are tied into a continuing and institutionalized process: hence, the explicit attention in almost all environmental agreements for provisions on regular meetings and the generation and publication of information; hence, the view of regimes as frameworks around which political pressure on states can be mobilized. What matters about the Kyoto Protocol, for example, is not that it would have a great impact on climate change (which it will not); but rather that it creates a political framework within which more effective agreements might be negotiated. Moreover, even in periods when governments of powerful states have rejected international agreements (as with the United States in relation to the 1991 Convention on Biological Diversity, the 1997 Kyoto Protocol, and the 2000 Cartegena Protocol on Biosafety), changes can still be taking place at the domestic and transnational levels. Hence, the action taken by several US states on climate change or the way in which US firms have had to adapt to international regulation in the area of biotechnology and transgenic crops.

Fourth, optimists point to the extent to which conflict over sovereignty has eased. Attitudes to sovereignty, particularly in the developing world, have shifted very substantially since the Stockholm Conference in 1972. Developing countries such as China, India, or Brazil have moved away from the rigid dichotomy between environment and development visible at Stockholm. They have come to lay greater weight on the importance of protecting the environment and on moving towards more sustainable patterns of economic development. There is, then, increasing consensus on the ways in which environmental protection can reinforce economic development. There is also increased awareness of the threats posed to the South by unchecked environmental degradation. In addition, the South has come to accept that

[21] For more detailed legal analysis see, in particular, Patricia Birnie and Alan Boyle, *International Law and the Environment*, 2nd edn. (Oxford: Oxford University Press, 2002).

environmental degradation within states is a matter of legitimate interest to the outside world, being both a matter of 'international concern' (suggesting that it is legitimate for other states to become involved), and, increasingly, of the 'common concern to humankind'. Recent declarations have also acknowledged the rights of NGOs both to involve themselves within the 'domestic' environmental affairs of developing countries and to participate in global negotiations.

Finally, a great deal of optimistic case depends on confidence in scientific knowledge: both to generate solutions to environmental problems, but also to promote and facilitate international cooperation. Indeed, one dominant theme of the literature has been the extent to which increasingly levels of scientific knowledge can work to redirect state interests, to facilitate international cooperation, and to promote 'environmental learning'. Within this context much attention has been given to the role of transnational 'epistemic communities' of scientists and experts.[22] From the liberal perspective, increased scientific understanding of environmental problems will work to redirect state interests and to facilitate international cooperation. 'The norms, rules and strategies for environmental governance are no longer widely contested'.[23]

Complex governance beyond the state

On many issues (such as deforestation, biodiversity, ozone, fisheries, and hazardous waste) environmental governance is characterized by a complex and shifting array of actors, including states, NGOs, transnational social movements and civil society organizations (CSOs), and specialist transnational communities.[24] This is, of course, related to the greatly increased role that non-governmental groups (NGOs) have come to play in global environmental politics: in shifting public and political attitudes towards the environment and placing environmental issues high on the political agendas of an increasing number of states; in publicizing the nature and seriousness of environmental problems; in acting as a conduit for the dissemination of scientific research; in organizing and orchestrating pressure on states, companies, and international organizations; and in providing one of the most important

[22] See Peter M. Haas, 'Epistemic Communities and the Dynamics of International Environmental Governance', in Volker Rittberger (ed.), *Regime Theory and International Relations* (Oxford: Oxford University Press, 1995).

[23] Haas (1999: 103).

[24] On this theme see, in particular, Ken Conca, 'Old States in New Bottles? The Hybridization of Authority in Global Environmental Governance', in John Barry and Robyn Eckersley (eds.), *The State and the Global Ecological Crisis* (Cambridge, MA: MIT Press, 2005), 181–205; and Frank Bierman, 'Global Governance and the Environment', in Michele Betsill, Kathryn Hochstetler, and Dimistris Stevis (eds.), *Palgrave Guide to Environmental Politics* (New York: Palgrave, 2005).

mechanisms for helping to ensure effective implementation of environmental agreements.[25] Impatient as ever with states, liberals are inclined to see the emergence of this transnational civil society as an inherently positive development.[26]

As discussed in Chapter 4, environmental thinking and environmental practice has tended to develop along two streams. The first presses in a functional–contractual direction. Under this heading we would place those aspects of environmental governance that involve epistemic communities of technical specialists and the many regulatory networks that are responsible for the development, diffusion, and implementation of an increasing range of environmental norms, rules, and regulations. On this view, institutions, including state institutions, should not be seen at representative of sovereign power or as embodiments of a particular community; but rather as functional bodies that compete with one another to provide efficient solutions to governance problems. There is no prior normative preference as to what governance functions should be undertaken at what level, by what kinds of actors, or by what social mechanism (state, market, and civil society). State functions are substitutable and may be assumed by external agencies, by private actors and, given the nature of the ecological challenge, by a range of transnational actors. On this account, states would still exist; but the status and the protection conferred by the norm of sovereignty would disappear. A second stream presses in a deliberative-democratic direction. The nature of the ecological challenge pushes towards more open and diverse governance arrangements, with substantially greater power for local communities, increased autonomy for various ethnic and territorial groups, and legal recognition for civil society organization. Here international law becomes the law of a cosmopolitan community. It regulates states but does not depend on the will of the state for its existence, content, or implementation. The state is at least partially constituted by the will of this transnational civil society. Again the state continues to exist, but it loses its place as an autonomous institution and instead become one of many participants in a broader and far more complex social, political, and legal process.

Power and values

Liberals remain inclined to believe that the reality of ecological interdependence will create problems that can only be solved by new and more

[25] Thomas Princen and Matthias Finger (eds.), *Environmental NGOs in World Politics: Linking the Local with the Global* (London: Routledge, 1994).

[26] For an analysis of the role of different non-state groups within a specific negotiation, see Christoph Bail, Robert Falkner, and Helen Marquand (eds.), *The Cartegena Protocol on Biosafety* (London: Earthscan for RIIA, 2002), chs. 27, 28, and 29.

far-reaching mechanisms of cooperation. Radical environmental degradation of the planet will involve losses for all and states are locked into a situation from which they cannot escape and about which will be forced to cooperate. Thus, for modern liberals, the seriousness of environmental problems and the inescapability of ecological interdependence will increasingly force states to cooperate. Rosenau, for example, talks of environmental issues 'impelling national and sub-national governments towards ever greater transnational cooperation.'[27] The language of environmentalism is full of talk of 'necessities' and 'imperatives' and often rests on the idea that fear of impending catastrophe will inevitably help to bring forth reform.

Sceptics, on the other hand, continue to highlight the many obstacles to cooperation. In the first place, the loose rhetoric of 'global environmental interdependence' disguises a wide variety of problems whose specific character may sometimes work to promote cooperation (as in the case of ozone) but may also militate against cooperation (as in the case of global climate change). Second, the weaknesses of many existing legal regimes are too great to be ignored. The numbers of agreements may well be large but sanctions for compliance are weak. States have shown a marked preference for nonbinding targets/guidelines which they are free to implement at whatever pace they see fit rather the acceptance of firm and unambiguous obligations. Most agreements are peppered with caveats, qualifications, and escape holes, and lacking in clear measurable commitments, and few existing environmental treaties contain inescapable requirements that states resort to binding third-party procedures for settlement of disputes. States remain extremely keen to maintain firm control over reporting, monitoring, and inspection procedures. The reluctance of the United States in the 1990s to join regimes dealing with biological diversity, climate change, and biosafety provided graphic evidence of the on-going problem of managing unequal power.

Third, there are powerful pressures on states and state representatives to place a high priority on their immediate short-term interests and on the protection of political autonomy. There is a clear mismatch between the time horizons of politicians and political processes on the one hand and the extended time frames needed to address and deal with many of the most serious environmental problems on the other. In addition, there is no easy link between increased scientific knowledge, the political salience of the environment, and the growth of international cooperation. Although environmental issues have generally grown in importance over the past thirty years, this process is neither linear nor can it be divorced from politics. The high levels of environmental activism of the late 1980s fell away and environmental

[27] James Rosenau, 'Environmental Challenges in a Turbulent World', in Ronnie D. Lipschutz and Ken Conca (eds.), *The State and Social Power in Global Environmental Politics* (New York: Columbia University Press, 1983), 71–93.

parties lost support in many countries through the 1990s. On the one side, the issue concerns the politicization of science and scientific knowledge and the far from simple ways in which scientific consensus forms and presses towards a particular policy response. On the other, the political salience of environmental concerns depends on a wide range of political factors, often wholly unrelated either to the environment per se or to scientific knowledge and understanding.

Fourth, there are the serious difficulties facing states in their efforts to manage the global economy in the interest of ecological rationality. International environmental regulation has traditionally relied on separating issues and negotiating particular agreements to deal with particular problems. However, it has become increasingly difficult to treat ecology and international political economy as separate spheres. For example the institutions that matter cannot be confined to those that have a specifically 'environmental' label (such as UN Environment Programme, Commission on Sustainable Development, or the Global Environment Fund), but rather are the core institutions that manage (or at least seek to manage) the world economy (the World Bank/IMF, the GATT, and the Group of Seven). The intrinsic and complex interconnections between different environmental issues, and between the environment and many other domains of social and economic life place the dominant techniques of international environmental cooperation under increasing strain. It is increasingly difficult to separate the issues. Attempting to give meaning to sustainability at the international level is necessarily about managing the environmental implications of a diverse and highly politicized sets of relationships (e.g. links between trade and environment, between debt and environment, between military spending and environment, and so on). Unsurprisingly, international society has found this task to be a daunting one and the most notable step in this direction (the negotiation at Rio in 1992 of the 800-page Agenda 21) was marked by omissions, by lack of overall coherence, and by a reluctance to prioritize and to specify any too clear link between impressive aspirations and effective action. The more recent impasse on trade and environment linkages within the WTO provides a further clear example of the difficulties involved.

Sceptics include political realists, always willing to point to the 'false promise of international institutions'. But they also include radical ecologists who doubt the reformist liberalism that has characterized so much international thinking on the environment—the idea that a revitalization of global growth (albeit of a more sustainable character) is an essential part of averting future environmental catastrophe. For those who see a deep contradiction between this continued emphasis on growth and the finite nature of the earth's ecosystem, the distributional conflicts, above all between rich and poor, are likely to be far more intense and politically significant than the comforting rhetoric of 'sustainable development' would suggest.

The environment provides a particularly significant example of how the problem of capturing common interest is exacerbated by inequalities and conflicts over values and perceptions of justice.

Power and inequality

The environment is deeply implicated in the patterns of unequal power that continue to dominate world politics—in at least four ways.

First, there is the role that the past use of environmental resources has played in the practices of imperialism, in the successful development of the industrialized world, and in the creation of present inequalities.[28] The enormous disparities in resource use and the relative size of the 'ecological footprint' cast by rich and poor frame the contemporary global politics of the environment and open up the most fundamental distributional dilemma: how can developing countries increase the welfare of their citizens and their power and wealth as states without copying the profligate lifestyles and unsustainable patterns of consumption and resource use of the now rich and dominant? What will be the future ecological impact of the policies chosen by the developing world and how will the global environment be politically managed in a system in which the OECD countries represent a diminishing share of the world's population and the global economy?

Second, there is the unequal impact of environmental change on different states and communities and the vastly different capacity of states and communities to cope and adapt to environmental change. One recurring theme in this book has been how processes of globalization impact very differently across the world and how this differential impact is a major feature of global inequality. Developing countries are already threatened by the expanding scale of many originally local problems, such as the erosion of topsoil and water scarcity. They will also be disproportionately affected by unchecked climate change, through rising water stress, falling farm incomes, increased malnutrition and disease, and the likely exacerbation of armed conflict resulting from environmental stress. Moreover, the generation of many apparently 'local' environmental problems and the capacity of states to confront those problems is heavily influenced by the pressures and constraints of an increasingly globalized capitalist economy—for example, the linkages between structural adjustment policies and environmental degradation, or, more broadly, the transmission via the market of Western lifestyles and of a particular vision of modernity and progress.

Third, there is the role of power in setting the agenda of environmental politics, including the deeply contested issue of what counts as a *global*

---

[28] On imperialism, see Alfred W. Crosby, *Ecological Imperialism: The Biological Expansion of Europe, 900–1900*, 2nd edn. (Cambridge: Cambridge University Press, 2004).

challenge and the way in which ecological ideas are translated into policy. In part this has to do with the setting of the broad agenda, for example the way in which the environmental debate becomes dominated by those issues in which Northern countries have a particular interest (biodiversity, climate change, and tropical deforestation) or which particularly engage the emotions of Northern publics; and away from often less headline-grabing problems that are of greatest concern to the peoples of the South (desertification, water- and fuel-wood scarcity, lack of access to safe drinking water, clean air, and decent sanitation) and, above all, from the pressing need for continued economic development. Attention is therefore diverted away from the pressing need for the industrialized world to adopt changed patterns of economic development involving lower resource use, the full internalization of environmental externalities, strict pollution abatement measures, and a lower relative share of both the Earth's resources and its 'sinks'. But power can also shape how particular environmental ideas are understood and developed. The case of 'liberal environmentalism' provides a good example—the way in which the concept of sustainability was picked up in the later 1980s by the OECD and the international financial institutions and transformed into a set of technical understandings that purged it of its radical elements so as to do as little harm as possible to orthodox ideas of economic development.[29]

In the period from around 1985 to 1992, the principal axis of confrontation was clearly focused between North and South. How could environment and development be reconciled? To what extent was the North willing to accept the responsibility for its past contribution to environmental problems and to transfer the technology and financial resources necessary to enable and persuade developing countries to adopt more sustainable patterns of development? In addition, developing countries were highly resistant to moves that would further legitimize external intervention in domestic environmental matters (with forests remaining a particularly contentious issue); and there were conflicts over the institutional control over the mechanisms designed to assist the move towards sustainability (such as the relative voting power within the Global Environmental Facility). For much of the 1990s, the debate about power swung in a different direction and concerned the response of international society in the face of a global hegemon that either failed to support efforts to build environmental regimes or actively sought to counter them?[30] Here it is worth noting that the United States rejected the Kyoto Treaty not only because it saw it as a flawed agreement and because it went against its own economic interests but also because it rejected the exemption of major developing countries such as China and India as intrinsically unfair.

[29] Stephen Bernstein, *The Compromise of Liberal Environmentalism* (New York: Columbia University Press, 2001).
[30] See Robert Falkner, 'American Hegemony and the Global Environment', *International Studies Review*, 7/4 (2005), 585–99.

As the United States re-engages with environmental issues and, especially, with the problem of climate change, so the centrality of North–South axis has re-emerged and so have the distributional and the institutional conflicts (to do with the control over the transfer of technology and resources and with the creation of the sort of effective enforcement mechanism that the Kyoto Protocol has lacked). However, the extent to which the developed world needs an agreement on climate change and the extent to which that agreement will have to include major emerging states such as China, India, and Brazil opens up a potentially rather different distribution of power. In this case, the problem of effective and legitimate governance may well revolve around the relationship between a club of major environmental players on the one hand and the broader problem of rich–poor relations on the other.

Justice, values, and context

In relation to the environment, Henry Shue has written of the 'inevitability of justice'. [31] Environmental challenges, most notably climate change, pose a wide range of difficult ethical issues. [32] Many of these follow directly from the distributional and procedural questions sketched above: how should historic responsibilities in relation to the environment be understood and acted upon? How should the costs of preventing avoidable change be allocated? Who should assume responsibility for adapting to those changes that cannot be avoided? How to ensure procedural fairness within the institutions of global environmental governance, especially given existing inequalities in the distribution of wealth and power? But reflecting on the changing nature of environmental problems has also stimulated debate on the normative framework within which these many specific issues can be debated.

For many people the emergence of global environmental problems and the greatly strengthened awareness of a global common interest amongst all peoples in protecting the environment and safeguarding the future of humanity has provided a powerful stimulus to the growth of a cosmopolitan moral consciousness. The notion of sharing a world, the essential interconnectedness and interdependence of the global environment, and the scarcity of the resources available to humanity that need to be distributed both within and between generations all create conditions within which it becomes much harder than in the past to accept that consideration of justice in general, and of distributive justice in particular, end at the borders of states. For

---

[31] Henry Shue, 'The Unavoidability of Justice', in Andrew Hurrell and Benedict Kingsbury (eds.), *The International Politics of the Environment* (Oxford: Oxford University Press, 1992), 373–97.
[32] For an excellent analytical survey, see Stephen M. Gardiner, 'Ethics and Global Climate Change', *Ethics*, 114 (April 2004), 555–600.

many people, then, global environmental interdependence has given greater plausibility to visions of a cosmopolitan global community.

Yet one can also argue that the general communitarian argument in favour of pluralism and diversity assumes particular importance in the environmental field. The relationship to nature and the natural world is often a defining feature of a community's sense of itself. Moreover, there can be no universal definition of sustainable development that can be applied in a mechanistic fashion in all parts of the world. Environmental policies and priorities will inevitably and legitimately vary from one country (and from one community) to another. This reflects the immense variation that exists in the physical world, in the nature and scope of environmental challenges, and in the different perspectives on environmental problems that come from different levels of economic development. There is certainly a good deal of room for positive reinforcement between different goals and priorities. But sustainability is unavoidably about making trade-offs between different priorities: between the maximum preservation of the natural environment and the pursuit of continuously high levels of economic development; between rapid economic growth and the protection of traditional cultures or improvements in equity and social justice; or between the importation of the latest technology and the safeguarding of traditional practices and cultures. Liberal governance approaches to global environmental negotiations have often overlooked the absence of a shared cultural or cognitive script that allows the largely rhetorical consensus value of 'sustainability' to be translated into stable and effective operational rules. This is especially so when it comes to assessing the intrinsic value to be placed on the natural world and its preservation, the idea that what makes nature valuable to human beings is its very 'naturalness' and irreplaceability.

Understandings of a 'nature' and 'humanity' have been constructed very differently according to both culture and context. There is, for example, a very strong tradition within the United States that has led many people to see environmental protection in terms of the protection of wilderness.[33] This reflects a very particular social and environmental history. Even within the developed world, this is very different from the emphasis within German environmentalism on the critique of industrialized society. In the Anglo-Saxon world, a good deal of ecological thought has developed the distinction between an 'anthropocentric' position (where the value of nature derives from its role in fulfilling human interests and values) and an 'ecocentric' position (which insists on the moral standing of the natural world and the 'rights of nature').[34] In France, by contrast, an environmental thinking has tended

[33] Roderick Frazier Nash, *Wilderness and the American Mind*, 3rd edn. (New Haven, CT: Yale University Press, 1982).

[34] Robyn Eckersely, *Environmentalism and Political Theory* (London: UCL Press, 1992).

to probe and problematize the distinction between 'nature' and 'humanity' and the ways in which they are mutually constitutive.[35] In the case of the North–South divide, Guha and Allier have developed the distinction between a northern environmentalism that stresses the dichotomy between the rights of humans as against the rights of nature, and that is often structured around cultural and aesthetic goals and values; and a southern environmentalism that is built around the dichotomy between rich humans and poor humans, and that stresses the survival of communities and their rights to resources, and the need to transform global economic structures.[36] Finally, for many indigenous peoples nature simply cannot be understood in instrumental terms and, instead, we need to appreciate the very diverse ways in which nature's intrinsic values are related to community and identity.[37]

Conclusion

Three conclusions can be drawn from the increasingly close engagement between international society and the environment.

In the first place, there is little chance of escaping from the centrality of the state. The focus is likely to remain on the uneven and highly contested role of the state and on its ambiguous relationship with the environment: on the one hand, as an agent deeply implicated in many of the most serious processes of environmental harm; and, on the other, as the still-dominant form of political organization that will inevitably have to play a central role in facilitating progressive environmental change. Many enquiries of this kind stress the limits and obstacles that block progress and connect many of those limits to the state and the constraining logics of both domestic and international politics. The state may not be about to fade away any time soon but it is clear that the greening of sovereignty is an enormously difficult process. From this perspective the task is to imagine and think through innovative ways in which the environmentally destructive potential of the state can be tamed and its emancipatory potential enhanced.

Second, although the environment is in many ways the clearest embodiment of one-world logics and one-world dynamics, sustainability necessarily involves understanding and engaging with many different worlds, with many

[35] Kerry H. Whiteside, *Divided Natures: French Contribution to Political Ecology* (Cambridge, MA: MIT Press, 2002).

[36] Ramachandra Guha and Juan Martinez-Allier (eds.), *Varieties of Environmentalism* (London: Earthscan, 1997); and Juan Martinez-Allier, *The Environmentalism of the Poor: A Study of Ecological Conflicts and Valuation* (London: Edward Elgar, 2003).

[37] For one example, see Laura Rival, 'The Growth of Family Trees: Understanding Huaorani Perceptions of the Forest', *Man*, 28/4 (1993), 635–52. See also Darrell Posey and Graham Duttfield, *Beyond Intellectual Property: Toward Traditional Resource Rights for Indigenous Peoples and Local Communities* (Ottawa: IDRC, 1996).

different voices, and with many different understandings of what sustainability might mean. Politically, it is an issue on which top-down approaches to governance are very likely to fail on grounds of both effectiveness and legitimacy. Normatively, the common appeal in ecological thought and practice to moral intuition as a mode of reasoning and debate (rather than abstract rationalism) pushes environmentalism towards engagement with the different and varied moral cultures that exist across the world. The central role within environmental thinking and environmental practice of diversity and particularity, on the one hand, and commonality and community, on the other, make it a particularly rich source for thinking through the ethical relationship between the one world and the many worlds.

Third, considering global political order in relation to the environment highlights not just the one world and the many worlds, but also the close relationship between the old world and the new. Environmental problems lead naturally to claims that we are witnessing a fundamental discontinuity in the system of states. Environmental writing has often been well ahead of the field in suggesting that we are witnessing a reconfiguration of political space in which traditional notions of the state and of state sovereignty are being transformed. As this chapter has indicated, the ecological challenge has indeed been one of the most important factors contributing to the changes that have taken place in the changing normative structure of international society. And yet, even in relation to the environment, there is a real danger that transformationist claims overstate the scale of the changes that have actually taken place and, more important, that this exaggeration might lead to a misdiagnosis of the challenges to be faced. It is necessary *both* to understand and illuminate the still very important state-centred agenda of 'traditional' international environmental politics *and* to understand the ways in which environmental problems are altering dominant frames of reference and opening up new understandings about the nature of global political order. Rather than be seen as two different kinds of project, a very great deal of global environmental politics is likely to be concerned with the complex ways in which these two agendas relate and interact.

Part III

Alternatives

10

One world? Many worlds?

This chapter considers the place of regions within our understanding of global international society. As the title suggests, I am especially interested in asking questions about the relationship between the one world and the many worlds—on the one side, the one world of globalizing capitalism, of global security dynamics, of a global political system that, for many, revolves around a single hegemonic power, of global institutions and global governance, and of the drive to develop and embed a global cosmopolitan ethic; and, on the other side, the extent to which regions and the regional level of practice and of analysis have become more firmly established as important elements of the architecture of global political order; and the extent to which we are witnessing an emerging multi-regional system of international relations.

The chapter addresses three questions:

1. What has been the place of regionalism and what is included under the heading of regionalism?

2. What has been the place of regionalism within international society and what accounts for the renewed move towards regionalism?

3. In what ways might regionalism be related to international order and global governance? I consider four notions: regions as containers for diversity and difference; regions as poles or powers; regions as levels in a system of multilevel global governance; and regions as harbingers of change in the character of international society.

The place of regionalism in international society

From the development of the earliest political communities, economic and political relations came naturally to have a strong regionalist focus, above all because of the limits of technology, trade, and communications. There was a strong regional focus to the development of many imperial systems: both contiguous expansion as with the United States and Russia, and overseas expansion, as with France in north and west Africa. In the inter-war period both Germany and Japan sought to construct coercively imposed regional orders. Up until the Second World War, the Inter-American System was exceptional in terms of the development of a formal, if weak, institutional framework. The post-1945 era, however, was to be built around the twin pillars of the sovereign state on the one hand, and multilateral institutions on the other. The UN and the Bretton Woods institutions were to provide security and some degree of economic stability for a world of sovereign nation-states, not to replace the state. Regionalism was not totally written out of the script. The widespread belief that the nation-state had had its day and the strong revulsion against excesses committed in the name of nationalism stimulated regionalist thinking, above all in Europe. Others (both politicians such as Churchill and commentators such as Walter Lippmann) favoured a system of international order built around regional spheres of responsibility. But, overall, regionalism was to play a subordinate and secondary role.

This changed, above all, because of the pressures of the Cold War.[1] There had been regionalist exceptions in the multilateral order and these became increasingly important (especially Article 24 of the GATT and Article 52 of the Charter). And, of course, it was the success of economic regionalism in Europe that was the most important catalyst, and the success of European regionalism encouraged a wave of attempts at imitation and export across many parts of the post-colonial world. These, we should remember, were not intended as limited exercises in interstate cooperation but often fully fledged federations complete with airlines, common currencies, and flags. This wave of activism was followed by a slow-down in the progress of the movement of European integration from the mid-1960s and the near total failure of regionalist economic arrangements outside Europe. However, after a decade or more of disillusion, regionalism began to gather pace once again from the late 1980s, with commentators pointing to the success and durability of the Association of Southeast Asian Nations (ASEAN) and the expansion of security cooperation in Asia; and the wide-ranging return of economic regionalism, often involving exercises in deep integration and ambitious regional economic integration schemes, with NAFTA and Mercosur amongst the most notable developments outside Europe. Of fifty-eight regional groupings, twenty were created after the end of the Cold War. A wide variety of regional groupings were appearing in almost every part of the world, and increasing attention was being given to the 'new regionalism'.[2]

---

[1] On the historical evolution, see Louise Fawcett, 'Exploring Regional Domains: A Comparative History of Regionalism', *International Affairs*, 80/3 (2004), 429–46.

[2] On the new regionalism, see Louise Fawcett and Andrew Hurrell (eds.), *Regionalism in World Politics* (Oxford: Oxford University Press, 1995); Andrew Gamble and Anthony Payne (eds.), *Regionalism and World Order* (Basingstoke, UK: Palgrave/Macmillan, 1996); Edward D. Mansfield and Helen V. Milner, 'The New Wave of Regionalism', *International Organization*,

It is clear even from the above very brief sketch that 'regionalism' is a blanket term covering a wide range of very different developments and processes. The terrain is contested. The precise terms are not in themselves important. But the underlying distinctions matter greatly and much regionalist analysis is muddled precisely because commentators are seeking to explain very different phenomena or because they are insufficiently clear about the relationship amongst the varied processes described under the banner of 'regionalism'. Although geographical proximity and contiguity in themselves tell us very little about either the definitions of regions or the dynamics of regionalism, they do helpfully distinguish regionalism from other forms of 'less than global' organization. Without some geographical limits, the term 'regionalism' becomes diffuse and unmanageable. The problem of defining regions and regionalism attracted a good deal of academic attention in the late 1960s and early 1970s but the results yielded few clear conclusions. Regionalism was often analysed in terms of the degree of social cohesiveness (ethnicity, race, language, religion, culture, history, and consciousness of a common heritage), economic cohesiveness (trade patterns and economic complementarity), political cohesiveness (regime type and ideology), and organizational cohesiveness (existence of formal regional institutions).[3] Particular attention was given to the idea of regional interdependence.[4] Nevertheless, attempts to define and delineate regions 'scientifically' produced little clear result.[5] There are no 'natural' regions, and definitions of 'region' and indicators of 'regionness' vary according to the particular problem or question under investigation.[6] Moreover, it is how political actors perceive and interpret the idea of a region that is critical: all regions are socially constructed and hence politically contested. This makes it especially important to distinguish between

53/3 (1999), 602–8; Björn Hettne, András Inotai, and Oswaldo Sunkel (eds.), *Globalism and the New Regionalism* (Basingstoke, UK: Macmillan, 1999); and Shaun Breslin, Christopher W. Hughes, Nicola Phillips, and Ben Rosamond, *New Regionalisms in the Global Political Economy* (London: Routledge, 2002). See also Mary Farrell, Björn Hettne, and Luk van Langenbove (eds.), *Global Politics of Regionalism: Theory and Practice* (London: Pluto, 2005); and Amitav Acharya and Alistair Ian Johnston (eds.), *Crafting Cooperation: Regional International Institutions in Comparative Perspective* (Cambridge: Cambridge University Press, 2007).

[3] See e.g. Louis J. Cantori and Steven L. Spiegel, 'International Regions: A Comparative Approach to Five Subordinate Systems', *International Studies Quarterly*, 13/4 (December 1969), 361–80; Louis J. Cantori and Steven L. Spiegel (eds.), *The International Politics of Regions: A Comparative Approach* (Englewood Cliffs, NJ: Prentice-Hall, 1970); William Thompson, 'The Regional Subsystem: A Conceptual Explication and a Propositional Inventory', *International Studies Quarterly*, 17/1 (1973), 89–117.

[4] A good example is Joseph S. Nye (ed.), *International Regionalism: Readings* (Boston, MA: Little, Brown and Co., 1968).

[5] See Bruce Russett, *International Regions and the International System* (Chicago, IL: Rand McNally, 1967).

[6] For a still very relevant discussion of the problems of classifying regional systems, see David Grigg, 'The Logic of Regional Systems', *Annals of the Association of American Geographers*, 55/3 (September 1965), 465–91.

regionalism as description and regionalism as prescription—regionalism as a moral position or as a doctrine as to how international relations ought to be organized.

It is useful to make a distinction between five different kinds of processes. (1) *Regionalization*: This refers to societal integration and the often undirected processes of social and economic interaction. It is what the early writers on regionalism talked of as informal integration or soft integration and is not based on the conscious policy of states or groups of states but is the outcome of a broad range of economic, social, and cultural forces. Examples of informal but densely integrated economic and social spaces would include the Greater China Zone (around Hong Kong, Taiwan, and southern China) or the northern Mexico–southern California area, or the various cross-national growth triangles within Europe. (2) *Regional Awareness and Identity*: 'Regional awareness', 'regional identity', and 'regional consciousness' are inherently imprecise and fuzzy notions. Nevertheless, they are impossible to ignore and, within the broader politics of identity, have become more central to the analysis of contemporary regionalism. As with nations, so regions can be seen as imagined communities which rest on mental maps whose lines highlight some features whilst ignoring others. Discussions of regional awareness lay great emphasis on language and rhetoric; on the discourse of regionalism and the political processes by which definitions of regionalism and regional identity are constantly defined and redefined; and on the historically constructed shared understandings and the meanings given to political activity by the actors involved. (3) *Interstate cooperation*: This refers to closer interstate cooperation and the construction of overlapping sets of intergovernmental agreements or a region-wide network of regimes in a variety of issue areas. Such cooperative arrangements can serve a wide variety of purposes. On the one hand, they can serve as a means of responding to external challenges and of coordinating regional positions in international institutions or negotiating forums. On the other, they can be developed to secure welfare gains, to promote common values, or to solve common problems, especially problems arising from increased levels of regional interdependence. (4) *State-led integration*: This refers to specific policy decisions by states to reduce or remove barriers to mutual exchange of goods, services, capital, and people. This is a subset of the previous category and forms the heartland of what many people take as the natural definition of regionalism and regional integration. (5) *Regional consolidation*: Early theorists of integration were obsessed by the idea of an end-goal that would transform the role of nation-states via the pooling of sovereignty and lead to the emergence of some new form of political community. In fact, we can think about the possible emergence of a consolidated region along various dimensions. One might indeed refer to some measure of identity or community. Another would involve a situation in which the region plays a defining role in the relations between the states of that region and the rest of the world, or comes to form the organizing basis for policy within the region across a range of issues. For those outside the region, regionalism is politically significant to the extent that it can impose costs on outsiders: whether through the detrimental impact of preferential regional economic arrangements (so-called malign regionalism that diverts trade and investment) or through causing a shift in the distribution of political power. It is also politically significant when outsiders are forced to define their policies towards individual regional states in regionalist terms. For those inside the region, regionalism matters when exclusion from regional arrangements imposes significant costs, both economic and political (such as loss of autonomy or a reduction in foreign policy options) and when the region becomes the organizing basis for policy within the region across a range of important issues.

The study of the new regionalism has underlined the degree to which, even if its form and dominant rhetoric are economic, regionalism is an extremely complex and dynamic process made up of not one but a series of interacting and often competing logics: logics of economic and technological transformation and societal integration; logics of power-political competition; logics of security (both interstate and societal); and logics of identity and community. Regionalism is best viewed as an unstable and indeterminate process of multiple and competing logics with no overriding teleology or single-end point. Dynamic regions are inherently unstable with little possibility of freezing the status quo. The analysis of the new regionalism has also underscored that, even if we lay emphasis on the construction of regions, including their discursive construction, power plays a central role. The power to name and shape the identity and boundaries of a region matters a great deal, as with the determination of the United States to pursue a trans-Pacific view of regionalism via APEC (Asia-Pacific Economic Cooperation) in such a way as to undercut narrower Asian variants;[7] or Brazil's efforts to create a form of South American regionalism that would exclude Mexico.

The one world into the many

In terms of explanation, the dominant tendency has been to look within regions. The heartland of the theory of regionalism focuses on the impact of rising levels of regional social and economic exchange and the links between economic integration, institutions and identity. The core logics most often

[7] An important feature of US power derives from its discretionary regional involvement and its refusal to become unconditionally committed. Being partially in and partially out, playing on the possibility of withdrawal, and sending mixed messages has consistently worked to Washington's power-political advantage. Think of Europe, Asia, and South America.

243

reflect the liberal institutionalism analysed in Chapter 3, but with many sub-varieties and important constructivist alternatives. As is well known, most of this work grew out of the European experience. It tended to take as its starting point the desire to create a common market and to intentionally privilege transnational economic interests, both to avoid the recurrence of war and conflict and to promote economic welfare in general as well as to protect a particular kind of economic model. The most important division is between those who see regionalism principally in terms of state interests and interstate arrangements and those who see integration as producing more complex regional polities.[8]

Although intra-regional constellations of power, interest, and identity remain of fundamental importance, the relationship between the one world of the international system and the many worlds of different regionalism has been given less prominence than it deserves.[9] All regionalist arrangements have to be understood in relation to systemic or 'outside-in' factors—even if the most important condition for regionalism in a specific case is the relative weakness of such factors. Let me look briefly at four areas.

In the first place, as has been frequently noted, the age of economic global-ization has also been the age of regionalization and much of the analysis of the new regionalism has been devoted to these linkages. Thus regionalism is seen as a critical part of the political economy of globalization and the strategies that states (and other actors) have adopted in the face of globalization. Some-times regionalism is seen as one amongst a range of contending world order projects and, in particular, as a conscious attempt to reassert political control over increased economic liberalization and globalization. For others, regional-ism takes on a more specifically political economy focus—either reproducing dominant forms of neo-liberal economic governance at the regional level, or serving as a form of resistance to globalization and as a platform where alternative norms and practices can be developed, as in the recent emergence of a vehemently anti-liberalizing (and often anti-liberal) regionalism in South America. But, from this perspective, the crucial point is that the emergence

---

[8] The literature is vast. For overviews, see Ben Rosamund, *Theories of European Integration* (Basingstoke, UK: Macmillan, 2000); and Jack Hayward and Anand Menon (eds.), *Governing Europe* (Oxford: Oxford University Press, 2003). Amongst the most important perspectives, see Moravcsik (1998); Philippe Schmitter, 'Neo-Neo-Functionalism', in Antje Wiener, and Thomas Diez (eds.), *European Integration Theory* (Oxford: Oxford University Press, 2003); and Wayne Sandholtz and Alec Stone Sweet (eds.), *European Integration and Supranational Governance* (Oxford: Oxford University Press, 1998).

[9] For all its sweep and sophistication, Buzan and Waever are primarily concerned with intra-regional security logics and they tend to view regions as mutually exclusive. Barry Buzan and Ole Waever, *Regions as Powers: The Structure of International Security* (Cambridge: Cambridge University Press, 2003). Katzenstein's important study does look at the place of regions within the broader system, but mostly from the perspective of a US hegemonic order. Peter Katzenstein, *A World of Regions: Asia and Europe in the American Imperium* (Ithaca, NY: Cornell University Press, 2005).

and the fate of regionalism need to be understood within the global restructuring of power and production. The many worlds are very closely intertwined with the character and fate of the one. It may be the case, for example, that the dense network of regionalized production chains in China and Southeast Asia in the electronics and computer industries are best seen as the product of decisions taken in the boardrooms of major corporations in the United States. The core driving logic is global even if the manifestation is regional.

A number of related arguments can be listed here in very bald summary: that the region is the most appropriate and viable level to reconcile the changing and intensifying pressures of global capitalist competition on the one hand with the need for political regulation and management on the other; that it is easier to negotiate 'deep integration' and the sorts of deeply intrusive rules needed to manage globalization at the regional level, given that value and societal consensus is likely to be higher and that the political problems of governance beyond the state are likely to be more manageable; that, for many developing countries, regionalism can be part of a process of controlled or negotiated integration into the global economy; and that, especially for developed countries, it offers a favourable level at which to recast the post-1945 bargain between market liberalization and social protection.

What of geopolitics and the international political system? Systemic factors were clearly fundamental to the emergence and success of European integration. They are also central to understanding the very different pattern of security relationships in Cold War Asia. For many analysts, the end of the Cold War removed the security overlay that had either dominated, or at least, strongly influenced, patterns of regional security in many parts of the world. Regions were 'set free'; and regional logics came to predominate in the production of insecurity (often related to the negative externalities produced by increasing levels of regional exchange and interdependence and often located on the problematic peripheries of strongly integrating regional cores); and in terms of the management of insecurity, with increased incentives for regional states to deal with their own problems and a decreased incentive for outside powers to intervene or become involved.[10] Note that this pattern contrasted not just with the Cold War but also with the globalizing security patterns of the classic age of European imperialism and, arguably, also with the ideological conflicts of the inter-war period which took on, if not a global, then certainly a strongly trans-regional character.

In the early years of this century we have, however, seen a very powerful reassertion of arguments stressing the importance of global and globalizing

---

[10] See especially Buzan and Waever (2003).

security logics—both directly in relation to terrorism and weapons of mass destruction as well as the extent to which these threats are themselves tied to processes of globalization; and in relation to the way in which the United States has responded to these threats, imposing a very powerful global perspective and set of policies. Recent practice and a great deal of recent analysis have therefore propounded and reinforced the notion of 'one world'. The impact on regionalism is contradictory. On the one side, these developments help revive the old idea of regionalism as a means of insulating the region from external interventionism, or, more ambitiously, of using the region as means of counterbalancing or resisting the power of the United States. On the other hand, they can undermine regionalism—because of divisions over the relative priority to be attached to terrorism and proliferation issues and over the appropriateness of different sorts of response; and because a more engaged United States provides opportunities for regional states to seek to draw in and enmesh the United States to their own regional advantage. Analytically the challenge is to look critically at the balance between the one world and the many. In particular, there is good reason to question the excessive globalism of the recent security debate. Even if they also have global connections and ramifications, most security threats are tied to local and regional circumstances and have to be understood through complex cultural and contextual filters. As during the Cold War, there is a real danger of imposing external categories onto regional realities (as in the simplistic and self-defeating attempt to divide the Middle East into 'moderates' and 'radicals').

There are two other sets of 'outside-in' factors to be noted. The first involves the relationship between the UN and regional bodies. We have become accustomed to the argument that weak states continue to exist because of external recognition: their juridical sovereignty is more important than their empirical sovereignty. In a similar way, many regional organizations are supported and held together at least in part because of the way in which outside actors support and legitimize them. The legitimacy of regional organizations comes from the role that they play (or at least are intended to play) in the broader structure of global governance. The other factor concerns the diffusion of the idea of regionalism itself: both the idea that regions matter and the way in which specific regionalist models come to be diffused across the world—through institutional competition (especially between the EU and NAFTA as providers of models of regional economic integration); through teaching and support (as with the active support that the EU has given to regionalism elsewhere); and through the operation of membership conditionality (as with the process of EU enlargement). Understanding more about these processes and how they occur and concentrating more on the broader phenomenon of 'inter-regionalism' is an important subject of future research.

The Many Worlds into the One

This section considers four arguments as to how the many worlds of regionalism have been, or might be, related to international order: regions as containers for diversity and difference; regions as poles or powers; regions as levels in a system of multilevel global governance; and regions as harbingers of change in the character of international society.

Regions as containers for culture and for value diversity

As we have seen, one of perennial attractions of a statist, pluralist conception of international society is that it has seemed to provide one way—and perhaps the least bad way—of organizing global politics in a world where actual consensus on fundamental values is limited or where there is widespread scepticism as to how a cross-cultural morality might be grounded. The massive movement of peoples, the intensification of contacts and interconnections between societies, and the multiple dislocations of established ways of thinking and of doing have intensified identity politics in many parts of the world. They have given a sharper and often destructive twist to struggles for cultural recognition. They have undermined the adequacy (and moral viability) of states as containers of cultural pluralism. If this is true, what of the possibility of recreating a form of global pluralism built around denser more solidaristic regions?

The idea that regions are, and should be, the embodiments of cultural distinctiveness is an old one. It can be seen in the long history of pan-regional ideas and movements. The tendency to assume that all roads would lead inevitably to the nation-state has perhaps distorted our reading of such movements, or at least led us to consign them rather too readily to a historical dead-end road. Such a view underplays the persistence of such views and the degree to which they continue to provide a powerful set of collective ideas and imaginings that can be tapped into by a range of political actors. Think of the continued power of pan-Islamic ideas and the ways in which globalization has given a new impetus to the possibility of a transnational Islamic community; or the revival of Bolivarianism; or of the many different ways in which ideas about Asian identity recur. Moreover, even if the nation-state 'wins out', posing the choices in terms of a stark conflict of pan-regionalism and the nation-state misses the ways in which both of these powerful forces have continued to interact across time and to feed into debates about global political order.

And yet seeking to recreate identity-based pluralism on a regional level confronts serious difficulties. This is a central lesson that emerges from the debates over Asian values in the 1990s. Faced by an increasingly interventionist Western-dominated international society and empowered by the success of regional economic development, the early and mid-1990s saw frequent claims that there was a distinctive Asian approach to human rights built around the idea of 'shared values': a different conception of the relationship between the individual and the state; respect for the community; the central importance of the duties that individuals owe towards the group; and the particular differences that follow from these values in terms of freedom of speech and freedom of association.[11]

Yet the working out of the debate on Asian values highlighted the diversity of voices within this allegedly coherent regionalist construction: the diversity of cultures and cultural traditions; the equally wide range of economic and political systems; the tremendous pace of social and economic change that was transforming societies and remoulding traditions; the fact that several major states (most notably Japan) kept their distance from the discussion of Asian values. Thus, even at the official level, notions of a unified and coherent set of Asian values needed to be taken with a large pinch of salt. Beyond the level of governments, NGOs propounded a very different message on human rights, upholding strong conceptions of universality, and arguing both for greater weight for civil and political rights and for social justice and grassroots empowerment. As noted previously, cultures are not best understood as closed and impermeable systems. Nor is it clear that the substantive differences across regions are as deep as often suggested. For example, the communitarian and social values of the Catholic and Christian Democratic tradition of human rights are just as much as part of the West as Anglo-American individualist liberalism. Finally, a great deal of the conflict over human rights in Asia had to do with traditional and straightforwardly political factors: the internal political dimension, and the building-up of the discourse of Asian values and of a 'threat' to those values as a means to increase political legitimacy; and the developmentalist claim and the revival of the idea that the imperative of economic development and state-building should trump Western liberal notions of civil and political rights.

Similar lessons emerge from the current debates over Islam in Europe; from the 'who are we' arguments in the United States; and even from the dynamism of change underway within the Islamic world, with there being no better case of complexity and dynamism than contemporary Iran. Spengler's image of windowless cultures was always nonsense as an empirical claim and dangerous as a normative argument. The globalization and the deterritorialization of identity politics is one of the most important reasons why a neat pluralist global order has been rendered obsolete, and this is true at the regional as well as the national level. As Tully reminds us:

[11] For a prominent example, see Bilahari Kausikan, 'Asia's Different Standard', *Foreign Policy*, 92 (Fall 1993); For an excellent elaboration of the debate, see Yash Ghai, 'Human Rights and Governance: The Asia Debate', Occasional Paper, Center for Asian Pacific Affairs, November 1994.

... cultures are not internally homogeneous. They are continuously contested, imagined and re-imagined, transformed and negotiated, both by their members and through their interaction with others.... Cultural diversity is a tangled labyrinth of intertwining cultural differences *and* similarities, not a panopticon of fixed, independent and incommensurable worldviews in which we are either prisoners or cosmopolitan spectators in the central tower.[12]

Regions as poles and as powers

Many regionalist arrangements have been central to efforts to maximize bargaining power in a globalized world.[13] Even if it is dressed up in other terms, a great deal of regionalist activity does have the character of an outwardly directed coalition. One form of potential power is directly focused on bargaining and coalitional strategies: but behind this lurks the critical issue (certainly in terms of trade) of market size which, in turn, shapes both the capacity to negotiate effectively; to retaliate within the structures of the WTO; and, to engage in 'regulatory mercantilism'—the way in which norms, practices, and standards that develop within large economic areas become internationally established.

The idea of regions as poles has been a perennial feature of the debate over Europe's role. Some stress the notion of Europe as a pole or a counterweight to the United States. Whatever new forms of governance, statehood, and sovereignty may have been developed within Europe, its impact outside will be through the creation of a power in a classic sense. The second route is very different. Here Europe serves not as a counterweight but as a counterpoint. Power is not bringing projected, at least not in its traditional hard, form. Instead it is Europe's civilian power, its normative power, and its transformative power that matters. Europe's influence rests on its provision of a model—a model of social order and of a particular brand of advanced capitalism that lays emphasis on the need for equality and solidarity; but, above all, as a model of governance beyond the state. For many it is this kind of soft power that Europe should seek to project. Europe, in other words, should seek to externalize its internal political project and the social and political values associated with it. And it is these values and this model that other countries and regions can invoke or appeal to. Even as Europe seeks to build up its military capacity, military power is not to be deployed primarily for war-fighting but in support of softer goals of state-building and governance.[14]

---

[12] Tully (1995: 11).

[13] For earlier discussions, see Roger D. Masters, 'A Multi-Bloc Model of the International System', *American Political Science Review*, LV/4 (1961), 780–98; and Bull (2003: 254–7, 294–9).

[14] See e.g. Kalypso Nicolaidis and Robert Howse, ' "This is my EUtopia..." Narrative as Power', *Journal of Common Market Studies*, 40/4 (2002), 767–92; Ian Manners, 'Normative Power Europe: A Contradiction in Terms?', *Journal of Common Market Studies*, 40/2 (2002),

However, problems affect both of these options. There is no consensus on the power-political projection model. Despite its edging away from being a purely civilian power, the weaknesses of Europe as a power-political player are well known, especially in the military field. And the severity of recent challenges make one doubt whether Kissingerian questions as to the seriousness of Europe as 'real' political player in the military and geopolitical sense have been overcome or are likely to be so in the short or even medium term. The European paradox remains. Europe's tremendous success was in overcoming the old Hobbesian world of wars and conflict precisely by creating a set of political arrangements that simply could not function according to the old-style power-political logic of traditional nation-states.

The soft power route is far more plausible and attractive. And yet the difficulties are also apparent here. In part, this is because the projection of effective soft power also involves opportunity costs, risks, and long-term commitment. Soft power is not a soft option. In part, the difficulties follow from the uncomfortable gap and the many inconsistencies between European internal practices and many of its external actions (for example in terms of its policies on agriculture; the way in which its migration and asylum policies undermine its purported valuing of human rights; the way in which its accession policy provides almost no space for dialogue or negotiation; or the way in which its relationship with the ACP countries continues to reflect colonial attitudes and practices). In part, they follow from the tension between Europe's position as a model of governance designed to mediate difference on the one hand and its promotion of a set of universal values on the other. Seen from other parts of the world, US and EU positions on international order are strikingly similar—in their substantive content, in the degree to which they involve revising limited pluralist notions of international society, and in the absence of sustained engagement with the views of other states and regions.

Outside Europe it is certainly the case that power dynamics play a central role inside many regions—as in Asia where soft forms of security multilateralism are promoted as a means of managing the rise of Chinese power and of working against a tightening of the broader balance of power in the region. It is also important to underscore the more defensive imperatives that have come to characterize many recent examples of regionalism. Hence we can see a continued emphasis on regionalism as a response to economic crisis and failure and to the shared regional perception of needing one's neighbours as partners in a politically and economically nasty and threatening world. The political imperative to keep trying to 'relaunch' Mercosur with a strong emphasis on its character as a 'political project' provides one example. Asian regionalism provides a further example, whether in the face of the financial

235–58. Zaki Laïdi, *La Norme sans la Force: L'énigme et la puissance europénne* (Paris: Presses Sciences-Po, 2005).

crisis or the diversion of foreign direct investment to China. Whatever the actual limits to purely Asian responses to the financial crises of the late 1990s, there has been a significant sense that the region needs to develop a greater sense of its own identity and of its own capacity to deal with economic vulnerability (especially in the financial and monetary field). The African case provides an even more striking example of regionalism launched on the back of crisis, human disasters, and widespread political and economic failure.

There is, however, very little evidence that regions can become powers on the back of sorts of regional institutions that have developed in any region outside Europe, or that seem likely to develop. There is a tremendous difference between the relative success of various regional groupings in ensuring that regional states do fewer nasty things to each other and creating the conditions for actively cooperating in face of the outside world on the other.

But what of regions centred around powerful states? Such a situation may arise because the regional state is so overwhelmingly dominant within a region that it is the 'natural hegemon' and can enforce its will; or because it succeeds in creating consensual hegemony within a region (maybe by providing economic benefits or underpinning regional security, or by claiming to embody a particular view of the world or a set of values). All regional leaders need regional followers. But we should also recognize that the practice of regional power is often problematic. Regions can be snares that reduce rather than increase the projection of power; regional great powers can be enmeshed in very unstable regional 'backyards' and 'near-abroads'; and the other states in the region can be very resistant to being led by what outsiders may consider to be the 'natural' leader of the region (think of the opposition to Brazilian and Indian membership of the Security Council).

Support for a regional power might also come from the outside. For example the United States has sometimes sought to build up regional powers or 'regional influentials' and to engage in a policy of regional devolution—particularly at times when its own imperial credentials are called into question (as in the late 1960s or in the current period). An alternative external form of support for would-be regional powers comes from the calls for existing oligarchical forms of global governance built around a relatively small group of major Western states (as in the G8) to be broadened to include key regional powers, especially in the interests of representational legitimacy. There is every reason to expect these kinds of arguments to continue.

Despite these difficulties over the longer term, it is important to hold open the possibility of a world order made up of large 'region-states', which might have a variety of internal forms of political organization (old-style spheres of influence, hegemonically centred institutionalism, and different forms of federal union). Such a pattern of global political order might follow from the sheer power of attraction of dynamic economic cores (Europe, North America, and China); it might follow from the recurring functionalist argument that, for all the tenacity of the nation-state, there is an underlying and long-term shift towards larger scale units of economic and social organization; or it might follow from a return of major power rivalry in which spheres of influence come once more to play a central role.

The region as a level in a system of multilevel governance

As institutionalization and governance develop at the global, the regional, and the local levels, we find a recurrent liberal vision of a productive partnership between these different levels. Three ideas are frequently highlighted: delegation, policing, and mutual reinforcement. The idea of delegation has been common in the security arena, especially in terms of the relationship between the UN and regional bodies. The rationale is clear. The UN is massively overburdened. Regional states have a greater incentive to bear the costs and assume the risks of security management, and regional organizations and regional coalitions can contribute to burden sharing, provide greater knowledge of the problems involved, and ensure greater legitimacy within the region, especially for peace operations that demand deep and long-term intervention. And yet the natural advantages of letting regional states assume primary responsibility can be questioned. It is not clear that the balance of interests and incentives will press regional states to take up the burden of responsibility for regional security. The complications of regional politics may on the contrary make it far harder for regional bodies to embark on risky and politically divisive action. Regional states and regional groupings may lack the resources to act effectively. Historic involvement and partisan interests may undermine the possibility of even-handed action at the regional level. And the lesson of the 1990s is surely that regional action remains dependent for its legitimacy on the uniquely one-world character of the UN.[15] Indeed there are important grounds for questioning the view that, in the global politics of legitimacy, endorsement of the use of force by a regional body is the next best thing to endorsement by the UN. In regions dominated by a hegemonic power (such as the Americas or the CIS), it is far from clear that agreement will be forthcoming or that the regional audience will see such legitimation in the same way.

The trading system provides an example of the idea of policing, with the image of a global institution in the form of the WTO monitoring the proliferation of regional economic arrangements. However, it also provides an example of the difficulties of such monitoring, with the WTO mostly unable

---

[15] On this issue, see Alex J. Bellamy and Paul D. Williams, 'Who's Keeping the Peace? Regionalization and Contemporary Peace Operations', *International Security*, 29/4 (2005), 157–95.

to ensure effective multilateral surveillance.[16] And the human rights system provides an example of the idea of positive reinforcement. The UN system should play the central role in the process of standard setting, as well as in the promotion and protection of human rights, with regional bodies entering the story principally in terms of a more detailed specification of rights and more effective implementation—what John Vincent called the 'local carriers of the global message'.[17] And yet the line between global promulgation and regional implementation has been a problematic one and regional groupings have sometimes served as vehicles for the promotion of conflicting conceptions of both the rights themselves and how they should be promoted.

Regions as harbingers of change and possible transformation

There is a long history of looking to regions as harbingers of change in the fundamental character of international society. In the 1950s, analysts looked to the existence of 'islands of peace' in Europe, Scandinavia, and North America that seemed to represent a challenge to realism and to underscore the real potential for cooperative institutions. More recently many have seen Europe as a new kind of polity. Hence John Ruggie's view of Europe as a postmodern region that had left the old pluralist world sovereignty and territoriality beyond; or Andrew Linklater's claim that '[I]ntimations of the post-Westphalian world are apparent in Western Europe'; or Jan Zielonka's view of 'Europe as Empire'—not a 'superstate but a polycentric polity penetrating rather than controlling its environment'.[18] For some, European politics have been so thoroughly domesticated that we should analyse them using the tools of Comparative Politics rather than of International Relations: Europe should be seen as a 'normal' federal state and the natural comparators are not other regional state systems, but rather other federal systems.

What are we to make of such claims? In the first place, it is obvious that Europe does provide evidence of hugely significant political, legal, and institutional change, but even in Europe it is also important to recognize the limits to change. Second, there is no evidence that Europe is indicative of some sort of generalizable post-Westphalian order that is either already apparent in other regions, or likely to emerge in those regions. But third, this does not mean that other regions have not witnessed significant processes of change in the patterns of governance that are emerging and in the extent to which intensified patterns of regionalization are challenging older

---

[16] See e.g. Hoekman and Kostecki (2001: ch. 10).   [17] Vincent (1986: 101).

[18] John G. Ruggie, 'Territoriality and beyond: Problematizing Modernity in International Relations', *International Organization*, 46/1 (1993), 139–74; Linklater (1998: 9); Jan Zielonka, *Europe as Empire: The Nature of the Enlarged European Union* (Oxford: Oxford University Press, 2006).

patterns of regional politics. Both textbooks and general commentary often gather together long lists of regional organizations as if the sheer weight of the acronyms were illustrative of a general move towards 'supranationalism' or of deep change in the legal and constitutional structure of different regions. Very important changes are indeed underway but looking at them through a European lens is a deeply misleading way of characterizing these changes.

Let me provide some brief illustration of these arguments, beginning with Europe and then moving to the world outside Europe.

There is no doubt at all that Europe represents a unique case of a group of states that have agreed to pool sovereignty in an increasing range of areas in pursuit of their common interests. The scope of change can be seen in the emergence of a structure of law and institutionalized governance that is qualitatively different from traditional international law (especially the constitutionalization of an originally treaty-system and the doctrines of supremacy and direct effect)[19]; in the growth of a system of governance that cannot be reduced to a set of interstate relations and in which high levels of delegation to supranational bodies, policy networks, the world of comitology, and cross-cutting interest group politics all play important roles[20]; and in a situation in which the logic and language of power has been fundamentally altered. The limits to change can be seen in the continued power of nationalism and the nation-state; in Europe's continued security dependence and the limits to its own military capacity, in the formal limits to the integration process and the limits to delegation[21]; and, perhaps most importantly, in the places where law and power meet and where informal norms and old-style pluralist practices continue to predominate. It is impossible here to try and capture the complexity of Europe. Rival theories are able to capture important explanatory logics and can often muster significant evidence in their support—but only at the cost of ignoring or downplaying countervailing trends and equally powerful developments. The point is simply to acknowledge the extent of change in terms of the consolidation of both solidarist institutions and complex governance beyond the state, and to highlight the very particular set of circumstances under which Europe has developed.

[19] Especially useful here is J. H. H. Weiler, 'The Transformation of Europe', in *The Constitution of Europe: 'Do the New Clothes Have an Emperor?' and Other Essays on European Integration* (Cambridge: Cambridge University Press, 1999), 10–101; and Alec Stone Sweet, Wayne Sandholtz, and Neil Fligstein, *The Institutionalization of Europe* (Oxford: Oxford University Press, 2001), especially ch. 1.

[20] Amongst the huge literature, see Dinan (1999); and Simon Hix, *The Political System of the European Union* (Basingstoke, UK: Palgrave, 1999).

[21] For a succinct statement of the limits, see Andrew Moravcsik, 'In Defence of the "Democratic Deficit": Reassessing the Legitimacy of the European Union', *Journal of Common Market Studies*, 40/4 (2002), 603–24.

Outside Europe, the Americas provide the clearest example of the move towards a regional liberal solidarism. Historically, Latin America can be placed firmly within a traditional pluralist conception of international law and international society. It is true that governments in the region (and still more Latin America's distinguished tradition of international lawyers) aspired from the earliest days of independence to a regional system of law that would accomplish ambitious goals and far-reaching purposes. These aspirations included the creation of formal regional organizations, mechanisms aiming at the peaceful settlement of disputes and, from the middle of the twentieth century, the incorporation into regional law of ideas concerning human rights and democracy. Although the achievements were not wholly negligible (e.g. diplomatic *concertation* and arbitration to manage contested borders), most of these aspirations towards more elaborate regional governance and more ambitious solidarist goals remained simply that—aspirations that were usually cloaked in legalistic and moralistic rhetoric. The norms that were politically most salient were those of the classical pluralist international society: sovereign equality, strict non-intervention, increasingly tight restrictions on the use of force; territoriality and the pragmatic use of *uti posseditis* to stabilize borders. Indeed, Latin American states were in the vanguard of the struggle to export pluralist understandings of European international society to the non-European world, playing a particularly central role in the struggle for equal sovereignty (e.g. in relation to the treatment of foreign firms and foreign nationals) and restrictions on the use of force (e.g. in relation to the collection of debts).

The 1990s witnessed a very significant expansion of regional institutions and important changes in the ambition, scope, and density of regional governance in the Americas. These changes followed partly from the creation of regional economic integration schemes (as with NAFTA and Mercosur) and from the ongoing process of negotiation of a Free Trade Area of the Americas (FTAA). In terms of political relations, the 1990s saw a revitalization of the efforts of the Organization of American States (OAS) and the agendas of successive Summits of the Americas (Miami, 1994; Santiago, 1998; and Quebec, 2001) revealed an extraordinary range of issues, many of which would have been very hard to imagine as legitimate topics for inter-American debate, let alone action, even a few years before—such as corruption, money laundering, or civil–military relations. Of particular relevance were the increased activity of the regional human rights system and the tightening of regional democratic norms in and around the OAS. The regional human rights system developed into a normatively intrusive regime with a far-reaching mandate to regulate domestic political norms and practices of regional states. The 1990s saw an increasing number of ratifications of regional human rights instruments and the increasing acceptance of the jurisdiction of the Inter-American Court. The regional 'democracy system' both created coordinating mechanisms to act in protection of democracy and linked sovereignty far more closely with

255

democratic legitimacy.[22] Even if a general international legal right to democratic governance may not have crystallized, many would see developments in the Americas in the 1990s as very much ahead of the curve, culminating in the adoption of the Inter-American Democratic Charter in 2001. There was also a move towards more coercive solidarism, both in the form of membership conditionality (with both the OAS and Mercosur having established explicit democratic criteria for membership) and in intervention (as with Haiti in 1994).

Twenty years on, the picture is significantly different. Patterns of interest have not been translated into effective regional institutions, above all because of the combination of interdependence and inequality (with the twin asymmetries of Brazil within South America and the United States within the hemisphere). The human rights and democracy regimes are clearly not embedded within a stable structure of hemispheric cooperation. The negotiations on hemispheric economic integration have broken down and there can hardly be a more striking contrast than that between the Miami Summit of the Americas in 1994 and the bitterly divided and contentious Mar del Plata Summit of 2005. Mercosur is in deep crisis; the prospects for an FTAA have receded and become highly politicized, and the OAS has become more marginalized from tackling the real sources of insecurity in the region. In addition, progress made in the 1990s in relation to monitoring elections and promoting democracy is threatened by growing divergence between the United States and much of South America. On the one side, the United States denounces both the alleged move to the left in the region and what it sees as the abuses of 'populism' and 'democratic cesarism'. On the other, there has been widespread discontent across the region with the results of democracy and liberal economic reform; calls for much greater attention to the social agenda; and the loud proclamation of more 'authentic', 'redistributive', and 'participatory' modes of democracy (most notably in Venezuela and Bolivia). Whatever the exact truth of these respective claims (with both sides presenting far too simplistic a picture of political change in the region), the point here is simply to note the difficulty of promoting democracy when there is so little consensus on the meaning of democracy and the direction in which democratic change should proceed.

---

[22] For an indication of how these changes were being viewed, see Heraldo Muñoz, 'The Right to Democracy in the Americas', *Journal of Interamerican Studies and World Affairs*, 40/1 (Spring 1998), 1–18; Domingo E. Acevedo and Claudio Grossman, 'The Organization of American States and the Protection of Democracy', in Tom Farer (ed.), *Beyond Sovereignty* (Baltimore, MD: Johns Hopkins University Press, 1996), 132–49; R. J. Bloomfield, 'Making the Western Hemisphere Safe for Democracy? The OAS Defense-of-Democracy Regime', in Carl Kaysen, Robert A. Pastor, and Laura W. Reed (eds.), *Collective Responses to Regional Problems: The Case of Latin America and the Caribbean* (Cambridge, MA: American Academy of Arts and Sciences, 1994), 15–28.

Within North America patterns of regionalization have intensified dramatically in terms of trade, investment, energy, environment, migration, and security.[23] Indeed, on many measures, the region is one of the most densely integrated places on earth. For some, the region appears as a textbook case of how integration and interdependence create increasing functional demand for cooperation, but where power-political interests, unequal levels of development, and very different patterns of historical, social, and cultural development work against that demand being met by formal and deeper institutionalization. It is, of course, important to underscore the limits of the institutionalized governance in the form of NAFTA and to show how the even formal dispute settlement within NAFTA has not created anything approaching a level playing field.[24] But, on the other side, it is noteworthy that NAFTA has proved relatively durable and effective, and that the United States has remained enmeshed within NAFTA, despite the strong unilateral inclinations of the Bush administration. In a region characterized by such asymmetric power, it is perhaps the existence of some degree of continued institutional engagement that is significant rather than the limits of that engagement. It is also important to note how a common antipathy towards formal institutions has stimulated different forms of complex government around and beyond the state, above all between Canada and the United States: around, for example, the 270 or so treaties that exist between Canada and the United States; the 60 bodies around NAFTA; the close informal coordination around North American Aerospace Defense Command and the 34 formal agreements on defence-related matters; and the multiple administrative networks on everything from law enforcement to the operation of cross-border power lines.

The region also provides a regional example of the broader argument about the limits to US effective power that will be developed in Chapter 11.[25] US power to control its own region has been reduced. Washington has certainly devoted enormous efforts to reasserting control of its borders and to border management, however much this runs counter to the logic of economic

---

[23] For an overview, see Robert A. Pastor, 'North America and the Americas: Integration among Unequal Partners', in Farrell, Hettne, and van Langenhoven (eds.), *The Global Politics of Regionalism*, 210–21.

[24] On NAFTA, see Frederick M. Abbott, 'NAFTA and the Legalization of World Politics: A Case Study', in Judith L. Goldstein, Miles Kahler, Robert O. Keohane, and Anne-Marie Slaughter (eds.), *Legalization and World Politics* (Cambridge, MA: MIT Press, 2001). For a powerful critique of existing regional governance, see Stephen Clarkson (with Sarah Davidson Ladly, Megan Merwart, and Carlton Thorne), 'The Primitive Realities of North America's Transnational Governance', in Edgar Grande and Louis W. Pauly (eds.), *Complex Sovereignty. Reconstituting Political Authority in the Twenty-first Century* (Toronto: University of Toronto Press, 2005).

[25] See Andrew Hurrell, 'Hegemony in a Region that Dares Not Speak its Name', *International Journal*, (Summer 2006), 545–66.

integration and to the sustainable management of migration.[26] Both Canada and then Mexico have had no alternative but to cooperate in intensified border security. And yet border-based and coercion-based drug and migration policies have had a very poor record of success. US security has become increasingly affected by the dense societal and economic integration that has developed; by the negative security externalities that this has produced—in the form of transnational organized crime, massive illicit flows of narcotics, and high and rising levels of undocumented migration—and by the weakness of the states around its southern periphery, including Mexico.

Perhaps the most important lesson of North America for this book is not about governance, but rather about the relationship between rising levels of integration on the one hand and the emergence of a regional community on the other. Whatever the data of the convergence or divergence of societal values and preferences across the North American region, the absence of any sense of a shared community or common ethos is abundantly clear. This is true even if we set the bar very low. For example, it has become common amongst both commentators and political theorists to argue that globalization and increased interaction and interconnection are changing our understandings of, and responsibilities to, distant others. But if arguments about ever-denser integration leading to shifting understandings of moral community were to have force, then North America, NAFTA and the relationship between the United States, Canada, and Mexico should be a likely candidate. It is a relationship characterized by extremely high levels of economic and societal interdependence; by high levels of deprivation in Mexico, a good deal of which can be implicated in problems likely to have negative spillover effects on the United States; and by two rich and privileged partners well able to afford assistance. Yet there is a total absence of debate on even minimal duties of assistance or distributive justice; and, whilst northern concerns over human rights within Mexico have expanded, the idea of an even minimalist regional rights-protecting community has made extremely little progress. Regionalization has done remarkably little to alter the moral geography of the region. Indeed it may well have pushed in the other direction given the extent to which it has rekindled old debates about race and identity. On the one side, even US liberals (and US courts) have tended to view rights as belonging to citizens within the borders of the state and to show a depressing lack of concern with the rights of 'aliens' both within the borders and around its periphery, including those who die seeking entry or whose rights are systematically abused in adjacent areas (most obviously in Guantanamo). On the other side, for all its moral posturing, Canada has joined the United States in remaining outside the regional human rights regime.

---

[26] See Peter Andreas and Thomas J. Biersteker (eds.), *The Rebordering of North America: Integration and Exclusion in a New Security Context* (New York: Routledge, 2003).

Africa provides one of the most interesting examples of the continued drive towards region-building and the increased elements of liberal solidarism, despite the long record of previous failures and the multiple problems besetting the region. The ECOWAS had been created in 1975 but shifted through the 1990s away from economic development and towards regional security. Within this new context, democracy and good governance came to occupy a far more central place within ECOWAS's formal normative structure and humanitarian justifications were offered for its interventions in Liberia and Sierra Leone. The South African Development Community (SADC), founded originally as SADCC in 1980, also moved towards a more overt emphasis on regional security within which the defence and maintenance of democracy again has a more formal place. And, most notably, the decision to replace the OAU with the new African Union involves not only a charter which drew heavily on European models but also gives member-states the right to intervene in the case of 'grave circumstances, namely: war crimes, genocide, and crimes against humanity' (Article 4(h) of the Constitutive Act of the African Union). Such developments stand against the common view of developing countries as uniformly resistant to emerging norms on humanitarian intervention.

The extent of normative change is contested. For some it is a clear example of normative change (most obviously in reaction to Rwanda) as well as of the broader spread of liberal values. For others, it is a cheap gesture or a move that, by institutionalizing the norm, allows for a reassertion of state control. The broader problem, however, concerns the acute weakness of African regional institutions: in terms of the capacity of their secretariats, in terms of the willingness of any of the member-states to delegate any significant powers, and in terms of the degree to which regionalism serves the direct and usually domestic interests of state leaders rather representing common responses to shared problems.[27] Africa has also seen the increasingly uncontrolled disjuncture between the political structures of interstate regionalism on the one hand and patterns of intensified social, economic, and military regionalization on the other. Together with the Middle East, it is the most important reminder of the paradox of regionalism, namely that a successful move beyond the state depends on the existence of reasonably well-functioning states.[28]

---

[27] For a forceful critique of Africa's regionalist pretensions, see Jeffrey Herbst, 'Crafting Regional Cooperation in Africa', in Amitav Acharya and Alistair Ian Johnston (eds.), *Crafting Cooperation: Regional International Institutions in Comparative Perspective* (Cambridge: Cambridge University Press, 2007).

[28] On the fundamental need to understand regional international politics in terms of the character of the African state, see Christopher Clapham, *Africa and the International System* (Cambridge: Cambridge University Press, 1996); and Douglas Lemke, 'African Lessons for International Relations Research', *World Politics*, 56 (2003), 114–38.

Building on the foundation of ASEAN (founded in 1967), Asia in the 1990s also saw an expansion of regionalist activity, including APEC (1989); the ASEAN Free Trade Area (AFTA, 1992); the ASEAN Regional Forum (ARF, 1994); and the ASEAN Plus Three (APT, 1997). For much of the 1990s much of the debate hinged on the success of ASEAN in developing a regional security community built around confidence-building measures and diplomatic coordination. Bolstered by economic dynamism, the success of ASEAN in the absence of European-style regional institutions was held to reflect an 'ASEAN way' based on a particular set of norms and a particular kind of diplomatic culture.[29] More recently, the harsher economic climate, the emergence of new transnational threats, and the sharpening of the political and economic challenge posed by China have pushed towards the functional expansion of regional cooperation but also raised questions about the durability of weakly institutionalized cooperation. The region is not moving towards an ASEAN version of post-Westphalia, nor are the prospects for strong regional institutions looking especially bright. However, increasingly dense patterns of social and economic regionalization are having a significant impact on patterns of power, both between states and within states. Moreover, although power-based stories of the region (which focus on the macro-power structure created by China, the United States, and, to a lesser extent, Japan) are increasingly prominent, the importance of regional institutions as a potential means of softening those power relationships has also continued to develop. In other words, it is not helpful to draw an overly sharp distinction between power-based accounts of the region on the one hand, and institutional and identity based accounts on the other.

Conclusions

In previous rounds of regionalism, the regionalist wave rose, but then broke and receded. Predictions that regionalism was here to stay proved unfounded. Outside Europe by the early 1970s various regions were littered with failed and discredited regionalist schemes, whether of economic integration or of political cooperation. This time around it is striking that, in many parts of the world, politicians and analysts seem convinced that regional cooperation has to move forward and has to be made to work—despite the strains besetting NAFTA, the fragility of Mercosur, ASEAN's difficult adjustment to a harsher regional environment, and the extremely limited results of regionalism in other parts of the world. From one perspective, this underscores the importance of distinguishing between regionalism as description and regionalism as

---

[29] See Amitav Acharya, *Constructing a Security Community in Southeast Asia: ASEAN and the Problem of Regional Order* (London: Routledge, 2001).

prescription—regionalism as a normative position, as a political programme, or as a doctrine as to how international society ought to be organized. As with the more general idea of interdependence, there is often a strong sense that the states of a given region are all in the same 'regional boat', ecologically, strategically, economically; that they are not pulling together; but that, either explicitly stated or implicitly implied, they should put aside national egoisms and devise new forms of cooperation. Regional projects, visions, and ethically constitutive stories are important for successful region-building, just as they have been with nation-building. But regionalism cannot be exempt from the hard reality of economic viability and the cold logic of power and interest.

For all of the limits the picture is not static. Martin Wight was famous for characterizing international relations as an arena of recurrence and reproduction and for arguing that states systems are the 'the loosest of all political organizations known to us'.[30] And yet when we survey the many worlds of different regional international societies it is clear that deep and significant changes have taken place, and that the regional societies, economies, and polities that have developed cannot usefully be characterized as 'loose'. They do not point in a neat or uniform direction—in most cases not towards stable and effective institutionalization, nor towards a cosy and comforting liberal solidarism, and still less towards some post-Westphalian transformation (even in Europe); but neither are they simply about recurrence and repetition. Within the many worlds these developments are crucial to understanding the many different directions in which governance is moving, the range of dilemmas being faced, and the different forms that regional politics beyond a state-based pluralism might take. For all its manifold frustrations, this is what Europe has been about, and what is most important about Europe, and, incidently, why we should welcome a renewed debate on the constitution of Europe.

Within the one world, I have discussed some of the ways in which regions can be related to international order and to global governance. None is without its problems. And none is more important than the role that regions may come to play in the search for global political legitimacy. The notion that the current distribution of global decision-making power can be defended in terms of the values propounded by the currently dominant is likely to come under increasing challenge. The organization of regions, the capacity of regions to generate and promote ideas of global order, and the claim of different regions to be represented more fully and more equally are likely to play a central role in the coming struggle for global political legitimacy.

[30] Wight (1977: 149).

11

Empire reborn?

This chapter considers the relationship between empire and global political order. Given the nature of the current international system, this means inevitably that we focus on the United States. But my aim is to set the role and position of the United States in a broad conceptual and historical context and to try and escape from the immediacy of the current discussion of the strategic choices that Washington has made, is in the course of making, or should make in the future. It is divided into three parts. In the first section, I would like to unsettle some of the assumptions that are often made about empire, in particular about the inevitability of the end of empire; the redundancy and outmodedness of empire as a form of political order, and the consequent implication that the natural focus of international relations should be the relations amongst states or nation-states. The sheer extent of the power of the United States and the apparent obviousness of the view that we are living in a unipolar world have brought back the language of empire and have led many to see the United States as an imperial power.

The second section considers how we should understand that power. I argue that notions of informal empire provide some analytical purchase but neglect both the consistently important role of military power and coercion in the evolution of US foreign policy, and the importance of rules, norms, and institutions—what one might call the formal side of so-called informal empire. I also argue that it is analytically more useful to understand the United States as a hegemonic rather than an imperial power, because doing so forces the analyst to focus directly on the crucial questions of negotiation, legitimacy, and 'followership'. Compared to empire, hegemony is commonly seen as a shallower and less intrusive mode of control. Although this is in some ways true, I suggest that US hegemony is complicated by a number of historical and structural forces which have pushed the United States towards deeper and more intrusive involvement and that are likely to continue to complicate the exercise of US power.

The third section examines five of the most commonly cited reasons for the demise of both empire and top-down hierarchical conceptions of international order more generally. Rather than comparing the extent and character of US power directly with that of other hegemonic states, I ask how these five factors may have changed in ways that would make a hegemonic order viable and potentially sustainable. Clearly, the power resources of the United States are enormous. And yet, especially when set against the way in which both international society and global politics have changed, it is the limits, instability, and uncertainties of that power that are most striking. These limits apply most directly to the exercise of coercive force, but their implications are broader and call into question the simplistic image of the United States as an unrivalled and all-powerful hegemonic power.

Empires and order

Empires have long been central to conceptions of world order. This was clearly true of international relations before the emergence of the classical European state system. But as we noted in Chapter 2, imperialism was also central to the political operation of the classical state system, to its economic development, to the character of the international legal and normative order, and, as so much recent work has shown, to its political theory. The classical state system was a world managed without embarrassment by the powerful. But what is more interesting than the historic centrality of empire is the way in which a range of commentators, of differing political persuasions, viewed empire not as some atavistic hangover from a feudal past, but rather as a central element of the international relations of the future and, in particular, as a response to the changes that were being wrought by capitalist development and by the forces of what comes to be called globalization. Let us look briefly at three moments.

Writing in the heyday of Victorian imperial self-confidence, John Seeley stressed the transformation in the scale of power, the 'vast uniting forces' of trade, investment, and migration; and the extent to which changes in technology and communication were facilitating new forms of political organization. 'I have suggested that in the modern world distance has very much lost its effect, and that there are signs of a time when states will be vaster than they have hitherto been'.[1] In common with much nineteenth-century thinking,[2] he saw the dominant logic of economic integration and interdependence as pointing towards fusion and the consolidation of political structures. And, like

[1] J. R. Seeley, *The Expansion of England*, edited and introduced by John Gross (Chicago, IL: University of Chicago Press, [1881] 1971), 234.

[2] For example, Richard Cobden, 'England, Ireland and America' and 'Russia', in *Political Writings of Richard Cobden*, 4th edn., reprinted by Kraus Reprint (New York), 5–119, and 122–258. On Cobden's admiring view of the power of the United States, see E. H. Cawley, *The American Diaries of Richard Cobden* (Princeton, NJ: Princeton University Press, 1952).

many of his contemporaries, he looked to the United States as a model: 'the most striking example of confident and successful expansion', a model of free institutions 'combined in the fullest degree with boundless expansion'; '. . . it is precisely the sort of union which the conditions of the time most naturally call into existence.'[3]

Writing in 1926, Alfred Zimmern, that quintessential liberal thinker and defender of the League of Nations, also saw empire as a necessary and beneficial element of a future world order. As with Seeley, it is economic transformation that is changing the imperatives of both national power and international governance. Within that search for governance, however, empire would continue to play a central role. On the one side, the British Commonwealth represented, for Zimmern, a model for the League of Nations—a model of a free and peaceful association of states and national communities. On the other side, the League of Nations was central to the survival and sustainability of the Commonwealth, hence Zimmern's notion of 'a league within a larger league, a society within that larger society'.[4] This easy slippage between liberal internationalism and liberal empire was certainly not confined to Zimmern. Thus Wilson defended the Monroe Doctrine at Paris, not as a hegemonic regional arrangement that reflected selfish US interests but as a model for the League. This idea had been discussed as early as November 1914 and was expressed both in a number of papers and in Wilson's speech to the Senate of 22 January 1917. It was, in part, the result of an attempt to make the League acceptable to US opinion. But it also reflected, as House proposed and as Wilson picked up with such enthusiasm and alacrity, a genuine belief that a Monroe-inspired pan-Americanism could indeed provide a model of post-war international organization.[5]

By the end of the Second World War, the tide seemed to be running still more powerfully against empire. Indeed, the war itself was crucial in the process of decolonization: the devastating weakening of the European core, the rise of the superpowers (with the term coined in 1944), the loss of direct control over colonial territories brought about by the war itself (especially in Asia), and the intensification of anti-colonial nationalism brought about by attempts to mobilize empires for war. The catastrophic conflicts of the first half of the twentieth century seem to reinforce a diffuse but pervasive sense that the day of the nation-state was over and that both international political forces and the development of global capitalism were pushing towards

---

[3] Seeley (1971: 235–6).

[4] Alfred Zimmern, *The Third British Empire*, 3rd edn. (Westport, CT: Greenwood [1934] 1979: 61).

[5] See Mark T. Gilderhus, *Pan-American Visions: Woodrow Wilson and the Western Hemisphere, 1913–1921* (Tucson, AZ: University of Arizona Press, 1986), 135–9; and 'Pan-American Initiatives: The Wilson Presidency and "Regional Integration", 1914–1917', *Diplomatic History* (Fall 1980), especially 415–17.

new forms of political ordering.[6] But, within these debates, hierarchy was to remain central. Sometimes the link between hierarchy and order was focused around institutions, as in the case of the UN with Churchill's (consistent) and Roosevelt's (initial) enthusiasm for an order built around the 'four policeman', each maintaining local order within their spheres of influence. Sometimes the focus was more directly on empire itself. Alexandre Kojève, the great interpreter of Hegel and French government official, provides a particularly interesting example of how these perceived changes pointed both to the continuing centrality of empire but also to its changing character.

In his *Outline of a Doctrine of French Policy*, written in August 1945, he wrote: 'At present, it is these nation-States which, irresistably, are gradually giving way to political formations which transgress national borders and which could be designated by the term "Empires". Nation-States, still powerful in the nineteenth century, are ceasing to be *political* realities.... The modern State, the current political reality, requires a larger foundation than that represented by Nations in the strict sense. To be *politically* viable, the modern State must rest upon a "vast 'imperial' union of affiliated Nations". The modern State is only truly a State if it is an Empire.'[7] In Kojève's view, Nazi Germany had certainly recognized these changes, as could be seen in the extensive debates over *Grossraumtheorien* and in Haushofer's geopolitics (that so influenced Spkyman and then Kennan).[8] But, for Kojève, Germany had sought a national solution that was bound to fail when faced by the 'imperial socialism' of the USSR on the one hand and the 'imperial capitalism of the Anglo-Saxons' on the other. 'It can therefore be said that Germany lost this war because she wanted to win it as a *nation*-State'. As with Zimmern, he saw the Commonwealth as a model, but argued that this was still too national a model. And again as with Zimmern, the future lay with the United States and in much more loosely structured de-territorialized arrangements. 'It is the Anglo-Saxon Empire, which is to say the Anglo-American politico-economic bloc, which is today the effective and actual political reality'.[9] Kojève's own 'solutions' pointed, presciently, to regionalism (the other obvious building-block of world order beyond the nation-state) and, deeply implausibly, to the notion of a 'Latin empire'.

Politically, of course, the post–Second World War period saw the challenge to the overseas European empires growing stronger and leading to

---

[6] For example E. H. Carr, *Nationalism and After* (London: Macmillan, 1945).

[7] Alexandre Kojève, 'Outline of a Doctrine of French Policy', (p. 2) 27 August 1945. Translated by Erik de Vries and with commentary by Robert Howse. Reprinted in *Policy Review* http://www.policyreview.org/aug04 accessed 05/11/2004.

[8] For Kojève's broader view of international relations see Jan-Werner Müller, *A Dangerous Mind: Carl Schmitt in Post-War European Thought* (New Haven, CT: Yale University Press, 2003), especially 'Visions of Global Order: Schmitt, Aron, and the Civil Servant of the World-Spirit', 87–103.

[9] Ibid. 3.

the completion of the third wave of decolonization (against the European overseas empires) and, eventually, to the fourth wave (with the breakup of the Soviet Empire and hegemonic system). Analytically, International Relations insisted evermore on describing its field of study as 'Politics among Nations' or as the politics of an anarchical interstate system, despite the important role of hierarchical ordering within both sides of the Cold War divide. George Liska was unusual in pointing to the dual or mixed character of the system. 'Contemporary international politics', he wrote in 1967, 'is a compound of two ingredients: the politics of reviving or reasserted nation-states and the politics of empire and interempire relations.'[10]

The emergence of the United States as the core of unipolar world refocused attention on the implications of a recentralization of global power—not simply in relation to the strategic choices for the United States, but, more broadly, in terms of the possibility of order through hierarchy, hegemony, or even empire. Talk of the United States as the indispensable nation grew more persistent and, to many people, more persuasive; and Krauthammer's characterization of a unipolar moment gave way to a belief that the world had entered a unipolar era.[11] Both empire and hegemony require power, purpose, and political support. As the many cataloguers and counters of power have noted, US power resources are unrivalled: the US military budget is greater than those of the next fifteen countries combined, and the US economy is larger than the next three combined. On some accounts, the United States possesses the largest margin of power in the history of the modern state system.[12] But it was, of course, the events following September 11 that seemed to provide a much clearer purpose (and perhaps a project), as well as much higher levels of domestic political support for an activist and engaged foreign policy. The emergence of a far starker unilateralist and nationalist foreign policy on the part of the United States reinforced still further the return of the language of empire. As a result, an increasing number of commentators came to talk of the US role in the world in imperialist terms.[13] And an increasing number (on both right and left) came to defend the virtues of an American Empire—as the policy best suited to the safeguarding the national interests of

---

[10] George Liska, *Imperial America: The International Politics of Primacy* (Baltimore, MD: Johns Hopkins University Press, 1967), 3.

[11] See Stephen G. Brooks and William C. Wohlforth, 'American Primacy in Perspective', *Foreign Affairs*, 81/4 (2002), 20–34.

[12] Stephen M. Walt, *Taming American Power: The Global Response to US Primacy* (New York: W.W. Norton, 2005), 31.

[13] The literature has expanded rapidly. For an overview, see Michael Cox, 'The Empire's Back in Town: Or America's Imperial Temptation—Again', *Millennium*, 32/1 (2003), 5–6. See, in particular, Andrew J. Bacevich, *American Empire: The Realities and Consequences of U.S. Diplomacy* (Cambridge, MA: Harvard University Press, 2002), 142–3; Niall Ferguson, *Empire: The Rise and Demise of the British World Order and the Lessons for Global Power* (New York: Basic Books, 2003); G. John Ikenberry, 'America's Imperial Ambition', *Foreign Affairs*, 81/5 (2002), 44–62; and Jack Snyder, 'Imperial Temptations', *The National Interest*, 71 (Spring 2003), 29–41.

the United States; as the only possible provider of global security and other international public goods; as the only state with the capacity to undertake the interventionist and state-building tasks that the changing character of security have rendered to vital; and as the essential power-political pivot for the expansion of global liberalism.

Definitions and distinctions

The characterization of the United States as an imperial power has always been difficult and contested. Thus Ernest May's classic portrayal of the absence of an imperial mindset within the United States can be contrasted with Williams's equally classic account of 'Empire as a Way of Life'.[14] It is clearly the case that the United States has long held a powerful image of itself as an anti-colonial power, with its rejection of European power politics; its sustained and recurring rhetoric of freedom and self-determination; its decisive role in establishing self-determination as an international political norm; and its direct pressure on the European states to divest themselves of empire from the Dutch in Indonesia to the French and British at Suez.

Against this, however, the United States must be seen as a product of European expansion which involved colonial settlement and the subjugation of indigenous and independent peoples. It was territorially strongly and successfully expansionist throughout the nineteenth century—through settlement, purchase, and war (using force over 100 times between 1807 and 1904). Moreover, when it did move away from territorial expansion and conquest, this was only in part because of liberal factors. It is certainly true that liberal concerns played a role—both in terms of the perceived dangers to freedom at home posed by imperial expansion abroad and the difficulty of reconciling the reality of empire and overseas rule with US values. But race and slavery were also dominant factors in explaining the end of southward expansion and in pushing the United States towards new forms of territorial control—as with the doctrine of non-incorporated territories or protectorate-style arrangements such as the Platt Amendment that served as the model for Haiti, Nicaragua, and the Dominican Republic, and that had in turn been taken from the model of British rule in Egypt. As Morgenthau and others have noted, there never appeared any strongly felt geopolitical imperative. 'Rarely, if ever, can a great power have embarked upon a policy of conquest with less conviction, determination and sense of purpose. For the United States, conquest beyond the limits of the North American continent was from the outset an unavoidable embarrassment rather than the achievement of

---

[14] Ernest R. May, *American Imperialism: A Speculative Essay* (New York: Atheneum, 1968); and William Appleman Williams, *Empire as a Way of Life* (Oxford: Oxford University Press, 1980).

267

a national purpose.'[15] Where such an imperative did exist, as in the case of the so-called Strategic Trust Territories, then conquest was not abjured. Equally, when geopolitics dictated territorial rearrangement and the bartering of peoples and sovereignties (as was true of both Paris in 1918 and Yalta in 1945), then the United States was willing to follow its interests rather than its professed values, opening itself, as Hoffmann notes, to the recurrent charge of Machiavellian scheming behind a Wilsonian façade.

And yet the United States did turn away from formal conquest and territorial annexation and towards external economic expansion and the Open Door. It is this which forces us to grapple with the non-territorial aspects of US power and with the distinction between formal and informal empire, between direct political rule (raising flags and painting maps) and informal economic control (opening economic doors).[16] This distinction remains crucial for understanding US power but suffers from two serious weaknesses. The first is its neglect of the continued willingness on the part of the United States to use force and coercion in pursuit of its interests. It is this willingness that is one of the most important characteristics which distinguishes hegemony from freely acknowledged primacy. In areas where its hegemony has been long established, as in Latin America, interventionism and the use of force have proved remarkably consistent even as the character of the broader international system underwent dramatic change. Interventionism cannot, for example, be understood as a function of the constraints of the Cold War. Moreover, as US relative power grew and as the constraints of the Cold War eased, so its willingness to use force has continued.[17]

The second problem is the tendency to overlook the 'formal' aspects of informal empire. This was a weakness of the original formulation and, still more, with its application to the United States. Historically, the practice of informal empire involved a complex set of institutional norms and arrangements (concerning, *inter alia*, extraterritoriality, protectorates, non-incorporated territories, spheres of influence, as well as norms relating to

[15] Hans J. Morgenthau, *The Purpose of American Politics* (New York: Alfred A. Knopf, 1960), 99–101. Morgenthau's discussion is fascinating as he grapples (rather unconvincingly) with the role of moral purpose. 'The hyperbolic moralisms with which American expansion has traditionally been justified, then, contain elements of subjective sincerity, but also of objective truth. The idea of the American mission to the less fortunate peoples of the world is certainly a political ideology, a rationalization and justification of policies that were undertaken for other and primarily selfish reasons. But the idea expresses also a serious commitment to a purpose that is merely the American purpose projected beyond the territorial limits of America and circumscribed only by the reach of American influence'. For an explanation of US expansion and its limits, see Fareed Zakaria, *From Wealth to Power: The Unusual Origins of America's World Role* (Princeton, NJ: Princeton University Press, 1998). On the role of race to which Zakaria pays too little attention, see Lars Schoultz, *Beneath the United States* (Cambridge, MA: Harvard University Press, 1999).

[16] For the classic exposition, see J. Gallagher and R. Robinson, 'The Imperialism of Free Trade', *Economic History Review*, VI/1 (1953), 1–15.

[17] On the use of force in the post-Cold War period, see Bacevich (2002: 142–3).

sovereignty, self-determination (or its absence), and the use of force). The ground rules of international society were indelibly marked by its dual character as both an interstate and an inter-imperial system. Today, the formal side of informal empire has become evermore crucial to the projection of power as the rules and institutions by which globalization is structured have become evermore ambitious, far-reaching, and intrusive. A great deal of US power is exercised through the changing legal and normative structure of international society—through US influence on core norms (e.g. those relating to the use of force or to the changing character of sovereignty); through US influence on regimes and institutions that it often chooses not to join; through its capacity to influence choices between market and political modes of governance; and through its cultivation of alternative modes of governance (e.g. the expansion of regulatory networks, or the externalization of its own domestic law). The view of the United States as being either 'for' or 'against' international law and institutions is highly misleading and runs the risk of diverting our attention from the ways in which US power is actually exercised.[18]

This leads to the second issue, namely the distinction between direct coercive control and control exercised through rules and institutions and mediated by negotiation. For many people, the unavoidability of the term 'empire' seems to flow naturally from the immense power resources at Washington's disposal and especially from the extraordinary military capabilities that give it such apparently crushing dominance over its adversaries. Empire (rather than hegemony or primacy) seems particularly appropriate for the direct use of coercion against weaker and subordinate states, unmediated by political negotiation, agreed rules, or shared institutions. Yet viewing power in purely coercive and material terms rests on a very narrow and essentially unhelpful understanding of power. To understand power in international relations, we must see it as a social relationship and place it side by side with other quintessentially social concepts such as prestige, authority, and legitimacy. A great deal of the struggle for political power is the quest for authoritative and legitimate control that avoids costly and dangerous reliance on brute force and coercion.

---

[18] US attitudes to international law cannot be simply read off the country's changing power-political position, as Robert Kagan suggests. [*Paradise and Power: America and Europe in the New World Order* (London: Atlantic Books, 2003), 8–41]. See Jonathan Zasloff, 'Law and the Shaping of American Foreign Policy From the Gilded Age to the New Era', *New York University Law Review*, 78 (2003), 239–373; on the post-1945 period, see Ikenberry (2001: ch. 6) and Edward C. Luck, 'Article 2 (4) and the Non-Use of Force: What Were We Thinking?' in David P. Forsythe, Patrice C. McMahon, and Andrew Wederon (eds.), *American Foreign Policy in a Globalized World* (London: Routledge, 2006).; on the recent period see Nico Krisch, 'Weak as Constraint, Strong as Tool: The Place of International Law in U.S. Foreign Policy', in David M. Malone and Yuen Foong Khong (eds.), *Unilateralism and U.S. Foreign Policy* (Boulder, CO: Lynne Rienner, 2003), 41–70.

Pericentric theorists of imperialism taught us a long time ago that formal empire depended on varieties of indirect rule and that, in a very important sense, the end of empire came when the imperialists ran out of willing collaborators. If this was true of formal empire, it is still more the case with informal empires and hegemonic systems. It is for this reason that the concept of hegemony is so important. After all, stable hegemony rests on a delicate balance between coercion and consensus, a balance between the exercise of the direct and indirect power by the hegemon on the one hand and the provision of a degree of autonomy of action and a degree of respect for the interests of weaker states on the other. Although emphases and implications may vary, this overall picture is true whether we adopt realist, liberal, or neo-Gramscian understandings of hegemony.[19] Unlike direct subordination, hegemony is necessarily based on a constant, and usually unstable, process of negotiation between the strong and the weak. Negotiation and the cultivation of legitimacy play an unavoidable role, especially, given the changing nature of policy content in a globalized world.

If the mode of control is best captured by the term hegemony, the third issue concerns the depth of involvement. The obvious intuition is that hegemony and informal empire imply shallower involvement and less intrusive efforts both to mould subordinate regimes to the hegemon's preferences and to fend off strategic rivals. On the Gallagher and Robinson view, informal empire is more flexible, cheaper, and less risky and that is why Britain preferred it whenever possible. As well as being far more in keeping with its values, the same logic and the same benefits should apply to the United States.

Against this, however, there have been clear examples where the United States has become deeply involved in attempts to remake and remould subordinate political units. One would point here to the attempts at colonial state-building during the high phase of interventionist fervour between 1898 and the Good Neighbour Policy of 1933, especially in Cuba, Haiti, and the Philippines. Kipling's 'The White Man's Burden' was, after all, addressed and dedicated not to the British Empire but to the US occupation of the Philippines.[20] Moreover, the constraints of the Cold War pressed the United States into still more expansive and ambitious attempts at promoting political democracy, economic development, and peaceful social reform, most notably in the case of the Alliance for Progress in the 1960s. This was the largest such effort between the occupations of Japan and Germany in the 1940s and the

---

[19] Liberal and neo-Gramscian approaches are very well covered in the literature. At the conservative end, the most important (and seriously neglected) theorist is Heinrich Triepel (1938).

[20] Paul A. Kramer, 'Empires, Exceptions, and Anglo-Saxons: Race and Rule between the British and United States Empires, 1880–1910', *The Journal of American History*, 88/4 (March 2002), 1348.

revival of attempts at nation-building in the 1990s. And it was a near total failure.[21]

But the more important question is whether there are not more abiding pressures towards deep involvement. One set of pressures arises from the recurring US political and moral ambition to improve the world and to export its values. 'I am seeking the very minimum of interference necessary to make them good' said Theodore Roosevelt in 1908 in relation to Cuba and Central America. But, whether we are talking about 1908 or 2004, it is highly improbable that making people good, or even moderately less bad, is ever going to be achieved by a minimum interference. Another set of pressures follow from the changing character of US economic interests. Unlike British involvement in trade and portfolio investment, the expansion of US economic interests through the twentieth century involved investment in production and the exploitation of raw materials, often behind the tariffs walls of the successful import substituting economies that dominated economic growth for much of the century. Being there and on the ground inevitably meant being far more deeply involved in domestic politics than had been the case of Britain. Moreover, the changing character of global economic regulation, most of which is related in one way or another to US interests, has increasingly come to involve deeply intrusive rules whose value depends on their internalization and implementation within domestic societies.

This crucial point can be made more generally. The promotion of US interests in a globalized age has come evermore to involve deep intrusion into how different societies are to be organized domestically. This is a structural

---

[21] The Alliance has been curiously neglected in recent debates about the viability of nation-building (and by historians more generally). Although there had been some successes, by the late 1960s the limits and failures were clear for all to see. And the reasons for failure remain relevant. Fist, the long-term goals of democracy and development were consistently undercut by the short-term needs of security and, especially, counter-insurgency. Second, the need to reduce burdens pushed the United States to embrace a range of dubious and distasteful proxies. These were the colonels and generals who assumed power in the twilight of democracy in the 1960s. As they became entrenched in power, Washington found indirect control increasingly difficult (proxy tails wagging hegemonic dogs) and the United States became tainted by its close support of the enemies of democracy and the nefarious activities of their torturing henchman. Indeed, it is this period which does so much to undermine the view of United States as a consistent supporter of democracy and human rights, and it is the apparent blindness to this reality that does so much to engender cynicism abroad today. And, third, the Alliance failed because of the sheer difficulties of nation-building even in a region where US power was so overwhelming, where the United States had both knowledge and cultural assets, and where it had made such a public commitment. It was this failure that contributed to some of the most influential analyses of the time, especially Robert Pakenham's *Liberal America and the Third World* (Princeton, NJ: Princeton University Press, 1973) and Samuel Huntington's *Political Order in Changing Societies* (New Haven, CT: Yale University Press, 1968)—the bible for those who sought justification of US support for authoritarian regimes, until the third wave of democratization and the end of the Cold War pushed many on the right from an extreme form of democratic impossibilism to an equally exaggerated belief in the universal possibilities of democracy and democracy promotion.

change. If states are to develop effective policies on economic development, environmental protection, human rights, the resolution of refugee crises, the fight against drugs, or the struggle against terrorism, then they need to engage with a wide range of international and transnational actors and to interact not just with central governments but with a much wider range of domestic political, economic, and social players. If you want to solve problems in a globalized world, you cannot simply persuade or bully governments into signing treaties and are therefore inevitably drawn to become involved with how other people organize their own societies. This trend has been reinforced by the transformation of the security agenda and, as I will suggest later, this is one of the most important factors that has reshaped the debate about legitimacy and, once more, complicated the exercise of hegemonic power.

Finally, it has always been extremely difficult for empires and hegemonic powers to define and limit their interests. International relations as a discipline has become far too used to thinking of the international political system in neo-realist terms: a world in which systems 'constrain' by pushing and shoving states to act in particular ways. Unequal power and the absence of traditional power-political competitors lead analysts naturally to a focus on domestic factors. Hence, the common argument that, in a period of unipolarity, US policy is to be explained in terms of interest groups (business or oil interests) or ideology (the rise of the neoconservatives). Hence, too, the focus on the ways in which hegemonic or imperial states can be driven to make policy choices and, in particular, be tempted to overexpansion, by domestic interest groups and by domestically engendered and propagated 'myths of empire' of the kind analysed so powerfully by Jack Snyder.[22]

This mode of thinking has great merits; but also real limits. Empires have always faced many genuine strategic dilemmas that are rooted in the nature of the system, and not in domestic politics; and the analyst needs to place much more emphasis on the way in which systems 'constrain' not by pushing and shoving but by entrapping and ensnaring. Maintaining a successful empire is an extraordinarily difficult task. In the case of Britain, what prompted the move away from informal empire was sometimes directly prompted by strategic rivalry in a way consistent with neo-realism; but it was also often the result of socio-economic change on the periphery, of local crises which appeared to threaten the stability of control and the prestige of the imperial power, and of the great variety of imperial bridgeheads which connected the imperial outside with the local inside.[23] As we move out of the age of formal empire, the options available to major states have been repeatedly constrained by the actions of the weak and by the instabilities of the periphery. Contrary

[22] Jack Snyder, *Myths of Empire: Domestic Politics and International Ambition* (Ithaca, NY: Cornell University Press, 1991).

[23] See John Darwin, 'Imperialism and the Victorians: The Dynamics of Territorial Expansion', *English Historical Review*, CXII/447 (1997), 614–42.

to the claims of neo-realists (especially defensive neo-realists), there can be no stable equilibrium of power and no uncontested definition of interest. As Hoffmann notes, 'almost anything can be described as a vital interest since even peripheral disorder can unravel the superpower's eminence.'[24] This should also caution against attempts to understand the policies of the United States in terms of its own grand strategic choices. As with the issue of followership and legitimacy, the focus of study needs to be on the objects of US power as much as on the objectives of US policy. Local balances and bargains can be just as vital as grand strategic bargains.

The debate on the consistency of US expansion and the balance between the varying components of US interest is too large to tackle here. It is not difficult to refute the view of the United States as purely reactive to events in the outside world. In an important sense, the United States has always been a revisionist state, whether this has been reflected in crusading or exemplarism.[25] But empire by invitation also remains a very important part of the historical picture (especially in relation to Europe), as does the acquisition of predominant power, if not by accident, then certainly as a result of pursuing other more important goals, especially winning major wars. But what I have sought to stress here is that the push factors behind US policy need to be set against the complex set of pull factors involved in maintaining power, even in the absence of a direct strategic rival.

The sustainability of hegemony

In this section, I examine five factors which have been commonly cited as lying behind the end of empire in the twentieth century: the declining utility of military force, resistance to alien rule, changes within the metropolitan core, changes in the international legal and moral climate, and the existence of opponents and challengers. These factors also underpinned the broader diffusion and decentralization of power that, for writers such as Bull and Watson, characterized the period from 1900 to the late 1970s. On this account, decolonization and the end of empire were only one element of the revolt against the previous Western dominance of the international system. Other elements

[24] Stanley Hoffmann, 'Why Don't they Like Us?', in Eugene R. Wittkopf and James M. MacCormick (eds.), *The Domestic Sources of American Foreign Policy: Insights and Evidence* (Lanham, MD: Rowman and Littlefield, 2004), 35.

[25] However we explain the balance between these two, the powerful sense of having a mission to revise the world perhaps explains what often looks so puzzling to outsiders—the subjective sense of vulnerability when, to the outside analyst, it is the absence of threats and challengers that is most striking. Williams puts it thus '... the faith in America's uniqueness coupled with the failure of others to copy the perfect revolution generated a deep sense of being *alone*. Americans considered themselves perpetually beleaguered' and quotes Weinberg's remark about 'a feeling of a preordained right to ideal security'. Williams (1980: 53–4).

included the struggle for equal sovereignty, racial equality, economic justice, and cultural liberation.[26] How far this diffusion or decentralization has been reversed is therefore not only central to understanding the role of the United States but also the character and development of the international system more generally.

The first factor concerns the utility of military force and arguments about its declining utility. This was a common theme in the 1970s, both of the broader literature on power and interdependence and of the more specific writing on military force and why big nations appeared increasingly to be losing small wars. The specific elements of these debates need not detain us here. Suffice to say that on a strong reading of this position we could trace a clear path from the self-assured dominance with which the imperial powers had collectively suppressed the Boxer Rebellion in 1900 to the military failures of the European empires in Algeria, southern Africa, or Indo-China, as well as to the defeat of the United States in Vietnam in 1975 and to the difficulties encountered by the Soviet Union in Afghanistan from its invasion in 1979 to its withdrawal in 1989.[27]

Military power is perhaps the most obvious area where the proponents of hegemonic reassertionism can point to significant and far-reaching change. Such claims often focus on the transformation of military technologies, the revolution in military affairs, and the astonishing gap that new technologies, enormous spending, and organizational capability have opened up between the United States and all other states. Hence, the stress on the impact of a range of overlapping technologies: the vast increase in the capacity to process information and to penetrate the fog of war, the increasing range, accuracy and lethality of weapons systems, the emergence of a new pattern of mobile, flexible and network-centric warfare.[28] Hence, too, the argument that, aside from winning militarily, these developments would serve to reduce the burdens and dangers of using military force: by reducing casualties, by allowing greater discrimination, helping to secure support at home and compliance with humanitarian law, abroad, and by reducing the reliance on allies and overseas bases.

---

[26] Bull and Watson (1984). A great deal of writing in the 1970s stressed the diffusion and decentralization of power which were seen as complicating not just old-style formal empires but also top-down conceptions of order, as with Kissingerian notions of a superpower-dominated system or an oligarchical ordering of Great Powers.

[27] For a wide-ranging account that stresses the increased difficulties of using military force, see Jeremy Black, *War and the World: Military Power and the Fate of Continents* (New Haven, CT: Yale University Press, 1998), especially chs. 7 and 9. For trends as seen in the 1970s, see Andrew Mack, 'Why Big Nations Lose Small Wars: The Politics of Asymmetric Conflict', *World Politics*, 27/2 (1975), 175–200; and Klaus Knorr, 'Is International Coercion Waning or Rising?', *International Security*, 1/4 (1975), 92–110.

[28] For a clear introduction, see Lawrence Freedman, *The Revolution in Strategic Affairs*, Adelphi Paper 318 (London: IISS, 1998).

In the light of these developments, some have been tempted to revise, if not reverse, the historical trajectory noted above. Thus Niall Ferguson compares contemporary US military power with the British victory at Omdurman in 1898 when 45,000 of 52,000 of the Mahdi's army were killed as against only 48 on the British side.[29] Hence too the tendency to recall Hilaire Belloc's lines: 'Whatever, happens we have got/the Maxim-gun; and they have not'. The US experience in the 1990s appeared to many to re-establish the utility of coercive military force at relatively low cost: not only had the 1991 Persian Gulf War involved far lower casualties than expected but losses in Haiti, Somalia, Bosnia, and Kosovo amounted to less than fifty deaths.

But if this portrayal sounds at first blush to represent a fundamental change, the reality is more complex. The first response is well known, namely that rational opponents will chose to avoid fighting on terms that favour the strongest—hence the notion of asymmetric response and the resort to terrorism, to insurgency, and to the pursuit of WMD. The two other reasons for doubt can both be loosely described as Clausewitzian. For Clausewitz, the successful use of coercive power is about breaking the will of an opponent through a complex mixture of physical and moral violence. The successful use of coercive power involves the capacity to change and control the minds of other human beings—to bend others to one's will and to impose particular vision of reality upon them. However technically efficient and destructive, military force that does not engage directly and brutally with the will of the opponent and which does not involve a willingness to bear costs and casualties is unlikely to meet this essential criterion for success.[30] The asymmetry of commitment (so-called wars of choice on the one hand vs. the extreme and literally self-destructive commitment of the suicide bomber on the other) therefore remains an important and limiting factor on US military power.

The other, and still more powerful, Clausewitzian doubt comes directly from the classic argument that the object of strategy is not purely military victory and that the sole purpose of military success is to change the terms of a political relationship. Victory on the battlefield should only be seen as a means to a political end. The difficulty of relating military objectives to sustainable political outcomes has always been the most important issue in debates about the utility of military force. It was central to many of the debates about counter-insurgency in the 1960s, as well as to analyses of why the United States failed in Vietnam in the 1970s. It arises also in those cases where 'militarization' has done little or nothing to allay or offset a broader policy failure whose roots are political and social, as with the war on drugs. And it is central to the immensely difficult task of moving from peacekeeping

---

[29] Ferguson (2003).

[30] Carl von Clausewitz, *On War*, edited and trans. by Michael Howard and Peter Paret (Princeton, NJ: Princeton University Press, 1978), bk I, chs. 1 & 2 and bk III ch. 3.

and peace-enforcement to post-conflict reconstruction and successful state-building.

This leads to the second factor, resistance to alien rule. Central to decolonization was the increasing social and political mobilization of previously subordinated peoples and societies. The reality of both general external involvement and more specific forms of direct alien rule, combined with the changes wrought by capitalist development, the dislocations caused by the world wars, the expansion of education and the spread of ideas about political freedom, all stimulated the development of anti-colonial nationalism. This was not true in all places and certainly not to the same extent; but the crucial intuition is that the successful development of empire carried with it the seeds of its own destruction. The power of anti-colonial nationalism, the power of the idea of national self-determination and the emergence of both mass and vanguardist resistance to alien rule reflected deep-rooted changes in the social structures and mental maps of previously subordinated peoples. In many ways, this represented a working out across the world of a general and universal process of social change and development.

In some cases, the continuities are striking and work to reinforce arguments about the difficulties of using military force. Faced by nationalist resistance, even states that are willing to bear very heavy casualties find controlling territory difficult. Chechnya has a population of only 1.05 million but in 1994–5 its nationalist movement defeated the Russian army and Moscow remains unable to reassert stable control despite willingness to bear heavy costs and to engage in brutal suppression. Other examples would include Israel in the occupied territories, or the situation in Sri Lanka. Nationalism also complicates the search for stable patterns of collaboration. As noted earlier, the high costs of direct involvement have consistently pushed imperial and hegemonic states towards the use of proxies. But the challenge here is steep and probably getting steeper: such proxies need to be efficient proxies at providing local security and at fulfilling broader security goals (as with anti-terrorism); they also need to be 'principled proxies', given the commitment of the United States and its allies to democracy and the human rights and the difficulties of evading the transnational politics of human rights; and they need to maintain both the confidence of their external backers and respond to the sentiments and needs of the populations on which their own position ultimately depends.

We might usefully enquire into why nationalism has been downgraded. In part, it may have to do with the powerful legacy of an excessively rosy reading of the history of decolonization—that independence had been part of the very purposes of empire, rather than a process in which armed resistance and violent conflict had played a fundamentally important role. In part, it may have to do with the implicit liberal assumptions that marked both the revived multilateralism of the 1990s and the more recent militant Wilsonianism—the view that, if one successfully gets internal self-determination right, then the power of external self-determination will naturally drain away.

And in part it may have to do with the tendency to see novelty in the patterns of violence that are most dangerous and most threatening. Many see the 'new wave' of transnational religious terrorism as representing a decisive breakpoint in the evolution of terrorism undertaken by non-state groups. It is certainly the case that much is new in terms of the conditions, means of operation, and, in some cases, goals and objectives. But nationalism and claims for national self-determination have been a long-standing and prominent feature of terrorism and remain so.[31] This was evidently the case in the role that terrorist acts played in the anti-colonial struggle and in the creation of states such as Ireland, Israel, Kenya, and Algeria. Equally, although many radical movements in the 1970s spoke the language of internationalism, nationalist goals remained prominent, as with the Basques, Irish, and Palestinians. And, in the so-called religious wave that developed from the late 1970s, the link between religious and ethnic identity is often close, as is the relationship between terrorist violence and the goal of self-determination and resistance to alien rule. From this perspective, truly transnational religious terrorist movements are the outlier. Focusing on suicide terrorism brings out the point still more clearly: 'From Lebanon to Israel to Sri Lanka to Kashmir to Chechnya, every suicide terrorist campaign from 1980 to 2001 has been waged by terrorist groups whose main goal has been to establish or maintain self-determination for their community's homeland by compelling an enemy to withdraw'.[32]

A great deal of hegemonic reassertionism depends on the belief that threats and enemies are localized (as with rogue states), or personalized (as with Saddam Hussein or Slobadan Miloševiæ); and that there is an absence of legitimating or unifying ideologies of revolt or resistance. There is no reason for believing that the specific form of twentieth-century anti-colonial nationalism was bound to continue indefinitely. Rather, anti-colonial nationalism should be seen as but one illustration of a broader phenomenon that might be labelled subaltern resistance. Such resistance might now be aimed at diffuse targets (such as the 'West' or 'globalization') and at local power-holders as much as external or alien forces; its aims may be far less well defined than those anti-colonial nationalists who sought the creation of new nation-states; and it may be closely tied to processes of transnationalization and de-territorialization.[33] It is possible that the broader sources of convergence and

[31] See David C. Rapoport, 'The Four Waves of Modern Terrorism', in Audrey Kurth Cronin and James M. Ludes (eds.), *Attacking Terrorism: Elements of Grand Strategy* (Washington, DC: Georgetown University Press, 2004), 46–73.

[32] Robert A. Pape, 'The Strategic Logic of Suicide Terrorism', *American Political Science Review*, 97/3 (2002), 344.

[33] Deterritorialization and the continuity of resistance are two of the most important themes discussed by Roy (2002, esp. 41–54 and 328–40).

integration associated with globalization, the spread of democratic rule, and the attractions and emulative potential of US soft power will make subaltern resistance to both alien control and top-down modes of governance far less important than in the past. But there are good grounds for questioning the current neglect of nationalism in discussions of hegemony, and for believing that subaltern resistance and the struggle for recognition on the part of the dominated and marginalized will remain powerful forces.[34] There are also important elements of continuity between the states, movements, ideologies, and crises produced by the superpower interventionism in the Third World during the Cold War and the conflicts and crises that beset the contemporary world.[35] We cannot understand contemporary resistance to the United States in, say, Iran, Bolivia, or Venezuela without taking into account US policy towards those countries during the Cold War.

The third factor to be considered concerns the politics of the metropolitan power. A major part of the story of the end of empire has focused on developments within the imperial metropole: the unwillingness to bear the costs of empire, the shift from warfare to welfare, the decline of the imperial mindset that was such a powerful part of dominant societies a century or so ago. European imperialism was not characterized solely by specific forms of foreign policy behaviour, but was related to the existence of extremely imperialistic societies and ideologies, both at the level of public opinion and within the 'official mind'. The debate is sometimes cast in terms of imperial willpower: the European empires collapsed when the Europeans lost the will to rule and the willingness to bear the costs of empire.

How does this play out in the case of the United States? In many ways, the position of the United States appears relatively favourable. Both Kojève and Negri and Hardt are simply wrong to suggest that modern imperial formations do not have a national core.[36] The United States is, after all, an imperial nation-state with an impressive capacity for nationalist mobilization and with a state that has long been much 'stronger' than the historical mythology suggests. Indeed, it is the combination of these features with the non-territorial and transnational characteristics of its power projection that underpins much of the case for its success and sustainability. Despite the many strains and fissures (especially during its greatest periods of expansion, immigration, and economic development) and despite the recurring doubts of conservatives (Kennan previously and Huntington most recently), by any

[34] In Stephen Krasner's recent discussion of suspending sovereignty and failed states, nationalism is not mentioned as a problem. On this account avarice, desperation, and elections will underpin the acceptability of semi-sovereignty. Krasner (2004: esp. 113–18).

[35] See Westad (2005).

[36] Michael Hardt and Antonio Negri, *Empire* (Cambridge, MA: Harvard University Press, 2000).

comparative standards the United States has been, and remains, an effective, socially cohesive nation-state.[37]

There are many aspects to the domestic prerequisites of hegemony, and these are often hard to balance and cash out in an overall judgement. The post-Vietnam view that US foreign policy, and especially the use of force, was severely constrained by public opinion appears to have given way to a view that stresses the consistency of public opinion, that sees public opinion as sensitive to casualties but not casualty-phobic, and that is pragmatically willing to support external projects that are both 'do-able' and consonant with US values. But the willingness to bear the costs of empire in terms of blood and treasure are not the only, nor necessarily the most important, way in which domestic factors matter—as in conventional debates about overcoming the ghosts of Vietnam. If, as suggested above, hegemony is about coercion and consensus and about being able to reward allies and strike deals with collaborators, then these complex and ever-changing external bargains have to be cashed out in US domestic politics. The real domestic constraint may therefore have to do less with the issue of costs and rather more to do with the extreme difficulty of meshing the external side of hegemonic management with the extreme complexity, closed and introspective character of US domestic politics.

Fourth, there is the role played by changes in the legal and normative climate. From this perspective, the progressive unfolding of the struggle against empire was reflected in a number of crucial changes in the dominant norms of international society and was reinforced by those changes: the increasing constraints on the use of force, especially in relation to conquest, forcible control and occupation; and the increased centrality of the norm of self-determination. In some ways, normative and legal change in the 1990s appeared to be running in the opposite direction. Examples would include: increased acceptance of the need to rethink and re-conceptualize sovereignty; increased acceptance of the argument that new security challenges necessarily involved deep involvement in domestic affairs of other, and especially weak, states; the establishment of international administrations to run territories whose sovereignty had been effectively suspended and the broader return of ideas about protectorates and of graduated notions of sovereignty of the kind familiar to lawyers writing at the turn of the twentieth century; and the spread of ideas about humanitarian intervention, human security, and the responsibility to protect.

However, four points need to be noted. First, although it may be true that the character of the legal order reflects patterns of hegemonic power and the interests of major states, it is also the case that controlling an increasingly complex and pluralist legal order is far harder today than it was a hundred

[37] Huntington (2004).

years ago. In the nineteenth century, international law was made by, and for, the imperial great powers; today, the international legal system has become far more complex, pluralist, and harder to control. This is a structural reason why the frustration of the United States with international law has grown sharper. Second, the major normative constraints are still there, especially in terms of norms against conquest and in favour of self-determination. Moreover, other normative developments, especially in the field of human rights, have greatly complicated the use of coercion. It is certainly true that the war on terror has represented a profound challenge to human rights in many parts of the world. But it is also the case that the reaction to these challenges demonstrates at least to some degree the embeddedness of the culture of human rights that has become such a central part of the liberal solidarist view of international society.

Third, to take advantage of the potential benefits of the legal order, the United States has to engage with it. Indeed, seen from outside, the most striking characteristic of the post-September 11 period was the failure to engage more systematically with the UN and international law at a time when so many aspects of the legal order were running in its favour. Fourth, and running in the opposite direction, the United States has picked up on two sets of norms for which consensus in international society is very hard to win—certainly outside a much deeper, offsetting commitment to process and procedure. One has to do with the use of force and the enunciation of a doctrine of both expanded pre-emption and prevention that clearly represents a far-reaching change in established legal understandings of the justifiable use of force. The other involves taking the already emerging notion of qualified or conditional sovereignty but giving it a much harder edge, for example, by arguing that certain sorts of states have lost the sovereign right to possess certain sorts of weapons, or that conditional or qualified sovereignty legitimizes intervention to change a political regime.

Finally, there is question of opponents and potential challengers. As I have tried to suggest above, this is not the only factor that needs to be considered, but it is an unavoidable one. The end of European empires was closely bound up with the existence of a global balance of power and with the dynamics of the competition between the superpowers and the opportunities that this created for weaker states and nationalist movements. Equally, whatever precise role we attribute to external pressure, the end of the Soviet Empire is impossible to understand outside the context of the Cold War and bipolar rivalry. Without claiming to be able to present a complete picture, We can identify two positions.

The first is heavily, but not exclusively, power-based. This account rests on three propositions. The first proposition is that US dominance is stable because of the sheer extent of US power and the impossibility of any foreseeable challenge or serious challenger. Second, enough deals can be done to secure sustained support for US positions. In some cases, support comes from security dependence, given the failures of collective security, the importance of US power for regional power balances, and the argument that only US power can tackle common challenges such as terrorism and WMD. In other cases, it rests on US economic power, both in terms of carrots and sticks. And third, US power is stable because it does rest on legitimate purpose. Even neo-conservatives have come to accept the importance of legitimacy, trying to argue that US power is legitimate because of the public goods that only the US can provide and because its power rests on broadly shared societal values, especially freedom and democracy.[38]

However, this argument encounters a number of serious difficulties. It sees balance of power politics solely in terms of military challenges and challengers. The problem of unbalanced power is not that unchecked power will lead inevitably to tanks rolling across borders. It is rather that radically unbalanced power will permit the powerful to 'lay down the law' to the less powerful, to skew the terms of cooperation in its own favour, to impose its own values and ways of doing things, and to undermine the procedural rules on which stable and sustained cooperation must inevitably depend. It is for this reason that the perceived need to 'contain' the power of the United States at the present time is a rational pluralist response that need not have anything to do with political or cultural anti-Americanism and still less with the notion that the United States represents a 'threat' in an old-fashioned military sense. Even if it remains only a background condition, the balance of power continues to matter and, on this account, it is no coincidence that two of the most elaborate instances of successful institution building, the EU and the WTO, reflect a relatively balanced set of power relations.

A second problem is that it downplays the willingness of major states affected by US power to engage in a modified form of balancing behaviour. Hard-balancing may be out, but soft or constrained balancing is certainly not. Hence potential rivals have certainly been willing to engage in deal-making with the United States, but they have also been willing to complicate and raise the costs of US policies in some international institutions (by denying legitimacy) and to challenge dominant US preferences in others (as with the developing world in the WTO). Balancing and bandwagonning are crude but they remain central to categories understanding the foreign policies of major second-tier states in the face of US power. And third, the claims to legitimacy quite clearly have not won over large parts of the world, even amongst those who share many of the same political and cultural values.

An alternative way of looking at the strategic choices of the hegemon is in terms of efforts to constitutionalize its power and to win acceptance for its

[38] See e.g. Robert Kagan, 'America's Crisis of Legitimacy', *Foreign Affairs*, 83/2 (2004), 65–88.

pre-eminence. The idea is an old one. For Aron, the choice for a potential hegemon is clear: 'Either a great power will not tolerate equals, and then must proceed to the last degree of empire, or else it consents to stand first among sovereign units, and must win acceptance for such pre-eminence.'[39] Of particular importance in terms of winning acceptance are the idea of strategic restraint and the role of institutions in signalling that strategic restraint. If the dominant power wishes to maintain its predominant position, it should act with strategic restraint so as to prevent the emergence of potential rivals. A rational hegemon will engage in a degree of self-restraint and institutional self-binding in order to undercut others' perceptions of threat. John Ikenberry provides one of the clearest accounts of this logic. In his many writings, he has stressed the distinctive, open, and institutionalized character of US hegemony and of the 'liberal' bargain that Washington has been able to deploy to address 'the uncertainties of American power'.

Asian and European states agree to accept American leadership and operate within an agreed-upon political–economic system. In return, the United States opens itself up and binds itself to its partners, in effect, building an institutionalized coalition of partners and reinforces the stability of these long-term relations by making itself more 'user friendly'—that is, by playing by the rules and creating ongoing political processes with these other states that facilitate consultation and joint decision-making.[40]

It is too early to judge whether the United States will be able to re-stabilize its hegemony via such a route, but there are three issues that will be crucial. The first is the degree to which there is genuine institutional engagement. Is it sufficient, as Richard Betts has suggested, for Washington to go 'through the motions of consultation, paying lip service to international institutions even as it shoves them along'?[41] After all, outside the North Atlantic, how far has Washington ever been willing to engage in anything approaching genuine consultation or 'joint decision-making'? The second is the degree to which institutional enmeshment with the dominant state dis-empowers rather than empowers. Yes, there are very powerful incentives that press weaker states towards institutions, but there also comes a tipping point when the substantive values and interests represented by the institution are so skewed in favour of the more powerful, or where the procedures that are held to mitigate unequal power cannot be effectively used by the weak (or can easily be circumvented by the strong). The third issue has to do with the balance of satisfactions and with the way in which that balance is, or is not, viewed as legitimate by a broad enough range of political opinion. The classic definition of a Great Power, after all, is one that is willing to take a broad

---

[39] Aron (1966: 70).   [40] Ikenberry (Winter 2001: 27); see also Ikenberry (2001).
[41] Richard Betts, 'The Political Support System for American Primacy', *International Affairs*, 81/1 (2005), 13.

enough definition of its own interests and to create a system in which the majority of states and peoples see themselves as having a stake.

Conclusions

The power resources of the United States are indeed enormous. But what is more striking is the instability of power, the uncertainties of power, and the perennial difficulty of translating power into desired outcomes, especially desired and durable outcomes in an increasingly complex world. In so far the United States seeks to pursue a hard, exclusivist conception of its own interests and to propound a narrow hegemonic conception of order, then it is likely to generate not a Pax Americana but rather an empire of insecurity, both for itself and for others. The challenges to the inherited structures of international society are likely to grow more serious and the difficulties of institutional repair will grow more intractable. But, just as importantly, even if we enter a period of hegemonic decompression, then we will need to ask how far the factors examined in this chapter also complicate the search for alternatives. After all, it is an illusion of the critics of the Bush administration that there is an easy, readymade multilateral alternative waiting in the wings. The legitimacy of the liberal multilateralism of the 1990s had already been called into question by many states (and by social movements) as that decade moved on. For many states and other groups, the rhetoric of liberal multilateralism covered the reality of its top-down, prescriptive, and often coercive character. The substantive outcomes appeared to be stacked in favour of the most powerful: collective security had become selective security; the agenda of human rights favoured democracy and civil and political rights but neglected economic and social rights, and ignored calls for greater economic justice; and although economic globalization was heavily promoted, there was little attention to its discontents and downsides. The hard-line hegemonist 'we can do it alone' is clearly wrong. But the liberal hegemonist version, 'we can do it together' depends on who 'we' are, on what 'it' is, and what is meant by 'together'.

Part IV

Conclusions

12

The state of international society and the pursuit of justice

This book has sought to map the changing structure of international society and to unpack some of the most important and most difficult dilemmas that arise. All such maps of a political terrain are necessarily interpretative and normative. This final chapter begins by drawing together the picture of international society that has been painted and then looks more directly at the normative implications. If international society has indeed been changing in the ways discussed in this book, what ought we to do? How ought we to proceed? And, still more crucially, who is the 'we' that is to be at the centre of this drive to create a morally more satisfactory form of international society?

The state of international society

A stable and legitimate form of international society faces three core challenges: capturing common interest, managing unequal power, and mediating difference and value conflict. This challenge is, in a profound sense, political. International society is characterized by a complex plurality of ideas, views, and values. It is also characterized by a plurality of political identities in search of recognition, some relatively secure within established states, many others standing in ambiguous or highly conflictual relation to existing institutional and political structures. Global inequality remains extreme with much of the day-to-day process of governance and many fundamental social choices being made in the shadow of unequal and often coercively exercised power. Many moral ideas and norms are now embedded within the institutions and practices of international society, but the plurality of views, values, and identities cannot be reconciled on the basis of any straightforward appeal to shared moral principles. And, although interest-driven cooperative logics play a fundamental role and although analytical International Relations has made great strides in understanding the conditions under which they may play such a role, global governance cannot be reduced to the provision of international public goods or the resolution of well-understood collective action problems.

The early years of the twenty-first century have seen many challenges to the fabric of international law and society and especially to the hopes of those who a decade earlier had seen the real possibility of moving towards a more ambitious, effective, and sustainable form of liberal solidarism. These challenges have been dramatized by the actions and rhetoric of the Bush administration, and there can be no doubt that US policies have posed a range of power-political, legal, and moral challenges to inherited understandings of international society. But the view that the problems facing international society are exclusively to do with the United States is a shallow and trivial one. The difficulties are historically and structurally deep-rooted.

Faced with the range and seriousness of the challenges, one temptation is to try to push back to a state-based pluralism. As we have seen, the pluralist view reflects a series of both principled and pragmatic arguments as to why nation-states should remain the building-blocks of global order, with a strong presumption in favour of upholding the traditional norm of non-intervention, or, at least highly constrained intervention. In addition, the pluralist continues to see this limited interstate order as providing a morally significant means of promoting coexistence and limiting conflict in a world in which consensus on more ambitious forms of cooperation is limited and in which more elaborate international institutions are liable to be captured by the special interests and particular values of the most powerful. For the pluralist, there is very little to suggest that politics without the state (certainly in the absence of secure and sustainable external suppliers of public order) represents a sustainable road to the containing or curtailing of social violence. She or he is also likely to reassert old liberal arguments deriving from Kant and Mill that point either to the moral unacceptability of attempts to export democracy or to their limited practical feasibility.

Second, the modern-day pluralist will point to the many qualifications and cautions that have emerged from the latest round of writing on globalization and its alleged impact on the state—not that the impact of globalization has not been profound but rather that its most important effect has been to exacerbate the inequalities that exist between those states that are better able to adapt and those that are not. In a related vein, the pluralist sees plenty of reasons for continuing to believe that we still live in a world of nations: that nationalism as a force and as a powerfully felt community of fate shows little sign of declining in many of the largest states of the world (and has been militantly reasserted in the United States); and that demands for national self-determination, as well as newer forms of resistance to alien rule continue to underlie a very great number of violent conflicts in the world, including many associated with the growth of terrorism.

Third, the contemporary pluralist will also insist on the contemporary relevance of the core institutions of international society. Faced by a superpower which listens little to the outside world and which in Thomas Franck's words, 'has never learnt to listen to itself as though it were the enemy speaking' and by a globalized world in which more and more communication seems to reflect less and less understanding, the role for diplomacy appears more important than ever. In the case of international law, the modern-day pluralist will highlight the dangers of overreach. Central to the pluralist understanding has been the belief that, unless law reconciled itself with the realities of the power-political order, it would, to repeat Stone's words, 'have a moth-like existence, fluttering inevitably and precariously year by year into the destructive flame of power'.[1] For the pluralist this is precisely what has occurred through the mistaken drive to constitutionalize international politics, most notably, in the period since September 11. Instead, many (especially in the United States) have suggested that we ought to recognize the power of the normative arguments in favour of a very limited, essentially Vattelian view of law and sovereignty,[2] and accept that the 'reality' of international law lies in the extent to which it reflects the reasonably immediate self-interest of states.[3]

Importantly, the pluralist argument rests on the continued role of power and the need to contain the exercise of power. The link between pluralism and the balance of power was historically very close, with the balance of power being seen as a principal means of preserving the independence of states (but not of all states); as a means of constraining and restraining the most powerful and would-be hegemonic; and as an inducement to moderation and restraint in foreign policy; and, finally, as an essential background condition for the operation of international law and institutions. Statements about the irrelevance of the balance of power have recently appeared from many parts of the political spectrum. However, for the modern-day pluralist, the view that the balance of power belongs to a vanished nineteenth century or to an almost equally distant Cold War world confuses particular historical manifestations of balance of power politics with the centrality of power in political life and the persistent pathologies to which it gives rise.

The problem of unbalanced power is not that it leads inexorably to a military threat. It is rather that radically unbalanced power will permit the powerful to 'lay down the law' to the less powerful, to skew the terms of cooperation in its own favour, to impose its own values and ways of doing things, and to undermine the procedural rules on which stable and legitimate cooperation must inevitably depend. The relevance and utility of balance of

---

[1] Stone (1969: 386).

[2] See e.g. Jeremy Rabkin, *The Case for Sovereignty: Why the World Should Welcome American Independence* (Washington, DC: AEI Press, 2004).

[3] See the deeply flawed but highly influential views of Jack L. Goldsmith and Eric A Posner, *The Limits of International Law* (Oxford: Oxford University Press, 2005).

power theory is not limited to those cases where unbalanced power poses a direct security challenge to other states, and needs to include 'soft' as well as 'hard' balancing strategies.[4] It is for this reason that balance of power thinking continues to play such a central role in the foreign policy of second-tier states such as China, India, Russia, or Brazil, and helps shape US policy towards major regions (as in the case of the United States seeking to build up an alliance with India). Equally, it is impossible to make analytical sense of security in many parts of the world except with reference to the balance of power. Think, most obviously, of the Asia-Pacific region. And balance of power politics often plays a decisive role in the operation of multilateral institutions, especially in terms of the informal understandings and trade-offs amongst the major states without which effective multilateralism is unlikely to prove effective. The link, then, between the old pluralist world of power politics and the solidarist world of institutions is close and persistent.

In his impressive elaboration of a justice-based conception of international legal legitimacy, Allen Buchanan accepts that moving beyond procedural legitimacy and, more specifically, beyond the norm of state consent may involve a danger of predation by strong states upon weaker ones. But he goes on to argue, first, that 'how best to curb predation is a complex issue of constitutional design for the international legal system'; and second, that '. . . even if it were true that adherence to the state consent super-norm, as an instrument for curbing predation, is now a necessary condition for system legitimacy, this might well change. What is necessary for system legitimacy now may no longer be required in the future, if alternative protections for weak states can be established'.[5] To this the pluralist will reply that legal or constitutional solutions depend on international political arrangements. There is little firm reason for believing that constitutional design in the absence of either a balance of power or at least the capacity of smaller states to raise the costs of coercion is likely to prove a sustainable solution to the problem of predation. Indeed, the continued structural failings of collective security place severe limits on the effectiveness of these alternative means of security and protection. More generally, the pluralist defender of a limited society of states does not argue that the state system represents the optimal way of obtaining such objectives as security, economic justice, or environmental sustainability. Such a form of limited global political order is, on the contrary, deeply flawed. The point is rather than it remains the best on offer.[6]

[4] See Andrew Hurrell, 'Hegemony, Liberalism and Global Order', *International Affairs*, 82/1 (January 2006): 12–16; Stephen G. Brooks and William C. Wohlforth, 'Hard Times for Soft Balancing', *International Security*, 30/1 (Summer 2005), 103.

[5] Allen Buchanan, *Justice, Legitimacy and Self-determination: Moral Foundations of International Law* (Oxford: Oxford University Press, 2004), 312.

[6] On this point, see Caney's critique of Bull in Simon Caney, *Justice Beyond Borders: A Global Political Theory* (Oxford: Oxford University Press, 2005), 160–7.

Simply pointing to the existence of the WTO, the EU, or the UN does not demonstrate that other forms of collaboration are possible—partly because of the weaknesses and fragility of such bodies but also because of the degree to which their functioning both reflects and depends on the macro-political order embodied in a viable society of states. However strong the moral case for alternative cosmopolitan political structures, the pluralist remains sceptical as to their viability and suspicious of the disorder (and potential for injustice) involved in attempts to build such structures.

Fourth, the modern-day pluralist remains deeply sceptical about claims regarding either the homogenization of values and cultures or the spread of Western liberal values. On this view, there is little reason for believing that the problematic issues of value conflict and cultural division have become obsolete. Quite the contrary. Much writing within Western political theory centres on the loss of faith and religious reassurance and on the absence of metaphysical anchors or transcendental guarantees. Postmodern theorists tell us that we should accept the contingency of our moral commitments and, very plausibly, that the chances of tolerance will be increased if we adopt an ironic attitude towards them. And yet the problem in global politics is precisely the opposite. The problem is not scepticism, but the excesses of faith. The political challenge is that the world is full of people who have all too clear a view of what the universal moral order ought to be; who are all too certain that their own moral vision is founded on some absolutely secure foundation; and who believe that their vision of the world should be extended and imposed upon others, if necessary by force of arms. The idea that the faithful should adopt an ironic stance towards the truth would be treated as absurd. For religious fundamentalists of all stripes, moral truth is God-given and obedience to that truth is central to their faith. Political action should be directed to the liberation of the religiously sanctioned state, region, or community, to the creation of an ideal world, and to the destruction of evil. It is, then, hardly surprising to see the return within international society of the language of the holy war and of the belief that violence in pursuit of religiously sanctioned goals is legitimate, whether on behalf of states or of terrorist movements. In highlighting the role of values, it is important not just to focus on the most obvious examples of clashing values and deeply incompatible world views (as in debates about Islam and the West), but to recognize that the diversity of culture and of context and the differences to which they give rise pervade many aspects of solidarist law and institutions.

This pluralist view continues to be upheld by many influential theorists;[7] and continues to express the core preferences of many major states. For all their accommodations to the changes of the post–Cold War years, China,

[7] See, in particular, Robert Jackson, *The Global Covenant: Human Conduct in a World of States* (Oxford: Oxford University Press, 2000).

Russia, India, and Brazil have continued to share a preference for relatively hard conceptions of national sovereignty and, although sometimes professing a liking for multilateralism, have tended to resist the effective delegation of authority to international bodies. In this, of course, they have much in common with the United States. Within this company, the European preference for more elaborate forms of institutionalized global governance represents the outlier. Certainly in terms of its political power but also in terms of a range of principled arguments, it is therefore wholly wrong to see pluralism as belonging solely to a vanished Westphalian world.

A retreat to pluralism?

But, however powerful the attractions of pluralism may be, there is no acceptable or viable way of reasserting a pluralist view of international society. There are five powerful reasons for this.

First, the complexity of governance challenges necessarily involves intervention and deep engagement. The management of globalization inevitably involves the creation of deeply intrusive rules and institutions and debate on how different societies are to be organized domestically. This is a structural change. If states are to develop effective policies on economic development, environmental protection, human rights, the resolution of refugee crises, the fight against drugs, or the struggle against terrorism, then they need to engage with a wide range of international and transnational actors and to interact not just with central governments but with a much wider range of domestic political, economic, and social players. This tendency has been increased by the erosion of states and state capacity and by the decreasing capacity of states in many parts of the world to play their allotted role as the provider of local order. It is, therefore, very hard to foresee a form of international society in which the norms and practices of intervention do not play a major and probably increasing role.

The structural logic at play in the generation of demands for governance is also reflected in the evermore complex ways in which different issues are linked. As we have seen, the contemporary security agenda reflects the importance of new forms of interconnectivity that relate the many different forms of contemporary violence (religious, political, entrepreneurial, and criminal), global communications, patterns of migration and diaspora politics, and patterns of economic and social inequality. As always, it is important to ask critical questions about such linkages and not to assume that such linkages are somehow natural. The link between migration and security—the so-called 'migration–security nexus'—is a good example of how Western states have sought to shape the migration and asylum agenda in ways that reflect their own interests and concerns. But, even allowing for the operation of power and even remaining persistently sceptical, there are important structural connections between different areas and domains of global governance—between the environment and development (as in the idea of sustainable development); between trade regulation and health, labour standards, and the environment; or between democracy, state-building, and conflict resolution. As bargaining theory suggests, 'issue-linkage' may serve a positive role in facilitating agreements, allowing governments to trade-off different issues and to engage in side-payments. But it also creates a powerful functional logic towards the expansion of governance which, in turn, raises difficult questions of legitimacy and of how different institutions or bodies of law and regulation are to be related to each other. How, for example, can one make any sense of global environmental governance without tackling the ways in which trade and environment relate to each other and without facing up to institutional and legal questions that emerge when we consider the relationship of the WTO to multilateral environmental treaties?

In addition, the scale of the governance challenges facing international society is also likely to be profoundly affected by the multiple uncertainties and the multiple instabilities of many aspects of globalization. Think of the relationship between an enormously complex and under-regulated global financial system; a complex biosphere characterized by non-linearity, multiple feedback loops and unpredictability; a global energy structure subject to unstable technological, market and geopolitical constraints; and increasingly diffuse patterns of interstate and transnational violence. Within each of these domains, there is evident potential for instability. When taken together, their robustness and capacity to sustain shocks decline dramatically and cumulative destabilizing dynamics are potentially very serious. Natural and human systems display high levels of dynamic complexity and existing theories struggle to understand complex systems.[8] That struggle is being rendered harder by accelerating changes in technology, economic activity, and forms of social organization.

This is not the place to engage in elaborate exercises in futurology. However, it is important to recognize the extent to which social, environmental and, above all, technological change is likely to affect the *scale* of governance challenges, the *sources* of control and governance, and the *subjects* of control.[9] Uncontrolled climate change, continued loss of forests and topsoil, worsening shortages of water and the global spread of new strains of disease are all likely to have long-term and global ramifications and have the potential to erode states and to foment new forms of conflict. Governance will need to confront

[8] See Robert Jervis, *System Effects: Complexity in Political and Social Life* (Princeton, NJ: Princeton University Press, 1997).

[9] For one view of these potential changes, see James Martin, *The Meaning of the 21st Century* (London: Eden Project Books, 2006).

the still poorly understood complexity of natural systems, the increasing complexity of human and social systems, and increasing rates of technological change. New technologies (especially the exponential growth of bandwidth, optical fibres, and computing power) are likely to continue to enmesh global society within ever-denser networks of production, computation, and communication. Such technologies may strengthen the attractiveness and viability of decentralized modes of governance beyond the state, via markets, networks, and self-regulation. But other aspects of technological change (such as genetic modification of plants and, in the future of humans, the long-term impact of persistent organic pollutants, nanotechnology, self-evolving technology, the continued spread and use of nuclear technologies, and the possibilities of bioterrorism) all create new dangers to be controlled by means of institutions that have the capacity to regulate, to monitor, and to enforce. The triple challenge of capturing common interests, managing unequal (and possibly increasingly unequal) power, and mediating value conflict is likely to remain central. But it is very hard to imagine a future in which this challenge can be met via a narrow state-based conception of global political order.

Second, there is the question of identity politics and the struggle for recognition. The massive movement of peoples, the intensification of contacts and interconnections between societies, and the multiple dislocations of established ways of thinking and of doing have intensified identity politics and have given a sharper and often destructive twist to struggles for cultural recognition. But these same developments undermine the view of states as empirically viable or morally acceptable containers of cultural pluralism. The globalization and the de-territorialization of identity politics is one of the most important reasons why a neat pluralist global order has been rendered obsolete. Even seeking to recreate identity-based pluralism on a regional level confronts serious difficulties.

Third, pluralism is vulnerable because of the degree to which dealing the governance challenges in a globalized world requires socialized power. This is most obviously true in the field of security. Even if states have succeeded in increasing the collective element in security management, the dilemma of preponderant power has not been displaced: except in a small subset of cases, collective responses to insecurity continue to depend on the resources, will, and interest of major states. In the case of any moderately serious security threat, this is likely to involve the United States. But the need for socialized power also applies to economic order. Think, for example, of the need for effective states with sufficient legitimate power and authority to tax transnational corporations; or to enforce equitable burden-sharing in the management of financial crises. One classic strand of liberal theory stressed the importance of disarmament; others have promoted a view of international (and regional) order in which sovereignty is dispersed and power disaggregated.[10] But the fundamental problem with models of dispersed sovereignty is that, whilst they correctly acknowledge the dangers of centralized power, they fail to acknowledge the necessity of such power for social order and the promotion of common moral purposes. For all the contributions of non-state groups, networks and transnational communities, this is also a central limitation to transnational models and modes of governance.

Fourth, there is the question of global inequality. Previous chapters have traced the way in which different forms of inequality are reflected both in the changing character of international society and in the new forms of global governance that have developed. They have also sought to illustrate the ways in which this institutional inequality relates to the broader inequalities that define the global system—in relation to the global economy, to the environment, and to insecurity and violent conflict. The pluralist instinct is to seek to isolate those areas where inequality gives rise to direct political challenges. In most cases, they argue, this does not result from radical deprivation or from the protests of the poorest. It comes instead from rising and revisionist states: those currently excluded from the councils of the rich and powerful and for whom this exclusion is seen both to threaten material interests and to be a potent cause of nationalist resentment. The pluralist answer lies in accommodating rising powers within the balance of power and in socializing rising states into a stable system of great power management. In a related vein, others highlight the historic role of hierarchy and oligarchy and see this as fundamental to contemporary governance challenges. This might involve ad hoc bodies of the powerful, perhaps involving an expansion of the G8 to include major emerging and regional powers. Or it might involve drawing in those developing states that are most crucial to the management of a particular issue: China, India, and Brazil on climate change, for example. The rules and the character of the Great Power club may change, but the underlying pluralist logic of a club of major powers remains the same.

There is every reason to believe that this aspect of pluralist order will continue to play a crucial role in the twenty-first century. At the same time, however, it is highly doubtful whether this limited pluralist response is adequate to manage the challenges posed by inequality—the insecurities and violence in which inequality and poverty are implicated, the degree to which poverty lies at the heart of many aspects of unsustainable modes of development; and the perceived illegitimacy of a system of global governance that creates new patterns of inclusion and exclusion. Certainly any form of governance that appears to reflect the values and preferences of a privileged elite in the

---

[10] See e.g. Thomas Pogge, 'Cosmopolitanism and Sovereignty', in *World Poverty and Human Rights* (Cambridge: Polity Press, 2002), 168–95.

developed world whose share of the world's population has declined and will decline still further is likely to face insuperable problems of legitimacy. However difficult it may be to measure and assess particular linkages, it is highly implausible to believe that the 20 percent of the world's population living in the high-income countries can insulate itself from the instability and insecurity of the rest and from revisionist demands for change. More extensive and expansive modes of governance are likely to be necessary to deal with the linkages between inequality and a wide range of security, political, and environmental problems and, within these modes of governance, the problem of global democracy will come to play a more central part of the politics of global order.

Finally, there is the question of demands for justice. Here it is important to distinguish between the general issue of how justice is to be related to global order and the fate of a particular justice agenda. The old pluralist impulse to separate order from justice has long confronted many difficulties. The value of order is not placed within any general ethical account or framework.[11] Order as analysed by Bull, Kissinger, or Kennan implies an ethical view and hence a view of justice: to argue that certain goals should be pursued is to suggest that it is right to pursue them and that those who do so act justly. However, these particular goals are not argued for in a clear and consistent manner. Nor are they coherently related to other values. In addition, the retreat to power as the final arbiter of all politics and the removal of all concern with morality manifestly fails. As Hoffmann pointed out long ago, the meaning of the alleged trumping claims of realism—defending the national interest, even guaranteeing national survival—are necessarily contested and involve a range of normative assumptions.

As previous chapters have argued, questions of justice inevitably arise in the context of changing patterns of global governance because of the way in which conflicting societal values and different social, cultural, and economic preferences are to be ordered. Moreover, none of the world's major religious systems accepts the idea of a neat separation between 'interstate order' and 'global justice', and the diffusion of power, especially towards large developing countries, is likely to increase the stridency of justice-driven demands for change.

The fate of the particular justice agenda of liberal solidarism is, however, a different matter. Earlier chapters have highlighted the very significant changes that have taken place in the normative structure of international society as it concerns human rights, humanitarian intervention, and the responsibilities entailed in the idea of sovereignty. They sought to illustrate how far these changes have been reflected in transnational practices and in the

---

[11] Ian Harris, 'Order and Justice in "The Anarchical Society"', *International Affairs*, 69 (1993), 725–41.

consolidation of a relatively broad and deep human rights culture. But it also stressed the hypocrisy, double standards, and incoherence of the Western promotion of human rights, and the legitimate doubts that have arisen as to how far human rights norms have in fact been securely internalized in the foreign policies and public attitudes of even core Western liberal states.

Similar questions and problems arise with respect to the Western pursuit of democracy. But against the background of historical growth of social mobilization in developing world and the empowering possibilities of globalization, it is unlikely that the democratic genie will easily be put back into the bottle. This does not mean that the power of the democratic idea will mesh neatly or easily with the interests of the currently powerful. There is already clear evidence of the ways in which efforts to promote the spread of democracy can clash with the other more immediate foreign policy priorities. More importantly, crucial questions are likely to recur as to the proper scope of democratic ideas beyond the state and as to how the values of democracy should be applied to global governance and to global social choices that will shape the life chances of individuals and communities in the twenty-first century. Pressed by revisionist powers such as China and India, the notion that the current distribution of decision-making power can be defended in democratic terms is likely to come under increasing attack. Indeed, such arguments may well come to play the sort of critical role in the twenty-first century that the idea of national self-determination played in the twentieth century.

The changes associated with globalization and the increased interaction and connectedness across global society have therefore undermined both the practical viability and the moral acceptability of a traditional state-based pluralism. It no longer makes any sense to think of world politics in terms of the distinction drawn by Martin Wight that does so much analytical work in the classical pluralist conception: on the one hand, we have domestic society as the political arena within which understandings of the 'good life' might be debated, developed, and, potentially, realized; on the other, we have international relations which is condemned to remain forever an arena concerned with the imperatives of 'mere survival'.[12] To take only the most obvious example, 'mere survival' in relation to the protection of the global environment depends fundamentally on how societies are organized domestically and on how their various conceptions of what the good life entails can be brought together and reconciled. As suggested in earlier chapters, material and moral circumstances have already taken as beyond an international society conceived in Nardin's terms as a practical association—'an association of

---

[12] Martin Wight, 'Why Is There No International Theory?', in Martin Wight and Herbert Butterfield (eds.), *Diplomatic Investigations* (London: Allen and Unwin, 1966).

independent and diverse political communities, each devoted to its own ends and its own conception of the good'.[13]

The conservative ideal, embodied in the work of Hayek and Oakeshott, that political life should be concerned only with limited procedural rules governing coexistence cannot be applied satisfactorily to the conditions of global political life in the twenty-first century which require the identification of substantive collective goals and the creation of institutionalized structures of governance to implement them. These changes also decisively undercut the strong pluralism that one finds in such major contemporary liberal theorists such as Rawls. Given the changed nature of global politics and the changes that have taken place in the normative structure of international society, it cannot make any sense for one's normative vision of global politics to be built around the idea of states as bounded political communities whose basic structure is defined in terms of 'self-sufficient schemes of cooperation *for all the essential purposes of human life*'.[14] These changes also work against the postmodern celebration of difference and diversity. It is not that difference and diversity are in any way unworthy of celebration. But it is intellectually vacuous to celebrate difference and diversity in a closely integrated world without confronting the need to specify the general global principles and procedures by which interaction *necessarily* and *unavoidably* has to be regulated.

The pursuit of justice

One of the attractions of an old-fashioned state-based pluralism and of a very thin view of international society was precisely that it appeared to offer a way of dealing with diversity and disagreement. If diversity and value conflict are such important features of international life, then we should seek to organize global politics in such a way as to give groups scope for collective self-government and cultural autonomy in their own affairs and to reduce the degree to which they will clash over how the world should be ordered. Equally, if the dangers of predation by the powerful are deep-rooted, even if not structurally determined, then we should continue to place a heavy emphasis on sovereignty and on the balance of power. In addition, the sceptical pluralist is attracted to the idea that it might also be possible to develop a cross-cultural consensus over the minimal rules around which such a limited international society might be built. Hence the attraction to international society writers of Hart's notion of a minimum content of

[13] Terry Nardin, *Law, Morality and the Relations of States* (Princeton, NJ: Princeton University Press, 1983), 9.

[14] John Rawls, *Political Liberalism* (New York: Columbia University Press, 1993), 301, emphasis added.

natural law built around Hobbesian assumptions.[15] Hence, too, Bull's emphasis on the 'elementary conditions of social life', his attempt to isolate the elementary, primary, and universal goals of a society of states; and his analytical effort to link these goals to the historical institutions of international society.

But if, as I have suggested, there is no viable retreat to pluralism and to a world in which each group can sit undisturbed under their own fig tree, then negotiating the terms of limited coexistence is no longer adequate. We are condemned instead to negotiate the terms of ongoing and evermore extensive forms of collaboration and active cooperation. This does not mean that there is no space for pluralism and toleration of difference. Nor does it mean that there are not examples of governance at the international or transnational level that should be repatriated within domestic political systems. But it is does mean that that this space has diminished and that the disagreements surrounding the terms of cooperation have become far more intractable. It is also the case that the costs of failure are likely to become increasingly intolerable, both from a moral as well as practical standpoint. Thinking of global governance in terms of interest-based cooperation within particular issue-areas remains central to both academic analysis and political practice. However, the changing character of governance increases the importance of reaching agreement on the common purposes and common values which influence how problems within issue-areas are to be understood, how issue areas are themselves constructed, and how they are linked.

Negotiating the terms of cooperation is certainly a quintessentially political exercise. But it is also an inherently normative one both because acting in the world requires that we think about morally desirable change and because moral debate forms one part of how that political exercise will unfold. As noted in many places in this book, debates on global justice within political theory and political philosophy have increased enormously in scope and sophistication. There is an increasingly rich array of potential answers to the problems of global political theory, including those related to just war, to humanitarian intervention, distributive justice, and to global democracy. But, at least in my own view, the basis on which particular moral principles can be meaningfully and persuasively defended, justified, and criticized within global society as a whole has received less attention than it deserves. The fragility of global political order makes it unconvincing to see this challenge as a second-order issue of moral methodology. I suggest that three problems are crucial: moral accessibility; institutional authority, and political agency.

[15] Hart (1961: 188–95).

Moral accessibility

How might we establish some minimally secure basis for rational moral debate in a diverse and deeply divided world and for developing arguments for global justice that enjoy broad accessibility? There are two broad and recurring patterns of thought on these questions. The first trusts to human reason. Surely, say many political theorists, it is precisely human reason and the universality of human reason that provides both the foundation of moral argument and the best hope that it can be openly debated and acted upon globally. The goal is to ground arguments about justice in ways that are as free as possible from any particular historical or cultural tradition and to locate moral principles to which no reasonable person could reject. We can escape from circumstance and contingency by appealing to genuinely universal and tradition-independent norms. Human reason has the potential to elaborate an internally consistent and universally applicable set of rules and evaluative criteria that can serve as the framework for thinking about global justice. The normative theorist begins with his or her best considered judgement based on reasons that are suitably coherent and generalizable and develops arguments to which no reasonable person could reject. Whatever people may actually believe, the theorist seeks to find good reasons why others should alter their beliefs and their patterns of behaviour.

But there are serious problems with such a position. What moral meaning can be attached to even the purest and most serene universalist voice—whether of the religious believer, the natural lawyer, or the Kantian liberal—echoing down from the mountain if those to whom it is addressed do not understand themselves to be part of even the thinnest and most fragile shared community? Sometimes the subversive and recurring whispering of the sceptics follows simply from the empirical fact of deep difference and from the epistemological force of particularism. As the critics of natural law have repeatedly reminded us, there are simply too many cases where the obviousness of moral intuition turns out to depend on specific social and historical circumstances. For many others it follows naturally and inevitably from a grand narrative about the end of moral, religious and perhaps also scientific certainty. Faith in notions of natural law, in rationalism, and in stories of progressive human development has been undermined by the same questioning, doubt and suspicion that underpinned the Enlightenment's attack on religion and superstition.

For the arch-sceptic and the committed anti-foundationalist, doubt often centres on the idea of reason itself. What do we mean by 'reason', and whose reason are we talking about? As Alastair MacIntyre has written, '... the legacy of the Enlightenment has been the problem of an ideal of rational justification which it has proved impossible to attain'.[16]

... the history of attempts to construct a morality for tradition-free individuals, whether by appeal to one out of several conceptions of universalizability or to one out of equally multifarious conceptions of utility or to shared intuitions or to some combination of these, has in its outcome ... been a history of continuously unresolved disputes, so that there emerges no uncontested and incontestable account of what tradition-independent morality consists in and consequently no neutral set of criteria by means of which the claims of rival and contending traditions could be adjudicated.[17]

But doubts about the universality of reason can also rest on more modest forms of sceptical humanism. Such sceptics do not deny the importance of human reason, but rather see it as fickle, changeable, and corruptible; they suspect that universal reason, whatever its formal claims to generality, in practice works against the diversity of values and the multiplicity of forms of human society. When the great open spaces left by the Kantian moral imperative are filled, the specific contents have a distressing habit of reflecting rather closely the parochial perspectives and particular values of the theorist concerned.[18] Moreover, excessive faith in formal and rationalist models of justice can lead to insensitivity over the wrongs committed in the name of that justice. One can see reason as providing a fragile basis for cross-cultural comparison and evaluation and for making different conceptions of moral life mutually intelligible. But one might still doubt that Human Reason is capable of producing compelling global principles of justice and of providing guidance as to how these global principles should be translated into reasons for or against particular policies in particular and very diverse places; or that moral conflict can be resolved by resort to the grand imaginative exercises of reason of a Rawlsian kind, however sophisticated. Such, at least, is my own position.

Left here we have not moved very far forward. But, importantly, even many of those who wish to start with reason and with their own best considered judgements as to what justice requires and who seek to build theories of justice around universal principles that could be chosen by any rational individual do not end the story there. There is an insistence that valid principles of justice must be publicly justifiable. They must be related to the values and

---

[16] Alasdair MacIntyre, *Whose Justice? Whose Rationality?* (London: Duckworth, 1985), 6.

[17] Ibid. 334.

[18] As an example, Rogers Smith has analysed the way in which Rawls's thought fits within and grows out of a distinctively American liberal tradition. Rogers M. Smith, *Civic Ideals: Conflicting Visions of Citizenship in US History* (New Haven, CT: Yale University Press, 1997), 481–5. For a broader critique of the ideological character of Western liberal political thought, see Michael Freeden, *Ideologies and Political Theory: A Conceptual Approach* (Oxford: Oxford University Press, 1996), ch. 6.

the discursive resources that are available within the political or moral culture of a given society. One option is to conclude that such a course is only possible within a given society, indeed perhaps only within societies that are already committed to some form of political liberalism.[19] Another option is both to advance arguments about global justice and to justify those arguments explicitly within the evolving political and moral culture of international and transnational society—partly in terms of the substantive values represented in that culture and partly as a community of persons who respect a shared process of rational deliberation.

A second, and equally deep-rooted, way of thinking begins not with abstract reason, but with the normative practices of existing communities and cultural traditions. As Michael Walzer puts it, 'principles of justice are . . . the inevitable product of historical and cultural particularism'.[20] Normative theory needs to be grounded in the existing normative practices of particular communities. Political theory should uncover, interpret, and critically development understandings of justice and morality that exist within specific historical and cultural contexts. The theorist or social critic 'gives expression to his people's deepest sense of who they ought to live'; he or she should not seek some hidden moral truth but should rather uncover and interpret the 'social meanings' that exist within the 'common life' of particular communities. On this view, as David Miller has written, 'There are no universal principles of justice. Instead, we must see justice as the creation of a particular political community at a particular time, and the account we give must be given from within such a community'.[21] Theory, then, should interpret and uncover the normative understandings that have come to develop within a particular society and build arguments and proposals for greater justice out of the values and modes of reasoning that have already begun to take root.

Clearly, this sort of tradition or norm-based moral reasoning carries a very high risk of ethnocentrism and parochialism. As O'Neill puts it:

Once upon a time it might not have mattered if those who lived in homogeneous but isolated societies reasoned in ways that could not have been accessible to hypothetical others with whom they had no connection. But today's societies, cultures and traditions are not bounded or impervious. . . . Ethnocentric reasoning will fail or falter for those who attempt communication across boundaries; it will lack authority—and may prove inaccessible to others. Norm-based conceptions of reason will not suffice in a pluralist

[19] This move is central to Rawls's shift from the ostensibly universalist claims of *A Theory of Justice* (Cambridge: Cambridge University Press, 1971) to the argument of *Political Liberalism* (New York: Columbia University Press, 1993) where theory is to be constructed from the fundamental ideas implicit in the public political culture.

[20] Michael Walzer, *Spheres of Justice: A Defence of Pluralism and Equality* (Oxford: Martin Robertson, 1983), 5–6.

[21] David Miller, 'Introduction', in David Miller and Michael Walzer (eds.), *Pluralism, Justice, and Equality* (Oxford: Oxford University Press, 1995), 2.

world. If any ways of organizing either thinking or action are to have quite general authority, they cannot presuppose the norms and opinions of a particular time or place.[22]

But the strength of this criticism depends on how we interpret the 'particular time or place' and on the scope of our moral enquiry. A more open version of the interpretative or hermeneutic approach to global justice would look beyond the claims of particular communities and seek to uncover the values and moral arguments that have become embedded within the discourses, practices, and institutions of international and world society. There is no reason in principle why interpretative or conventionalist accounts of justice need to be confined within state borders and used to buttress communitarian positions. The theorist can move back and forth both between moral abstraction and moral immediacy but also between the shared moral meanings that exist within particular states and societies on the one hand, and of international society as a whole on the other.

What, then, does tackling the problem of moral accessibility involve? In the first place, it means locating stable, public, and shared vocabularies of justice that can serve as a medium for argumentative exchange across the world as a whole and not simply within the limited confines of the Western world, or the still more limited confines of liberal political theory. Both analytical enquiry and rational normative debate require the production of clear and coherent definitions and categories. And yet both endeavours are necessarily built around concepts whose connotations and meaning have shifted dramatically over time even within the liberal West—state, nation, democracy, rights, security; and whose production and evolution have been the subject of social conflict and contestation. Second, tackling the problem of moral accessibility involves seeking a stable institutional framework for the idea of a global moral community within which these moral ideas and projects can achieve some deliberative purchase, and perhaps even persuasion. And third, achieving these goals means that arguments need to be related to the values, patterns of argument and normative structures of both international society and global society as part of a broad process of public justification and persuasion. The core focus, then, should be on the idea of a moral community, not as posited, or imagined, or argued for by human reason alone, but as reflected in the shared practices, shared understandings, and broader moral consciousness of international and global society.

In earlier chapters, I have traced how the institutional and constitutional structure of international society has moved away from its inherited emphasis on pluralism and towards the expansion of both liberal solidarist norms and institutions and emerging practices of governance beyond the state. There is now a denser and more integrated network of shared institutions, discourses,

---

[22] Onora O'Neill, *Bounds of Justice* (Cambridge: Cambridge University Press, 2000), 22–3.

and practices within which social expectations of global justice and injustice have become more securely established. Alongside the old idea that actors create and uphold international law because it provides them with functional benefits, the post-1945 period has seen the emergence of a range of internationally agreed core principles—respect for fundamental human rights, prohibition of aggression, and self-determination—which may underpin some notion of a world common good and some broader basis for evaluating specific rules. Thus the density, scope, and complexity of the agreements, norms and rules in which states and societies are already enmeshed provide some basis for positing a community interest or an agreed set of purposes and values against which new substantive norms may be judged—the idea of an objective community interest or of the common interest of global society. This is not best viewed in terms of the surreptitious return of natural law ideas but should rather be understood as a philosophically anchorless, but nevertheless reasonably solid pragmatic consensus.

The normative structure of international society has evolved in ways which help to undercut the arguments of those who deny the existence of a global justice community or who take a restrictionist or strongly pluralist position towards global justice. For classical realists such as Morgenthau, '[T]he appeal to moral principles in the international sphere has *no universal meaning* [my emphasis]. It is either so vague as to have no concrete meaning that could provide rational guidance for political action, or it will be nothing but the reflection of the moral perceptions of a particular nation'.[23] For Carr the 'inability to provide any absolute and disinterested standard for the conduct of international affairs' means that international law and morality is necessarily revealed as 'the transparent disguises of selfish vested interests'.[24] Or, still more starkly, for Schmitt, 'Whoever speaks for humanity lies'. But these dichotomies are too stark. The meaning of many moral principles might not be universal, but it is certainly widely diffused across the world and embedded in many institutions and practices. There is now a denser and more integrated network of shared institutions and practices within which social expectations of global justice and injustice have become more securely established.

There are good reasons for believing that the density of international society provides a meaningful basis for debate over our responsibilities to the most vulnerable and most deprived of distant strangers. Thus we have seen the emergence of an international and transnational culture of human rights that involves a widely shared common language, an inclusive moral vocabulary, and an authoritative and well-developed normative structure from which very few groups are prepared to try and exempt themselves. This shared discourse implies a general acceptance of certain general principles and processes and

[23] Hans Morgenthau, *American Foreign Policy* (New York: Alfred A. Knopf, 1951), 35.
[24] E. H. Carr (2001: 80).

of a particular kind of rationality and argumentation. It limits the range of permissible justifications and motivations; it empowers particular groups and particular institutions; and it helps create incentives for socialization and internalization. It is, of course, shaped by its historical origins within a particular culture; but it is open, dynamic, and resistant to permanent capture by a particular interest or power-political grouping. However varied the philosophical, political, or cultural backgrounds from which it is approached, the emergence and spread of this transnational moral and legal discourse represents a major historical development.

But whilst the density of international society has undoubtedly increased, the elements of deformity have remained all too prominent. There is deformity in terms of the distribution of advantages and disadvantages: in the way, for example, security is defined or in the choices taken by institutions and states as to whose security is to be protected; and, very obviously, in the massive inequalities of the global economic order. There is deformity in terms of who sets the rules of international society. Institutions are not, as much liberal, neutral theory has suggested instruments for resolving common problems but rather sites of power, even of dominance. The vast majority of smaller states are 'rule takers', with externally promulgated rules increasingly affecting many aspects of social, economic, and political life. There is deformity in terms of the very different capacity of states and societies to adapt to the demands of a global economy, combined with the extent to which the economic choices of developing counties are, if not dictated, then certainly shaped by the institutions dominated by the strong and often backed by coercion in the form of an expanding range of conditionalities. And finally, deformity is evident in the limited capacity of international law and institutions to constrain effectively the unilateral and often illegal acts of the strong. To pick up the refrain of earlier writers on international society, there is ample evidence that we should be deeply suspicious of the claims of those who set themselves up as local agents of a global common good (Bull) or local carriers of a global message (Vincent).

None of this is to suggest that the increased normative ambition of international society is not part of the fabric of contemporary international relations. But it is to say that this society remains deeply contaminated by power and that the political theorist can only ignore the persistence of this structural contamination at the cost of idealization; that where solidarist cooperation is weak or breaks down, the older imperatives of pluralist order continue to flourish; and that even when genuinely consensual, the promotion of solidarist values both depends on, and reinforces, the power and on privileges of the dominant state or states.

What of the world beyond the society of states? The increasing integration of markets—not just cross-border transactions but also integrated transnational production structures—seems intuitively to have important normative implications and to buttress claims for moral cosmopolitanism. Globalization has done much to erode the boundedness of political communities whose particular cultures, traditions, and ways of living are given so much weight by communitarians. For many people in many parts of the world, it has also given a new reality to the sense of sharing a single world and to the nature of plurality, connection, and finitude.[25] The circumstances of justice and the nature of social cooperation have been altered in important and morally significant ways. For one very important strand of thought, the expansion of global interdependence has helped to create or reinforce a global 'basic structure' that is the primary subject of justice.[26] On some interactionist accounts, issues of justice arise amongst all those engaged in cooperation within this basic structure; for others, it is precisely the harms caused by the global basic structure and our participation in those harming activities that gives rise to moral obligations.[27]

But there are real problems with arguments that place such great weight on economic globalization. In part, these have to do with empirical work showing the limits of economic globalization and the extent to which it is neither self-evidently new nor any more far-reaching than in the past. In part, they reflect ambiguity as to whether the global basic structure is an empirical fact which a theory of justice seeks to regulate or something that is itself to be constituted through the implementation of principles of justice. To what extent, in other words, are the moral obligations pressed by interactionist theorists contingent on (contested) empirical analysis of the degree of economic interdependence and institutional development that has in fact occurred and the actual (and again contested) distribution of goods and bads within it?[28] And in part, the problems reflect the old difficulty of relating empirical accounts of an increasingly unified world to normative accounts of the emergence of a world community.[29] However dense and intense economic exchange may be, it does not translate easily or automatically into a shared awareness of a common identity or a shared community. As we saw in Chapter 10, even within regions characterized by extremely dense patterns of

---

[25] Onora O'Neill, *Towards Justice and Virtue: A Constructive Account of Practical Reasoning* (Cambridge: Cambridge University Press, 1996), ch. 4.

[26] For neo-Rawlsians, the global basic structure is defined very broadly to include the way in which major social institutions (including both market and political institutions) work to distribute all kinds of material resources. See Charles R. Beitz, 'International Liberalism and Distributive Justice: A Survey of Recent Thought', *World Politics*, 51 (1999), 269–96.

[27] Especially Charles Beitz, *Political Theory and International Relations* (Princeton, NJ: Princeton University Press, 1979); and Thomas Pogge, *Realizing Rawls* (Ithaca, NY: Cornell University Press, 1999) and Pogge (2002).

[28] I owe this argument to Terry MacDonald.

[29] See Chris Brown, 'International Political Theory and the Idea of a World Community', in Ken Booth and Steve Smith (eds.), *International Relations Theory Today* (Cambridge: Polity, 1995).

integration there is little clear relationship between material integration and conceptions of political or moral community.

Much of the rhetoric of an economically globalizing and unifying world, then, fails to distinguish between three senses of the idea of unity: unity as interdependence and interconnection; unity as uniformity in the character of the states and societies that make up the global system; and unity as consciousness of a shared humanity or commitment to some shared set of purposes.

Earlier chapters of this book have pointed to the important roles that transnational advocacy groups, social movements, and transnational networks have played within global politics and, more specifically, within both solidarist and transnational governance models of international society. Very important claims have been made about the normative potentiality of global civil society as an arena of politics that is able to transcend the inside–outside character of traditional politics and to fashion and provide space for new forms of political community, solidarity, and identity. Sometimes, the emphasis is on global civil society as a relatively autonomous, self-organized public sphere in which genuine deliberation amongst competing positions can take place and through which some notion of international public reason can be developed. In other cases, global civil society and its linked network of 'domestic' civil societies feed positively into state-based order through the provision of legitimacy and consent, and into market-based order as the repository of the trust and other forms of social capital without which markets will not function. But on both views global civil society represents a pluralist and open arena for the negotiation of rules and norms based on genuine and unforced consent. It serves as a regulative ideal but one whose potential can be gauged from the changing real practices of world politics.

But, as with markets, there are real problems and, consequently, a need to counter a certain romanticization of the potentialities of transnational civil society—although not, as is the current danger, to go too far in the other direction. Civil society is, after all, an arena of politics like any other, in which the good and thoroughly awful coexist, in which the pervasive claims made by social movements and NGOs to authenticity and representativeness need to be tested and challenged, and in which outcomes may be just as subject to direct manipulation by powerful actors as in the world of interstate politics. While state action may be shaped by global civil society, it is often state action that is crucial in fostering the emergence of civil society in the first place and in providing the institutional framework that enables it to flourish. And, critically, state power is increasingly determined by the ability of governments to work successfully within civil society and to exploit transnational and trans-governmental coalitions for their own purposes. There is a constant danger of global civil society becoming an arena of politics which states and other economic and social organizations seek to dominate and exploit precisely in order to legitimize their own claims to power.

Institutional authority

There are three major reasons why institutions are so important: as a means of helping to secure a framework for mutually intelligible moral debate; as a way of securing the stable implementation of shared rules; and in terms of the potential for the progressive development of a global moral community.

In the first place, if we are looking for cross-cultural universals, a good case can be made for starting with process and with the near-universality of ideas about fairness of process: hearing the other side, providing arguments for one's actions, finding some mechanism for adjudicating between conflicting moral claims. All stable societies have to find some agreed process and procedure by which moral conflicts can be adjudicated and managed, if not resolved. Within world politics the challenge is still more daunting, given the diversity and divisiveness of sentiments, attachments, languages, cultures and ways-of-living, combined with the massive inequalities of power, wealth, and capacity. Stuart Hampshire has suggested that there is an irreducible minimum to notions of just process.

Particular institutions, each with its specific procedures for deciding between rival conceptions of what is substantially just and fair, come and go in history. The one most general feature of the process of decision is preserved as the necessary condition that qualifies a process, whatever it happens to be, to be accounted as an essentially just and fair one: that contrary claims are heard. An unjust procedure, violating this necessary condition of procedural fairness, is unjust, always, and everywhere and without reference to any distinct conception of the good.[30]

This kind of focus on process feeds into a view of reason and rationality not as abstract and universal but rather as developing 'naturally from necessities of social life, that is from the inevitably recurrent conflicts which must be resolved if communities are to survive'.[31] Global justice is not something that can be deduced from abstract rational principles, nor can it be reflective of a single world view, religious or secular; it is, rather, a negotiated product of dialogue and deliberation and therefore always subject to revision and re-evaluation.

Second, institutions are also necessary because rules have to be applied. The cry of the liberal solidarist or the cosmopolitan moralist is that we need new rules to meet new circumstances. Terrorism requires that international society rethink rules relating to self-defence and the use of force. The degree to

[30] Stuart Hampshire, *Justice Is Conflict* (London: Duckworth, 1999), 27–8.
[31] Ibid. 25.

which international society is affected morally and practically by humanitarian catastrophe means that we need new rules on humanitarian intervention. There are good arguments in favour of both these propositions. But it is a myth that, for example, a new rule on humanitarian intervention would obviate the need for institutions and institutional debate. Even if the rule is agreed and even if the background criteria for evaluation are agreed, all rules have to be interpreted and applied. The promulgation of a new rule of humanitarian intervention will not avoid the need for that rule to be applied to the circumstances of a particular case. On the one side, this inevitably raises the fundamental political issue: who is the body that has the authority to interpret and to apply the rule? As Dallmayr argues:

The notion of *praxis*, however, brings to the fore a domain usually shunned or sidelined by universalist morality: the domain of politics.... Even assuming widespread acceptance of universal norms, we know at least since Aristotle that rules do not translate directly into *praxis* but require careful interpretation and application. At this point eminently political questions arise: who has the right of interpretation? And, in the case of conflict: who is entitled to rule between different interpretations? This right or competence cannot simply be left to "universal" theorists or intellectuals—in the absence of an explicitly *political* delegation or empowerment. These considerations indicate that it is insufficient—on moral and practical grounds—to throw a mantle of universal rules over humankind without paying simultaneous attention to public debate and the role of political will formation.[32]

On the other side, we are faced by problems intrinsic to the idea of interpretation and application. Thus cultural and historical complexity make it difficult to read off judgements in particular cases from general or universal moral laws and there is good reason for supposing that a great deal of the debate over values and ethics in the twenty-first century will necessarily have to be context-rich and interpretative. At one level, this might simply mean that universal principles need to show sensitivity to local context. But the challenge is deeper. Thus Tully follows Wittgenstein in criticizing those who show an excessive craving for generality and, still more, those who demonstrate a contemptuous attitude to the particular case. 'To understand a general term, and so know your way around its maze of uses, it is always necessary to enter into a dialogue with interlocutors from other regions of the city, to listen to their "further descriptions" and come to recognize the aspects of the phenomenon in question that they bring to light, aspect which go unnoticed from one's own familiar set of examples'.[33] In terms of institutionalizing global order such a position lends support to a form of practical reasoning that is constantly navigating between the general rule, whether legal or moral, and

---

[32] Fred Dallmayr, 'Cosmopolitanism, Moral and Political', *Political Theory*, 31/3 (June 2003), 434.

[33] Tully (1995: 110).

its always contestable application to the facts and circumstances of a particular case.

Third, institutions matter because of their potential for a self-reinforcing dynamic. Once created, institutions act as platforms for ongoing normative debate, for the mobilization of concern and for debating and revising ideas about how international society should be organized. However much social scientists (and technocratic practitioners) insist on analysing international institutions solely in terms of the provision of international public goods, normative issues cannot be kept out of the picture. In addition, there is an inherent tendency for all normative systems (especially reasonably well-institutionalized judicial systems) to expand and develop, and to enmesh actors within certain patterns of discourse, reasoning, and argumentation. Finally, as we have seen, there are good reasons for believing that international institutions have acted as powerful agents for the diffusion and socialization of norms.

Assessing the very mixed empirical record of actually existing institutions can have important implications for our views of global justice. Thomas Nagel, for example, has developed a political conception of global justice. Drawing on Hobbesian traditions, he argues that justice arises amongst those jointly subject to coercive authority.

On the political conception, sovereign states are not merely instruments for realizing the preinstitutional value of justice among human beings. Instead, their existence is precisely what gives the value of justice its application, by putting the fellow citizens of a sovereign state into a relation that they do not have with the rest of humanity, an institutional relationship which must then be evaluated by the special standards of fairness and equality that fill out the content of justice.[34]

His assessment of where international institutions and global governance are *'for the moment'* [my emphasis] is that they fail to meet a crucial test, namely '[T]hey are not collectively enacted and coercively imposed in the name of all the individuals whose lives they affect'.[35] Yet this view of justice places too much weight on the difference between coercive and non-coercive situations; and, more importantly, underplays the extent of the changes that have in fact taken place in the density of international institutions, in the extent to which they do in tact exercise power and can be said to be co-authored, and in the relationship of both states and individuals to those institutions.[36]

[34] Thomas Nagel, 'The Problem of Global Justice', *Philosophy and Public Affairs*, 33/2 (2005), 120.

[35] Ibid. 138.

[36] See Andrew Hurrell, 'Global Inequality and International Institutions', in Thomas Pogge (ed.), *Global Justice* (Cambridge: Polity Press, 2001), 32–54; and Joshua Cohen and Charles Sabel, 'Extra Rempublicam Nulla Justitia?', *Philosophy and Public Affairs*, 34/2 (2006), 147–75.

Others who either deny the possibility of international distributive justice or see it only in highly constrained forms also place great emphasis on the absence or weakness of international institutions or other cooperative arrangements.

Now although in the contemporary world there are clearly forms of interaction and cooperation occurring at the global level—the international economy provides the most obvious example, but there are also many forms of political cooperation, ranging from defence treaties through to environmental protection agreements—these are not sufficient to constitute a global community. They do not by themselves create either a shared sense of identity or a common ethos. And above all there is no common institutional structure that would justify us in describing unequal outcomes as forms of unequal treatment'.[37]

As it stands, this argument raises a number of questions. In the first place, it says nothing about the criteria that would help us decide when we had reached a point of institutional change when something morally significant was happening. What might 'sufficient to constitute a global community' mean? This is particularly important because we are not dealing with a black and white choice but with an uncertain and highly variable process of institutionalization and governance. And, secondly, institutions cannot be understood as simple reflections of some pre-existing and static community. Institutions reflect but also actively shape communities. Thus state institutions have been tremendously important in the creation and development of national communities. So how can we arrive at a more dynamic view of the link between institutions and morally relevant communities? Curiously perhaps, elements of an answer can be found in Rawls. Now on the one side what is most striking about *The Law of Peoples* is its static, backward-looking character. The image of the international system that Rawls presents is strikingly old-fashioned and profoundly at odds with even modest claims about international change and evolution. But, on the other hand, Rawls's own work highlights the potential for a two-way and self-reinforcing link between the institutions of the basic structure and the political culture of the people governed within those institutions.

Thus society's 'main political, social and economic institutions and how they fit into one unified system of social co-operation' determine the basic structure and govern 'the initial focus' of how to think about matters of justice.[38] But the emphasis here should be on 'initial' since Rawls also recognizes the possibility of self-reinforcing change. 'In addition, the institutions of the basic structure have deep and long-term social effects and in fundamental ways shape citizens' character and aims, the kinds of persons they are and

---

[37] David Miller, 'Justice and Global Inequality', in Andrew Hurrell and Ngarie Woods (eds.), *Globalization and Inequality* (Oxford: Oxford University Press, 1999), 190.

[38] Rawls (1993: 11–12).

aspire to be'.[39] When writing about domestic society, there is a strong sense that institutions play a central role in moving from self-interested cooperation towards a full overlapping consensus. They have important socializing influences on citizens and Rawls presents a psychological account of how people come to accept and internalize principles of justice. Equally—when looking at international life—change, evolution, and learning are all recognized. 'The idea of a reasonably just society of well-ordered peoples will not have an important place in a theory of international politics until such peoples exist and have learned to coordinate their actions in wider forms of political, economic and social cooperation.'[40] Or again: 'What encourages the statesman's work is that relations of affinity are not a fixed thing, but may continually grow stronger over time as peoples come to work together in cooperative institutions they have developed.... The relatively narrow circle of mutually caring peoples in the world may expand over time and must never be viewed as fixed'.[41]

A global moral community in which claims about justice can secure both authority and be genuinely accessible to a broad swathe of humanity will be one that is built around some minimal notion of just process, that prioritizes institutions that embed procedural fairness, and that cultivates the shared political culture and the habits of argumentation and deliberation on which such institutions necessarily depend. As Judith Shklar puts it: 'Procedural justice is not merely a formal ritual, as is so often charged. It is a system that in principle gives everyone some access to the agencies of rectification and, more significantly, the possibility of expressing a sense of injustice to some effect, at least occasionally'.[42]

Within political theory, much work needs to be done on the potential principles of global political justice, including identifying the different faces of global public power that need to be made subject to different kinds of regulative principles and detaching specific principles of political justice from overarching conceptions of global justice. Within international law, thinking in this way pushes us back towards a revalidation of process and the historically embedded practices of legal argumentation and justification. The positivist claim that an appeal to the 'law' can provide a secure means of securing international cooperation has long faced many powerful and persuasive objections, as has the positivist attempt to separate law and morality. But the core intuition remains a powerful one: that, in an international society characterized by deep and fundamental value conflict and by the constant difficulty of managing unequal power, a viable and stable international legal order must be built around shared processes and procedures, accepted understandings of

---

[39] Rawls (1993: 68).

[40] John Rawls, *The Law of Peoples* (Cambridge, MA: Harvard University Press, 1999), 19.

[41] Ibid. 112–13.

[42] Judith Shklar, *Faces of Injustice* (New Haven, CT: Yale University Press, 1990), 124.

legal sources, and a commitment to diplomatic negotiation and dialogue. The alternative is both normatively unacceptable and politically unviable, namely to open the door to a situation in which it is the strength of a single state or group of states that decides what shall count as law. Moral imperatives cannot themselves create law, and there is no legitimate substitute for showing that moral commitment reflects shared understandings that are embodied within shared rules and institutions.

It is important here to avoid too sharp a distinction between a consent-based view of international legal legitimacy and a justice-based view.[43] Procedural legitimacy is not simply about state consent. On the one hand, consent itself may be moderated and mediated by the complexities of legal process, even without disappearing entirely from the international legal order. On the other hand, there are other important values located within the processes of international law. This may be understood in terms of the old arguments about the 'inner morality' of law and the rule of law (for example, that law be coherent, general and impartial in its application, prospective, stable, and public).[44] Or it may involve principles of public law that can be employed to guide international and global law-making (such as those of procedural transparency, reasoned decision, opportunities for review, or substantive standards such as proportionality).[45] Or, most generally, it may simply involve an insistence that the justification of a position or a case follows an articulated, discernible, and coherent pattern of legal argument that draws on analogies, precedents, and principles that are compatible with already widely accepted values. Finally, law can be viewed as a sociologically embedded transnational cultural practice in which claims and counterclaims can be articulated and debated and from which norms can emerge that can have at least some determinacy and argumentative purchase. Law, then, can play a communicative and epistemic role, shaping the conditions within which claims, including justice claims, can be made and debated. The modern-day Grotian will be inclined to stress the ongoing, unstable and subtle interplay between the sources of law and legal process on the one hand, and the content of the law and of legal rules on the other.

In the light of the picture of actually existing international society presented in this book, it would be naive to sanctify process. Process can never be the whole story for four reasons. In the first place, our own ethical commitments demand that we engage politically on the basis of our own values and seek to promote and uphold them. Second, even the most open process will always presuppose certain kinds of implied normative assumptions about who should be there and how the process should be conducted. Third, even on grounds

---

[43] See Buchanan (2004: esp. ch. 7).

[44] See, most importantly, Lon Fuller, *The Morality of Law*, rev. edn. (New Haven, CT: Yale University Press, 1969).

[45] See Kingsbury, Krisch, and Stewart (2005: 37–42).

of efficiency, some commitment to equity and fairness of outcomes may be necessary to secure the effectiveness and legitimacy of cooperative endeavours and shared institutions. Finally, the relationship between process and power is never a simple one. In general, the argument defended in this book has been that power expressed through shared rules and norms is potentially more acceptable than power unmediated by rules. Yet I have also tried to show how the balance between law as a reflection and reinforcement of power and law as a moderator of power is often a very fine one. Moreover, the specialized legal and institutional processes that characterize so many aspects of global governance are also exclusionary. In particular, they exclude those who lack the knowledge, the technical language, and the navigational skills of transnationalized modernity. It is this that leads to the importance of thinking about the conditions for effective political agency.

Political agency

That we should focus on institutions, on negotiation, and on dialogue and deliberation is hardly an original suggestion. Albeit with significant variation, many have been tempted to go down a broadly Habermasian road—stressing the extent to which the terms of a just global order cannot be based on coercion nor on whatever bargain states and societies happen to be able to strike with one another, but require instead critical reflection, uncoerced agreement of rational agents via a shared process of deliberation and reasoned justification.[46] There have also been important arguments in favour of creating global institutional frameworks which widen the boundaries of the dialogic community.[47]

If we try to move down this road, there are many open questions as to whose voices are to be included and how, in institutional terms, they are to be included. The first and the easiest thing that we can say is that the participants in global moral politics will have to come from a wide variety of cultural, religious, and linguistic backgrounds. One does not have to believe in clashing civilizations or in radical incommensurability to believe that human diversity and value conflict remain important and that perspectives on issues of international order and justice vary enormously from one part of the world to another. This may be because of cultural differences in the strong sense; but, as I have argued in earlier chapters, it is just as likely to be result of differences in national and regional histories, in social and economic circumstances and conditions, and in political contexts and trajectories. But, whichever is the case, the premium is on understanding those different world views and appreciating the difficulties of communication. It seems highly

---

[46] For an introduction to Habermas's political thought, see Chris Thornhill, *Political Theory in Modern Germany: An Introduction* (Cambridge: Polity Press, 2000), ch. 4.

[47] Most notably, Linklater (1998).

unlikely that any single ideology or world view will provide an overarching framework or meta-narrative for values and ethics in the twenty-first century. Instead, debate, deliberation, and contestation over issues of justice will take place in a wide variety of spheres and domains involving a wide variety of actors: states, NGOs, firms, and international organizations. To the extent that such convergence around a single world view does emerge, it will only be viable in so far as it comes from persuasion and un-coerced acceptance rather than imposition and imperialism—both for moral reasons, but also because imperial or hegemonic ordering, including liberal imperialism, is unlikely to prove stable, effective, or legitimate.

But even assuming the presence of these multiple voices, the location of a stable and shared moral vocabulary and some degree of institutional stability, one still needs to ask about the conditions of effective political agency. Within domestic society, Habermas is ambiguous as to how far the discourse principle requires changes merely in the procedures of bargaining or changes to the underlying balance of bargaining power itself.

The discourse principle, which is supposed to secure an uncoerced consensus, can thus be brought to bear only indirectly, namely, through procedures that *regulate* bargaining from the standpoint of fairness. In this way, non-neutralizable bargaining power should at least be disciplined by its equal distribution among the parties. More specifically, the negotiation of compromises should follow procedures that provide all the interested parties with an equal opportunity for pressure, that is, an equal opportunity to influence one another during the actual bargaining, so that all the affected interests can come into play and have equal chances of prevailing. To the extent that these conditions are met, there are grounds for presuming that negotiated agreements are fair.[48]

But however we might think about power within domestic society, the conditions of global society make it impossible to evade the issue of unequal bargaining power. The massive inequalities of power and condition; the continued occurrence of war and intervention and the continued willingness of major states to use military power as an instrument of state policy; the role of power in skewing the terms of the capitalist global economy and the close links that exist between globalization and inequality; and the deformity of many of the core institutions of international society—all these point towards the pressing need to consider the minimal political preconditions that might underpin a global moral community in which reasoned deliberation and un-coerced consensus could even begin to be possible. Although political theorists are perhaps naturally tempted to argue from the ceiling down, the wholly different scale of inequalities that exist in world politics should push us to think hard about the minimum preconditions for an acceptable international political process. At a minimum this might include: some acceptance

[48] Jürgen Habermas, *Between Facts and Norms: Contributions to a Discourse Theory of Law and Democracy* (Cambridge: Polity Press, 1996), 166–7.

of equality of status, respect, and consideration; some commitment to reciprocity and to the public justification of one's actions; some capacity for autonomous decision-making on the basis of reasonable information; a degree of un-coerced willingness to participate; a situation in which the most disadvantaged perceive themselves as having some stake in the system; and some institutional processes by which the weak and disadvantaged are able to make their voice heard and to express claims about unjust treatment.

Apart from concern with the suffering of the most disadvantaged, Rawls gives two very good reasons why we should be concerned with inequality: first, that a large gap between rich and poor 'often leads to some citizens being stigmatized and treated as inferiors, and that is unjust'; and second, because of the 'important role of fairness in the political processes of the basic structure of the Society of Peoples'. Yet, despite ample evidence that some peoples are stigmatized and treated as inferiors and still more evidence of the massive unfairness of international political processes, Rawls draws only the most feeble of conclusions as to what needs to be changed globally in the interests of justice.[49]

Recent liberal discourses on global justice sometimes appear to be a discourses about what the rich and powerful owe to the poor, weak, and oppressed. The weak, the oppressed, and the dispossessed appear mostly as the passive objects of (potential) benevolence. Their voices, visions, and understandings of the world are seldom heard or seldom deliberated upon. This is one of the dangers of too sharp a separation between moral cosmopolitanism and political cosmopolitanism. Now one answer is, of course, to open up decision-making and political process to a much broader range of constituencies. As we have seen, the democratizing agenda of global governance includes both proposed reforms in the ways in which states are represented within international organizations and increased attention to the claims of civil society groups to represent and speak for particular cultural and transnational constituencies.

But opening up decision-making in the absence of a genuine capacity to engage is at best a very partial answer. Participation in a political process requires more than simply presence. Having an effective voice requires material capacities and the material conditions on which meaningful political participation depends. Fair process, then, does not diminish our concern with global inequality and with distributive justice. Quite the reverse. It provides one of the most powerful moral reasons why we should take distribution seriously. There is, then, a very strong argument that improving fair political process in global political life will require substantial redistribution of resources from the rich to the poor. Equally, we might argue, upholding an ideal of global human rights requires that we include within the agenda of

[49] Rawls (1999: 114–15).

316

rights itself a serious concern with rights of access to law and to effective legal process. Again the substance of the justice claim has to be linked to the material and political conditions by which those claims might be effectively pressed.

But does even significant redistribution amongst individuals address the crucial issue of political agency? Politically, the advance of justice has rarely been conceded easily by the strong and still more rarely has it been the result of altruism. It has rather been the result of political struggle, and political struggle requires effective political agency. For liberals, agency matters, or should matter. As we have noted, many have been tempted to rehabilitate imperialism. Yet imperialism is morally problematic because it represents a wholesale denial of the political agency of those ruled over. There are many forms of such agency and many potentially successful instruments. As against the realist emphasis on hard power, it is important to note the many cases where civilian power and the power of moral ideas have been central to progressive political change. Equally, not all forms of political agency involve the state: different forms of internationalism have a long history and, as noted earlier in this book, the material circumstances of globalization have opened up new possibilities for effective transnational political activity.

But, to return to where this book started, even in the twenty-first century it is very difficult to avoid the state. It is all too easy for those who live comfortably within viable and prosperous states to talk glibly of the virtues of a post-Westphalian world. Even if we share a cosmopolitan concern for individuals, we need to recognize that state strength is an important determinant of the capacity of individuals and groups to manage the costs and benefits of globalization; that states play a crucial political role in securing and protecting cultural identity; and that the political agency of states acting internationally is necessary to achieve the mutuality and reciprocity that has surely to be central to a *shared* scheme of global social cooperation and to a meaningful global justice community. The critics of state-based pluralism have no difficulty in highlighting the oppressive character of many states, nor in showing how the organization of humanity into particular political peoples creates unjust practices of exclusion, conflict, and the denial of rights. Cosmopolitan political theorists have rightly drawn attention to the manifold weaknesses of the so-called 'morality of states' and of claims that the subjects of distributive justice should be states rather than individuals. And yet, for all the serious problems of mixed motives and cross-cutting interests, achieving even a minimum degree of procedural justice is likely to require a significant redistribution of political power and the creation by the weak and marginalized of the effective collective political agency needed to challenge the currently strong and dominant.

I have argued, then, that we need to give far greater attention to the links between political and moral cosmopolitanism and to the possible principles of global political justice that might inform those links. A revalidation of process legitimacy and procedural justice is crucial for the development of a stable, effective, and legitimate international society and for the nurturing of meaningfully shared foundations for the discussion of global justice. In a very important sense, the ethical claims of international society rest on the contention that such a society continues to be the most stable set of globally institutionalized political processes by which norms and rules can be negotiated on the basis of dialogue and consent, rather than simply being imposed by the most powerful. There is very little reason for supposing that progress in the direction of moral accessibility, institutional stability, or more balanced and equitable forms of political agency is likely to be easy. It may not be possible at all. There are nevertheless good reasons for believing that it is a direction which continues to be of crucial importance. Understanding how the rope bridge may be spun out across the canyon is central both to the chances of world order in the twenty-first century and to the promotion of greater global justice.

Bibliography

Abbott, Frederick M., 'NAFTA and the Legalization of World Politics: A Case Study', in Judith L. Goldstein, Miles Kahler, Robert O. Keohane, and Anne-Marie Slaughter (eds.), *Legalization and World Politics* (Cambridge, MA: MIT Press, 2001).

Abbott, Kenneth W. and Duncan Snidal, 'Why States Act Through Formal International Organizations', *Journal of Conflict Resolution*, 42/1 (1998), 3–32.

Acevedo, Domingo E. and Claudio Grossman, 'The Organization of American States and the Protection of Democracy', in Tom Farer (ed.), *Beyond Sovereignty* (Baltimore, MD: Johns Hopkins University Press, 1996), 132–49.

Acharya, Amitav, *Constructing a Security Community in Southeast Asia: ASEAN and the Problem of Regional Order* (London: Routledge, 2001).

—— 'How Ideas Spread: Whose Norms Matter? Norm Localization and Institutional Change in Asian Regionalism', *International Organization*, 58/2 (Spring 2004), 239–75.

—— and Alistair Ian Johnston (eds.), *Crafting Cooperation: Regional International Institutions in Comparative Perspective* (Cambridge: Cambridge University Press, 2007).

Adler, Emanuel and Michael Barnett (eds.), *Governing Anarchy: Security Communities in Theory, History and Comparison* (Cambridge: Cambridge University Press, 1998).

Alderson, Kai and Andrew Hurrell (eds.), *Hedley Bull on International Society* (Basingstoke, UK: Macmillan, 2000).

Allott, Philip, *The Health of Nations: Society and Law Beyond the State* (Cambridge: Cambridge University Press, 2002).

Alston, Philip, 'Conjuring up New Human Rights: A Proposal for Quality Control', *The American Journal of International Law*, 78/3 (July 1984), 607–21.

—— 'The Myopia of the Handmaidens: International Lawyers and Globalization', *European Journal of International Law*, 8/3 (1997), 435–48.

Andreas, Peter and Thomas J. Biersteker (eds.), *The Rebordering of North America: Integration and Exclusion in a New Security Context* (New York: Routledge, 2003).

Angell, Norman, *The Great Illusion: A Study of the Relation of Military Power in Nations to the Economic and Social Advantage* (London: Heinemann, 1910).

Anheier, Helmut, Marlies Glasius, and Mary Kaldor, 'Introducing Global Civil Society', in *Global Civil Society 2001* (Oxford: Oxford University Press, 2001).

Arendt, Hannah, *The Life of the Mind* (San Diego, CA: Harcourt, 1978).

Armstrong, David, *Revolutions and World Order* (Oxford: Oxford University Press, 1993).

—— Lorna Lylod, and John Redmond, *International Organization*, 3rd edn. (Basingstoke, UK: Macmillan, 2004).

Aron, Raymond, *Les Sociétés modernes* (Paris: Quadrige/PUF, 2006).

Bibliography

Aron, Raymond, *Peace and War: A Theory of International Relations* (London: Weidenfeld & Nicolson, 1966).

Axelrod, Robert, 'An Evolutionary Approach to Norms', *American Political Science Review*, 80/4 (December 1986), 1095–111.

Avant, Deborah, *The Market for Force* (Cambridge: Cambridge University Press, 2005).

Avineri, Shlomo (ed.), *Karl Marx on Colonisation and Modernisation* (New York: Doubleday, 1968).

Ayoob, Mohammed, *The Third World Security Predicament: State Making, Regional Conflict, and the International System* (Boulder, CO: Lynne Rienner, 1995).

—— 'Humanitarian Intervention and State Sovereignty', *The International Journal of Human Rights*, 6/1 (Spring 2002), 81–102.

Bacevich, Andrew J., *American Empire: The Realities and Consequences of U.S. Diplomacy* (Cambridge, MA: Harvard University Press, 2002).

Bail, Christoph, Robert Falkner, and Helen Marquand (eds.), *The Cartegena Protocol on Biosafety* (London: Earthscan for Chatham House (RIIA), 2002).

Barnett, Michael and Martha Finnemore, *Rules for the World: International Organizations in Global Politics* (Ithaca, NY: Cornell University Press, 2001).

—— and Raymond Duvall (eds.), *Power and Global Governance* (Cambridge: Cambridge University Press, 2005).

Barry, Brian, *Sociologist, Economists and Democracy* (London: Collier, 1970), 75–98.

Barry, John and Robyn Eckersley (eds.), *The State and the Global Ecological Crisis* (Cambridge, MA: MIT Press, 2005).

Beck, Robert J., Anthony Clark Arend, and Robert D. van der Lugt (eds.), *International Rules: Approaches from International Law and International Relations* (Oxford: Oxford University Press, 1996).

Beitz, Charles, *Political Theory and International Relations* (Princeton, NJ: Princeton University Press, 1979).

—— 'International Liberalism and Distributive Justice: A Survey of Recent Thought', *World Politics*, 51 (1999), 269–96.

Beetham, David, *The Legitimation of Power* (Basingstoke, UK: Macmillan, 1991).

Bellamy, Alex J. and Paul D. Williams, 'Who's Keeping the Peace? Regionalization and Contemporary Peace Operations', *International Security*, 29/4 (2005), 157–95.

Benner, Erica, 'Is There a Core National Doctrine?', *Nations and Nationalism*, 7/2 (2001), 155–74.

—— 'The Liberal Limits to Republican Nationalism,' in Daniel A. Bell and Avner de-Shalit (eds.), *Forms of Justice* (Lanham: Rowan and Littlefield, 2003).

Benner, Thorsten, Wolfgang H. Reinecke, and Jan Martin Witte, 'Multisectoral networks in Global Governance: Towards a Pluralistic System of Accountability', *Government and Opposition*, 39/2 (Spring 2004), 191–210.

Bentham, Jeremy, *A Plan for a Universal and Perpetual Peace* (London: Grotius Society Publications, 1927).

Berdal, Mats, 'How "New" are "New Wars"? Global Economic Change and the Study of Civil War', *Global Governance*, 9/4 (2003), 477–502.

—— 'The UN Security Council: Ineffective but Indispensable', *Survival*, 45/2 (2003), 7–30.

_____ and David M. Malone (eds.), *Greed and Grievance: Economic Agendas and Civil Wars* (Boulder, CO: Lynne Rienner, 2000).

Berlin, Isaiah, 'Two Concepts of Liberty,' in *Four Essays on Liberty* (Oxford: Oxford University Press, 1969).

Bernard, Montague, *On the Principle of Non-intervention* (Oxford: J.J. and J.A.S. Parker, 1860).

Bernstein, Stephen, *The Compromise of Liberal Environmentalism* (New York: Columbia University Press, 2001).

Betts, Richard, 'The Political Support System for American Primacy', *International Affairs*, 81/1 (2005), 1–14.

Bierman, Frank, 'Global Governance and the Environment', in Michele Betsill, Kathryn Hochstetler, and Dimistris Stevis (eds.), *Palgrave Guide to International Environmental Politics* (New York: Palgrave, 2005).

Biersteker, Thomas J., 'Globalization as a Mode of Thinking in Major Institutional Actors', in Ngaire Woods (ed.), *The Political Economy of Globalization* (Basingstoke, UK: Macmillan, 2000), 147–72.

_____ and Rodney Bruce Hall (eds.), *The Emergence of Private Authority in Global Governance* (Cambridge: Cambridge University Press, 2002).

Bircham, Emma and John Charlton (eds.), *Anti-Capitalism: A Guide to the Movement* (London: Bookmark, 2001).

Birnie, Patricia and Alan Boyle, *International Law and the Environment*, 2nd edn. (Oxford: Oxford University Press, 2002).

Black, Jeremy, *War and the World: Military Power and the Fate of Continents* (New Haven, CT: Yale University Press, 1998).

Bloomfield, Richard J., 'Making the Western Hemisphere Safe for Democracy? The OAS Defense-of-Democracy Regime', in Carl Kaysen, Robert A. Pastor, and Laura W. Reed (eds.), *Collective Responses to Regional Problems: The Case of Latin America and the Caribbean* (Cambridge, MA: American Academy of Arts and Sciences, 1994), 15–28.

Bobbitt, Philip, *The Sword of Achilles: War, Peace and the Course of History* (London: Penguin, 2003).

Bohman, James and Matthias Lutz-Bachmann (eds.), *Perpetual Peace: Essays on Kant's Cosmopolitan Ideal* (Cambridge, MA: MIT Press, 1997).

Bolton, John R., ' "Legitimacy" in International Affairs: The American Perspecitve in Theory and Operation', Remarks to the Fedaralist Society, November 2003, http://www.state.gov/t/us/rm26143.htm accessed on 10.08.05.

Bourquin, Maurice (ed.), *Collective Security: A Record of the Seventh and Eighth International Studies Conference, Paris 1934—London 1935* (Paris: International Institute of Intellectual Cooperation, 1936).

Boutros-Ghali, Boutros, 'A Grotian Moment', *Fordham International Law Journal*, 18/5 (1995), 1609–16.

Braithwaite, John and Peter Drahos, *Global Business Regulation* (Cambridge: Cambridge University Press, 2000).

Breslin, Shaun, Christopher W. Hughes, Nicola Phillips, and Ben Rosamond (eds.), *New Regionalisms in the Global Political Economy* (London: Routledge, 2002).

Brierly, James L., edited by Humphrey Waldock, *The Law of Nations: An Introduction to the International Law of Peace*, 6th edn. (Oxford: Clarendon Press, 1963).

Brooks, Stephen G. and William C. Wohlforth, 'American Primacy in Perspective', *Foreign Affairs*, 81/4 (2002), 20–34.

Brooks, Stephen G. and William C. Wohlforth, 'Hard Times for Soft Balancing', *International Security*, 30/1 (Summer 2005), 103.

Broomhall, Bruce, *International Justice and the International Criminal Court* (Oxford: Oxford University Press, 2003).

Brown, Chris, 'International Political Theory and the Idea of a World Community', in Ken Booth and Steve Smith (eds.), *International Relations Theory Today* (Cambridge: Polity Press, 1995).

Brown, Michael, Sean Lynn-Jones, and Steven Miller (eds.), *Debating the Democratic Peace* (Cambridge, MA: MIT Press, 1996).

Brownlie, Ian, 'The Reality and Efficiency of International Law', *The British Yearbook of International Law 1981* (Oxford: Clarendon Press), 1–8.

Brubaker, Rogers, *Nationalism Reformed: Nationhood and the National Question in the New Europe* (Cambridge: Cambridge University Press, 1996).

Buchanan, Allen, *Justice, Legitimacy and Self-determination: Moral Foundations of International Law* (Oxford: Oxford University Press, 2004)

Buchheit, Lee C., *Secession: The Legitimacy of Self-Determination* (New Haven, CT: Yale University Press, 1978).

Bull, Hedley 'The Grotian Conception of International Society', in Alderson and Hurrell (2000).

—— *The Anarchical Society: A Study in World Politics*, 3rd edn. (Basingstoke, UK: Macmillan, [1977] 2003).

—— 'The Third World and International Society', in George W. Keeton and George Schwarzenberger (eds.), *The Year Book of World Affairs 1979*, The London Institute of World Affairs (London: Stevens and Sons, 1979), 15–31.

—— 'The Great Irresponsibles? The United States, the Soviet Union and World Order', *International Journal*, XXV (1979–80), 439.

—— 'The Revolt Against Western Dominance', *The Hagey Lectures* (Waterloo: University of Waterloo, 1984).

—— and Adam Watson (eds.), *The Expansion of International Society* (Oxford: Oxford University Press, 1984).

Burrow, John, *The Crisis of Reason: European Thought, 1848–1914* (New Haven, CT: Yale University Press, 2000).

Butterfield, Herbert, 'The Balance of Power,' in Herbert Butterfield and Martin Wight (eds.), *Diplomatic Investigations: Essays in the Theory of International Politics* (London: Allen and Unwin, 1966), 132–48.

Buzan, Barry, *From International to World Society? English School Theory and the Social Structure of Globalisation* (Cambridge: Cambridge University Press, 2004).

—— and Ole Waever, *Regions as Powers: The Structure of International Security* (Cambridge: Cambridge University Press, 2003).

—— —— and Jaap de Wilde, *Security: A New Framework for Analysis* (Boulder, CO: Lynne Rienner, 1998).

Byers, Michael and Simon Chesterman, 'Changing the Rules About Rules? Unilateral Humanitarian Intervention and the Future of International Law', in J. L. Holzgrefe and Robert O. Keohane (eds.), *Humanitarian Intervention: Ethical, Legal and Political Dilemmas* (Cambridge: Cambridge University Press, 2003), 177–203.

Caldwell, Lynton Keith, *Between Two Worlds: Science, the Environmental Movement and Policy Choice* (Cambridge: Cambridge University Press, 1992).

Camillieri, Joseph A. and Jim Falk, *The End of Sovereignty? The Politics of a Shrinking and Fragmenting World* (London: Edward Elgar, 1992).

Caney, Simon, *Justice Beyond Borders: A Global Political Theory* (Oxford: Oxford University Press, 2005).

Cantori, Louis J. and Steven L. Spiegel (eds.), *The International Politics of Regions: A Comparative Approach* (Englewood Cliffs, NJ: Prentice-Hall, 1970).

Cardoso, Fernando Henrique and Enzo Faletto, *Dependency and Development in Latin America* (Beverly Hills, CA: University of California Press, 1979).

―― 'Relações Norte-Sul no Contexto Atual: Uma Nova Dependência', in Renato Baumann (ed.), *O Brasil e a Economia Global* (Rio de Janeiro: Editora Campus, 1996), 5–15.

Caron, David D., 'The Legitimacy of the Collective Authority of the Security Council', *American Journal of International Law*, 87/3 (1993), 552–88.

Carothers, Thomas, *Aiding Democracy Abroad: The Learning Curve* (Washington, DC: Carnegie Endowment for International Peace, 1999).

Carr, E. H., *The Twenty Years' Crisis, 1919–1939: An Introduction to the Study of International Relations* (reissued with a new introduction and additional material by Michael Cox, Palgrave, Basingstoke, [1939] 2001).

―― *Nationalism and After* (London: Macmillan, 1945).

Cassese, Antonio, *Self-Determination of Peoples: A Legal Reappraisal* (Cambridge: Cambridge University Press, 1995).

Cawley, Elizabeth H., *The American Diaries of Richard Cobden* (Princeton, NJ: Princeton University Press, 1952).

Ceadel, Martin, *The Origins of War Prevention: The British Peace Movement and International Relations, 1730–1854* (Oxford: Clarendon Press, 1996).

Cederman, Lars-Erik, 'Nationalism and Ethnicity', in Walter Carlsnaes, Thomas Risse, and Beth Simmons (eds.), *The Handbook of International Relations* (London: Sage, 2002), 409–28.

Chan, Steve, 'In Search of Democratic Peace: Problems and Promise', *Mershon International Studies Review*, 41/1 (1997), 59–91.

Chang, Ha-Joon, *Kicking Away the Ladder: Development Strategies in Historical Perspective* (London: Anthem Press, 2002).

Chase-Dunn, Christopher, 'World State Formation: Historical Processes and Emergent Necessity', *Political Geography Quarterly*, 9/2 (1996), 108–30.

Chayes, Abram and Antonia Handler Chayes, 'Regime Architecture: Elements and Principles', in Janne Nolan (ed.), *Global Engagement. Cooperation and Security in the 21st Century* (Washington, DC: Brookings Institution, 1994), 65–130.

―― ―― *The New Sovereignty: Compliance with International Regulatory Agreements* (Cambridge, MA: Harvard University Press, 1995).

Chinkin, Christine, 'Human Rights and the Politics of Representation', in Michael Byers (ed.), *The Role of Law in International Politics* (Oxford: Oxford University Press, 2000), 131–47.

Clapham, Christopher, *Africa and the International System* (Cambridge: Cambridge University Press, 1996).

Clark, Ann Marie, Elisabeth J. Friedeman, and Kathryn Hochstetler, 'The Sovereign Limits of Global Civil Society. A Comparison of NGO Participation in UN World Conferences on the Environment, Human Rights and Women', *World Politics*, 51 (October 1998), 1–35.

Clark, Ian, *Legitimacy in International Society* (Oxford: Oxford University Press, 2005).

Clarke, Michael, 'War in the New International Order', *International Affairs*, 77/3 (2001), 663–71.

Clarkson, Stephen (with Sarah Davidson Ladly, Megan Merwart, and Carlton Thorne), 'The Primitive Realities of North America's Transnational Governance', in Edgar Grande and Louis W. Pauly (eds.), *Complex Sovereignty. Reconstituting Political Authority in the Twenty-First Century* (Toronto: University of Toronto Press, 2005).

Claude, Inis L., *Power and International Relations* (New York: Random House, 1962).

—— 'Collective Legitimation as a Political Function of the United Nations', *International Organization*, 20/3 (Summer 1966), 367–79.

Cobban, Alfred, *The Nation State and National Self-determination* (London: Collins, [1945] 1969).

Cobden, Richard, 'England, Ireland and America' and 'Russia', in *The Political Writing of Richard Cobden*, 4th edn. (reprinted by Kraus Reprint; New York, 1969).

—— *Political Writings of Richard Cobden* (London: Routledge/Thoemmes Press, [1867] 1995).

Cohen, Jean and Andrew Arato, *Civil Society and Political Theory* (Cambridge, MA: MIT Press, 1992).

Cohen, Joel E., *How Many People Can the Earth Support?* (New York: W.W. Norton, 1995).

Cohen, Joshua and Charles Sabel, 'Extra Rempublicam Nulla Justitia?', *Philosophy and Public Affairs*, 34/2 (2006), 147–75.

Coleman, James S., *Foundations of Social Theory* (Cambridge, MA: Harvard University Press, 1990).

Collingwood, Vivien, 'Assistance with Strings Attached: Good Governance Conditionality in International Society', D. Phil. thesis, Oxford University, 2003.

Commission on Global Governance, *Our Global Neighbourhood* (New York: Oxford University Press, 1995).

Conca, Ken, 'Old States in New Bottles? The Hybridization of Authority in Global Environmental Governance', in John Barry and Robyn Eckersley (eds.), *The State and the Global Ecological Crisis* (Cambridge, MA: MIT Press, 2005), 181–205.

—— and Ronnie D. Lipschutz, 'A Tale of Two Forests', in Ronnie D. Lipschutz and Ken Conca (eds.), *The State and Social Power in Global Environmental Politics* (New York: Columbia University Press, 1993), 1–18.

Cooper, Richard, *The Economics of Interdependence: Economic Policy in the Atlantic Community* (New York: McGraw-Hill, 1968).

Cooper, Robert, *The Breaking of Nations: Order and Chaos in the 21st Century* (London: Atlantic Books, 2003).

Cox, Michael, 'The Empire's Back in Town: Or America's Imperial Temptation—Again', *Millennium*, 32/1 (2003), 1–29.

Cox, Robert, *Production, Power, and World Order: Social Forces in the Making of History* (New York: Columbia University Press, 1987).

—— (with T. Sinclair), *Approaches to World Order* (Cambridge: Cambridge University Press, 1996).

Crawford, James, 'Democracy and International Law', *British Yearbook of International Law*, No. 64 (1993), 113–33.

Crosby, Alfred W., *Ecological Imperialism: The Biological Expansion of Europe, 900–1900*, 2nd edn. (Cambridge: Cambridge University Press, 2004).

Cutler, A. Claire, Virginia Hauffler, and Tony Porter (eds.), *Private Authority and International Affairs* (Albany, NY: State University of New York Press, 1999).

Dallmayr, Fred, 'Cosmopolitanism, Moral and Political', *Political Theory*, 31/3 (June 2003), 421–42.

Daly, Herman E. and John B. Cobb, *For the Common Good* (London: Earthscan, 1990).

Darwin, John, 'Imperialism and the Victorians: The Dynamics of Territorial Expansion', *English Historical Review*, 112/447 (1997), 614–42.

Davis, Natalie Zemon, *The Gift in Sixteenth-Century France* (Oxford: Oxford University Press, 2000).

DeSombre, Elizabeth R., *The Global Environment and World Politics* (London: Continuum, 2002).

Deudney, Daniel, 'Regrounding Realism', *Security Studies*, 10/1 (2000), 1–45.

De Vattel, Emerich, *The Law of Nations* or *The Principles of Natural Law*, vol. III, trans. Charles G. Fenwick (Washington, DC: Carnegie Institution, 1916).

Deutsch, Karl W., Sidney A. Burrell, and Robert A. Kann, *Political Community in the North Atlantic Area* (Princeton, NJ: Princeton University Press, 1957).

Diehl, Paul F. (ed.), *The Politics of Global Governance: International Organizations in an Interdependent World* (Boulder, CO: Lynne Rienner, 1997).

—— and Nils Petter Gleditsch (eds.), *Environmental Conflict* (Boulder, CO: Westview, 2001).

Digeser, Peter, 'The Fourth Face of Power', *Journal of Politics*, 54/4 (1992), 977–1007.

Dinan, Desmond, *Ever Closer Union: An Introduction to European Union*: 2nd edn. (Basingstoke, UK: Palgrave, 1999).

Dixit, Avinash, 'On Modes of Economic Governance', *Econometrica*, 71/2 (March 2003), 449–81.

—— 'Economic Governance', in *The New Palgrave Dictionary of Economics*, 2nd edn. (London: Palgrave, 2006).

Dobson, Andrew, *Green Political Theory*, 3rd edn. (London: Routledge, 2000).

Dollar, David and Aart Kraay, 'Spreading the Wealth', *Foreign Affairs*, 81/1 (2002), 120–33.

Donnelly, Jack, *Universal Human Rights in Theory and Practice*, 2nd edn. (Ithaca, NY: Cornell University Press, 2003).

Dowding, Keith, 'Model or Metaphor? A Critical Review of the Policy Network Approach', *Political Studies*, XLIII/1 (1995), 136–58.

Downs, George W. (ed.), *Collective Security Beyond the Cold War* (Ann Arbor, MI: University of Michigan Press, 1994).

Doyle, Michael, 'Kant, Liberal Legacies and Foreign Affairs', *Philosophy and Public Affairs*, 12/3/4 (Summer and Fall 1983), 205–35, 323–53.

—— Ian Johnstone, and Robert Orr (eds.), *Keeping the Peace: Multidimensional UN Operations in Cambodia and El Salvador* (Cambridge: Cambridge University Press, 1997).

—— and Nicholas Sambanis, 'International Peacebuilding: A Theoretical and Quantitative Analysis', *American Political Science Review*, 94/4 (2000), 778–801.

Drori, Gili S., John W. Meyer, and Hokyu Hwan (eds.), *Globalization and Organization: World Society and Organizational Change* (Oxford: Oxford University Press, 2006).

Drucker, Peter F., *The Age of Discontinuity: Guidelines to Our Changing Society* (New York: Harper & Row, 1969).

Dryzek, John S., *Rational Ecology: Environment and Political Economy* (Oxford: Blackwell, 1987).

Dryzek, John S., David Downes, Christian Hunold, Hans-Kristian Hernes, and David Scholsberg (eds.), *Green States and Social Movements: Environmental Movements in the United States, United Kingdom, Germany and Norway* (Oxford: Oxford University Press, 2003).

Dunbabin, John, 'The League of Nations' Place in the International System', *History*, 78/254 (October 1993), 421–42.

Dunn, John, 'Nation State and Human Community', published in Italian in *Stato Nazionale e Communitá Umana* (Milan: Anabasi, 1994).

Dunne, Tim, *Inventing International Society: A History of the English School* (Basingstoke, UK: Macmillan, 1998).

Dyzenhaus, David, *Legality and Legitimacy: Carl Schmitt, Hans Kelsen and Herman Heller in Weimar* (Oxford: Oxford University Press, 1999).

Eckersley, Robyn, *Environmentalism and Political Theory* (London: UCL Press, 1992).

Ellickson, Robert C., *Order Without Law: How Neighbours Settle Disputes* (Cambridge: Cambridge University Press, 1991).

Elliott, Kimberly Ann, Jeffrey J. Schott, and Gary Hufbauer, *Economic Sanctions Reconsidered*, 3rd edn. (Washington, DC: Institute for International Economics, 1999).

Elster, Jon, *The Cement of Society: A Study of Social Order* (Cambridge: Cambridge University Press, 1989).

—— 'Majoritarian Rule and Individual Rights', in Stephen Shute and Susan Hurley (eds.), *On Human Rights: The Oxford Amnesty Lectures* (New York: Basic Books, 1993), 111–34.

Evans, Peter, *Dependent Development: The Alliance of Multinational, State and Local Capital in Brazil* (Princeton, NJ: Princeton University Press, 1981).

—— *Embedded Autonomy: States and Industrial Transformation* (Princeton, NJ: Princeton University Press, 1995).

—— 'The Eclipse of the State? Reflections on Stateness in an Era of Globalization', *World Politics*, 50/1 (1997), 62–87.

Falk, Richard, *On Humane Governance: Towards a New Global Politics* (Cambridge: Polity Press, 1995).

Falkner, Robert, 'American Hegemony and the Global Environment', *International Studies Review*, 7/4 (December 2005), 585–99.

Farrell, Mary, Björn Hettne, and Luk van Langenbove (eds.), *The Global Politics of Regionalism: Theory and Practice* (London: Pluto, 2005).

Fawcett, Louise, 'Exploring Regional Domains: A Comparative History of Regionalism', *International Affairs*, 80/3 (2004), 429–46.

—— and Andrew Hurrell (eds.), *Regionalism in World Politics* (Oxford: Oxford University Press, 1995).

Ferejohn, John, 'Judicializing Politics, Politicizing Law', *Law and Contemporary Problems*, 41 (Summer 2002).

Ferguson, Niall, *Empire: The Rise and Demise of the British World Order and the Lessons for Global Power* (New York: Basic Books, 2003).

Finnemore, Martha and Kathryn Sikkink, 'International Norm Dynamics and Political Change', *International Organization*, 52/4 (1998), 887–917.

—— and Stephen J. Toope, 'Alternatives to "Legalization": Richer Views of Law and Politics', *International Organization*, 55/3 (2001).

—— *The Purposes of Intervention: Changing Beliefs about the Use of Force* (Ithaca, NY: Cornell University Press, 2003).

Florini, Anne (ed.), *The Third Force: The Rise of Transnational Civil Society* (Washington, DC: Carnegie, 2000).

Fonseca Jr, Gelson, *A Legitimidade e Outras Questões Internacionais* (São Paulo: Paz e Terra, 1998).

Foot, Rosemary, *Rights Beyond Borders. The Global Community and the Struggle over Human Rights in China* (Oxford: Oxford University Press, 2000).

—— Neil MacFarlane, and Michael Mastanduno, 'Conclusion: Instrumental Multilateralism in US Foreign Policy', in Rosemary Foot, Neil MacFarlane, and Michael Mastanduno (eds.), *US Hegemony and International Organizations* (Oxford: Oxford Univeristy Press, 2003).

—— 'Human Rights and Counterterrorism in Global Governance: Reputation and Resistance', *Global Governance*, 11/3 (Summer 2005), 291–310.

Forsythe, David P., *Human Rights in International Relations* (Cambridge: Cambridge University Press, 2000).

Fox, Gregory H., 'Democratization', in David M. Malone (ed.) *The UN Security Council: From the Cold War to the 21st Century* (Boulder, CO: Lynne Rienner, 2004).

—— and Brad R. Roth, 'Democracy and International Law', *Review of International Studies*, 27/3 (2001), 327–52.

Franck, Thomas M., *The Power of Legitimacy Among Nations* (Oxford: Oxford University Press, 1990).

—— 'The Emerging Right to Democratic Governance', *American Journal of International Law*, 86/1 (January 1992), 46–91.

—— *Fairness in International Law and Institutions* (Oxford: Clarendon Press, 1995).

Freeden, Michael, *Ideologies and Political Theory: A Conceptual Approach* (Oxford: Oxford University Press, 1996).

Freedman, Lawrence, *The Revolution in Strategic Affairs*, Adelphi Paper 318 (London: International Institute for Strategic Studies, 1998).

Friedman, Thomas L., *The World Is Flat: A Brief History of the Twenty-First Century* (New York: Farrar, Straus and Goroux, 2005).

Fukuyama, Francis, *The End of History and the Last Man* (London: Penguin, 1992).

Fuller, Lon, *The Morality of Law*, rev. edn. (New Haven, CT: Yale University Press, 1969).

Gallagher, John and Ronald Robinson, 'The Imperialism of Free Trade', *Economic History Review*, 6/1 (1953), 1–15.

Gambetta, Diego, *The Sicilian Mafia: The Business of Private Protection* (Cambridge, MA: Harvard University Press, 1993).

Gamble, Andrew and Anthony Payne (eds.), *Regionalism and World Order* (Basingstoke, UK: Palgrave, 1996).

Gardiner, Stephen M., 'Ethics and Global Climate Change', *Ethics*, 114 (April 2004), 555–600.

Garrett, Geoff, 'Global Markets and National Politics: Collision Course or Virtuous Circle', *International Organization*, 52/4 (1998), 787–824.

Gat, Azar, *War in Human Civilization* (Oxford: Oxford University Press, 2006).

Gellner, Ernest, *Nations and Nationalism* (Oxford: Basil Blackwell, 1983).

Ghai, Yash, 'Human Rights and Governance: The Asia Debate', Occasional Paper, Center for Asian Pacific Affairs, November 1994.

Gilderhus, Mark T., 'Pan-American Initiatives: The Wilson Presidency and "Regional Integration", 1914–1917', *Diplomatic History* (Fall 1980), esp. 415–17.

—— *Pan-American Visions: Woodrow Wilson and the Western Hemisphere, 1913–1921* (Tucson, AZ: University of Arizona Press, 1986).

Gilpin, Robert, *War and Change in World Politics* (New York: Cambridge University Press, 1981).

—— *The Political Economy of International Relations* (Princeton, NJ: Princeton University Press, 1987).

Gleditsch, Nils Pieter, 'Armed Conflict and the Environment: A Critique of the Literature', *Journal of Peace Research*, 35/3 (May 1998), 381–400.

Glennon, Michael J., 'Why the Security Council Failed', *Foreign Affairs*, 82/3 (May/June 2003), 16–35.

Goldsmith, Jack L. and Eric A. Posner, *The Limits of International Law* (Oxford: Oxford University Press, 2005).

Goodin, Robert E., *Green Political Theory* (Cambridge: Polity Press, 1992).

Grant, Ruth and Robert O. Keohane, 'Accountability and Abuses of Power in World Politics', *American Political Science Review*, 99/1 (February 2004), 29–43.

Griffin, James, 'Discrepancies between the Best Philosophical Account of Human Rights and International Law of Human Rights' *Proceedings of the Aristotelian Society*, 101 (2000), 1–28.

Grigg, David, 'The Logic of Regional Systems', *Annals of the Association of American Geographers*, 55/3 (September 1965), 465–91.

Grotius, Hugo, *The Rights of War and Peace* (ed. with an introduction) Richard Tuck (Philadelphia: Liberty Fund, 2005), book 1, ch. 1. Available at: http://oll.Libertyfund. org/Intros/Grotius.php

Grubb, Michael, 'Seeking Fair Weather: Ethics and the International Debate on Climate Change', *International Affairs*, 71/3 (1995), 465–6.

Gruber, Lloyd, *Ruling the World: Power Politics and the Rise of Supranational Institutions* (Princeton, NJ: Princeton University Press, 2000).

Guha, Ramachandra and Juan Martinez-Allier (eds.), *Varieties of Environmentalism* (London: Earthscan, 1997).

Gurr, Ted Robert, 'Peoples Against States: Ethnopolitical Conflict and the Changing World System', *International Studies Quarterly*, 38/3 (1994), 347–77.

Haas, Peter M. (ed.), 'Knowledge, Power and International Policy Coordination', special issue of *International Organization*, 46/1 (1992).

——— 'Epistemic Communities and the Dynamics of International Environmental Governance', in Volker Rittberger (ed.), *Regime Theory and International Relations* (Oxford: Oxford University Press, 1995).

——— 'Social Constructivism and the Evolution of Multilateral Environmental Governance', in Aseem Prakash and Jeffrey A. Hart (eds.), *Globalization and Governance* (New York: Routledge, 1999), 103–33.

——— Robert O. Keohane, and Mark Levy (eds.), *Institutions for the Earth* (Cambridge, MA: MIT Press, 1993).

Habermas, Jürgen, *Between Facts and Norms: Contributions to a Discourse Theory of Law and Democracy* (Cambridge: Polity Press, 1996).

Hafner-Burton, Emilie and Kiyotera Tsutsui, 'Human Rights in a Globalizing World: The Paradox of Empty Promises', *American Journal of Sociology*, 110/5 (2005), 1373–411.

Halliday, Fred, *Revolution and World Politics: The Rise and Fall of the Sixth Great Power* (Basingstoke, UK: Macmillan, 1999).

Hampshire, Stuart, *Justice is Conflict* (London: Duckworth, 1999).

Hardin, Russell, *One for All: The Logic of Group Conflict* (Princeton, UK: Princeton University Press, 1995).

Hardt, Michael, 'Today's Bandung?', *New Left Review*, II/14 (March–April 2002) 112–18.

——— and Antonio Negri, *Empire* (Cambridge, MA: Harvard University Press, 2000).

Harris, Ian, 'Order and Justice in "The Anarchical Society"', *International Affairs*, 69 (1993), 725–41.

Hart, H. L. A., *The Concept of Law* (Oxford: Oxford University Press, 1961).

Hasenclever, Andreas, Peter, Mayer, and Volker Rittberger, *Theories of International Regimes* (Cambridge: Cambridge University Press, 1997).

Hashmi, Sohail H., 'Political Boundaries and Moral Communities: Islamic Perspectives', in Allen Buchanan and Margaret Moore (eds.), *States, Nations and Borders: The Ethics of Making Boundaries* (Cambridge: Cambridge University Press, 2003), 181–213.

Haslam, Jonathan, *No Virtue Like Necessity: Realist Thought in International Relations Since Machiavelli* (New Haven, CT: Yale University Press, 2002).

Hayward, Jack and Anand Menon (eds.), *Governing Europe* (Oxford: Oxford University Press, 2003).

Hechter, Michael, 'The Role of Values in Rational Choice Theory', *Rationality and Society*, 6/3 (July 1994), 318–33.

Held, David, *Democracy and Global Order: From the Modern State to Cosmopolitan Governance* (Cambridge: Polity Press, 1995).

——— and Anthony McGrew (eds.), *The Global Transformations Reader*, 2nd edn. (Cambridge: Polity Press, 2003).

——— ——— David Goldblatt, and Jonathan Perraton, *Global Transformations* (Stanford, CA: Stanford University Press, 1999).

Henkin, Louis, 'International Human Rights and Rights in the United States', in Theodor Meron (ed.), *Human Rights in International Law: Legal and Policy Issues* (Oxford: Oxford University Press, 1989).

Herbst, Jeffrey, 'Responding to State Failure in Africa', *International Security*, 21/3 (Winter 1996–7), 120–44.

—— 'Crafting Regional Cooperation in Africa,' in Amitav Acharya and Alistair Ian Johnston (eds.), *Crafting Cooperation: Regional International Institutions in Comparative Perspective* (Cambridge: Cambridge University Press, 2007).

Hettne, Björn, András Inotai, and Oswaldo Sunkel (eds.), *Globalism and the New Regionalism* (Basingstoke, UK: Macmillan, 1999).

Higgins, Rosalyn, *Problems and Process: International Law and How We Use It* (Oxford: Oxford University Press, 1994).

Hinsley, F. H., *Power and the Pursuit of Peace: Theory and Practice in the History of Relations between States* (Cambridge: Cambridge University Press, 1963; (reprinted in 1980).

Hirschman, Albert O., *The Passions and the Interests: Political Arguments for Capitalism before Its Triumph* (Princeton, NJ: Princeton University Press, 1977).

Hirst, Paul, *War and Power in the 21st Century* (Cambridge: Polity Press, 2001).

Hirst, Paul, and Graham Thompson, *Globalization in Question: The International Economy and the Possibilities of Governance* (Cambridge: Polity Press, 1996).

Hix, Simon, *The Political System of the European Union* (Basingstoke, UK: Palgrave, 1999).

Hobbes, Thomas, *Leviathan* Richard Tuck ed., (Cambridge: Cambridge University Press, 1996).

Hobsbawm, E. J., *Nations and Nationalism Since 1870: Programme, Myth, Reality* (Cambridge: Cambridge University Press, 1992).

Hoekman, Bernard M. and Michel M. Kostecki, *The Political Economy of the World Trading System: The WTO and Beyond*, 2nd edn. (Oxford: Oxford University Press, 2001).

Hoffmann, Stanley, 'Conference Report on the Conditions of World Order', *Daedalus*, 95/2 (1966), 455–78.

—— 'An American Social Science: International Relations', in *Janus and Minerva: Essays in the Theory and Practice of International Politics* (Boulder, CO: Westview, 1987).

—— 'Why Don't They Like Us?', in Eugene R. Wittkopf and James M. MacCormick (eds.), *The Domestic Sources of American Foreign Policy. Insights and Evidence* (Lanham, MD: Rowman & Littlefield, 2004), 33–41.

Hollis, Martin, 'Why Elster is Stuck and Needs to Recover His Faith', *London Review of Books*, 13/2 (24 January 1991).

Holmes, James R., *Theodore Roosevelt and World Order: International Police Power in International Relations* (Washington, DC: Potomac Books, 2006).

Holzgrefe, J. L. and Robert O. Keohane (eds.), *Humanitarian Intervention: Ethical, Legal and Political Dilemmas* (Cambridge: Cambridge University Press, 2004).

Homer-Dixon, Thomas F., 'Environmental Scarcities and Violent Conflict: Evidence from Cases', *International Security*, 19/1 (1994), 5–40.

Hopgood, Stephen, *Keepers of the Flame. Understanding Amnesty International* (Ithaca, NY: Cornell University Press, 2006).

Houweling, Jenk W., 'Destabilizing Consequences of Sequential Development', in Luc van de Goor, Kumar Rupesinghe, and Paul Sciarone (eds.), *Between Development and Destruction: An Enquiry into the Causes of Conflict in Post-Colonial States* (Basingstoke, UK: Macmillan, 1996), 143–69.

Howard, Michael, *War and the Liberal Conscience* (Oxford: Oxford University Press, 1989).

____ *The Lessons of History* (Oxford: Oxford University Press, 1991).

____ 'The United Nations and International Security,' in Adam Roberts and Benedict Kingsbury (eds.), *United Nations, Divided World*, 2nd edn. (Oxford: Oxford University Press, 1993).

Howse, Robert and Kalypso Nicolaidis, 'Enhancing WTO Legitimacy: Constitutionalization or Global Subsidiarity?' *Governance*, 16/1 (2003), 73–4. Multilateral Organization.

Huntington, Samuel P., *Political Order in Changing Societies* (New Haven, CT: Yale University Press, 1968).

____ *The Third Wave: Democratization in the Late Twentieth Century* (London: University of Oklahoma Press/Norman, 1991).

____ *The Clash of Civilizations and the Remaking of World Order* (New York: Simon and Schuster, 1996).

____ *Who Are We? America's Great Debate* (New York: Free Press, 2004).

Hurd, Ian, 'Legitimacy and Authority in International Politics', *International Organization*, 32/2 (1999), 379–408.

Hurrell, Andrew, 'Kant and the Kantian Paradigm in International Relations', *Review of International Studies*, 16 (1990), 183–205.

____ and Ngaire Woods, 'Globalisation and Inequality', *Millennium*, 24/3 (1995), 447–70.

____ 'Vattel: Pluralism and Its Limits', in Ian Clark and Iver Neumann (eds.), *Classical Theories of International Relations* (Basingstoke, UK: Macmillan, 1996), 233–55.

____ 'Global Inequality and International Institutions', in Thomas Pogge (ed.), *Global Justice* (Cambridge: Polity Press, 2001), 32–54.

____ 'Norms and Ethics in International Relations,' in Walter Carlsnaes, Thomas Risse, and Beth Simmons (eds.), *The Handbook of International Relations* (London: Sage, 2002), 137–54.

____ ' "There Are No Rules" (George W Bush): International Order after September 11', *International Relations*, 16/2 (2002), 186–93.

____ 'Hegemony in a Region That Dares not Speak Its Name', *International Journal*, 61/3 (Fall 2006), 545–66.

____ 'Hegemony, Liberalism and Global Order', *International Affairs*, 82/1 (January 2006): 12–16.

Hutchinson, John and Anthony D. Smith, *Nationalism* (Oxford: Oxford University Press, 1994).

Huxley, Aldous, *Ends and Means: An Enquiry into the Nature of Ideals and into the Methods Employed for Their Realization* (London: Chatto & Windus, 1937).

ICISS, *The Responsibility to Protect: Report of the International Commission on Intervention and State Sovereignty* (Ottawa: IDRC, 2001).

Ignatieff, Michael, *Blood and Belonging: Journeys into the New Nationalism* (London: Vintage Books, 1993).

Ikenberry, G. John, 'American Grand Strategy in the Age of Terror', *Survival*, 43/4 (Winter 2001), 19–34.

____ *After Victory: Institutions, Strategic Restraint, and the Rebuilding of Order After Major Wars* (Princeton, NJ: Princeton University Press, 2001).

Ikenberry, G. John, 'America's Imperial Ambition', *Foreign Affairs*, 81/5 (2002), 44–60.

Iriye, Akira, *Global Community: The Role of International Organizations in the Making of the Contemporary World* (Berkeley, CA: University of California Press, 2002).

Jackson, Robert, *The Global Covenant: Human Conduct in a World of States* (Oxford: Oxford University Press, 2000).

Jennings, R. Y., *The Acquisition of Territory in International Law* (Manchester, UK: Manchester University Press, 1963).

Jervis, Robert, 'A Political Science Perspective on the Balance of Power', *American Journal of Political Science*, 97/3 (June 1992), 716–24.

____ *System Effects: Complexity in Political and Social Life* (Princeton, NJ: Princeton University Press, 1997).

____ 'Theories of War in an Era of Leading-Power Peace', *American Political Science Review*, 96/1 (March 2002), 1–14.

Joerges, Christian and Ellen Vos, *EU Committees: Social Regulation, Law and Politics* (Oxford: Hart, 1999).

Jones, Candace, William S. Hesterly, and Stephen P. Borgatti, 'A General Theory of Network Governance: Exchange Conditions and Social Mechanisms', *The Academy of Management Review*, 22/4 (1997), 911–45.

Johnson, Douglas M., *Consent and Commitment in the World Community: The Classification and Analysis of International Instruments* (New York: Transnational, 1997), 8.

Jordan, Andrew, Rüdiger K. W. Wurzel, and Anthony Zito, 'The Rise of "New" Policy Instruments in Comparative Perspective: Has Governance Eclipsed Government?', *Political Studies*, 53/3 (2005), 477–96.

Joyner, Christopher C., 'The United Nations and Democracy', *Global Governance*, 5/3 (1999), 333–57.

Judt, Tony, *Postwar: A History of Europe since 1945* (London: Heineman, 2005).

Kagan, Robert, *Paradise and Power: America and Europe in the New World Order* (London: Atlantic Books, 2003).

____ 'America's Crisis of Legitimacy', *Foreign Affairs*, 83/2 (March–April 2004), 65–87.

Kahler, Miles, 'Inventing International Relations: International Relations Since 1945', in Michael W. Doyle and G. John Ikenberry (eds.), *New Thinking in International Relations* (Oxford: Westview Press, 1997), 20–53.

____ and David A. Lake (eds.), *Governance in a Global Economy* (Princeton, NJ: Princeton University Press, 2003).

Kaldor, Mary, *New and Old Wars: Organized Violence in a Global Era* (Cambridge: Polity Press, 2002).

Kant, Immanuel, 'Perpetual Peace: A Philosophical Sketch', in Hans Reiss (ed.), *Kant: Political Writings*, 2nd edn. (Cambridge: Cambridge University Press, 1991), 93–115.

Kaplan, Robert D., *The Coming Anarchy: Shattering the Dreams of the Post-Cold War World* (New York: Vintage, 2001).

Kassim, Hussein, 'Policy Networks, Networks and European Union Policy Making: A Sceptical View', *West European Politics*, 17/4 (1994), 15–27.

Katzenstein, Peter, *A World of Regions: Asia and Europe in the American Imperium* (Ithaca, NY: Cornell University Press, 2005).

Kausikan, Bilahari, 'Asia's Different Standard', *Foreign Policy*, 92 (Fall 1993), 24–41.

Keane, John, *Democracy and Civil Society: On the Predicaments of European Socialism, the Prospects for Democracy, and the Problem of Controlling Social and Political Power* (London: Verso, 1988).

——— *Reflections on Violence* (London: Verso, 1996).

Keck, Margaret and Kathryn Sikkink, *Activists Beyond Borders* (Ithaca, NY: Cornell University Press, 1998).

Kedourie, Elie, *Nationalism*, 4th edn. (Oxford: Blackwell, 1993).

Keene, Edward, *Beyond the Anarchical Society: Grotius, Colonialism and Order in World Politics* (Cambridge: Cambridge University Press, 2002).

Kennedy, David, 'New Approaches to Comparative Law: Comparativism and International Governance', *Utah Law Review*, 2 (1997), 545–637.

——— *The Dark Sides of Virtue: Reassessing International Humanitarianism* (Princeton, NJ: Princeton University Press, 2004).

Kennedy, Paul, *The Parliament of Man: The United Nations and the Quest for World Government* (London: Allen Lane, 2006).

Kenwood, A. G., and Lougheed A. L. 'The Conception of an Order in International Economic Relations'. Unpublished paper, 1978.

Keohane, Robert O., 'Institutionalist Theory and the Realist Challenge after the Cold War', in David A. Baldwin (ed.), *Neorealism and Neoliberalism: The Contemporary Debate* (New York: Columbia University Press, 1993), 269–301.

——— and Joseph S. Nye, 'Introduction,' in Joseph S. Nye and John D. Donahue (eds.), *Governance in a Globalising World* (Washington, DC: Brookings Institute, 2000).

——— *Power and Governance in a Partially Globalized World* (London: Routledge, 2002).

——— and Joseph S. Nye Jr, 'Redefining Accountability for Global Governance', in Miles Kahler and David A. Lake (2003), 386–411.

Khilnani, Sunil, 'The Development of Civil Society', in Sudipta Kaviraj and Sunil Khilnani (eds.), *Civil Society: History and Possibilities* (Cambridge: Cambridge University Press, 2001), 11–32.

Killick,Tony, *Aid and the Political Economy of Policy Change* (London: Routledge, 1998).

Kindleberger, Charles, *Europe and the Dollar* (Cambridge, MA: MIT Press, 1966).

Kingsbury, Benedict, 'A Grotian Tradition of Theory and Practice: Grotius, Law and Moral Skepticism in the Thought of Hedley Bull', in Ian Clark and Iver B. Neumann (eds.), *Classical Theories of International Relations* (Basingstoke, UK: Palgrave, 1996), 42–70.

——— 'Legal Positivism as Normative Politics: International Society, Balance of Power, and Lassa Oppenheim's Positive International Law', *European Journal of International Law*, 13/2 (April 2002), 401–37.

——— 'The International Legal Order', in Peter Cane and Makr Tushnet (eds.), *Oxford Handbook of Legal Studies* (Oxford: Oxford University Press, 2003), 271–97.

——— Nico, Krisch and Richard B. Stewart, 'The Emergence of Global Administrative Law', *Law and Contemporary Problems*, 68/3/4 (2005), 15–62.

Kissinger, Henry A., *A World Restored* (London: Weidenfeld & Nicolson, 1957).

——— *American Foreign Policy*, 3rd edn. (New York: W.W. Norton, 1977).

——— *Diplomacy* (London: Simon and Schuster, 1994).

Klare, Michael T., *Resource Wars: The New Landscape of Global Conflict* (New York: Henry Holt, 2002).

Klayvas, Stathis N., ' "New" and "Old" Civil Wars: A Valid Distinction', *World Politics*, 54/1 (2001), 99–118.

—— *The Logic of Violence in Civil War* (Cambridge: Cambridge University Press, 2006).

Klein, Pierre, 'The Effects of US Predominance on the Elaboration of Treaty Regimes and on the Evolution of the Law of Treaties', in Michael Byers and Georg Nolte (eds.), *United States Hegemony and the Foundations of International Law* (Cambridge: Cambridge University Press, 2003), 363–91.

Knorr, Klaus, 'Is International Coercion Waning or Rising?', *International Security*, 1/4 (1977), 92–110.

Koh, Harold, 'Why Do Nations Obey International Law?', *Yale Law Journal*, 106/8 (1997), 2599–659.

Kojève, Alexandre, 'Outline of a Doctrine of French Policy', trans. by Erik de Vries, commentary by Robert Howse, *Policy Review* (27 August 1945), http://www.policyreview.org/aug04 accessed 05/11/2004.

Koreniewiecz, Roberto P. and William C. Smith, 'Transnational Social Movements Elite Projects, and Collective Action from Below in the Americas', in Louise Fawcett and Monica Serrano (eds.), *Regionalism and Governance in the Americas* (Basingstoke, UK: Palgrave, 2005).

Koskenniemi, Martti, 'The Pull of the Mainstream', review of Theodor Meron, in *Human Rights and Humanitarian Norms as Customary Law* (Oxford: Clarendon Press, 1989), *Michigan Law Review*, 88/6, 1990, 1946–62.

—— *The Gentle Civilizer of Nations: The Rise and Fall of International Law, 1870–1960* (Cambridge: Cambridge University Press, 2002).

Kramer, Paul A., 'Empires, Exceptions, and Anglo-Saxons: Race and Rule between the British and United States Empires, 1880–1910', *The Journal of American History*, 88/4 (March 2002), 1315–53.

Krasner, Stephen D., *Sovereignty: Organized Hypocrisy* (Princeton, NJ: Princeton University Press, 1999).

—— 'Sharing Sovereignty: New Institutions for Collapsed and Failing States', *International Security*, 29/2 (Fall 2004), 85–120.

Krause, Keith and Michael C. Williams (eds.), *Critical Security Studies: Concepts and Cases* (Minneapolis, MN: University of Minnesota Press, 1998).

Krisch, Nico, 'Weak as Constraint, Strong as Tool: The Place of International Law in U.S. Foreign Policy', in David M. Malone and Yuen Foong Khong (eds.), *Unilateralism and U.S. Foreign Policy* (Boulder, CO: Lynne Rienner, 2003), 41–70.

—— 'More Equal Than the Rest? Hierarchy, Equality and US Predominance in International Law', in Georg Nolte and Michael Byers (eds.), *United States Hegemony and the Foundations of International Law* (Cambridge: Cambridge University Press, 2003), 135–75.

—— 'International Law in Times of Hegemony: Unequal Power and the Shaping of the International Legal Order', *European Journal of International Law*, 16/3 (June 2005), 369–408.

Laïdi, Zaki, *La Norme sans la Force: L'énigme e la puissance européne* (Paris: Presses Sciences-Po, 2005).

Laitin, David, *Identity Formation: The Russian Speaking Populations in the Near Abroad* (Ithaca, NY: Cornell University Press, 1998).

Lake, David A., 'Anarchy, Hierarchy, and the Variety of International Relations', *International Organization*, 50/1 (Winter 1996), 1–33.

Lal, Deepak, *Reviving the Invisible Hand: The Case for Classical Liberalism in the 21st Century* (Princeton, NJ: Princeton University Press, 2006).

Lansing, Robert, *The Peace Negotiations: A Personal Narrative* (Boston, MA: Houghton Mifflin, 1921).

Lauterpacht, Hersch, 'The Grotian Tradition in International Law', *British Yearbook of International Law* (1946), 1–53.

League of Nations, *The Aaland Islands Question: Report Presented to the Council of the League by the Commission of Rapporteurs*, League of Nations Doc.B.7.21/68/106,1921.

Leffler, Melvin, *A Preponderance of Power: National Security, the Truman Administration and the Cold War* (Stanford, CA: Stanford University Press, 2002).

Lemke, Douglas, 'African Lessons for International Relations Research', *World Politics*, 56/1 (2003), 114–38.

Levy, Marc, 'Is the Environment a National Security Issue?', *International Security*, 20/2 (1995), 35–62.

Lichbach, March Irving, 'An Evaluation of "Does Economic Inequality Breed Political Conflict?" Studies', *World Politics*, 41/4 (July 1989), 431–70.

Linklater, Andrew, *The Transformation of Political Community. Ethical Foundations of the Post-Wetphalian Era* (Cambridge: Polity Press, 1998).

——— and Hidemi Suganami, *The English School of International Relations: A Contemporary Reassessment* (Cambridge: Cambridge University Press, 2006).

Lipshutz, Ronnie D., 'Reconstructing World Politics: The Emergence of Global Civil Society', *Millennium*, 21/3 (1992), 389–420.

——— and Ken Conca, 'The Implications of Global Ecological Interdependence', in Ronnie D. Lipschutz and Ken Conca (eds.), *The State and Social Power in Global Environmental Politics* (New York: Columbia University Press, 1993), 327–43.

Liska, George, *Imperial America: The International Politics of Primacy* (Baltimore, MD: Johns Hopkins University Press, 1967).

Litfin, Karen T. (ed.), *The Greening of Sovereignty in World Politics* (Cambridge, MA: MIT Press, 1998).

Lomborg, Bjørn, *The Skeptical Environmentalist: Measuring the Real State of the World* (Cambridge: Cambridge University Press, 2001).

Lowe, Vaughan, Inaugural Lecture, Oxford, 14 May 2001.

Luck, Edward C., 'Article 2(4) on the Non-Use of Force: What Were We Thinking?', in David P. Forsythe, Patrice C. McMahon, and Andrew Wedeman (eds.), *American Foreign Policy in a Globalized World* (London: Routledge, 2006), 77–121.

Lukes, Steven, *Power: A Radical Analysis* (London: Macmillan, 1974).

Lutz, Ellen and Kathryn Sikkink, 'The Justice Cascade: The Evolution and Impact of Human Rights Trials in Latin America', *Chicago Journal of International Law*, 2/1 (2001), 1–34.

MacCormick, Neil, 'Liberalism, Nationalism and the Post-sovereign State', *Political Studies*, 44/Special Issue (1996), 553–67.

Macdonald, Terry, ' "We the Peoples": NGOS and Democratic Representation in Global Politics'. (DPhil thesis, Oxford University Press, 2005).

MacFarlane, S. Neil and Yuen Foong Khong, *Human Security and the UN: A Critical History* (Bloomington, MN: Indiana University Press, 2006).

MacIntyre, Alasdair, *Whose Justice? Whose Rationality?* (London: Duckworth, 1985), 6.

Mack, Andrew, 'Why Big Nations Lose Small Wars: The Politics of Asymmetric Conflict', *World Politics*, 27/2 (January 1975), 175–200.

Macmillan, Margaret, *Paris 1919: Six Months That Changed the World* (New York: Random House, 2003).

Majone, Giandomenico, 'From the Positive to the Regulatory State: Causes and Consequences of Changes in the Mode of Governance', *Journal of Public Policy*, 17/2 (1997), 139–67.

Malcolm, Noel, 'Hobbes' Theory of International Relations', in *Aspects of Hobbes* (Oxford: Oxford University Press, 2002), 432–56.

Malone, David, *The International Struggle over Iraq: Politics in the UN Security Council, 1980–2005* (Oxford: Oxford University Press, 2006).

Manners, Ian, 'Normative Power Europe: A Contradiction in Terms?', *Journal of Common Market Studies*, 40/2 (2002), 235–58.

Mannoni, Stefano, *Potenza e Ragione: La Scienza del Diritto Internazionale nella Crisi Dell'Equlibrio Europeo (1870–1914)* (Milan: Editore Guiffre, 1999).

Mansfield, Edward D. and Helen V. Milner, 'The New Wave of Regionalism', *International Organization*, 53/3 (1999), 602–8.

—— and Jack Snyder, 'Democratization and the Danger of War', *International Security*, 20/1 (Summer 1995), 5–38.

March, James G. and Johan P. Olson, *Rediscovering Institutions: The Organizational Basis of Politics* (New York: Free Press, 1989).

Martin, James, *The Meaning of the 21st Century* (London: Edenprojectbooks, 2006).

Martinez-Allier, Juan, *The Environmentalism of the Poor: A Study of Ecological Conflicts and Valuation* (London: Edward Elgar, 2003).

Mastanduno, Michael, 'Preserving the Unipolar Moment: Realist Theories and U.S. Grand Strategy After the Cold War', in Ethan B. Kapstein and Michael Mastanduno (eds.), *Unipolar Politics: Realism and State Strategies After the Cold War* (New York: Columbia University Press, 1999).

Masters, Roger D., 'A Multi-Bloc Model of the International System', *American Political Science Review*, LV/4 (1961), 780–98.

Matthews, Jessica Tuchman, 'Redefining Security', *Foreign Affairs*, 68/2 (Spring 1989), 162–77.

Mattli, Walter, 'Private Justice in a Global Economy: From Litigation to Arbitration', *International Organization*, 55/4 (Autumn 2001), 919–47.

—— and Tim Büthe, 'Setting International Standards. Technological Rationality or the Primacy of Power', *World Politics*, 56/1 (October 2003), 1–42.

May, Ernest R., *American Imperialism: A Speculative Essay* (New York: Atheneum, 1968).

Mayall, James, *Nationalism and International Society* (Cambridge: Cambridge University Press, 1990).

—— *World Politics: Progress and Its Limits* (Cambridge: Polity Press, 2000).

Mazower, Mark, *Dark Continent: Europe's Twentieth Century* (Harmondsworth, UK: Penguin Books, 1999).

McLellan, David (ed.), *Karl Marx: Selected Writings* (Oxford: Oxford University Press, 1977).

McNeill, W. H., *The Rise of the West: A History of the Human Community* (Chicago, IL: Chicago University Press, 1963).

—— *Arnold J Toynbee: A Life* (Oxford: Oxford University Press, 1989).

Mearsheimer, John J., 'The False Promise of International Institutions', *International Institutions*, 19/3 (Winter 1994–5), 5–49.

—— *The Tragedy of Great Power Politics* (New York: W.W. Norton, 2001).

Mertens, Hans-Joachim, '*Lex Mercatoria*: A Self-Applying System Beyond National Law', in Gunther Teubner (ed.), *Global Law Without a State* (Aldershot, UK: Dartmouth, 1997), 31–43.

Meyer, John W., John Boli, George M. Thomas, and Francisco O. Ramirez, 'World Society and the Nation-State', *American Journal of Sociology*, 103/1 (1997), 144–81.

Milanovic, Branko, 'The Two Faces of Globalization: Against Globalization as We Know It', *World Development*, 4/4 (2003), 667–83.

Miller, David, 'Introduction', in David Miller and Michael Walzer (eds.), *Pluralism, Justice, and Equality* (Oxford: Oxford University Press, 1995), 2.

—— *On Nationality* (Oxford: Clarendon Press, 1995).

—— 'Justice and Global Inequality', in Andrew Hurrell and Ngarie Woods (eds.), *Globalization and Inequality* (Oxford: Oxford University Press, 1999), 190.

Mitchell, Ronald B., 'International Environment', in Walter Carlsnaes, Thomas Risse, and Beth Simmons (eds.), *The Handbook of International Relations* (London: Sage, 2002), 500–16.

Moravcsik, Andrew, *The Choice for Europe: Social Purpose and State Power from Messina to Maastricht* (Ithaca, NY: Cornell University Press, 1998).

—— 'The Origins of Human Rights Regimes: Democratic Delegation in Postwar Europe', *International Organization*, 54/2 (2000), 217–52.

—— 'Liberal International Relations Theory: A Scientific Assessment', in Colin Elman and Miriam Fendius Elman (eds.), *Progress in International Relations Theory* (Cambridge, MA: MIT Press, 2002), 159–204.

—— 'In Defence of the "Democratic Deficit": Reassessing the Legitimacy of the European Union', *Journal of Common Market Studies*, 40/4 (2002), 603–24.

Morgenthau, Hans J., 'Positivism, Functionalism and International Law', *American Journal of International Law*, 34/2 (April 1940), 260–84.

—— *American Foreign Policy* (New York: Alfred A. Knopf, 1951), 35.

—— *Politics Among Nations: The Struggle for Power and Peace*, 2nd edn. (New York: Alfred A. Knopf, 1959).

—— *The Purpose of American Politics* (New York: Alfred A. Knopf, 1960).

Müller, Jan-Werner, *A Dangerous Mind: Carl Schmitt in Post-war European Thought* (New Haven, UK: Yale University Press, 2003).

Mueller, John, *Retreat from Doomsday: The Obsolescence of Major War* (New York: Basic Books, 1990).

Muñoz, Heraldo, 'The Right to Democracy in the Americas', *Journal of Interamerican Studies and World Affairs*, 40/1 (Spring 1998), 1–18.

Murphy, Craig, *International Organizations and Industrial Change* (Oxford: Oxford University Press, 1994).

Musil, Robert, *The Man Without Qualities*, trans. Sophie Wilkins and Burton Pike (London: Picador, 1995).

Muthu, Sankar, *Enlightenment Against Empire* (Princeton, NJ: Princeton University Press, 2003).

Myers, Norman, *Ultimate Security: The Environmental Basis of Political Security* (New York: W.W. Norton, 1993).

Nagel, Thomas, *The View from Nowhere* (Oxford: Oxford University Press, 1986).

—— 'The Problem of Global Justice', *Philosophy and Public Affairs*, 33/2 (2005).

Nardin, Terry, *Law, Morality and the Relations of States* (Princeton, NJ: Princeton University Press, 1983), 9.

Narlikar, Amrita, *The World Trade Organization: A Very Short Introduction* (Oxford: Oxford University Press, 2005).

—— and Ngaire Woods, 'Governance and Accountability: The WTO, the IMF, and the World Bank', *International Social Science Journal*, 53/170 (2001), 569–83.

Nash, Roderick Frazier, *Wilderness and the American Mind*, 3rd edn. (New Haven, CT: Yale University Press, 1982).

Nau, Henry R., 'The Truth about American Unilateralism', *The American Outlook* (Fall 2003).

Neff, Stephen C., 'A Short History of Internaitonal Law', in Malcom Evans (ed.), *International Law* (Oxford: Oxford University Press, 2003), 41–5.

Nicolaidis, Kalypso and Robert Howse, ' "This is my EUtopia" Narrative as Power', *Journal of Common Market Studies*, 40/4 (2002), 767–92.

Niebuhr, Reinhold, 'The Illusion of World Government', *Foreign Affairs*, 27 (1948–9), 379.

Nielsen, Kai, 'World Government, Security and Global Justice', in Steven Luper-Foy (ed.), *Problems of International Justice* (Boulder, CO: Westview, 1988), 263–82.

Nielson, Daniel L. and Michael J. Tierney, 'Delegation to International Organizations: Agency Theory and World Bank Environmental Reform', *International Organizaton*, 57 (Spring 2003), 241–76.

Niño, Carlos Santiago, *The Ethics of Human Rights* (Oxford: Clarendon Press, 1991).

Northedge, F. S., *The League of Nations: Its Life and Times, 1920–1946* (Leicester, UK: Leicester University Press, 1986).

Nye, Joseph S. (ed.), *International Regionalism: Readings* (Boston, MA: Little, Brown and Co., 1968).

—— and John D. Donahue (eds.), *Governance in a Globalizing World* (Washington, DC: Brookings Institution, 2000).

—— and Robert O. Keohane, 'Globalization: What's New? And What's Not? (And So What?)', *Foreign Policy*, 118 (Spring 2000), 104–19.

—— *Soft Power: The Means to Succeed in World Politics* (New York: Public Affairs, 2004).

O'Brien, Conor Cruise, *The United Nations: Sacred Drama* (London: Hutchinson, 1968).

Offer, Avner, 'Going to War in 1914: A Matter of Honour?', *Politics and Society*, 23/2 (June 1995), 213–41.

Ohmae, Kenichi, 'The Rise of the Region State', *Foreign Affairs*, 72/2 (Spring 1993), 78–87.

Ondaatje, Michael, *Anil's Ghost* (London: Picador, 2001).

O'Neill, Onora, *Towards Justice and Virtue: A Constructive Account of Practical Reasoning* (Cambridge: Cambridge University Press, 1996), ch. 4.

—— *Bounds of Justice* (Cambridge: Cambridge University Press, 2000), 22.

Onuma, Yasuaki, 'Eurocentrism in the History of International Law', in Yasuaki Onuma (ed.), *A Normative Approach to War: Peace, War and Justice in Hugo Grotius* (Oxford: Clarendon Press, 1993), 371–86.

Ophuls Jr, William, *Ecology and the Politics of Scarcity Revisited* (New York: W.H. Freeman, 1992).

Oppenheim, Lassa, *International Law: A Treatise*, vol. 1 (London: Longman, Green & Co, 1905).

O'Rourke, Kevin H. and Jeffrey G. Williamson, *Globalization and History. The Evolution of a Nineteenth Century Atlantic Economy* (Cambridge, MA: MIT Press, 1999).

Osiander, Andreas, 'Sovereignty, International Relations and the Westphalian Myth', *International Organization*, 55/2 (Spring 2001), 251–87.

Palma, Gabriel, 'Dependency and Development: A Critical Overview', in Dudley Seers (ed.), *Dependency Theory. A Critical Reassessment* (London: Pinter, 1981), 20–78.

Pakenham, Robert, *Liberal America and the Third World* (Princeton, NJ: Princeton University Press, 1973).

Pape, Robert A., 'The Strategic Logic of Suicide Terrorism', *American Political Science Review*, 97/3 (2002), 343–61.

Pastor, Robert A., 'North America and the Americas: Integration among Unequal Partners', in Mary Farrell, Björn Hettne, and Luk van Langenbove (eds.), *The Global Politics of Regionalism: Theory and Practice* (London: Pluto, 2005), 210–21.

Pasquino, Pasquale, 'Political Theory of Peace and War: Foucault and the History of Modern Political Theory', *Economy and Society*, 22/1 (February 1993), 77–88.

Paterson, Matthew, 'Interpreting Trends in Global Environmental Governance', *International Affairs*, 75/4 (1999), 793–802.

Paul, T. V. and John Hall (eds.), *International Order and the Future of World Politics* (Cambridge: Cambridge University Press, 1999).

Paulus, Andreas, *Die internationale Gemeinschaft im Völkerrecht* (Munich: Beck, 2001).

Percy, Sarah, *Regulating the Private Security Industry*, Adelphi Paper 384 (London: International Institute for Strategic Studies, 2007).

Pettit, Philip, 'Democracy, Electoral and Contestatory', *Nomos*, 42 (2000), 105–44.

Pierre, Jon, *Debating Governance. Authority, Steering and Democracy* (Oxford: Oxford University Press, 2000).

—— and B. Guy Peters, *Governance, Politics and the State* (Basingstoke, UK: Macmillan, 2000).

Piscatori, James, *Islam in a World of Nation-States* (Cambridge: Cambridge University Press, 1986).

—— 'Order, Justice and Global Islam', in Rosemary Foot, John L. Gaddis, and Andrew Hurrell (eds.), *Order and Justice in International Relations* (Oxford: Oxford University Press, 2003), 262–86.

Pitts, Jennifer, *A Turn to Empire: The Rise of Imperial Liberalism in Britain and France* (Princeton, NJ: Princeton University Press, 2005).

Podolny, Joel M. and Karen L. Page, 'Network Forms of Organization', *Annual Review of Sociology*, 24 (1998), 57–76.

Pogge, Thomas, *World Poverty and Human Rights* (Cambridge: Polity Press, 2002), 169.

―― 'Cosmopolitanism and Sovereignty', in *World Poverty and Human Rights* (Cambridge: Polity Press, 2002), 168–95.

―― *Realizing Rawls* (Ithaca, NY: Cornell University Press, 1999).

Posey, Darrell and Graham Duttfield, *Beyond Intellectual Property: Toward Traditional Resource Rights for Indigenous Peoples and Local Communities* (Ottawa: IDRC, 1996).

Prantl, Jochen, 'Informal Groups of States and the UN Security Council', *International Organization*, 59/3 (2005), 559–92.

Preece, Jennifer Jackson, 'Ethnic Cleansing as an Instrument of Nation-State Creation: Changing State Practices and Evolving Legal Norms', *Human Rights Quarterly*, 20/4 (1998), 817–42.

Princen, Thomas and Matthias Finger (eds.), *Environmental NGOs in World Politics. Linking the Local with the Global* (London: Routledge, 1994).

Rabkin, Jeremy, *The Case for Sovereignty: Why the World Should Welcome American Independence* (Washington, DC: AEI Press, 2004).

Rapoport, David C., 'The Four Waves of Modern Terrorism', in Audrey Kurth Cronin and James M. Ludes (eds.), *Attacking Terrorism. Elements of Grand Strategy* (Washington, DC: Georgetown University Press, 2004), 46–73.

Rawls, John, *A Theory of Justice* (Cambridge: Cambridge University Press, 1971)

―― 'The Law of Peoples', in Stephen Shute and Susan Hurley (eds.), *On Human Rights* (New York: Basic Books, 1993).

―― *Political Liberalism* (New York: Columbia University Press, 1993), 301.

―― *The Law of Peoples* (Cambridge, MA: Harvard University Press, 1999), 19.

Reinecke, Wolfgang, *Global Public Policy: Governing Without Government?* (Washington, DC: Brookings Institute, 1998).

Reisman, W. Michael, 'The United States and International Institutions', *Survival* 41/4 (1999–2000), 71–2.

Rengger, N. J., *International Relations, Political Theory and the Problem of Order: Beyond International Relations Theory?* (London: Routledge, 2000).

Reus-Smit, Christian, *The Moral Purpose of the State* (Princeton, NJ: Princeton University Press, 1999).

Richter, Rosemary, *Utopia Lost: The United Nations and World Order* (New York: Twentieth Century Fund Press, 1995).

Rilke, Rainer Maria, *Duino Elegies* (London: Hogarth Press, 1968).

Risse-Kappen, Thomas (ed.), *Bringing Transnational Relations Back in Non-State Actors, Domestic Structures, and International Institutions* (Cambridge: Cambridge University Press, 1995).

Rival, Laura, 'The Growth of Family Trees: Understanding Huaorani Perceptions of the Forest', *Man*, 28/4 (1993), 635–52.

Roberts, Adam, 'Willing the End but not the Means', *The World Today*, 55/5 (May 1999), 8–12.

____ 'The So-called "Right" of Humanitarian Intervention', *Yearbook of International Humanitarian Law*, 3 (Summer 2000), 3–51.

____ 'Legal Controversies in the War on Terror', Keynote Address, US Pacific Command, International Military Operations and Law Conference, Singapore, 21–4 March 2005, 4–5.

____ and Benedict Kingsbury (eds.), *United Nations, Divided World: The UN's Roles in International Relations*, 2nd edn. (Oxford: Oxford University Press, 1993).

Rogers, Paul F., 'Politics in the Next 50 Years: The Changing Nature of International Conflict', *Peace Studies Papers*, Working Paper 1, Fourth Series, Department of Peace Studies, University of Bradford (October 2000) http://www.brad.ac.uk/peace/pubs/pspl1.pdf

Ronit, Karsten and Volker Schneider, 'Global Governance Through Private Organizations', *Governance*, 12/3 (1999), 243–66.

Rosamund, Ben, *Theories of European Integration* (Basingstoke, UK: Macmillan, 2000).

Rosato, Sebastian, 'The Flawed Logic of Democratic Peace Theory', *American Political Science Review*, 97/4 (2003), 585–602.

Rosenau, James N., 'Environmental Challenges in a Turbulent World', in Ronnie D. Lipschutz and Ken Conca, 'The Implications of Global Ecological Interdependence', in Ronnie D. Lipschutz and Ken Conca (eds.), *The State and Social Power in Global Environmental Politics* (New York: Columbia University Press, 1993), 71–93.

____ and Ernst-Otto Czempiel (eds.), *Governance without Government. Order and Change in World Politics* (Cambridge: Cambridge University Press, 1992).

Rothschild, Emma, 'What Is Security?', *Deadalus*, 124/3 (Summer 1995).

Rousseau, Jean-Jacques, *Lettres. de la Montagne* , in C. E. Vaughan (ed.), *The Political Writings of Jean Jacques Rousseau* (Cambridge: Cambridge University Press, 1915), vol. II. Available at: http://oll.libertyfund.org/Texts/Rousseau0284/PoliticalWritings/HTMLs/0065-2_pt03_Passages.html.

____ 'Abstract and Judgement of Saint-Pierre's Project for Perpetual Peace', in Stanley Hoffmann and David Fidler (eds.), *Rousseau on International Relations* (Oxford: Clarendon Press, 1991), 54.

____ *L'Etat de Guerre* (Arles: Actes Sud, 2000).

Roy, Olivier, *Globalised Islam: The Search for a New Ummah* (London: Hurst, 2002).

Ruggie, John G., 'Territoriality and Beyond: Problematizing Modernity in International Relations', *International Organization*, 46/1 (1993), 139–74.

____ *Constructing the World Polity: Essays on International Institutionalization* (London: Routledge, 1998).

Rummel, Rudolph J., *Never Again: Ending War, Democide and Famine Through Democratic Freedom* (Coral Springs: Llumina Press, 2005).

Russett, Bruce, *Grasping the Democratic Peace: Principles for a Post-Cold War World* (Princeton, NJ: Princeton University Press, 1993).

____ *International Regions and the International System* (Chicago, IL: Rand McNally, 1967).

Sandholtz, Wayne and Alec Stone Sweet (eds.), *European Integration and Supranational Governance* (Oxford: Oxford University Press, 1998).

Sarooshi, Danesh, *The United Nations and the Development of Collective Security: The Delegation by the UN Security Council of Its Chapter VII Powers* (Oxford: Oxford University Press, 1999).

Sassen, Saskia, 'Embedding the Global in the National', in David A. Smith, Dorothy J. Solinger, and Stephen C. Topik (eds.), *States and Sovereignty in the Global Economy* (London: Routledge, 1999).

Scharpf, Fritz, *Governing Europe: Effective and Democratic?* (Oxford: Oxford University Press, 1999).

Scheffler, Samuel, *Boundaries and Allegiances: Problems of Justice and Responsibility in Liberal Thought* (Oxford: Oxford University Press, 2001).

Schiffer, Walter, *The Legal Community of Mankind* (New York, Columbia University Press, 1954).

Schmitt, Carl, *The Concept of the Political*, trans. Georg Schwab (New Brunswick, NJ: Rutgers University Press, 1976).

Schmitter, Philippe, 'Neo-Neo-Functionalism', in Antje Wiener and Thomas Diez (eds.), *European Integration Theory* (Oxford: Oxford University Press, 2003).

Scholte, Jan Art, *Globalization: A Critical Introduction*, 2nd edn. (Basingstoke, UK: Palgrave, 2005).

Schoultz, Lars, *Beneath the United States: A History of U.S. Policy Towards Latin America* (Cambridge, MA: Harvard University Press, 1999).

Schroeder, Paul, *The Transformation of European Politics 1763–1848* (Oxford: Clarendon Press, 1994).

Scott, James C., *Seeing Like a State: How Certain Schemes to Improve the Human Condition Have Failed* (New Haven, CT: Yale University Press, 1998).

Scruton, Roger, 'Conservatism', in Andrew Dobson and Robyn Eckersely (eds.), *Political Theory and the Ecological Challenge* (Cambridge: Cambridge University Press, 2006), 7–19.

Seeley, John R., *The Expansion of England*, edited and introduced by John Gross (Chicago, IL: University of Chicago Press, [1881] 1971).

Sen, Amartya, *Inequality Reexamined* (Oxford: Oxford University Press, 1992).

―――― 'Six Billion and All That'. Lecture delivered at Economic Development Seminar on poverty, inequality, and other issues raised by the work of A. K. Sen, Queen Elizabeth House, Oxford, 3 February 2000.

Shapiro, Ian, *The State of Democratic Theory* (Princeton, NJ: Princeton University Press, 2003), 147.

―――― and Russell Hardin (eds.), *Political Order*, Nomos No. 38 (New York: New York University Press, 1993).

Shapiro, Judith, *Mao's War Against Nature: Politics and the Environment in Revolutionary China* (Cambridge: Cambridge University Press, 2001).

Shapiro, Martin, 'The Giving Reason Requirement', in Martin Shapiro and Alec Stone Sweet (eds.), *On Law, Politics and Judicialization* (Oxford: Oxford University Press, 2002), 228–57.

Shaw, M. N., *International Law*, 3rd edn. (Cambridge: Cambridge University Press, 1994), 98–9.

Shklar, Judith, *Faces of Injustice* (New Haven, CT: Yale University Press, 1990).

Shue, Henry, *Basic Rights: Subsistence, Affluence and US Foreign Policy* (Princeton, UK: Princeton University Press, 1980).

―――― 'The Unavoidability of Justice', in Andrew Hurrell and Benedict Kingsbury (eds.), *The International Politics of the Environment* (Oxford: Oxford University Press, 1992), 373–97.

Sikkink, Kathyrn, *Mixed Signals: U.S. Human Rights Policy Towards Latin America* (Ithaca, NY: Cornell University Press, 2004).

Simma, Bruno (ed.), *The Charter of the United Nations: A Commentary*, 2nd edn. (Oxford: Oxford University Press, 2002).

Singer, Max and Aaron Wildavsky, *The Real World Order Zones of Peace/Zones of Turmoil* (Chatham, NJ: Chatham House, 1993).

Singer, Peter, *Corporate Warriors: The Rise of the Privatized Military Industry* (Ithaca, NY/London: Cornell University Press, 2003).

Skinner, Quentin, 'Some Problems in the Analysis of Political Thought and Action', in James Tully (ed.), *Meaning and Context: Quentin Skinner and his Critics* (Cambridge: Polity Press, 1988), 97–119.

Slaughter, Anne-Marie, *A New World Order* (Princeton, NJ: Princeton University Press, 2004).

—— 'Governing the Global Economy Through Government Networks', in Michael Byers (ed.), *The Role of Law in International Politics* (Oxford: Oxford University Press, 2000), 177–206.

Smith, Adam, *An Inquiry into the Nature and Causes of the Wealth of Nations* (Chicago: University of Chicago Press, [1775] 1976).

—— *The Wealth of Nations*, with an introduction by D. D. Raphael (London: David Campbell, 1991).

Smith, Anthony D., *The Ethnic Origins of Nations* (Oxford: Basil Blackwell, 1986).

Smith, Rhona K. M. and Christien van den Anker (eds.), *The Essentials of Human Rights* (London: Hodder Arnold, 2005).

Smith, Rogers M., *Civic Ideals: Conflicting Visions of Citizenship in US History* (New Haven, CT: Yale University Press, 1997).

—— *Stories of Peoplehood: The Politics and Morals of Political Membership* (Cambridge: Cambridge University Press, 2003).

Smith, Tony, *America's Mission: The United States and the Worldwide Struggle for Democracy in the Twentieth Century* (Princeton, NJ: Princeton University Press, 1994).

Snidal, Duncan, 'The Limits of Hegemonic Stability Theory', *International Organization*, 39 (1985), 579–614.

Snyder, Jack, *Myths of Empire: Domestic Politics and International Ambition* (Ithaca, NJ: Cornell University Press, 1991).

—— 'Imperial Temptations', *The National Interest*, 71 (Spring 2003), 29–41.

Soltan, Karol, Eric M. Uslaner, and Virginia Haufler (eds.), *Institutions and Social Order* (Ann Arbor, MI: University of Michigan Press, 1998).

Spengler, Oswald, *Der Untergang des Abendlandes* (Munich: C. H. Beck, [1922] 1963).

Steiner, George, *The Death of Tragedy* (London: Faber and Faber, 1961).

Stokke, Olav (ed.), *Aid and Political Conditionality* (London: Frank Cass, 1995).

Stone, Julius, 'Approaches to the Notion of International Justice', in C. E. Black and Richard Falk (eds.), *The Future of the International Legal Order*, vol. 1 (Princeton, NJ: Princeton University Press, 1969), 372–462.

Streeck, Wolfgang and Philippe C. Schmitter, 'Community, Market, State—and Associations? The Prospective Contribution of Interest Governance to Social Order', *European Sociological Review*, 1/2 (September 1985), 119–38.

Sweet, Alec Stone, 'Judicialization and the Construction of Governance', *Comparative Political Studies*, 32/2 (April 1999), 147–84.

—— Wayne Sandholtz, and Neil Fligstein, *The Institutionalization of Europe* (Oxford: Oxford University Press, 2001).

—— 'Islands of Transnational Governance', in Christopher K. Ansell and Giuseppe di Palma (eds.), *Restructuring Territoriality: Europe and the United States Compared* (Cambridge: Cambridge University Press, 2004), 122–44.

Tanzi, Vito and Ludger Schuknecht, *Public Spending in the 20th Century* (Cambridge: Cambridge University Press, 2000).

Tarrow, Sydney, *The New Transnational Activism* (Cambridge: Cambridge University Press, 2005).

Taylor, Charles, 'Conditions of an Unforced Consensus on Human Rights,' in Joanne R. Bauer and Daniel A. Bell (eds.), *The East Asian Challenge for Human Rights* (Cambridge: Cambridge University Press, 1999), 137–8.

Teivainen, Teivo, 'The World Social Forum and Global Democratization: Learning from Porto Alegre', *Third World Quarterly*, 23/4 (2002), 621–32.

Teubner, Gunther (ed.), *Global Law Without a State* (Aldershot, UK: Dartmouth, 1997).

Thompson, William, 'The Regional Subsystem: A Conceptual Explication and a Propositional Inventory', *International Studies Quarterly*, 17/1: (1973), 89–117.

Thornhill, Chris, *Political Theory in Modern Germany: An Introduction* (Cambridge: Polity Press, 2000), ch. 4.

Tickner, J. Ann, 'Re-visioning Security', in Ken Booth and Steve Smith (eds.), *International Political Theory Today* (Cambridge: Polity Press, 1995), 175–97.

Toynbee, Arnold, *A Study of History* (Oxford: Oxford University Press, 1934)

Tuck, Richard, *The Rights of War and Peace: Political Thought and International Order from Grotius to Kant* (Oxford: Oxford University Press, 1999).

Triepel, Heinrich, *Die Hegemonie: Ein Buch von den Führenden Staaten* (Stuttgart: Kohlhammer, 1938).

Tully, James, *Strange Multiplicity: Constitutionalism in an Age of Diversity* (Cambridge: Cambridge University Press, 1995).

Ullman, Richard H., 'Redefining Security', *International Security*, 8/1 (Summer 1983), 129–53.

United Nations, 'A More Secure World: Our Shared Responsibility'. Report of the Secretary-General's High Level Panel on Threats, Challenges and Change, United Nations (December 2004), http://www.un.org/secureworld/report2.pdf

—— *Human Development Report 2000* (New York: UNDP, 2001), http://hdr.undp.org/reports/global/2000/en/

Vagts, Alfred and Detlev F. Vagts, 'The Balance of Power in International Law: A History of an Idea', *American Journal of International Law*, 73/4 (October 1979), 555–80.

van Creveld, Martin, *The Transformation of War* (New York: Free Press, 1991).

Varshney, Ashutosh, 'Nationalism, Ethnic Conflict and Rationality', *Perspectives on Politics*, 1/1 (March 2003), 85–99.

Vaughan, C. E. (ed.) *The Political Writings of Jean Jaeques Rousseau (Cambridge: Cambridge University Press, 1915)* vol. II.

Vigezzi, Brunello, *The British Committee on the Theory of International Politics (1954–1985): The Rediscovery of History* (Milan: Edizioni Unicopli, 2005).

Vincent, R. J., *Human Rights and International Relations* (Cambridge: Cambridge University Press, 1986).

von Clausewitz, Carl, *On War*, ed. and trans. Michael Howard and Peter Paret (Princeton, NJ: Princeton University Press, 1978).

von Gentz, Friedrich, *Fragments upon the Balance of Power in Europe*, Printed for M. Peltier (London, 1806).

Wade, Robert, *Governing the Market: Economic Theory and the Role of Government in East Asian Industrialization* (Princeton, NJ: Princeton University Press, 1990).

—— 'Is Globalization Reducing Poverty and Inequality', *World Development*, 32/4 (2004), 567–89.

Wallensteen, Peter and Margareta Sollenberg, 'Armed Conflict, 1989–99', *Journal of Peace Research*, 37/5 (2000), 635–49.

Walt, Stephen M., *Taming American Power: The Global Response to US Primacy* (New York: W.W. Norton, 2005).

Waltz, Kenneth, *Theory of International Politics* (Reading, MA: Addison-Wesley, 1979).

Walzer, Michael, *Just and Unjust Wars: A Moral Argument with Historical Illustrations* (New York: Basic Books, 1977).

—— 'The Moral Standing of States: A Response to Four Critics', *Philosophy and Public Affairs*, 9/3 (1980), 210–6.

—— *Spheres of Justice: A Defence of Pluralism and Equality* (Oxford: Martin Robertson, 1983).

—— 'The Reform of the International System,' in Oyvind Osterud (ed.), *Studies in War and Peace* (Oslo: Norwegian University Press, 1986), 227–50.

Wapner, Paul, *Environmental Activism and World Civic Politics* (Albany, NY: State University of New York Press, 1996).

Watson, Adam, *The Evolution of International Society: A Comparative Historical Analysis* (London: Routledge, 1992).

Weber, Max, 'The Profession and Vocation of Politics', in Peter Lassman and Ronald Spiers (eds.), *Weber: Political Writings* (Cambridge: Cambridge University Press, 1994), 309–69.

Weiler, J. H. H., *The Constitution of Europe: 'Do the New Clothes Have an Emperor?' and Other Essays on European Integration* (Cambridge: Cambridge University Press, 1999).

—— 'The Geology of International Law: Governance, Democracy, and Legitimacy', *Heidelberg Journal of International Law*, 64 (2004), 547–62.

Welsh, Jennifer (ed.), *Humanitarian Intervention and International Relations* (Oxford: Oxford University Press, 2004).

Wendt, Alexander, 'Why a World State Is Inevitable', *European Journal of International Relations*, 9/4 (2003), 491–542.

—— and Raymond Duvall, 'Institutions and International Order', in Ersnt-Otto Cziempiel and James N. Rosenau (eds.), *Global Changes and Theoretical Challenges* (Lexington: Lexington Books, 1989), 51–73.

Westad, Odd Arne, *The Global Cold War* (Cambridge: Cambridge University Press, 2005).

Wheeler, Nicholas, *Saving Strangers: Humanitarian Intervention in International Society* (Oxford: Oxford University Press, 2000).

Whitehead, Laurence, 'Afterword: On Cultures and Contexts', in Hans Antlov and Tak-Wing Ngo (eds.), *The Cultural Construction of Politics in Asia* (Richmond: Curzon Press, 2000), 223–40.

—— *Democratization: Theory and Experience* (Oxford: Oxford University Press, 2002).

Whiteside, Kerry H., *Divided Natures. French Contribution to Political Ecology* (Cambridge, MA: MIT Press, 2002).

Widner, Jennifer, 'States and Statelessness in Africa', *Daedalus*, 124/3 (Summer 1995), 129–55.

Williamson, Oliver E., *The Economic Institutions of Capitalism: Firms, Markets, Relational Contracting* (New York: Free Press, 1985).

Wilson, Peter, *The International Theory of Leonard Woolf* (New York Palgrave, 2003).

Wilson, Woodrow, *The Public Papers of Woodrow Wilson, Volume I. War and Peace: Presidential Messages, Addresses and Public Papers 1917–1924* ed. R. S. Baker and W. E. Dodd (London and New York: Harper and Brothers, 1927).

—— 'Address to the United States Senate, 22 January 1917', in Arthur S. Link (ed.), The Papers of Woodrow Wilson, vol. 40, 20, November 1916–23, January 1917, 536–7 (Princeton, NJ: Princeton University Press, 1982).

Wight, Martin, 'Why Is There No International Theory?', in Martin Wight and Herbert Butterfield (eds.), *Diplomatic Investigations* (London: Allen and Unwin, 1966).

—— *Systems of States* (Leicester, UK: Leicester University Press, 1977).

—— *Power Politics* (London: Penguin Books, 1979).

—— *International Theory: The Three Traditions*, ed. by Gabriele Wight and Brian Porter (Leicester, UK: Leicester University Press, 1991).

Wight, Martin, *The International Thought of Martin Wight* (Basingstoke, UK: Palgrave, 2006)

Williams, William A., *Empire as a Way of Life: An Essay on the Causes and Character of America's Present Predicament Along with a Few Thoughts About an Alternative* (Oxford: Oxford University Press, 1980).

Wolf, Martin, *Why Globalization Works* (New Haven, CT: Yale University Press, 2004).

Wolff, Stefan, *Ethnic Conflict: A Global Perspective* (Oxford: Oxford University Press, 2006).

Woods, Ngaire (ed.), *The Political Economy of Globalization* (Basingstoke, UK: Macmillan, 2000).

—— 'Order, Justice, the IMF and the World Bank', in Rosemary Foot, John Gaddis, and Andrew Hurrell (eds.), *Order and Justice in World Politics* (Oxford: Oxford University Press, 2003), 80–103.

—— *The Globalizers: The IMF, the World Bank, and Their Borrowers* (Ithaca, NY: Cornell University Press, 2006).

—— and Amrita Narlikar, 'Governance and Accountability: The WTO, the IMF and the World Bank', *International Social Science Journal*, 53/170 (December 2001), 569–83.

Wrong, Dennis, *The Problem of Order: What Unites and Divides Society* (New York: Free Press, 1994).

Young, Oran R., *International Governance: Protecting the Environment in a Stateless Society* (Ithaca, NY, and London: Cornell University Press, 1994).

____ (ed.), *Global Governance: Drawing Insights from the Environmental Experience* (Cambridge, MA: MIT Press, 1997).

____ *Governance in World Affairs* (Ithaca, NY: Cornell University Press, 1999).

Zakaria, Fareed, *From Wealth to Power: The Unusual Origins of America's World Role* (Princeton, NJ: Princeton University Press, 1998).

Zasloff, Jonathan, 'Law and the Shaping of American Foreign Policy from the Gilded Age to the New Era', *New York University Law Review*, 78/1 (April 2003), 239–373.

Zielonka, Jan, *Europe as Empire: The Nature of the Enlarged European Union* (Oxford: Oxford University Press, 2006).

Zimmermann, Warren, *First Great Triumph: How Five Americans Made Their Country a World Power* (New York: Farrar, Straus and Giroux, 2002).

Zimmern, Alfred E., *Nationalism and Government* (London: Chatto and Windus, 1923).

____ 'Nationalism and Internationalism', *Foreign Affairs*, 1/4 (1923), 115–26.

____ *The Third British Empire*, 3rd edn. 1934 (Westport, CT: Greenwood, 1979).

Zürn, Michael, 'The Rise of International Environmental Research: A Review of Current Research', *World Politics*, 50/4 (1998), 617–49.

____ 'From Interdependence to Globalization', in Walter Carlsnaes, Thomas Risse, and Beth Simmons (eds.), *The Handbook of International Relations* (London: Sage, 2002), 255–74.

Index